D1483662

FROM POSTMODERNISM
TO POSTSECULARISM

FROM POSTMODERNISM TO POSTSECULARISM

Re-Emerging Islamic Civilization

Eric Walberg

Clarity Press

In-house editor: Diana G. Collier
Cover: R. Jordan P. Santos

Library of Congress Cataloging-in-Publication Data

Library of Congress Cataloging-in-Publication Data

Walberg, Eric.
  From postmodernism to postsecularism : re-emerging Islamic civilization / by Eric Walberg.
      p. cm.
  ISBN 978-0-9853353-8-0 -- ISBN 978-0-9860362-4-8
  1. Islamic civilization--21st century. 2. Islam--Relations--Christianity. 3. Christianity and other religions--Islam. 4. Islam--Relations--Judaism. 5. Judaism--Relations--Islam. I. Title.

BP190.5.C54W35 2013
909'.09767--dc23

2013014269

Clarity Press, Inc.
Ste. 469, 3277 Roswell Rd. NE
Atlanta, GA. 30305 , USA
http://www.claritypress.com

TABLE OF CONTENTS

GLOSSARY

adl	justice
aql	reason
asabiya	tribalism, national consciousness
awqaf	see waqf
ayat	a verse in the Quran
bid'a	"innovation, novelty, heretical doctrine, heresy" (Hans Wehr, *Arabic-English Dictionary*), generally having a negative connotation (something new in opposition to the Quran and sunna); however, it can be positive.
caliph	steward/ spiritual leader of the caliphate, literally a successor to the prophet Muhammad
caliphate	stewardship. Historically, the term came to refer to a territory defined by Islamic governance over multinational populations based on belief rather than ethnicity.
center	as used in discussions concerning imperialism, the dominant or 'mother' country
dawa	invitation to / proselytizing Islam
dar al-harb	abode of war
dar al-islam	abode of peace
darura	need
deen	an all-embracing way of life, which makes Islam more than a personal religion. Religion in the western world deals with private affairs whereas deen covers all aspects of life.
dhimmi	People of the Book living in a Muslim society, who receive special rights of self-governance and are relieved of certain duties in exchange for a tax (jizya).
faqih	jurist
fard ayn	individual duty
fard kifaya	collective duty of the umma
fatwa	ruling by religious scholar concerning Islamic law. In Sunni Islam any fatwa is non-binding, whereas in Shia Islam it could be considered by an individual as binding, depending on his or her relation to the scholar.
fiqh	Islamic jurisprudence

fitna	civil strife, sedition, riot, intrigue, treason
gharar	risk, uncertainty, deception, fraud or undue advantage in a business transaction
hadd (hudud)	fixed penalty established in the Quran/ sharia (rights of God, God's law)
hadith(s)	documented sayings and traditions of the Prophet
hajj	pilgrimage to Mecca
haram	forbidden
Hejaz	the western Arabian Peninsula, including Medina and Mecca
hijab	literally screen, referring to modesty in dress for both men and women as revealed in the Quran and hadiths. It now is used to refer to a headscarf for women.
hijra	literally emigration, referring to the journey of Muhammad and his followers from Mecca to Medina in 622.
hiraba	organized crime, armed robbery, "wag[ing] war against Allah and His Messenger, and striv[ing] with might and main for mischief through the land"
Hizb ut-Tahrir	Party of Liberation, international party advocating renewal of the caliphate
ijma	consensus
ijtihad	independent reasoning, legal interpretation based on tajdid
ijtima	society, assembly
ilm	knowledge
imam	prayer leader (Sunni), spiritual leader (Shia)
infitah	opening
islah	reform
Ismaili	a branch of Shiism, the 'Seveners' who believe there were only seven Imams
istihsan	legal preference, used by liberal reformers
istislah	determining what is in the interests of human welfare by one's own deliberations
jahiliya	state of ignorance of divine guidance, referring to the condition Arabs found themselves in prior to the revelation of the Quran, now referring to backsliders and non-Muslims in the absence of the rule of sharia
Jamaat i-Islami	Islamic Society (Pakistan, Indonesia and Egypt)
jihad	struggle, effort (greater and lesser jihad)
jizya	tax paid by non-Muslims exempting them from military service
kaaba	the sacred stone in Mecca where Abraham was to have worshipped. It provides the direction for Muslims to face when saying their prayers.
kafir (kufar)	unbeliever(s), referring to those who reject God

Kharijites	Ali was murdered in 661 by these extremist followers, who rejected both power-seekers like Muawiya and Ali for his irresolution
khilafa	stewardship, governance (anglicized as caliphate)
Khilafat Mov't	post-WWI movement to support the Caliphate
khutba	sermon
Levant	present-day Syria, Lebanon Palestine, Jordan, Israel
madhhab	school of Islamic jurisprudence
mahdi	the guided one (redeemer)
majlis al-shura	consultative parliament
mahdi	the guided one, messiah
maqsid (maqasid)	goal(s)
maslaha	consideration of public interest
Mesopotamia	present-day Iraq
mufti	an Islamic scholar qualified to issue fatwas. This is not always a formal position as most Muslims consider someone trained in Islamic law can issue an opinion on its teachings.
mujahid(een)	one who pursues jihad
mujtahid(een)	highly skilled interpreter of hadiths, authorized to use ijtihad in legal rulings
mukrih	coercion
naksa	reverse, referring to the 1967 defeat in the Arab-Israeli war
neo-Wahhabi	the al-Qaeda-type terrorism arising from the Wahhab doctrine
niqab	a stricter form of hijab, a black head cover that reveals only the woman's eyes. Not to be confused with the burqa which covers the entire body from head to foot, with a net to allow vision.
periphery	in imperialism, the colonies
privateering	legalized piracy chartered by a monarch (i.e., Dutch VOC, British East India Company)
qadi	a judge
qiyas	analogical reasoning
riba	usury, interest, literally excess
Salaf(i)	earliest generation of Muslims, and those who emulate them today
salat	prayer
sharia	laws based on the Quran and hadiths
shura	advice, consultation
Sufi	literally wool, referring to asceticism. Sufis emphasize revelation and immanence
sunna	traditions of the Prophet derived from hadiths
sura	chapter of the Quran

Tablighi Jamaat	information society
tajdid	renewal, referring to rereading 'the text' (Quran)
takfir	charge of unbelief
Tanzimat	nineteenth century Ottoman reform movement, literally "regulations"
taqlid	use of precedents
tariqa (turuq)	a Sufi order, literally 'way'
tawhid	the oneness of God. Shirk is belief in more than one god and is the primary sin in Islam
ta'zir	discretionary penalty in absence of explicit punishment in the Quran/ sharia
ulama (sing.alim)	elite of scholars
umma	community of Muslims
urf	local custom which is not in direct conflict with established Islamic principles
ushur	literally "one tenth" referring to the legally required zakat tithe. Zakat on wealth is 2.5%. Production involving both labor and capital is subject to a 5% tax (10% if only labor or capital is involved). For earnings from finding treasure, the rate is 20%.
usul	foundation
waqf (awqaf)	religious endowment or foundation, land, a building or cash
zakat	charity, traditionally by a tithe on income/ wealth
zina	adultery, fornication, rape, sexual misconduct

ACRONYMS

AKP	Turkish Justice and Development Party (2001)
AQAP	al-Qaeda in the Arab Peninsula (2009)
AQIM	al-Qaeda in the Islamic Maghreb (1999)
AU	African Union (2002), successor to the Organization of African Unity (1963)
BRIC(S)	Informal economic bloc (2008), members Brazil, Russia, India, China, as of 2010 including South Africa, making it BRICS
CUP	Committee for Unity and Progress (1889) secular reformers during the last years of the Ottoman Caliphate
D-8	Developing 8 refers to the Organization for Economic Cooperation (1997) consisting of Bangladesh, Egypt, Indonesia, Iran, Malaysia, Nigeria, Pakistan, and Turkey
ECOWAS	Economic Community of West African States (1974)
EIJ	Egyptian Islamic Jihad (late 1970s)
FJP	Egyptian MB Freedom and Justice Party (2011)
FIS	Algerian Front Islamique de Salut (1989)
FLN	Algerian Front Liberation National (1954)
GCC	Gulf Cooperation Council (1981)
JCP	Libyan MB Justice and Construction Party (2011)

JDP	Moroccan MB Justice and Development Party (1960s, since 1998 JDP)
MB	Muslim Brotherhood (1928, Egypt)
MEK	Mujahideen-e-Khalq (1965, People's Mujahideen) Iranian insurgency
MSP	Algerian MB Movement of Society for Peace (1953, formally MSP early 1990s)
NU	Indonesian Nahdlatul Ulama (1926, Renaissance scholars)
OIC	Organization of Islamic Cooperation (1969)
PLO	Palestinian Liberation Organization (1964)
RIC	Informal economic bloc (2001), member Russia, India, China
SCO	Shanghai Cooperation Organization (1996), members China, Kazakhstan, Kyrgyzstan, Russia, Tajikistan, and Uzbekistan
UAR	United Arab Republic (1958–1961), union of Egypt and Syria
UEMOA	West African Monetary Union (1994)
UMNO	United Malays National Organization (1946)

ACKNOWLEDGMENTS

First of all I must thank my editor Diana Collier for her encouragement to undertake this far-reaching survey of what can only be described as the most exciting and hopeful development in the world today, and her careful and thoughtful work in editing my MS.

There are tmany people whose work in understanding and making accessible the wealth of Islamic civilization has been essential reading. I hope the reader will browse the Bibliography and endnotes for many fascinating byways. As with my *Postmodern Imperialism: Geopolitics and the Great Games*, the internet has provided a virtual resource that gives access to information on an unprecedented scale, making an ambitious work like this possible.

Thanks go to my many Muslim friends and colleagues in Egypt, who helped me understand from the inside both the revolution of 2011 and the deeper traditional way of life grounded in Islam. Thanks go to my editors at *Al-Ahram Weekly*, who gave me the opportunity to write uncensored about Islam and the West, about the great celebration of Ramadan, and the exciting events of the past two years following the Arab Spring.

Thanks go to my sister Carol, who provided a quiet retreat for writing, and to my librarian friends in Bruce County, whose help was essential. Once again, I would like to thank my parents Alf and Betty whose deeply felt Christian faith was grounded in both revelation and reason, much like Islam.

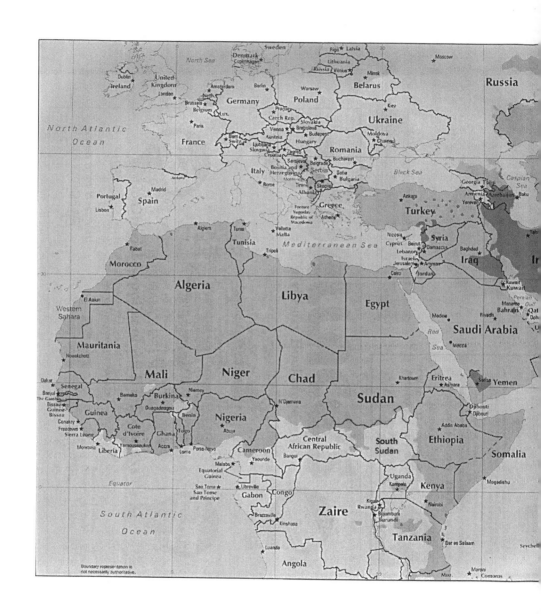

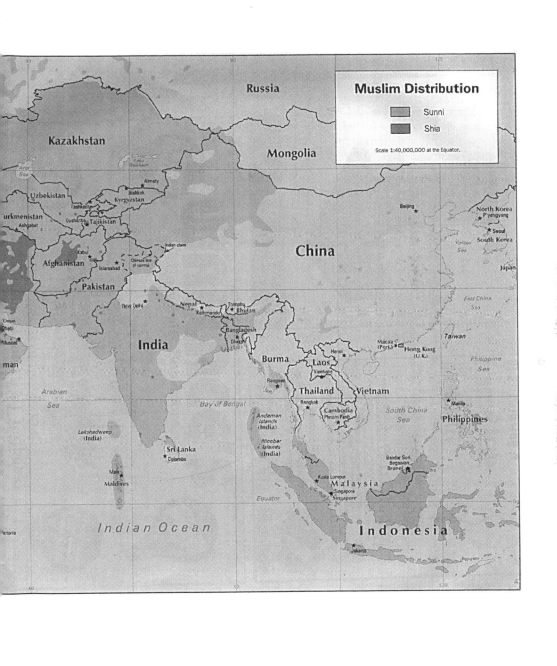

Muslim Distribution

Sunni
Shia

Scale 1:40,000,000 at the Equator.

Russia

Kazakhstan

Mongolia

Uzbekistan

Almaty

Bishkek
Kyrgyzstan

urkmenistan

Tashkent

Dushanbe Tajikistan

Ashgabat

Indian claim

Beijing

North Korea
P'yongyang

Kabul

Chinese line
of control

China

Seoul
South Korea

Afghanistan

Islamabad

Yellow
Sea

Japan

Pakistan

Oman

New Delhi

Nepal

Thimphu

Bhutan

East China
Sea

Dhabi

Kathmandu

Bangladesh

Muscat

Dhaka

Macau
(Port.)

Taiwan

man

India

Burma

Laos

Hanoi

Hong Kong
(U.K.)

Vientiane

Philippine
Sea

Arabian
Sea

Bay of Bengal

Rangoon

Thailand

Vietnam

Bangkok

Cambodia
Phnom Penh

South China
Sea

Manila

Philippines

Lakshadweep
(India)

Andaman
Islands
(India)

Nicobar
Islands
(India)

Sri Lanka

Colombo

Bandar Seri
Begawan
Brunei

Male

Maldives

Kuala Lumpur

M a l a y s i a

Singapore
Singapore

Equator

Indian Ocean

I n d o n e s i a

ictoria

Jakarta

PREFACE

This book is a continuation of my earlier work, *Postmodern Imperialism: Geopolitics and the Great Games* (2011), though it stands on its own. My purpose in *Postmodern Imperialism* was to give a picture of the world from the viewpoint of those on the receiving end of imperialism. It traces the manipulation of Islamists by imperialism, and poses the question: What are the implications of the revival of Islamic thought and activism for the western imperial project?

The subject of this work is the expansion of Islam since the seventh century, when revelations delivered to the Prophet Muhammad led to its consolidation as the renewal and culmination of Abrahamic monotheism. It looks at the parallels between the Muslim world today and past crises in Islamic civilization, which gave impetus to reforms and renewal from within, relying on the Quran and hadiths,[1] and attempts to interpret recent history from the viewpoint of the Muslim world—how it sees the imposition on it of western systems and beliefs, and how it is dealing with this.

The period up to and including the occupation of the Muslim world by the western imperialists corresponds to *Postmodern Imperialism*'s Great Game I (GGI). For Asians, the most important event heralding the possibility of a new post-GGI 'game' was the Japanese victory in 1905 over Russia. Japan had successfully reformed via the Meiji Restoration in 1868, inspiring all Asia, including China and the Muslim world, which saw Japan's determination to develop independently of the imperial powers as a way out of the colonial trap that they were rapidly falling into.

The subsequent movement for secular reform in the Muslim world took place in a world economic and political order that was both capitalist and socialist. This was the period I termed Great Game II (GGII), the period of neocolonialism, when newly 'independent' colonies attempted to imitate either their former western masters or at best, the now communist Russia. This period began by the early twentieth century, but really got underway only after WWII, when GGI pretensions were finally done away with.

Apart from the resurgence of Islam as an alternative world order, there were parallel anti-imperialist movements among non-Muslim Asians. Japan's own entry into GGI as a rival to the western empires made it a center of resistance to the West for Chinese and Indians alike, the leading figures being Liang Qichao, who called for a reformed Confucianism in China, and Gandhi and Tagore, who called for a return to classical Indian culture as embodied in the Vedas, and advocated self-reliance and rural life as opposed to incorporation in the world trade system and urban industrialization.

However, Buddhism, Confucianism and Hinduism could not resist the imperial onslaught. In Japan, Buddhism was shunted aside and a military-led development ruthlessly imitated the imperialists. In China, the invasion by imperialists, starting with the opium trade and culminating in the suppression of the Boxer Rebellion, led to the overthrow of the monarchy and eventually the victory of the communists, who alone were not compromised by association with the imperialists, and were able to unite the people around a strong secular state. Persia and Turkey tried to go the Japanese route as secular states imitating the West. The resistance by Indians culminated in a secular socialism and a tragic sectarian partition, which both divided the world's largest Muslim community and pushed Indians into secular states.

Neither Confucianism, Buddhism nor Hinduism survived as alternative worldviews opposed to empire. At the same time, in the Muslim world there were the tentative beginnings of a movement to mobilize the people around a strong and holistic spiritual tradition combining moral and ethical values. This led to the rise of the Muslim Brotherhood, and other more radical groups. (Saudi tribalism and Pakistan's 'Muslim nationalism' have operated within the imperialist system). The Iranian revolution in 1979 marked the first substantive break with the secular world order, heralding a new Great Game III, culminating in the Arab Spring. On a visit to revolutionary Tehran in 1979, Michel Foucault called it "the first great insurrection" against the "global systems" of the West—in which he clearly included communism and its secular socialist variants. "Islam has a good chance to become a gigantic powder keg, at the level of hundreds of millions of men."[2]

Islamic civilization is the most complete alternative world system, a "universalist response" that confronts imperialism, incorporating a transcendent spirituality (unlike Confucianism) and with a clear political and economic program (unlike Buddhism and Hinduism). The goal of those following the Islamic response is to outlast the imperialists, adapt modern technology, while avoiding the pitfalls of militarism and usury/ interest.

The current Great Game being played in the world by the powers-that-be will come to an end, bang- or whimper-style. The gathering financial crisis could lead to collapse on a world scale of the subjective acceptance of capitalist hierarchy and its socio-economic underpinnings.

Given the bankruptcy of the values and operation of the current world system, an appreciation of Islam as a viable alternative system with robust moral/

ethical limits, grounded in community and Nature, not money and commoditization, is long overdue. Islam, like communism—and unlike capitalism—is not a conspiracy. It openly proclaims itself as an alternative socio-economic system which strives to eliminate exploitation. Capitalism, on the contrary, hides the surplus produced by society in order that it can be expropriated without causing protest by those who do the producing.

Understanding Islam as a basis of social organization requires considering first methodology (how we see the world) and epistemology (the nature of knowledge and its limits). The most developed critical analysis of capitalism, Marx's theory of abstract capitalism, based on Hegel's *Logic*, employed a dialectical method to show a perfect correspondence of the logic-of-the-phenomenon with the phenomenon itself (capitalism), allowing the subject (us) to see the truth of the object, to 'know' it, though the logic of capitalism manifests itself in history imperfectly (as does Hegel's *Logic* in its unfolding in Nature). Marx's materialism inverted the overly idealistic Hegelian theory, focusing on political economy, based on his famous equation "forces of production determine relations of production", positing a revolutionary future where the contradictions of the real world are resolved, based on reason.

The Hegel-Marx dialectical theory, which brings together the cultural values of art, science, and morality in a grand synthesis including politics and economics, stands in sharp contrast to the positivist methodology which has became dominant in the West, which rejects such 'metaphysics', instead putting quantitative science above art and morals, reducing scientific 'truth' to what can be physically measured, effectively consigning art and morals to the metaphysical trashcan. There can be no 'truth' there, and by implication, in politics and economics.

Fourteen centuries ago, Muhammad's revelations presented a vision much like Hegel's and Marx's combined, at the same time avoiding the degeneration inherent in the modernist project. Like Hegel's Christian revelation-reason dialectic, Islam similarly posits an immanent God, where through devout religious practice, man can find spiritual truth in his daily life, reflecting the will of God, by following the path laid out in the Quran. Through revelations from the Archangel Gabriel, Muhammad critiqued both past religious beliefs and past economic and political customs, forging a way of life where the contradictions of the real world are resolved through faith and reason. This experience was recorded and transmitted through the generations, providing a rich empirical repository of civilizational social experience for future guidance. The 'truth' of this is embodied in all aspects of life, including art, science and morals. However, just as there is no detailed blueprint for communism, there is no detailed blueprint for the "straight path" of Islam. This is something that depends on the real world and how Muslims engage with it.

'What is truth?' and 'How can we find the truth?' are the crux of the ideological struggle between western civilization and re-emerging Islamic civilization. Matter confronts spirit, the individual—society, appearance—inner experience, reason—revelation. Those of us educated in the West have a certain mindset which inevitably colors the lenses through which we see the world, by which we identify 'truth'. To understand the world from the viewpoint of re-emerging Islamic civilization requires taking off these glasses and looking at the world through different lenses, using a different 'map' by to navigate our lives. The main purpose of this book is to help the reader to understand the alternative map which Islam offers.

The collapse of the Soviet Union and the fatal weakening of the socialist movement for a better future pushed me to reflect on what was missing in Marx, and to investigate what I saw as the strongest force resisting imperialism—Islam.

Neither life in the Soviet Union, nor life in Islamic societies was/is particular attractive to someone brought up in the cradle of western luxury. But it doesn't require much investigation to realize that the small proportion of the world's population who live lives of luxury today have been very lucky, that for the vast majority (the so-called 99%) of the world's population, the security and communal values of both the failed socialist experiment and the ongoing Islamic one have their pluses. And further investigation reveals that, regardless of material considerations, there is a spiritual richness in Islam that in many ways is unrivaled in other social systems. And I mean 'social systems' as opposed to just 'religions', because Islam strives to be more than just a religion, as the word is understood today in the West.

I have been fortunate to live under both these alternative social systems. Both were/are frustrating, defective, messy, far from fulfilling their promise, full of hierarchy. But they could be worse. The post-collapse Soviet Union is far worse for most of its inhabitants than the defective Soviet way of life. It is hard to imagine a worse fate than being poor and born into Mubarak's secular Egypt.

My concern in *Postmodern Imperialism* was to expose the logic of empire and give readers a sense of what the real world *really* looks like. My concern here is to give the reader a glimpse of the sweep of Islamic civilization and to see its re-emergence today as a positive development, possibly the most important one for realigning ourselves with Nature, and rediscovering humanity's spiritual evolutionary path.

There have been many societies in the past where life was 'superior' to western civilization today, and there will be in the future. To appreciate alternatives to western civilization requires an open mind and a fresh look at the past—and the present. What Islam adds to the socialist alternative is a sense of the miracle of life, acknowledgment of our humble part in the universe, without abandoning the vital role of reason.

ENDNOTES

1   Stories relating sayings and traditions of the Prophet
2   "A Powder Keg Called Islam", *Corriere della sera*, 13, February 1979. Quoted in Janet Afary and Kevin Anderson, *Foucault and the Iranian Revolution: Gender and the Seductions of Islamism*, USA: University of Chicago Press, 2005, 4.

INTRODUCTION

Surely never will Allah change the condition of a people until they change it themselves (with their own souls). But when Allah wills a people's punishment, there can be no turning it back, nor will they find, besides Him, any to protect. (13:11)

Definitions

Over the past two centuries, the entire world has been force-marched into **modernity**. The modern paradigm is variously called Newtonian, Cartesian, mechanistic, referring to the rational-industrial worldview arising from Enlightenment. Its cheerleaders laud the West's empirical sciences, the spectacular material wealth which the application of science to the material world has resulted in, democracy and the "move from ethnocentric to worldcentric morality", "the great antireligious movement, the great movement of rational secularization, which 'killed' God",[1] replaced by science and man. Its detractors argue that the belief that science provides a 'true' understanding of a mechanistic Nature has led to genocidal wars, ecological crisis, an Age of Anxiety.[2]

The cornerstone of modernity and postmodernism[3] is **secularism**, a term which here is "used to describe any philosophy which forms its ethics without reference to religious dogmas".[4]

The dangers inherent in modernity's reduction of truth to what can be measured were soon recognized. Friedrich Nietzsche signaled the beginning of the postmodern era: "Against the positivism which stops before phenomena, saying 'there are only *facts*', I say it is precisely facts that do not exist, only *interpretations*."[5] **Postmodernism** rejects this worship of science, and recognizes that there is a big hole in the Enlightenment representation paradigm: it "leaves out the mapmaker",[6] the 'fact' that the subject is reflected in the map, and that all maps are therefore subjective.[7] There is no absolute truth, even where truth is limited to what can be rigorously measured. This skepticism is salutary, but we must not just treat all interpretations as equally valid (or invalid), which would amount to nihilism, and leave us helpless.

So far, postmodernism has not presented a compelling alternative to the crisis of modernity, yet the yearning for spirit remains in the face of society's confrontation with modernity. A Zen saying asserts, "That which one can deviate from is not the true Tao." We need to find this deeper path, which embodies the truth, express it, celebrate it, at the same time, recognizing that our maps of it are always in need of adjusting. In moving beyond secularism, we must move towards modes of consciousness that go beyond mere rationality, that are "trans-rational and trans-industrial", with "a self integrated in its networks of responsibility and service."[8]

Islam's claim against modernity parallels that of westerners dissatisfied with the rational-industrial worldview, but it has been drowned out by the noise of modernity and postmodernism, and ignored by New Agers.[9]

Modernist icon Newton's third law is that for every action, there is an equal and opposite reaction. Using this law as a metaphor, in the face of the 'modern' West's soulless secularism and outright hostility to Islam, there is an inexorable reaction, as the eternal values of Islam continue to manifest themselves. This is especially witnessed in the month of Ramadan, which continues to demonstrate the powerful spiritual calling of Islam. More than one billion people around the world endure a month of dry fasting from sunrise to sunset, not just as some grueling health gimmick, but a test of the spirit, the will, as proof of devotion. And it is precisely this cultivation of mass 'mind over matter' that frustrates western secularists, so used to indulging every consumer fetish.

Why are Muslims so stubborn in nurturing ancient beliefs and rituals when they fly in the face of modern science and the touted (albeit deceptive) prospect of material plenty? Secular critics dismiss Islam as a harmful, even dangerous anachronism. Why disrupt one's busy day five times to pray, slow down the whole economic order for an entire month every year, ban alcohol and interest—the bedrock of western society?

The now rich and self-satisfied secular West, after centuries of conquest and imposition of its colonial and now neocolonial order, has found itself at a nightmarish deadend. Wars, riots, drug addiction, corruption, famine, and ahead, ecological Armageddon. There is little to cheer for and no coherent explanation for the impasse and the way forward. So the demand that the Muslim world follow in western footsteps rings hollow.

For non-believers, the **social laws underlying modern western society** can help them to understand Islam's continued relevance. One is Mayer Rothschild's dictum: "Give me control of a nation's money and I care not who makes its laws." The other is Carl Clausewitz's "War is the continuation of policy by other means." Together, they point to the underlying western economic and political dynamic which has led to the current crisis. In a nutshell, the dominance of banks in controlling economic affairs (as opposed to governments acting in the popular interest) has created a world where economics is forced to serve their particular needs (speculation, interest and exorbitant profits), and the politics which promotes the interests of banks is—just look around—war.

This is the 'logic' of western society, especially in the past three decades, now that the alternative to capitalism, the Soviet Union, has been dismantled, discredited, and more or less absorbed into the western economic order. This triumph over the 'enemy' left the field open to the Rothschild-Clausewitz logic. Electoral democracy is vaunted, but is a threadbare facade, for while the popular will consistently rejects war and banker hegemony, no political party is able to get elected to represent this popular will.

Even sophisticated postmodernists can be inspired by Islam, which rejects the Rothschild-Clausewitz laws, to see through the fog of our Enlightenment world. Perhaps the most renowned postmodernist, Michel Foucault (1926–1984), shocked his acolytes with his embrace of the Iranian revolution, which he realized was organized around a different concept from previous revolutions—"political spirituality"—a fundamental cultural, social and political break with the modern western order as well as with the Soviet Union and China. The affinity between this European critic of modernity and the antimodernist Islamist radicals on the streets of Iran is startling, but makes sense. Both were searching for "a new politics as a counterdiscourse to a thoroughly materialistic world"; both were disdainful of modern liberal judicial systems; both "admired individuals who risked death in attempts to reach a more authentic existence".[10]

Though Foucault did not produce a study of modern banking, his studies of modern mental institutions, schools, hospitals and prisons revealed the importance of "technologies of power" in creating docile, utilitarian bodies, and more subtle, hidden forms of controlling humans as 'social units', leading him to reject the emancipatory claims of the Enlightenment. This insight was shared by the conservative thinker Gai Eaton, a convert to Islam, who argues, "The whip may be cruel compared with the model prison, but the whipped man recovers. The prisoner who suffers daily humiliation and deprivation of his manhood may never recover."[11] Orthodox Muslim and postmodern neo-Marxist meet in their rejection of Enlightenment secularism.

Believers need no postmodern explanation for the why and how of Islam and the devilish deadend the West now faces. Islam advocates a social order where peace (*islam* means peace, submission, reconciliation) is the highest attainment of society, the goal of all 'policy', to which all should submit. If presented with the choice between the current chaos and the genuine Islamic alternative, the latter would surely be the overwhelming choice of the common people, both in Europe and

America, despite the fact that Muslims represent only 2–8% of the population in the West. Rather than the 'clash of civilizations' advocated by Islamophobes, those who seek social and economic justice can find inspiration in the eternal truths of Islam, looking to Europe's own Islamo-Christian heritage—past and present—to discover an 'alliance of civilizations' that rejects war, usury, moral degeneration and racism—the bane of today's secular world.

For more than a century now, Islam has been bombarded with calls for reform, to bring it into the modern age. I will look at the wide array of **reform movements** here, though after sifting through them, I have come to the conclusion that there is no need for a new Islam. Rather, as Seyyed Hossein Nasr argues, the accumulated tradition of the centuries of Islamic civilization prior to the rise of capitalism is a valuable heritage which merely needs thoughtful application. The all-encompassing nature of Islam meant that a degree of perfection was achieved in art, architecture, and the governing of the rhythms of daily life that has embedded in it the wisdom of ages, where revelation and reason achieved a balance that endures, despite the onslaught of western modernity. "The decline of the Muslims is not due to shortcomings of Islam but to their own failure to live up to it."[12] Thus, *re*-emerging Islamic civilization.

Even secularists such as Vali Nasr are not particularly concerned about reforming Islam, though, reflecting his own understanding of religion, for the opposite reason. He approves of the inherently conservative Muslim worldview and advocates business-friendly policies by the West to build up Muslim middle class entrepreneurs, who will ensure that their countries integrate with the global market economy. He confidently predicts that these forces in Muslim-majority nations will demand the same secularism as the West's middle class does (and that westernized Muslim leaders have been trying to impose for more than a century), where religion is a private affair with no effect on politics and economics. He sees Turkey as the pre-eminent example of how the consolidation of a dynamic pro-business middle class (which just happens to pray and observe Islamic rituals) is perfectly compatible with western values. Though an advocate of assimilation, Vali Nasr nonetheless admires Islam's success over the centuries, which he argues is not due to the use of violence, but due to its perennial embrace of "cultural diversity and intellectual curiosity".[13] This was an attitude that the Prophet Muhammad[14] encouraged in his Bedouin followers, telling them: "Seek knowledge even unto China."[15]

Reflecting these two very different views of the interaction of Islam and modernity, the past two centuries have witnessed two overriding trends in the Muslim world. In the first place, there are some variants of what Vali Nasr calls **Kemalism**, after the founder of the secular Turkish republic, Mustafa Kemal Ataturk, though this could also be called Tanzimat (Arabic for reforms, reorganization), a process begun by Kemal's Ottoman predecessor Sultan Mahmud II a century before the founding of the Turkish Republic in 1924.

This is the path of top-down forced adoption to western modernity, characterized by accepting an imposed economic system of capitalism and a political system composed of 'sovereign' ethnically distinct nation states. The entire Muslim world was subjected to this in some form, be it by a monarch, a military dictator, a colonial administration or a neocolonial 'independent' administration. This includes Turkey, Egypt, Syria, India and Pakistan, Iran, Indonesia and Malaysia, which are the focus of this work, with Saudi Arabia and the Gulf states the 'exceptions that prove the rule'. This policy of western-inspired reform, carried out voluntarily or involuntarily by local elites, by definition operates within the colonial/ neocolonial system, and has had a head-start over those who aim to build a system not based on western modernity and which is contrary to the interests of existing elites.

This trend, which is also called here **assimilationist** or **accommodationist**, contrasts with that of the stubborn **traditionalists** who on the whole reject the modernity which has arisen on the ashes of the Christian—now secular—civilization of the West, who developed a response to this modernity based on the Quran and traditions of the Prophet and the Islamic civilizations of the past 14 centuries. These forces by definition have had to work outside the imperial system, as they were/are, like the communists, fundamentally opposed to it, quasi-revolutionaries, and they have only come into their own to some extent since the fateful year 1979, when the traditionalists achieved their first major breakthrough with the Islamic revolution in Iran. This revolution was the culmination of a process that had begun in the nineteenth century with reformers al-Afghani and Abduh, was furthered by Rida and Iqbal, suffered a mortal shock in the 1948 and 1967 defeats of the Arab world by Israel, given a more militant edge by Maududi and Qutb, and since then has been perverted by the likes of bin Laden. However, it is alive in the writings and activism of dozens of thinkers and activists today, and given further force and meaning by anti-imperialist fighters across the Muslim world. With the Arab Spring the ferment has reached all corners of the world, Muslim and non-Muslim, a cause of celebration for some, and worry for others.

Where in this process to put Saudi Arabia and the Gulf states is problematic, as Saudi Arabia has actively allied with the imperialist order from the establishment of the Saudi state in the 1920s, as have the Gulf states, first as British colonies and then as 'independent' states from the 1970s. As for al-Qaeda and similar organizations, like anti-capitalist revolutionary groups of yore, they are a direct spin-off of the modernist project, and must be seen in this context—the Enlightenment 'mapmaker' is responsible for 'putting them on the map'.

The current reform movements in the Muslim world began two centuries ago, but Islamic thinker-doers only became prominent at the end of the nineteenth century, with the most sustained movements arising in Egypt. There have been 3 waves of Islamic activism in Egypt, which are the focus of this book:

- 1880s+ Afghani/ Abduh (who inspired both secularists and Islamists),
- 1920s+ Banna and the Muslim Brotherhood (MB) movement,
- 1970s+ militant radicals such as Egypt's Islamic Society and the transnational al-Qaeda.

The bedrock of these waves of activism is opposition to western assimilation, focusing on family values, traditional sexual mores and cultural authenticity. The most recent wave is a colorful alliance of sheikhs, informal street preachers, women, scholars, doctors, lawyers, "groping their way toward a new, Islamic order".[16] It is more middle class, 'democratic', characterized by increased attendance at mosques, broad adoption of Islamic dress by men and women, proliferation of religious literature and recordings, and the burgeoning of Islamic organizations.

"The state's blunders over several decades, combined with the historical, social and economic conditions, had laid the groundwork for society's return to religion."[17] In 1979, on the cusp of the Iranian revolution, a young Egyptian MBer, Essam El-Erian (now Freedom and Justice Party vice-chairman and MP) said, "Young people believe Islam is the solution to the ills in society after the failure of western democracy, socialism and communism to address the political and socio-economic difficulties."[18] Three decades later, the Muslim Brotherhood is riding a wave of youthful idealism and reaping the rewards of its 84 years of experience both in organization and as the persecuted shadow of Egypt's march towards modernity, though it is faced by powerful enemies who reject the new 'map' being proposed for society.

The other great centre of Islamic thinking has been Iran, both before and after its 1979 revolution, though the revolution quickly bogged down due to war with Iraq, internal power struggles, economic crisis, and hostility and sanctions imposed by the West. Other Islamic revolutions—in Algeria and Afghanistan—were aborted under western pressure. Turkey's transformation beginning in 2001 with the sweep by Islamists at the polls has been no less fateful in its own way.

Like those earlier upheavals, the Arab Spring is really an Islamic one, the logical reaction to a century and a half of intrigues to incorporate the Middle East and Central/ South Asia into the imperial project. The overthrow of Ben Ali in Tunisia and Mubarak in Egypt in 2011 recap both Turkey and Iran's history in the twentieth century—from secular pro-western dictatorship to an independent democracy inspired by Islam, though this means something very different in each case (see Chapter 4). But Egypt is also charting a new course—re-Islamization of society from below, arguably providing a greater challenge to western interests than terrorists, Turkey's "secular Islam" or even Iran's Islamic experiment.[19]

How Did the Arab Spring Come About?

Pankaj Mishra argues that decolonisation is an ongoing process, and that the Arab Spring is really just a continuation of this, its first concrete manifestation being the founding of the MB in Egypt in 1928, striving to bring about a social system independent of the colonial one imposed on Egypt (and the world) at the time.[20] In this context, the Arab Spring can also be seen as a continuation of the Iranian and Algerian Islamic revolutions (1979, 1990), and the Palestinian Intifadas (1987, 2000).

Even further back are Islamic societies which arose and prospered in southeast Asia and central Africa before the western imperial invasion and have resonance today. Africa itself would have become an Islamic continent if it had not been for the western occupation. The imperialists occupied Africa at gunpoint in the name of Jesus and empire, and managed to stop the overland wave of Islamization, which had been coming peacefully with trade relations, as it was in southeast Asia at the time.

We can keep going back in history, to see ever earlier waves of Islamic awakening, finally arriving at the seventh century message of Muhammad to spread Islam—peacefully—around the world, with the goal a loosely-organized caliphate[21] composed of communities united in faith, relating through trade and sharing their wealth. This is still the vision that Muslims have, though the overpowering might of the imperialists has put it on a back burner, requiring a more complex strategy of unification today.

What explains this adherence to Islam as the basis of Muslims' lives, unlike the case of Christians, Jews or other religions, and for which there is no secular equivalent?[22] For a Muslim, the reason is simple: "Islam is the solution" as the Egyptian MB's slogan succinctly puts it, and always has been. For while the lives of the original Israelites and Christians are shrouded in the mists of history and myth, the lives of the founder and first disciples of Islam are well documented, inspiring the Salafis to dedicate themselves to observing as closely as possible the dress and way of life of the Prophet, and the Sufis to dedicate themselves to trying to simulate the Prophet's state of mind that allowed him to receive the divine revelations.

Apologists for empire predict the current revolutionary surge will fail, in the sense of achieving the aims of the revolutionaries, who, as in all revolutions, are a small minority, and are typically discarded as the traditional political forces reassert themselves. They point out that the systemic economic forces are (so far) unaddressed. In their self-complacent view, the new alignment of forces, now dominated by the Islamists, will simply be forced to reach a *modus vivendi* with imperialism, which will in turn force it to adjust to preserve its position in the Middle East, supported by its economic hegemony and the local cadres of the ruling elite, trained in the West. "There are precedents: in the 1950s and 1960s, Islamists in the region sided with the West and Saudi Arabia against Nasser's Egypt; not long ago they supported Jordan's monarch against the PLO and domestic dissidents; and, today, supposedly Islamist Turkey is both in Washington's good graces and an active NATO member."[23]

The utopian demands of February 2011 will no doubt remain unfulfilled. However, Zhou Enlai's comment about the effects of the French revolution—It is too early to tell[24]—is apropos here. The political forces will shift and be redefined. The MB's 'radical' oppositional role will be passed on—possibly to the Salafis or some new Islamic political alignment. Islam will continue to reveal new Newtonian 'reactions'.

What are the chances of the Muslim world asserting an independent position in the face of American empire and today's rising non-imperialist world bloc, as represented by BRIC and other groupings? The Middle East countries, shaped by a century and a half of imperialism, and incorporated in a forced and haphazard way into the western economic and political order, have a brief moment now when the old sureties have been cast into doubt. But the elites in the Arab world have been educated largely in the West or at least by western expats at English/ French/ German-language schools in their westernized major cities.

Breaking away from the current world order requires bold thinking, leaders who are not in awe of IMF delegations and US senators, with frozen smiles hiding their real intentions. Egypt, the most important of the Arab Spring countries, imports most of its grain to feed the 40% living in poverty. It also produces kiwis and other luxury agricultural goods for export, as a result of foreign advice about how to develop its economy. This may be rational from the point of view of a globalized market, but makes no sense if one's 'map' includes social justice.

Are the Muslim Brotherhoods and other Islamic political forces in the region aware of the scope of the problem? Are they willing and able to take the necessary measures to confront the imperialist system? Will they be allowed to by their own national armies, which for 30 years or more have been trained, armed and financed by US and NATO forces, and take regular part in NATO/US-conducted exercises? Most Egyptians (largely representative of the Arabs of north Africa and the Mediterranean) are suspicious of US intentions in their region, despite a fascination with western pop culture, which subtly glorifies western life and its activities around the world. Whether or not they can extract themselves from the vise they find themselves in is far from clear.

In all cases, the Islamists are fighting to institute a political-economic system—to draw their social map—to help them move towards a society inspired by Islam. Maps—both physical and metaphorical—inherited from their colonial masters are certainly not going to lead them there. But what that means in the twenty-first century is also unclear. Is capitalism compatible with Islam? If not, how can a transition from capitalism to an alternative system be made?

The massive problems that all these countries face are the problems of all third world countries around the world—urban sprawl and ghettos filled with dispossessed illiterate peasants, dysfunctional health and education systems, corruption, civil war/ violence. Fortunately, there are countries elsewhere in the third world, apart from Islamic Iran, which have begun this process, such as Ecuador and Argentina on confronting the IMF, and Cuba, Venezuela, Brazil and Bolivia on resource management and land reform. There are many proven policies that can mitigate the situation—nationalization, co-operatives, multiple exchange rates, debt reduction, bilateral and multilateral cooperation with countries in the region. Non-interest banking has been developed in the Gulf and Malaysia, and is spreading throughout the region. Islam alone cannot possibly have all the answers to the problems raised by imperialism. Islamists will have to learn from their friends who have done battle with the imperialists and survived.

The Russians had Lenin and Marx, and support from disaffected elements in the West in 1917, and were able to forge a new system in the face of bitter enmity from the West. The Islamists have the Quran and their own cadres today, but face a much more powerful and experienced protagonist, albeit in economic disarray. The key will be if the Islamists can take control of security and mobilize their cadres across the country to bring people together on an altruistic basis, as the communists tried to do with mixed success.

When it comes down to it, Islam could be replaced with almost any other religion (or, conceivably, reinvigorated communism), but only Islam has proved durable. The real-world bottom line is the return of morality to politics and economics, after it was banished with the rise of capitalism. After the era of imperialism, and the communist experiment, which tried to bring morality back to economics and failed, it is now the turn of the Islamists. For them, morality derives from spirituality; morality and ethics as concepts are invalid in isolation.

The dilemma of how to bring about this change is at the heart of Koestler's "The Yogi and the Commissar" (1942),[25] where he reflected on the failure of communism as the secular attempt to find a way out of the impasse created by capitalism after the collapse of Christianity and Judaism. The (communist) Commissar is concerned with the individual's relation to society, the Yogi with his relation to the universe. The commissar advocates transformation from without. He insists that all the evils of humanity can and must be cured by revolution and the reorganization of the system of production. The yogi holds that salvation is from within, and that only the spiritual effort of the individual can save the world. History, the disillusioned atheist Koestler concluded, had established the bankruptcy of both theories. The first had led to mass killings and the second led to the passive toleration of everything.

This work explores to what extent Islam avoids Koestler's dilemma, as the goal from the start has been to nurture a morally sound community based on the Quran, where the visions of Commissar and Yogi do not conflict—because they are not separated, Foucault's "political spirituality". Islam is neither capitalism nor communism. Despite tactical alliances by some with the imperialists, I argue here that the principles of Islam are not consistent with long-term accommodation with imperialism. In redrawing—and following—a new map, the stage is set for an exciting and hopeful confrontation, at both the personal and social level, both in the Muslim world and in the West.

***

Note on organization: The topic is broad and the choice of actors here is by no means comprehensive, but hopefully representative. I survey the Muslim world in three stages: the early period up to the era of occupation by imperialism (Great Game I), the period of neocolonial 'independence' (Great Game II), and the era of more genuine independence—of 're-emerging Islamic civilization'—beginning in the 1970s–1980s. Each survey starts with Turkey, Egypt, the Levant, and moves counterclockwise through Africa to Eurasia.

Note on translation: Quranic quotes are from the translation by Abdullah Yusuf Ali (1934). Muslims always add "peace be upon him (PBUH)" when referring to the Prophet Muhammad. This is to be understood throughout the text.

Note on transliteration: Arabic is difficult to transliterate. Texts in English use various methods to indicate the many sounds not used in English. In interest of simplicity,

- I have dispensed with most glottal stops (which foreigners usually ignore and can't pronounce anyway) except in a few cases where they are easy and essential to understanding by an Arabic speaker (al-Ma'mun, *ta'zir*).
- The Arabic soft and medium aitches are transliterated by h, the hard aitch—by kh. The silent "h" and the ending of feminine nouns (sunna, *ijma*, sura) is dropped, except for names which are widely spelt with it in English such as Abduh.
- al-Rahman is used in preference to ar-Rahman. Before 'sun' consonants the 'l' sound disappears but in written Arabic 'al' (the) does not become 'ar', which looks odd in English and only adds to the reader's confusion.
- Proper style should include al- before many 'surnames'; however, in keeping with common usage, Shafii, Wahhab, Gaddafi, etc. will

be written without al- after the first full expression of their names.

- Ibn (son) is capitalized for Ibn Khaldun but not if it is in the middle of a name, e.g., Amr ibn al-As. Similarly with Bin (son).
- I have left certain expressions such as Ahl-i Hadith and Jamaat-i Islam as they appear commonly in western media.
- Arab does not use capital letters, so only the main parts of a person's name are capitalized. Words such as Muslim and Sufi that are widely capitalized in English are capitalized, but otherwise, Arabic words are not capitalized.
- Plurals are complex in Arabic, are used only rarely here and noted in the glossary. In a few cases, anglicized plurals are used where the Arabic word is commonly used in English and the 's' 'works' (e.g., hadiths).

Note on terminology: In English, "Empire" is commonly used for the Ottoman, Safavid and Moghul state formations, though sultanate is more appropriate, the sultan being a Muslim ruler. The Ottomans were sultans, not presiding over a unitary caliphate, though the title caliph was adopted in the nineteenth century to add more authority as the Ottoman rule became more precarious. The various Muslim political formations after the Abbasid Caliphate were not empires comparable to the ones established under capitalism by the West from the sixteenth century on, which used private property and the market to thoroughly change and exploit their colonies. Caliphate rule was much less invasive. Thus I will use 'empire' in quotation marks to differentiate the Muslim from the capitalist political-economic formations. I will use the term Ottoman Caliphate, as after the demise of the Moghul and Safavid 'empires', the Ottomans became the *de facto* spiritual leaders of the Muslim world, if only in name, and were widely seen as such. While we don't speak of the "Christian world", the terms "Muslim world" and "Muslim history" are used, as Islam is much more encompassing, a way of life, as opposed to Christianity or Buddhism. *Dar al-islam* and umma are the Arabic equivalent of "Muslim world", literally "community".

Arabic words and English acronyms are listed in the glossary. Commonly used Arabic words such as sharia, Quran, Sufi, sunna, hadith are not italicized to avoid clutter. There are many legal terms which perhaps are not so necessary, but are included in the glossary for reference purposes. Words like *ijtihad* and *taqlid* are regularly encountered English-language texts about Islam. When a term is important to the discussion, it is in bold the first time.

For dates, (b. 1952) b. means 'born in', (c. 1952) means 'approximately', (r. 1952–1953) r. means 'ruled from', (d. 1953) means 'died in', and (1952–1953) gives lifespan dates.

ENDNOTES

1   Ken Wilber, *A Brief History of Everything*, USA: Shambhala, 2000, 63, 293.

2   W.H. Auden, *The Age of Anxiety: A Baroque Eclogue*, 1947.

3   I use postmodernism in preference to the clumsier postmodernity. The 'ism' can also refer to movements in the arts, but unless otherwise specified, refers to "the whole sweep of post-Enlightenment developments, which also includes postindustrial developments". Wilber, *A Brief History of Everything*, 48.

4   Austine Cline, *atheism.about.com*. It was first used by the agnostic George Holyoake in 1851 to describe his views of promoting a social order separate from religion. The vaguer definition of the principle of separation between government institutions and religious institutions is not particularly useful, making the term merely an antonym for theocracy.

5   Friedrich Nietzsche, *Toward a genealogy of morals,* in Walter Kaufmann (ed.), *The Portable Nietzsche,* 1954, 458.

6   Wilber, *A Brief History of Everything,* 54. A note on Ken Wilber (b. 1949), the guru of the New Age Integral Spirituality movement (integrating body, mind, heart, soul), whose 'integration' is a clear monism (see Chapter 1). While controversial and generally spurned by academia for his views on evolution and for claiming too much for his self-help system, his critique of postmodernity is accessible to the layman and sound, based largely on E.F. Schumacher and Jurgen Habermas. Wilber calls Habermas's subjective (aesthetic), objective (scientific) and intersubjective (moral) consciousness (*The Theory of Communicative Action* (1981)) "the Big Three" cultural value spheres of art, science and morality. See Ken Wilber, *The Marriage of Sense and Soul: Integrating Science and Religion*, USA: Random House, 1998. The Integral Spirituality movement best represents the 'left' wing of the growing spiritual revival in the West, the 'right' wing being the evangelical fundamentalists and Zionists. In a sense, these two wings are the western complements to the growing revival movements in the Muslim world, though there is no exact isomophism.

7   You are a postmodernist when you say that "John Doe's opinion tells more about *him* than about what he's describing."

8   Wilber, *A Brief History of Everything*, 64, 174.

9   Sufism has gained a following in the West, but traditional Islam, the foundation of Islamic civilization, is spurned. Wilber's 'integral spirituality' is arguably an attempt to highjack Sufism.

10 Afary, *Foucault and the Iranian Revolution*, 13.

11 Gai Eaton, *King of the Castle: Choice and Responsibility in the Modern World*, UK: Islamic Texts Society, 1977, 119.

12 Muhammad Asad, *The road to Mecca*, New York: [Simon and Schuster 1954,] Fons Vitae 2000, 162.

13 Vali Naser, *Forces of Fortune: The Rise of the New Muslim Middle Class and What It will Mean for Our World*, USA: Free Press, 2009, 146.

14 Muslims always add "peace be upon him" when referring the Prophet Muhammad. This is understood throughout this text.

15 Hadith narrated from Anas by al-Bayhaqi.

16 John Esposito, *Islam: the straight path*, UK: Oxford University Press, 1988 (1998), 8.

17 Geneive Abdo, *No God but God: Egypt and the Triumph of Islam*, Oxford: Oxford University Press, 2000, 132.

18 Ibid., 132.

19 Ali-Akbar Velayati, senior adviser to Ayatollah Ali Khamenei, Iran's supreme leader, called Turkey's model of "secular Islam" a version of western liberal democracy and unacceptable for countries that he said were going through an "Islamic awakening". "Iran criticises Turkey's 'secular Islam'", *Financial Times*, 13 December 2011.

20   Pankaj Mishra, *From the Ruins of Empire: The Intellectuals Who Remade Asia*, UK: Farrar, Straus and Giroux, 2012.

21   The term caliphate (stewardship) came into use only after Muhammad's death.

22   Except for the belief in communism in the Soviet Union, which was a kind of secular, socialist caliphate.

23   Hussein Agha and Robert Malley, "The Arab Counterrevolution", *New York Review of Books*, 29 September 2011.

24   In response to a question posed by Richard Nixon in 1972.

25   Arthur Koestler was an early (atheist) Zionist who went to Palestine in 1926 but later returned to Europe and joined the German Communist Party. He subsequently became disillusioned with communism, writing *The God That Failed* (1949).

CHAPTER ONE

ISLAM, CHRISTIANITY AND JUDAISM

Muhammad and Islam: 7th–16th Centuries

As the second largest and fastest growing religion in world today, Islam has proved hardier than its monotheistic predecessors, Christianity and Judaism, which have been compromised by their identification with the imperial onslaught of the past two centuries, and by the ongoing Zionist colonial project today. This has left Islam as the most universal religion, where conversion has a very different meaning than it does in Christianity or Judaism.

Advocates of Islam claim that it "is not a new or rival religion among the many competing for human allegiance; it is the natural and primordial religion,"[1] acknowledging all the biblical prophets, with an 'eternal text'[2] uncorrupted over time. Despite its origins in desert Arabia, only 18% of Muslims are Arab— 30% live in the Indian subcontinent, 17% in Asia (the largest Muslim nation is Indonesia), 20% in sub-Saharan Africa, 10% in Russia, China, America, Europe, and 10% in Turkey, Iran, Afghanistan. There are almost 2 billion Muslims, living in communities in virtually every country.

Monotheism developed in the Axial Age (800BC–200AD),[3] when urban civilization developed, together with new, more sophisticated faiths appropriate to it: Taoism and Confucianism in China, Hinduism and Buddhism in the Indian subcontinent, monotheism in the Middle East, all "concerned with the individual conscience, the good life and the question of justice in society."[4] Islam posits the essential unity of the great religions as deriving from a single source of revelation.[5] Eaton argues the wisdom expressed through these religions, as well as the myths of so-called primitive peoples, "inheres in the deepest level of our being so that we need only to be reminded of it in order to rediscover the truth within ourselves."[6] This truth, in a nutshell, is that the world of pain and hardship isn't the only reality, that our life consists of two journeys, requiring two 'maps'. The more obvious journey is downstream through time and space—one's physical life journey. The other is upstream, using time and locality only as starting points,

> a journey described in countless myths, towards the center of being, the passage from the illusory towards the eternally real. … The circumstances of the first journey provide supports for the second, and it was man's aim in the past to build a physical and social environment in which every element had a dual character, existing as a 'thing' in terms of the first journey, standing as a symbol and signpost in terms of the second.[7]

Unlike in Christianity, in Islam there is no doctrine of vicarious suffering or atonement, since there is no *original* sin as a result of which all humanity suffers. Adam, not Eve,[8] is tempted by devil, and the result is *personal* sin, disobedience. Sin is not a state of being but the result of acts of disobedience. Humans are not sinful by nature but are naturally limited, weak and subject to temptation. People are 'born Muslim' and the goal is to bring them back to their inherent being and to strive through life to overcome/ transcend their temptation to sin and be good Muslims. This belief has profound implications for all aspects of life-in-this-world. "In a Christian context, sexuality is traditionally seen as a consequence of the Fall, but for Muslims, it is an anticipation of paradise."[9] God is merciful to Adam. There is little emphasis on feelings of shame, disgrace and guilt. Death is due to the human condition, not due to sin/ the Fall, and was created by Allah as marking the termination of the test of human existence, to be followed by an afterlife in which deeds are rewarded accordingly.

As Islam encompasses the earlier monotheisms, the basic tenets, historical narratives and legends of Islam are to be found in both Judaism and Christianity though with important differences, recapitulating the historical transformations in human history. Adam's son, Abel, the shepherd, is murdered by his brother Cain, the farmer, reflecting the troubled transition from the 'primitive communism' of pastoral life to the sedentary life of agriculture, on which the great civilizations were built, but incorporating exploitation and social injustice. All of the Judaic prophets are recognized in addition to several others.

Jesus, the chief prophet of Christianity, was a radical reformer of Judaism, which had lost its universalism and promise to create a socially justice order, but he did not provide a practical program for doing so. The efforts by his followers to lead a simple, communal life were undone when Christianity was adopted by the Roman Empire. Islam would be the great synthesis of Judaism and Christianity, 're-forming' them as deen, incorporating guidelines for a political and socio-economic order in a 'map' which would guide all individuals pursuing the deeper spiritual journey, though like any temporal order requiring renewal over time, as historical conditions changed.

Pagan Arabia was poor prior to the advent of Islam, but Mecca had become the hub of a thriving trade route dominated by the Meccan Quraish tribe. The new wealth freed the rising merchant class from dependence on agricultural surplus, but along with wealth came inequality. A moral and ethical order was needed to overcome the old tribal prejudices and suspicions, putting the individual center stage and regulating human affairs according to principles of social justice. Tribal egalitarianism had to give way to the broader needs of communities now united by trade. "The Arabs were now ready for an Axial Age faith of their own." Individuals, competing and cooperating, governed by one transcendent God encouraging them to overcome egotism and greed, replaced the communal ideal.[10]

The germ of this 'Arab monotheism' was already present. Violence was prohibited during the festival of worship of the pagan gods at the Kaaba, the Arabs' ancient holy site in Mecca, when tribal hostilities were put in abeyance. Prior to Muhammad's revelations, there were Arabs who were attracted to monotheism, the *hanif*s, including friends and relatives of Muhammad.[11] Local legend nurtured by these *hanif*s had it that Abraham and his eldest son Ismail[12] had rebuilt the Kaaba which had first been built by Adam and fallen into disrepair, and that Ismail had stayed to become the father of the Arab nation.[13] There were some converts to Judaism and Christianity in the Arab world at the time of Muhammad, but they were looked on with suspicion since "both the Persians and the Byzantines had used the religions of Judaism and Christianity to promote their imperial designs in the region ... and Arabs had suffered enough cultural dislocation, as their own traditions eroded. The last thing they needed was a foreign ideology, couched in alien languages and traditions."[14] But Islam is more than just 'Christianity for the Arabs', as it was originally dubbed. Like Jesus, Muhammad was the prophet of a universal God, which the subsequent spread of Islam around the world corroborated.

Islam as deen struck a new balance between revelation and reason, which accounts both for its ability to absorb Greek rationalism (preserving this heritage at a time when Christendom was busy burning books), and for its resilience over time as a civilization, as Christianity and Judaism continued their decline as moral and ethical guides to humanity.[15] The revealed Quran constantly exhorts us to use our reason: "The worst of beasts in the sight of Allah are the deaf and the dumb—those who understand not." (8:22) God teaches Adam the names of things and instructs him to pass the information along. Numerous passages in the Quran and in hadiths attest to the need for Muslims to study, observe and understand the 'signs' of God in the world.[16] Abul Hasan al-Ashari (d. 935) more or less resolved the reason vs revelation debate—whether you can prove God's existence or must accept 'him' on faith as revealed by the prophets—by arguing that while we can study God's attributes, we can only contemplate his essence and must rely on revelation to experience God. (See Appendix A)

Where Islam stands out in relation to Judaism and Christianity is first Muhammad's undeniable historicity as a prophet whose life is thoroughly documented, and the Quran as an unadulterated divine message, while the existence of Jesus, let alone the Jewish prophets who are supposed to have lived hundreds of years previously, is still in dispute. The Torah and Gospels are similarly 'secondary sources',[17] which soon became off-limits to almost all believers, in 'dead' Hebrew and Latin, requiring a high degree of literacy in an age of mass illiteracy. In contrast, the Quran remained accessible—indeed was memorized by countless faithful from all social strata—over the ages, making sure the umma did not stray from the 'true path'.

Secondly, the Muslim social project, which Muhammad (570–632), a descendant of Abraham and Ismail and regarded as the final prophet of Allah, had begun to realize in Medina, was to build a just society on earth as a guide and a foretaste of the divine order. As such he is considered the most important prophet in Islam, though the Jewish prophets are acknowledged and Jesus holds a special place both as a messenger of God and the Messiah (*masih*).[18] The mission of the Prophet was to bring the final version of the word of God, which had been first transmitted to the Jews and then to the Christians, but in each case had been distorted. Muhammad was to establish a community of the faithful on earth, based on practices that were in accordance with and realized God's will, while preparing believers for their life-after-death, their spiritual journey.

By living in accordance with God's will, "a Muslim had to redeem history, and that meant that state affairs were not a distraction from spirituality but the stuff of religion itself."[19] Both politics and history itself are thus sacralized in Islam, rather than religious practice being separated from "real life" and confined to the unworldly. Though Muhammad died after only a decade as leader of the new community in Medina, the documentation of the life of the Prophet and the Muslim experience from 1HE[20] is indisputable and an inspiration to all Muslims. In today's context of foreign devastation of Muslim lands and the pervasive corruption of imposed leaders, it should come as no surprise that the current democratization of the Islamic world is not leading to secularization but sacralization, which is understandably focused on the political and governmental paradigms established during those precious early years in Medina.

All Muslims are reminded daily of their belonging to this earthly community, especially during the month of Ramadan each year, celebrating when Muhammad received the first revelations in 610AD.[21] 1EH (622) marks the *hijra*, the official beginning of the **umma** (community) when Muhammad and most of his followers escaped an increasingly hostile Mecca for Medina.

This is when Muhammad became founder of a state and legal system, creating a political union with the world's first written constitution—the Constitution of Medina—that placed faith above blood-ties, provided a legal framework for security of the community and individuals, religious freedoms and taxation. The ancient pilgrimage to Mecca, the **hajj**, became a pillar of Islam when the conquest of Mecca rid it of an accumulation of pagan gods and restored monotheism.

Muhammad's life is the stuff of legend—though one which is minutely documented. He was orphaned as a boy and was raised by his uncle Abu Talib. Poor and illiterate, but handsome and intelligent, at the age of 25, he married the wealthy Khadija, who was 40, already twice widowed and mother of two sons and a daughter. Together, they had two sons and four daughters, the only one to have children being Fatima. Muhammad and Khadija were married 25 years monogamously, which was unusual for the time, and only after Khadija died did Muhammad take other wives and concubines, mostly for dynastic and political alliances, or because the women were widows. Among them, Aisha, daughter of his companion Abu Bakr, was the most important and his favorite. Though he revealed that a Muslim is allowed only up to four wives, he received special dispensation from Allah (to help consolidate the growing umma, diplomatic relations, and Islamic educational outreach to women) for his 11–13 marriages. Islam in fact marked a revolutionary improvement in the status for all women—wives, daughters, mothers, widows and orphans.

A devout man, he often went to meditate and pray in a secluded cave. One day he returned, terrified, with the first of 23 years of revelations from the Archangel Gabriel. He abandoned his prosperous career as a trader, and for 13 years he chastised the Quraish for the way they were living, warning them of retribution in the afterlife, reciting exquisite verses which his growing band of followers memorized, recited and wrote down. His followers were both poor and rich, slaves and slave-owners. He was plotted against and fled assassination. Emigrating to Medina with some of his followers, [22] he was welcomed and the city effectively became the first Islamic state, its constitution regulating relations between the Medinans. It's the story of both a social and spiritual revolution, with the Quran recording its many stages, establishing a guide for the ages to social and spiritual renewal, a sourcebook of instruction for a kind of 'permanent revolution', renewing humanity's constant effort to establish God's way—'heaven on earth'. And what is the way? The way of concern for the poor and the orphan, against oppression, for the establishment not just of justice in social relations on a governmental level in this world, but purity, fairness and honesty in social dealings on an individual level. To produce good people, good government, each the key to the other.

While the Quran is considered the supreme guide as the direct word of God, the recollections of the prophetic tradition are essentially the first attempts to compile a more detailed explanation of how to live according to the Quran. These recollections are called **sunna,** traditions associated with the life of Muhammad as related in **hadiths** (sayings). Following the Prophet's death in 632, the text of the Quran was compiled and a definitive edition was issued under the rule of Caliph Uthman in 652. The hadiths were gathered over a longer period and there are many versions of them, the most authoritative generally considered that of al-Bukhari, published in 846.

Key dates in Islamic history include:

- the battle of Badr (624), the poorly armed Muslims' seemingly miraculous victory over the Quraish, who outnumbered them three to one,[23]
- the battle of Uhud (625), when the Muslims' army narrowly escaped defeat after internal dissent weakened it,
- the battle of the Trench (627), when the umma's enemies included Jewish tribes who had turned against the Muslims, were accused of treason and later expelled/ killed,
- the peaceful return to Mecca (629–630), involving no plunder and where amnesty was granted to the Muslims' enemies, leading to mass conversion of the Meccans and marking the beginning of the consolidation of Islam in Arabia,
- the death of Muhammad (632),
- the three unified caliphates:
  1. the four Rightly Guided **Caliphs**[24] **Abu Bakr** (Muhammad's father-in-law, father of Aisha), **Umar** ibn al-Khattab, **Uthman** ibn Affan (Muhammad's son-in-law, married to both Ruqayya and Um Kulthum) and **Ali** ibn Abi Talib (Muhammad's cousin and son-in-law, married to Fatima) (632–661),
  2. the **Umayyad** Caliphate (661–750), and
  3. the **Abbasid** Caliphate (750–944, though it formally existed until 1258).

Within a decade of Muhammad's death, the then reigning world powers of Byzantium, Persia and Egypt were incorporated into the Caliphate. The most rapid expansion took place under Umar, when more than two-thirds of the eastern Roman Empire was conquered by the Muslims. Under the Rightly Guided Caliphs, Islam soon dominated the Middle East and Central Asia, forming the most prosperous, peaceful and longest political and economic union/ federation in history.

The Caliphate differed from previous empires by its largely peaceful expansion, with almost no destruction of infrastructure or killing of natives. The Muslim armies were mostly welcomed by the subject peoples as new masters who brought peace and lighter taxation. "The new doctrine did not seem strange, and indeed increasing numbers found it quite a logical further step in their own religious development. "[25] The new rulers provided more flexible and tolerant rule than the Byzantines and Persians, tolerating Christian heterodox sects which had previously been persecuted by both Byzantium and Rome. The Muslims were seen as builders not destroyers. Suddenly across the continent, there arose a *pax islamica*. Imperial rivalries and sectarian bloodletting were suppressed as the new legal system based on the Quran was formulated. The Muslims ruled, but did not force conversion because forced conversion could never result in sincere adherence to Islam. Conversion was even discouraged as it meant losing the poll tax levied on non-Muslims (*dhimmi*), who were freed of obligations such as military service. [26]

> So powerful was the Muslim appeal that it was even able
> to make large-scale advances in territory where another
> major religion had prevailed ... Among 'primitive' peoples
> its preeminence was unrivalled. [It] came closer than any
> other medieval society to establishing a common world order
> of social and even cultural standards.[27]

Immediately after Muhammad's death, various Bedouin tribes reneged on their acceptance of Islam, refusing to pay zakat (charity) for the poor, and there were several false messiahs preaching the continuation of Muhammad's prophecy, which Abu Bakr had to deal with. After these battles, as Islam became the dominant force in the political world, raiding and expansion against hostile, non-Muslim neighbors became the logical activity of the Muslim armies. Later, Islamic law gave a religious interpretation to this conquest, "dividing the world into the **dar al-islam** (abode of peace) which was in perpetual conflict with the **dar al-harb** (abode of war)". After this initial expansion, "Muslims coexisted amicably with the non-Muslim world."[28] Jews welcomed the Muslim armies as they entered Jerusalem (*al-Quds*, meaning "the holy city") in 638, as the Muslims permitted their re-entry to the city from which they had been banned in 135AD.[29] Monophysite Copts[30] welcomed the pluralistic Muslims when they arrived in Egypt in 641, as liberators from their Byzantine Orthodox oppressors.

The umma was early on shaken by two periods of civil strife (*fitna*) over succession involving Muhammad's son-in-law and cousin, Ali, and his son Husayn. Medinan malcontents resented the Meccan caliphs Abu Bakir, Umar and Uthman, and murdered Uthman in 656. Ali was barely elected, dissent continued, culminating in the battle of the Camel led by Muhammad's widow, Aisha. The assertive Damascus Governor Muawiya, a relative of Uthman, declared himself Caliph, and Ali was murdered in 661 by his own extremist followers, the Kharijites, who rejected both power-seekers like Muawiya and Ali for his irresolution. Muawiya, son of Abu Sufyan and Hind,

Muhammad's mortal enemies prior to their surrender of Mecca in 630, was neither a companion of the Prophet nor respected for his religious standing, but a brilliant military leader and strongman who had every intention of establishing a dynasty and did. This marked the end of religious rule by the four rightly-guided caliphs, though Islamic civilization continued to develop and thrive.

The second *fitna* began in 680 when Muawiya tried to arrange the accession of his son Yazid I, opposed by Ali's younger son, Husayn. This was 'separation of religion and politics' with a vengeance, as a monarchy by last-minute Meccan converts, with no grounding in the Quran, replaced rule by consensus of the umma or rule by Muhammad's heirs, as some Medinans were calling for. The Meccan Umayyads, who were now ruling a Meccan Arab 'empire', refused to relinquish power to the more universalist Medinan faction, and in 680 Yazid's forces murdered Husayn, his wives, many of his children and followers in Kerbala (present-day Iraq), causing over 100 deaths.[31] These periods of civil strife came close to destroying the caliphate and left an indelible impression on future Islamic scholars, who sought to ensure stability and continuity of the umma above all.

The Umayyad Caliphate weakened under poor leadership—the bane of dynasties—and gave way to the Abbasids. Bernard Lewis claims the rise of the Abbasids was "a revolution in the history of Islam as important as the French or Russian revolutions in the history of Europe".[32] Eaton calls it "the marriage of the Persian genius with the Arab genius that made Islam the intellectual and imaginative marvel it eventually became,"[33] where the Persians brought the more authoritarian legacy of the Persian Empire to the free-spirited traditions of the Arabs. Previously the empire was run by an exclusively Arab military aristocracy, but under the Abbasids, it became a genuinely universal religion, where the social order was based on agriculture dominated by sophisticated irrigation systems and trade across the entire Eurasia, with a ruling class of officials, merchants and **ulama** (scholars). The upright merchant was taken as an ideal ethical type. A uniform legal system across the continent, sharia (see below), was built on egalitarian expectations of relative mobility. Trade flowered and a substantial, literate urban middle class exerted a democratic influence on the state. Unlike in Christian Europe, the trader and artisan were as respected and important as the landowner and general.

The first Abbasid caliph, Abu al-Abbas (r. 750–754), a descendant of the Prophet's uncle Abbas, liquidated the Umayyad elite, except for Abd al-Rahman, who was also distantly related to Muhammad[34] and who escaped and established himself as emir of the distant Andalus Caliphate in Cordoba, Spain (r. 755–788). Abbas's son Mansur moved the capital of the eastern caliphate to Baghdad in 762, which facilitated trade and expansion of Islam to both Africa and Asia.

The religious 'empire' was strong and united, and produced a powerful and attractive alternative for the merchant, scholar and peasant alike to the Christian one to the West. Until the eleventh century, conversion was seen as a serious threat by the Catholic Church. If the early Muslim caliphate had been more united, say, without the likes of Yazid I, it is quite possible that all of Europe would have 'fallen' to the Muslim armies, welcomed by oppressed peasants and Jews. This 'ideological' threat was an important motivation for the first Crusade (1096–1099)—to reassert western Christianity as the true monotheism, and weaken Islam.

Starting in 786 with Caliph Harun al-Rashid followed by his son al-Ma'mun, the caliphs were sons of slave-concubines to avoid the internecine complications of marrying into families of subjects. But the decline of the dynasty inevitably set in, compounded by the Christian crusades. The aristocracy succumbed to court intrigues, squeezing the peasants and merchants, and was pitched against the military (as mercenaries and Turkic slave officers gained control). Local bureaucracies allowed irrigation to decline and salination to set in. By the twelfth century the Caliphate existed in name only. Spain, Morocco and Tunisia became separate kingdoms, Persia autonomous, with an Ismaili[35] caliphate in Egypt, Syria and western Arabia. The last great military leader of this period was Salah al-Din (1138–1193), a Kurdish officer who established the Ayyubid Caliphate in Egypt and liberated Jerusalem in 1187 (after 88 years in 'Frankish' possession) and again in 1191. His dynasty, like the Abbasids, succumbed to rule by Turkic slave military officers (Mamluks).

From 1000–1250, the Caliphate crumbled under several centuries of war and invasion, first from the West, then from the East, when the Mongols (originally shamanists who later converted to Islam) and their successors, the Timurids, swept down through Eurasia from 1250–1500. But, after centuries of the ulama's quiet labors to construct a durable legal and social framework, "the umma had taken on a life of its own and had become spiritually and socially self-sustaining."[36] Islam continued to spread, now without an overriding political structure, "the trans-territorial autonomy of the religious community as a total moral society able to maintain local and even international solidarity independent of any particular political establishment."[37]

Over time there arose three lesser 'empires'[38] or better, sultanates:

- the Turkish Ottoman (centered in Istanbul, its zenith under Sultan Suleiman the Magnificent 1520–1566),
- the Persian Safavid (centered in Isfahan, its zenith under Shah Abbas 1587–1629), and
- the Indian Moghul (centered in Delhi, its zenith under Emperor Akbar 1556–1605).

They were not caliphates, as no one was leader of the whole Muslim umma anymore, though the Turkish sultan had the best claim to the title of caliph, being the ruler of the holy cities Mecca, Medina and al-Quds. Until their occupation by the western imperial powers from the eighteenth century on, they were characterized by ethnic and cultural diversity, without developing the western-style ethnic nationalisms, nation states and the economic system of capitalism, based strictly on profit.

The **Sunni-Shia** division is the major schism in Islam. "Sunni" comes from the term sunna, Shia from the word faction. The schism arose over the insistence by some Medinans after Muhammad's death that the caliph be a descendant of Muhammad, which meant Ali (Muhammad's cousin and son-in-law, married to Fatima, Muhammad's only child to have children) and Ali's sons Hasan and Husayn.[39] When Muawiya, governor of Damascus, proclaimed himself Caliph and murdered Husayn and his family and followers—a 'faction' of the umma—declared the succession leading to the Umayyad and later the Abbasid Caliphates to be illegitimate.

The Sunni-Shia divide is not the reflection of a reform movement like Protestantism, and never resulted in civil war as the schism in Christianity did. It is more an issue of political-religious authority, not destroying the unity of the umma (although antagonistic forces of course seek this), but expanding its spiritual types, "necessary in the divine 'economy'; for if a religion is to be truly universal and offer shelter to every variety of human temperament, then other faiths—different perspectives—must in some way be reflected in it, though always in images which do not conflict with the basic doctrine."[40] Shiism is associated more with scholarship and Sufism than is Sunni Islam.

"Traditionally Twelve-Imam Shiism avoided direct political power, leaving it to the Mahdi to take political power into his hands upon his reappearance on the historical stage."[41] Shiism elevates the concept of imam (prayer leader for Sunnis) to the level of spiritual leader, tracing twelve subsequent generations of descendants of Muhammad as represented by the 12 Imams, beginning with Ali and Husayn.[42] Apart from the issue of dynastic succession, Shia argue that the Medinans represent the more universalist strain in Islam vs the Meccans who represent the Arabic, tribal origins of Islam. The sharpness of the division waxed and waned, but hardened under the Abbasid Caliph Mansur in the eighth century. About 12% of the world's Muslims are Shia.

Early Islamic Reform

Islam—submission (*islam*) to the one God—was in fact a 'reform movement' of Judaism and Christianity, anticipating the fifteenth century Protestant Reformation 'return to fundamentals', though in a more radical way. The mission of Muhammad, as the last prophet, was to correct the 'map' of man's spiritual journey, to put monotheists back on the 'straight path'. Both Jews and Christians had been given their revelations—the Torah and Gospels—but had strayed over time, Judaism becoming an insular, tribal religion and Christianity the Roman Empire's religion, with pagan accretions. Islam as deen was both the spiritual path and a system of government, as Muhammad became the *de facto* ruler of the first 'Islamic state' in Medina (622–632), confronting him with the need to create order, to administer laws and conduct political and economic affairs—to establish a *pax islamica* based on God's will, a moral social order for the world based on God's laws, where a citizen would grow into a new higher moral and ethical being, *homo islamicus*. A tall order.

After a rocky start, with the threat of civil war and collapse of the umma barely averted, the first startling successes of the followers of Muhammad suggested that the aim was not so utopian. Islam was identified as the religion of success, and Muslims have the fervent belief that it is just a matter of time, not until the apocalypse, but until the 'kingdom of heaven'—Islam—will be realized in the here and now.

The strategy for achieving this at any particular moment in history necessarily changes, though the means (Islam) and the ends (Islamic civilization) are the same 'path', and thus the true path. The challenge from the start lay in

- interpreting the word of God, applying it in the real world, and reinterpreting it over time under changing conditions. From today's perspective, there are obvious anachronisms in the Quran such as slavery which have to be confronted in interpreting the Quran's message.
- just what constitutes a 'society governed by Islam', though there are clear statements in the Quran about providing for the welfare of the umma, and at the same time protecting property rights and regulating economic activity to avoid exploitation.
- the role in this process of the umma, as opposed to the ulama (Islamic scholars).

The unity of the umma is not in the first place reliant on politics, but on the commitment to the belief in the oneness of God and the obligation to follow God's law—which over the evolution of the Islamic community took on its civilizational dimension in **sharia**. "Islam was the community which succeeded perhaps most strongly in building for itself a total society, demarcated sharply from all culture before and beyond its limits ... [by] its own system of comprehensive law." The Christian communities took over pagan Roman law. For Muslims, "the laws and customs of humans are reoriented toward a universal justice."[43] Unlike Christianity's canonical law, sharia reform was and is the essence of social reform for Islamic civilization.

In 11 of the 50 Muslim-majority states today, constitutions acknowledge Islam as a source of national law,[44] but even without a constitution based on Islam, Muslims living in a non-Muslim nation, or under Muslim leaders who are corrupt, are obliged to "live according to the sharia" in the belief that a popular Islamic "counter-culture" can "transform the corrupt political order of their day, and make it submit to God's will".[45]

The history of Islamic civilization corroborates this, for it has gone through periods of stability and then upheaval and reform, and survived. Most revolutionary leaders do not make good administrators and their movements fail. However, Muhammad's ability to governor and adapt to changing circumstances, and the powerful message of social justice embodied in sharia, ensured that the movement would endure despite the *fitnas* of the first Caliphate, and replace the Byzantine and Persian empires with a new order, rather than being absorbed and compromised by them, as Christianity had been by the Roman Empire.

The first reform movement within Islam arose when those dissatisfied with the increasingly arbitrary monarchy of the Umayyads and their successors, the Abbasids, called for a return to the ideals of Muhammad and the Rightly Guided Caliphs. This resulted in the codification of sharia law, which became established over time as a detailed system of jurisprudence (*fiqh,* from the Arabic root "understand"), similar to the Torah of the Jews and the much later canonical law of the Christians, based on the Quran and sunna, as recorded in the hadiths. Islamic law emphasizes its vital role in "the understanding of divine commands"[46] and their implementation in daily life. The religious scholar in Islam is thus primarily a jurist, unlike in Christendom.

There are few specific legal injunctions in the Quran. Sharia (literally "way to the watering hole" for man or animals, emphasizing its role in returning us to God), as revealed there, is not a codified canon of unchanging law for all time, but rather values and principles which are eternal, a 'map' to help us return to "the water that leads to eternal life".[47] What is often implied in discussions of sharia today is in actuality *fiqh*, a socially-constructed product, conflating law and morality.

Islamic law does not pretend to be merely a neutral method to govern social relations, but a call to act morally; as stated in the Quran: Muslims are "a band of people ... enjoining what is right and forbidding what is wrong".[48] "We are judged, not by some alien despot who rules—or misrules—the universe [or the political sphere], but by the Norm inherent within us."[49] "Whosoever sins, sins only against himself." (4:3) Even when tyrants rule, the sharia governs Muslims' lives in conjunction with the ulama.

For the citizen, the question is, "What does God want me to do?" For the legal scholar, the *faqih*, it is, "Which means do I have to find this out?"[50] Sharia is akin to natural law, which holds that morality is a function of human nature, and that reason can reveal valid ethical and moral principles by looking at humanity in its social context, and deduce binding rules for society and the individual. It contrasts with positive law (arbitrary man-made law), which denies the existence of *a priori* ethical and moral principles. Of course, the *a priori* ethical and moral principles in the case of Islam are found in the Quran and sunna as related in the hadiths. The relationship between the sharia of the Quran and *fiqh* is similar to the relationship between the constitution and the body of laws based on the constitution—hence the popular slogan "The Quran is our Constitution".

Though there have been many attempts to cobble together international laws and treaties in the age of empire, secular international law is a poor imitation of the sharia that once regulated state relations from Africa to Eurasia. Without a common moral and ethical foundation and a means of enforcement, international law is little more than a reflection of the behavior and values of the most powerful states.[51]

But sharia encompasses much more than civil law codes as developed in the West. It deals with procedures of worship, personal hygiene, social relations and governance, and is regulated less by a state police force than by consensus of the community—hence the demand for it among Muslim peoples seeking to be freed from their colonial and neocolonial masters. There is the perception in the West that Islamists want to 'impose' sharia to limit the freedom of individuals. But in Muslim societies, the norms of personal behavior are already instilled in the customary practices of the people. What Islamists want is that the sharia apply to *the state*, regulating/ 'limiting' its activities to ensure that governance complies with Islam. A state that leads people away from an Islamic way of life violates sharia and is illegitimate.

The call for a return to the Quran and hadiths thus became the defining theme of all reform movements, not to 'rationalize' Islam and make it compatible with the prevailing 'modernity', but to revive the social and spiritual deen of the 'Golden Age of Islam', however short it might have actually been. "Revivalism is inherent in the logic and experience of Muslims in history."[52]

This reform zeal characterizes the great flowering of Islamic culture which took place under the Abbasid Caliphate beginning in 750. The growing class of scholars under the Abbasids, having preserved the intellectual traditions of the Greeks, and building on the earlier Islamic scholarship, established the body of work which is still the foundation of Islamic studies today: theology (*ilm al-kalam*), the schools of legal sciences or jurisprudence (*ilm al-fiqh*), and the Mutazilite and Asharite schools of thought (see Appendix A).

Fiqh developed as four major movements (*madhhabs*) founded by the Sunni scholars Hanifa, Malik, Shafii, Hanbal, and the Shia Jafari al-Sadiq. It emerged in the 8th–9th centuries, primarily under Caliph al-Mahdi (r. 775–785), based on the revelations about legal matters in the Quran's Medinan suras (especially suras 2–5, the later suras where the nuts and bolts of political and economic governance are laid out). The methodology for developing *fiqh* is called *usul al-fiqh*. Scholars used their reasoning to give "fresh views (*ijtihad*) on the basis of traditional legal principles ... *qiyas* (analogy),[53] *ijma* (consensus of opinion), *istihsan* (judicial preference)".[54] *Urf* (local customs) also played a role in the local manifestations of sharia, though less so after the ninth century, and not at all for Shia.

Ijtihad (independent reasoning) is the broadest term implying the use of reason to develop concrete answers to real problems based on the Quran and hadiths. It derives from the reflexive form of the root *j-h-d* (struggle), and has roots in a discourse between the Prophet and Muadh ibn Jabal when he was sent as a judge to Yemen.

Prophet: "Through what will you judge?"
Jabal: "Through the Book of God."
Prophet: "And if you find nothing in the Book of God?"
Jabal: "I shall judge according to the tradition [sunna] of God's Messenger."
Prophet: "And if you find nothing in the Messenger's tradition?"
Jabal: "I shall not fail to make an effort [*ajtahidu*] to reach an opinion."[55]

The importance to Islam of sharia is hard to overestimate, as it preserves the unity of the umma even in the absence of the overarching political structure of the caliphate, as occurred more than once in history, and is the case today, when Muslims are divided and even under the rule of non-Muslims.

Over time, the rising class of religious scholars and the law itself gradually became independent of the ruler, and legal decisions had to be "witnessed and validated by upstanding men of the Muslim community, bound by oath: a jury, some four hundred years older than its English equivalent".[56] *Taqlid* (use of precedence, literally imitation) was borrowed from the Persian and Roman empires to protect the position of scholars, and is the principle responsible for the accumulation of the many volumes of *fiqh,* which some consider precludes further *ijtihad*. What to do about legal issues not precisely addressed in the Quran and hadiths, whether they can be resolved using *ijtihad*, or whether society must rely only on the accumulated decisions of Muslim legal scholars (*taqlid*), lies at the heart of the controversy in Islam over the meaning of reform and how to pursue it.

The **Hanafi** school was founded by Abu Hanifa (699–767), and is the oldest and by far the most popular,[57] adopted as the official *madhhab* of the Abbasids, Ottomans and Moghuls, and followed today in Pakistan, India, Turkey and Egypt. It emphasizes the role of reason (*ijtihad* and *qiyas)* and consensus (*ijma*) if direct material cannot be found in the Quran or hadiths, and is considered more liberal than the other three schools. One notable ruling is that women may serve as qadis (judges).

This led to the more conservative **Maliki** school[58] founded by Malik ibn Anas (711–795). It stresses scholarly consensus, public interest, and relies heavily on the legal rulings of the four Rightly Guided Caliphs, primarily Umar, the Salafi (the Muslims of Medina at the time of the Prophet) and *urf*. Malik's best known work is *Al-Muwatta* (well-trodden path), the earliest authentic collection of hadiths.

The **Shafii** school, the official school of most traditional scholars and leading Sunni authorities (e.g., former Grand Mufti of Egypt Ali Gomaa), was founded by Muhammad ibn Idris al-Shafii (767–819) as a synthesis of the Hanafi and Maliki schools. Shafii developed a cohesive, systematic procedure for *ijtihad* where there is no clear rule governing the case at hand, based on the Quran and the sunna,[59] and broadened the definition of *ijma* as the consensus not only of the pious Muslims of Medina but of the leading jurists of the day. With Shafii, there is a unification of law across the Caliphate, ending local traditions, and independent *ijtihad* is discouraged.

These schools of jurisprudence are close and stand apart from the other Sunni school, the **Hanbali** school, founded by Ahmad ibn Hanbal (780–855), the most conservative one, which is followed in Saudi Arabia today. Hanbal studied under Shafii and traveled extensively through Iraq, Syria, and Arabia collecting traditions of the Prophet. He was opposed to any kind of innovation, rational methods or extensive philosophical interpretation, arguing that reported practices of the first three generations of Muslims and Salafi take priority over scholarly consensus and even hadiths.

The Shia use the **Jafari** school of jurisprudence. Jafar ibn Muhammad al-Sadiq (702–765) was a descendant of the Prophet's family and as such, for Shia, was the legitimate heir as caliph. He is considered by Shia as the sixth of the twelve Imams of Ahlul Bayt (Family of the House, referring to the family of the Prophet). He was a respected scholar and teacher of Hanifa, but, as the Shia's legitimate pretender, was imprisoned and finally poisoned by the second Abbasid Caliph Mansur. Jafar's four books of *usul* (foundations) are the main sources of hadiths for the Shia, who considered hadiths authentic only if the Quran confirms them.

These legal schools have defined the scope and direction of reform movements in Islam ever since. By the tenth century, following the argument of Hanbal, most Sunni jurists believed that *ijtihad* was no longer necessary or permitted, that *taqlid* built up over the previous two centuries was enough, especially as most Muslim scholars were by then non-Arab and Arabic was not understood by everyone throughout the caliphate. Critics contend the original dynamism of Islamic jurisprudence, characterized especially in the Hanafi school by *ijtihad,* was lost and **"the gates of ijtihad closed"** (*insidad bab al-ijtihad*).[60]

Ijtihad is in fact an obligation of Islam law and "the widespread notion that the 'door of *ijtihad* was closed' in later centuries as a matter of theological principle has been shown in recent scholarship to be without historical foundation."[61] Jurists could not always agree, and legal authorities known as muftis have always been issuing fatwas on legal matters, clear evidence of *ijtihad*. Rather, there were bursts of innovation and application of reasoning at different historical junctures. Despite being the most conservative in legal issues, Hanbali scholar Ahmad ibn Taymiya (1263–1328) urged Muslims to rise against the Mongols as illegitimate rulers, despite their claim to have converted to Islam, directly contradicting the accumulated *fiqh*.[62] Though most legal questions had precedents from the established Sunni schools of thought, *ijtihad* continued. The Shia ulama under the Safavids defied the shahs by denying their dynasty to be the successor of the Imams, and sided with the merchants and poor against arbitrary autocracy.

The very structure of the Caliphate precluded the policing of any attempt to 'close the gates'. The vast distances, the loose rule of very different cultures with different languages, gave local scholars the chance to exercise their intellects. The greatest thinkers in Islam came from distant outposts— Tunis (Ibn Khaldun), Andalus (Ibn Rushd), Turkestan/ Persia (Ibn Sina).[63] There were simultaneously *three* caliphates in the tenth century—Baghdad, Cairo, Cordoba—each with its own community of ulama, though this did not weaken Islam (as the existence of three popes in fifteenth century Europe weakened Christianity), as the caliph was not legislating the word of God, but rather was representing the umma in worldly affairs, in consultation with the leading scholars. His rule must, of course, be in accordance with God's will, and local scholars were there to advise him, using accepted traditions of *fiqh* to arrive at a consensus on important matters, both religious and worldly—*ijtihad*.

Islamic law became rigid, the conventional wisdom goes, and today's Islam is supposedly eight centuries out of date, in need of both a Christian-style Reformation and an Enlightenment to bring it into the twenty-first century. On the contrary, the burst of creativity in the 8th–11th centuries, when interpretation, reasoning by analogy, consensus and consultation flourished, resulted in the Islamic world being far more 'civilized' than a Europe stumbling through the Dark Ages. The Flemish ambassador of the Holy Roman Empire in Constantinople wrote: Muslims were "personally more gentle and sober than their opposite numbers in the Occident; even animals were treated with relative humanity."[64] Though Muslim rulers vied with each other (for instance, the Ottoman-Safavid rivalry), there was never a war between Muslim states, unlike in Christendom.[65]

This created a body of legal theory that did not so much "close" by the fourteenth century, but achieved a completeness that ensured that Islam would spread and remain the most vibrant of the world's religions over time.

The development of Islamic *fiqh* was an "immense achievement. Formulated over the course of a few centuries, it took root across three continents and outshone Christendom for almost a millennium." It adapted to local conditions and customs, and "helped bind civilizations that were as diverse as any the world has seen."[66]

In Islamic law, legal obligations fall into two categories: rights of God and rights of humanity, with corresponding punishments—***hadd*** and ***ta'zir***. All *hadd* (divinely revealed punishments, literally 'limit', plural *hudud*) and obligations set by revelation are rights of God.[67] The rights of God include "clear ones" (defining procedures of worship and ritual acts) and "ambiguous ones" requiring interpretation. Innovation (***bid'a***) is not acceptable concerning the rights of God, but is acceptable when undertaken by qualified jurists for the rights of humanity based on the perceived goals of the Quran (*maqasid*) (see below). Examples of recent acceptable *bid'a* include abolishing slavery and the call for universal literacy. Concerning the Sunni-Shia divide, the majority Sunni position is that Shia are "people of religious innovations", because of their "mistaken belief that Ali was the rightful successor of Prophet Muhammad"[68] and their revision of prayers to include Ali and Husayn.

Hudud penalties are specified only rarely in the Quran, and, in the case of theft and murder, can be cancelled if there is sincere repentance:

- Theft (amputation of the right hand) (5:38–40),[69]
- *Zina*, meaning fornication/ adultery (100 lashes) (24:2),
- False accusation of *zina* (80 lashes) (24:4–5),
- Murder (capital punishment only if the victim's family does not agree to settle for blood money) (2:178–179).
- *Hiraba*, meaning organized crime, armed robbery, "wag[ing] war against Allah and His Messenger, and striv[ing] with might and main for mischief through the land"[70] (execution, crucifixion, cutting off of hands and feet from opposite sides, or exile from the land) (5:32–33).
- *Fitna*, meaning tumult/ chaos, with connotations of sedition, is also condemned but without specifying a punishment,[71] the clear aim being to target those who joined the enemies in Medina, i.e., committed treason against the umma.

Other crimes (drinking alcohol, "lewdness") are mentioned but no punishment prescribed, and with the understanding, as in the case of theft, that repentance is an option. Homosexual acts are punished vaguely if at all: "If two men among you are guilty of lewdness, punish them both. If they repent and amend, leave them alone; for Allah is Oft-Returning, Most Merciful." (4:16) On the other hand the Sodom /Lot history is included as a lesson about willful, widespread violation of moral norms.

The subsequent *fiqh* laws prescribing stoning and capital punishment for crimes clearly reflect the weight of pre-Islamic tradition or imitation of western practices at the time. Stoning was a penalty from at least 2350BC in Mesopotamia and part of premodern Jewish practice. In fact, there was one stoning for fornication in 500 years of the Ottoman Caliphate.[72] This goes for attempts to extend *fitna* and *hiraba* to include religious disputes, under the charge of apostasy, and to apply capital punishment.[73] They contradict the Quran, where there is no penalty specified for religious doubters.[74]

It is not easy to impose *hadd* (four witnesses must testify in the case of fornication, and the punishment for false testimony is almost as severe as for the crime itself). Only *hiraba* cannot be forgiven and even it can be punished by mere exile.

Ta'zir punishments developed over time as state-imposed punishment for sins with no explicit sentence in the Quran. They do not have the safeguards of *hadd* which meant they could be arbitrary, and there was not the same requirement that crimes be rigorously proven. They are determined in accordance with public interest (*maslaha*), and are open to adjustment and judicial review. They can be introduced to modify *hadd* penalties under special circumstances. Umar's suspension of amputations for theft was an early example. All of this, of course, is only valid within a Muslim state governed by sharia.

Sharia in principle is more humane than other legal systems. The Quran emphasizes God's mercy and the preferability of forgiveness and repentance to the exaction of specific punishments, which are very few in the Quran. There is always God's punishment in the hereafter, even if miscreants slip through society's legal system. Muhammad made clear that it is better to ignore or hide lesser sins than to actively seek to prosecute them. "Whosoever covers (the sins of) a Muslim, Allah covers (his sins) on the Day of Judgment."[75] God is merciful and compassionate, as Muslims are reminded when they pray five times every day.

Maqasid (goals or purposes) is a branch of Islamic philosophy begun under Caliph Umar and associated with the Maliki school of *fiqh* that gives priority to the spirit of the message deriving from the Quran and sunna. As applied to sharia, there are five *maqasid* as developed by the twelfth century Islamic scholar Muhammad al-Ghazali (d. 1111), later added to by Ibn Taymiya and Abu Ishaq al-Shatibi (d. 1388): the preservation of religion, life, lineage, intellect and property. "Anything which furthers these aims is *maslaha* (public interest)."[76] Ibn Taymiya added fulfillment of contracts, preservation of kinship ties, honoring the rights of one's neighbors, sincerity, trustworthiness and moral purity. As opposed to reading verses of the Quran in isolation, the *maqasid* approach requires a comprehensive reading of the text as an integrated whole in order to identify the higher objectives and then interpreting particular verses on a given topic according to the identified *maqasid*. In one's actions it is necessary always to look at the context, to see if something will do more harm than good before one practices it.

The basic tenets of Islam are summarized in what has come to be known as the **five pillars** of Islam, as related in the sunna: belief in one God, regular five-times-a-day prayer, fasting during the month of Ramadan, zakat and pilgrimage. Our time on earth is short. These pillars are all coordinates on the 'map' of the 'second journey'. We need a "distraction from distraction", which these straightforward yet rigorous practices ensure.[77]

Though not one of the pillars of the faith, **jihad** (struggle, effort) in defense of the faith became a kind of "sixth pillar" following Muhammad's death. [78] Under the Prophet, raiding enemy caravans had provided income and an occupation for the converts. With the Persian and Byzantine empires and western Christendom ready to destroy the upstart Arab religious community, Muslims found inspiration in the so-called verse of the sword: "Fight and slay the pagans wherever you find them." (9:5) The context for this ayat was a specific instruction, a rally-the-troops call prior to the battle of Badr in 624, against "those with whom you make an agreement, then they break their agreement every time." (8:56) It was not meant to refer to all unbelievers, but those who betrayed the Muslims. Later it came to be interpreted as God commanding that the Hijaz (Arabian Peninsula) was to be cleared of all nonbelievers.

Similarly, the 'terror verse'—"Soon shall we cast terror into the hearts of the unbelievers" (3:151) —was addressed specifically to Muhammad before the battle of Uhud in 625, when the Muslims' small, ill-equipped army was going up against a much larger, well-equipped enemy. These verses cannot be taken as a *principle* for warfare.

The first instance of the root word *j-h-d* in the Quran is: "Therefore do not obey the negators, but strive against them (*jahid-hum*) with the Quran with the utmost resistance (*jihadan kabira*). (25:52) In other words, "God orders His Messenger to resist the Quraish's ill-treatment of him by relying on the Quran. The text is his spiritual and intellectual weapon against their aggression."[79] According to a hadith, Muhammad surprised his warriors on returning from the bloody Hunayn expedition, declaring: "We are back from the lesser jihad to the greater jihad." The transcendent, allegorical "greater jihad", he explained to them, is "fighting the self [ego]", the inner struggle "that takes people from the natural tension of passions to the peace of spiritual education".[80]

The only clear call to armed jihad in the Quran is: when you are directly attacked: it then is an 'individual duty' (*fard ayn*) to fight to defend yourself and your community. "To those against whom war is made, permission is given to fight, and ... [to] those who have been expelled from their homes in defiance of right for no cause except that they say: 'Our Lord is Allah!'" (22:39–40)[81] It is wrong to *start* a war: "Fight in the cause of God those who fight you, but do not commit aggression." (2:195) Jihad as war is only for defense of freedom of religion, one's country, for the liberty of one's community

(22:39–40, 2:190). A corollary of this (via *ijtihad*), is that only the leader of the umma can declare war.

"The root word [jihad] appears 41 times in 18 chapters of the Quran— and not always in the sense of sacred war—while prohibitions against warring occur more than 70 times."[82] There are 140 verses in favor of peace.[83] Far from being the militants' 'sixth pillar', jihad, be it greater or lesser, is really just a call to be energetic in observing the faith, and

> resides within all the other 'pillars'. From the spiritual point of view, all of the 'pillars' can be seen in the light of the inner jihad, which does not oppose, but rather complements contemplation and the attainment of peace that results from the contemplation of the One.[84]

The mystical **Sufi** tradition in Islam arose in the tenth century in reaction to the rationalist Mutazilites (see Appendix A). It insisted that reason cannot be applied to theology, that while God is transcendent, religious experience is first of all attained through the immediacy of revelation, achieved through trance-inducing rituals and asceticism. "The external gestures are not to be regarded as ends in themselves but as a means of acquiring *taqwa*, the 'God-consciousness' prescribed by the Quran and practiced by the Prophet, which consists of a constant remembrance of God (*dhikr*)."[85] Some have viewed Sufism as "the inner dimension or heart of the Islamic revelation" which is the belief/ brotherhood (*tariqa*) for those who wish to devote themselves entirely to "encounter their Creator here and now, and not a teaching meant to be followed by all members of the community."[86]

Islamic mysticism has a rich tradition and is much more accessible than Jewish and Christian mysticism. The Prophet spoke of three degrees in religion: *islam* (submission), *iman* (faith) and *ihsan* (excellence). Sufism "is the means of bringing both submission to God and faith in God to their logical conclusion."[87] Islam's lack of an all-powerful hierarchy, unlike the Christian church, facilitated the radical Sufi critique of orthodoxy. Sufism is the esoteric aspect of Islam, supported and complemented by Islam's exoteric practices and Islamic law. This dialectic of the esoteric/ exoteric is an important element in Islam's vitality, unlike its monotheistic cousins. Christianity ruthlessly repressed its mystics and Judaism successfully incorporated its mystical tradition into its elitist racial doctrines.

The otherworldiness of Sufis has thrived on contradiction and controversy. The metaphors commonly used in Sufi poetry are falling in love and being intoxicated with wine. Given its passionate nature, it is hardly surprising that Sufism is criticized by orthodox Muslims for verging on heresy, collapsing the Creator into his creation, which is the essence of animism and monism (Creator and creation are one). Al-Hallaj, one of a legendary handful to be executed as an apostate,[88] claimed it was possible to make a valid hajj in spirit, while staying at home. He claimed that his prayers allowed him to channel God: "I am the true one (*al-haqq*)." This was heretical, turning Islam, at least for him, into a monism.

In the absence of a pope and central authority (the pope authorized and controlled monastic orders), control of Sufism has always been exercised largely by public opinion, the consensus of the umma, curbing these mystics, who often disdain any concern for their appearance, apparel or outward behavior (which is un-Islamic), without preventing those with genuine vocation from following their destiny. Ghazali was

> the great bridge-builder between the two contrasting dimensions of Islam. No one could rival him either in his knowledge or his practice of the sharia, nor—in his own time—had he any equal as an exponent of Sufi doctrine. He 'legitimized' Sufism. His *Revival of Religious Sciences* was a synthesis which covered every aspect of the believer's lifepath [including] the mystical path.[89]

The rise of Sufism was a natural reaction to the rapid geographical expansion and new wealth of the Islamic community, which had resulted in decadence and a weakening of spirituality. After the first flush of expansion of the caliphate in the 7th–9th centuries, Islam was spread largely by both merchants and wandering Sufis, providing two very different approaches to spiritual life, one of which could find common ground with all potential converts and which could adapt to radically different cultures in India, Africa and Asia. It was not Christopher Columbus or Vasco da Gama, but rather countless Muslim merchants, scholars and Sufis who were the first great explorers—physically, intellectually, and of the human consciousness. Thirteenth century Persian poet Saadi, in *Golestan*, called merchants and Sufis "two almond kernels in the same shell".

Just as the legal schools and the ulama developed into formally recognized institutions, Sufi brotherhoods were formed, bringing together those devoted to pursuing a mystical experience inspired by the Quran. Kung calls this the "paradigm of the ulama and the Sufis",[90] which has defined Islam ever since. The most well known orders are the Chishti (India and Pakistan), the Mawlawis (Turkey and Egypt) and the Naqshbandis (started in Bukhara and spread throughout the Muslim world).[91]

At the very time of decline in the worldly status of Islam, Sufism gained new followers. In the thirteenth century, Sufis even became leaders within the umma, when Mongols attacked status quo rulers, and educated mediators were required. In the period between the Mongols and the Safavids, Sufism blossomed, producing Islam's greatest poet, the Persian Jalal al-Din Rumi (1207–1273), and became "a bridge between Sunnism and Shiism and in many instances prepared the ground for the spread of Shiism."[92] The great Muslim states of the Ottomans, Safavids and Moghuls all came about due to Sufi proselytizing and culture.

Over time, Sufism, once a reaction to decadence, itself became associated with decadence, as withdrawal from the world and asceticism—not part of the early traditions of Islam—are ill-suited to resisting an aggressive enemy intent on destruction, as happened when the Crusaders and then Mongols invaded Muslim lands from the 11th–14th centuries. Sufism never produced a viable social order, tending to degenerate into authoritarianism and become a cult of the Master.

At the same time, the contribution of Sufism to Islam's resilience over the ages, especially in the face of western secularism and imperialism cannot be exaggerated. From the 13th–16th centuries, Sufism was an essential element which contributed to a flourishing intellectual culture throughout the Islamic world. "Sufi *tariqa*s [orders], in an age when it was no longer feasible for a single conventional government to give unity to the whole of Islam, were able to offer not only a flexible element of social order, but also a correspondingly elastic sense of all-Islamic political unity."[93]

Sufis have been persecuted by both secularists (republican Turkey, the communist world) and Islamists (Iran, Saudi Arabia), and by definition—being focused on inner experience and dismissing the 'real world' as unreal—are not a significant direct factor in contemporary Islamic reform movements.[94] Though for the most part eschewing direct political activism,[95] Sufism retains a vigorous following around the world. Certainly it appears to be a particularly compelling introduction to Islam for disillusioned westerners (see Chapter 5). A taste of the headiness of Sufi thought is captured in this quote by Rumi:

> The greatest misfortune that could befall any human being is not to feel the pain of severance, which goads a man or woman to the religious quest. We must realize our inadequacy and that our sense of selfhood is illusory.

Rumi is the most popular poet in the US today, not to mention Turkey and Iran.[96]

In contrast to Islam, Judaism and Christianity's origins are shrouded in myth. Neither began as a political movement nor has much to say about **politics**. Early Jewish communities were tribal structures, and legends about the Hebrews' early political system describe kingdoms, rulers approved by God but whose dynasties suffered the fate of all dynasties. Both Jesus and Muhammad began their missions with revelations and a small band of followers. But 'separation of church and state' was inherent from the start in

Christianity: "Render unto Caesar the things which are Caesar's, and unto God the things that are God's" (Matthew 22:21). Jesus made clear that "my kingdom is not of this world" (John 18:36) and distanced his community from political power. His followers were left to pick up the pieces after his death, developing communities and rules to regulate them under the Apostle Paul. The church elders developed into a hierarchy of bishops, and as the church grew and the secular power of the Roman Empire waned, Christianity was adopted by the empire as a unifying ideology, an adjunct to political governance, which left the ruling structure of the empire intact. Christian law became an amalgam of Judaic and Roman secular law, the sacred and profane side-by-side.[97]

In contrast to Christianity, the Islamic order from the start was a "political spirituality", and Muhammad 'the politician' was replaced by the caliph, elected by consensus of his companions (although for the Shia, the caliph must be a descendant of the Prophet). The Muslim community, dedicated to the spiritual life journey, formed the core around which the Islamic 'state' was built. The journey is from the illusory towards the eternally real, in a world that is divine, and the new order was built around this deen, rather than being a compromise with a secular empire.

When a well-meaning western critic such as Hans Kung calls for the 'separation of religion and state' in the Muslim world today, he is projecting his own (secular) cultural heritage where it doesn't belong. Muslims interpret this call as the divorce of morality and politics, as abandoning the spiritual journey, as happened in the West. The secular West relies only on 'the will of the people' as confirmed in 'democratic elections' (i.e., the tyranny of the majority), without any moral and ethical touchstone, let alone religious sanction, other than what might be found in the state's constitution.

The priority of the spiritual journey meant that tribal Bedouin traditions of seventh century Arabia were replaced by a structured state governed by religious principles; thus, the inherent opposition between church and state of Christianity was absent from the start. The 'state' in Islam is special, as

> the umma has sacramental importance as a 'sign' that God has blessed this endeavor to redeem humanity from oppression and injustice. ... Debates about who and what manner of man should lead the umma proved to be as formative in Islam as debates about the person and nature of Jesus in Christianity.[98]

However, Islam is theo*centric* rather than theocratic. In religious succession, Muhammad 'the Prophet' was replaced by the Quran and sunna, which gave rise to the ulama to interpret these sources and advise the ruler.

The ruler occupies a peripheral role, not as a representative of God on earth and interpreter of His will, but rather as chief custodian who administers and strives for consensus of the umma, defending it against its enemies and maintaining the law. A stern, reluctant autocrat is conceivably better than an eager conciliatory leader if he is more effective in fulfilling the functions allotted to him.

Originally, the Rightly Guided Caliphs were 'elected', agreed upon by the senior, most respected Muslims by consensus, though the later rulers established dynasties, and the tradition of legitimacy through election gave way to 'might is right', as happened to the Hebrew kings of legend. Many rulers were nonetheless religiously inspired and just.[99]

Unlike the aphoristic sayings of Jesus and his emphasis on love as the overriding divine attribute and the key operating principle for humanity, the message Muhammad received was more directly imbued with instructions about how to regulate the umma's affairs, including political relations with other groups, the conduct of war and peace, and the role of religion in worldly affairs. Furthermore, Muhammad during his lifetime left many examples of how to conduct relations on both a personal and political level, unlike Jesus, whose sayings and stories about his behavior are very few and impossible to verify as authentic.

The guiding principles of Islamic governance, as evidenced in the Quran and hadiths, include:

- *shura* (consultation) Muslims have a responsibility to strive for good governance based on consulting the people. "Those who (conduct) affairs by mutual Consultation ... (are not cowed but) help and defend themselves." (42:38–39) This sura is called Consultation. And this includes the umma: "The best jihad is a speech of truth in the presence of a tyrant ruler."[100] A corollary is that a leader (and in the modern representative tradition, elected representatives) should be chosen through consultation from among the most worthy Muslims.
- *ijma* (consensus) and majority rule, based on the hadith: "My ummah will never agree upon an error."[101] There are two possibilities: the consensus of the entire Muslim community, or just of the religiously learned, the former asserted by the Shafii school and the latter by the Maliki school. For Shia, the status of *ijma* is ambiguous, the ulama traditionally being more powerful than for Sunnis.

Muhammad Asad's *Principles of State and Government in Islam* (1961) extracts political principles from the Quran and hadiths, and is summarized here as reflecting the political ideas inherent in Islam.[102] He begins with a critique of the secular state, where there is "no stable norm by which to judge between good and evil, and between right and wrong", only "national interest".[103] Left and right argue based on class/ group interests, which results in chaos. Instead, politics is based on absolute moral principles embodied in sharia, acknowledging that all derives from the Divine Will, and that we should act in accord with it. Sharia in the Quran is concise, intentionally vague,[104] and it is necessary to use *ijtihad* to adjust to the historical context.

Asad attempts to define theocracy in a new way, as a "social system in which all temporal legislation flows, in the last resort, from what the community considers to be Divine Law", rather than "to invest a priestly hierarchy with supreme political power". The goal of an Islamic state should be to present a framework for unity and cooperation based on Islam. The basis for the state should not be tribalism, or even nationalism, which is merely a modern version of tribalism.[105]

- The law of equity is the basis of Islamic society,[106] with the goals (*maqasid*) of security, freedom, dignity, cultural and social development. An elected government does not mean absolute sovereignty of the people in their own right. Real sovereignty rests in the "will of God as manifested in the ordinances of the sharia." Thus temporal laws must be formulated in the spirit of sharia.
- The leader must not obey a foreign power but the umma alone.
- The people must obey the government so long as it does not legalize actions forbidden by sharia or forbid regulating the umma's affairs according to the sharia.
- The government and leader must be based on people's free choice "from among you". The leader should be a Muslim who submits to the Divine Will. His term can be fixed or for life.
- Legislation is based on *ijtihad* derived from *ijma* of the whole community through a *shura* council motivated by public interest. It is wrong to "appoint to such work anyone who asks for it or who covets it."[107]
- The doors of *ijtihad* never close, but any innovations are subject to review by ulama/ experts and consensus of the umma.

There are clear duties of the state/ citizens:

- The amir is elected and "considered to have received a pledge of allegiance from the *whole* community, not only from the majority that voted for him but also from the minority whose votes had been cast against him ... the will of the majority is binding on every member of the community".
- Similarly the amir pledges to represent all citizens, not just those who voted for him.
- The majlis (parliament) can impeach the amir, as it 'enjoins right and forbids wrong' just as do all citizens.
- There is freedom of speech/ word but not "for incitement against the

law of Islam or sedition against the established government and one
must not be allowed to offend against common decency".

- The state is responsible for the umma's defense, education and
  economic security. It must provide for spiritual and bodily needs,
  "provide minimum material well-being without which there can be
  no human dignity, no real freedom, and in the last resort no spiritual
  progress." Caliph Umar: "Even the lonely shepherd in the mountains
  of Sanaa shall have his share of the wealth of the community."[108]

The western critique of any system that smacks of theocracy, even
this mild theocentric version proposed by Asad, is that it is totalitarian. But the
Islamic critique of the Enlightenment rise of secular politics (not to mention
that of Foucault), where politics is divorced from religious considerations, as
epitomized by the French revolution, is that *it* leads directly to totalitarianism.
Eaton critiques "totalitarian secular society from which every glimmer of
light has been finally excluded", pointing to both workers who have become
interchangeable units in the production process, and their apotheosis in
twentieth century labor camps, both of the Nazi and communist regimes.[109]
What is needed is a 'checks and balances' of faith and reason in governing
worldly affairs, a 'checks and balances' found in Islam, but absent in secularism,
where there are no absolute (God-given) principles underlying ethics or
obligations to others based on their common humanity.

Economics as a distinct discipline only arose in the West in the
eighteenth century, as a result of capitalism and the triumph of materialism.
In Islamic civilization, Quranic moral and ethical principles governed daily
life, including economic activity, much as religious principles once infused
traditional economic activity in the West. The very concept of 'Islamic
economics' only arose in the 1940s, as efforts to revive Islamic civilization in
the context of modern imperialism gathered momentum.

The Quran's main principles which reflect on economics include:

1. *Tawhid* (God as absolute 'owner') and humans are part of his creation.
   "To Him belongs all that is in the heavens and on earth: everything
   renders worship to Him." (2:116) Thus, the economy is inseparable
   from both Nature and our spiritual life. Morality infuses all life. So
   when the economic dimension is separated from the rest of man's
   activities, God's law is violated (morality and ethics are ignored,
   Nature is harmed).

2. Vicegerency (man's responsibilities/ duties as God's steward balance
   his individual rights). God created man as "a vicegerent on earth".[110]
   Since all material things come from Allah as *rizq* (property, wealth,
   blessing, sustenance), nothing 'belongs' to anyone except by the
   will of Allah. Private property, referring to personal possessions,

especially one's home, is a right, but a qualified one, [111] being balanced by man's duties to God and his fellow man. Wealth can be amassed only if this does not harm others, and should be used to help others. *All* people have a duty to give **zakat,**[112] which thus becomes a 'right' of the poor to charity.

3. The law of equity/ equality is the Quran's primary principle governing relations between people, revealed, for instance, in 2:178: "The law of equality is prescribed to you in cases of murder: the free for the free, the slave for the slave, the woman for the woman." 2:180 goes on to deal with principles of just distribution (inheritance laws, zakat and the prohibition of usury, all of which flow naturally from this concern with equity).

A commercial or business transaction is correct if based on equality: the value of the goods given must be equal to the countervalue of the goods received. If these values are not equal, the exchange becomes exploitative. Usury (**riba**, making money in the form of interest, literally excess) is forbidden (2:275–277), as it is a hidden form of exploitation of man and puts all the risk (**gharar**—also meaning deception) on the borrower, which in any contract is immoral.[113] The only 'loan' which pays interest is one's sacrifice in the service of God, the "beautiful loan, which Allah will double unto his credit and multiply many times." (2:245)

Deriving from equity is the principle that a person should receive a share in output in proportion to his input, and all 'investors' must take an active part in the undertaking.[114] The Quran does not specify punishments for violating these principles, leaving it up to the umma.

Citizens' rights are based on equity, and thus presented in a social context (which accounts for different shares in inheritance, at a time when husbands were the sole breadwinner), which implies social duties (zakat is a duty balancing the right to profit). There are family obligations and broader social obligations. The Quranic goals (*maqasid*) of the preservation of life, lineage, intellect, property, and the fulfillment of contracts lead naturally to certain economic norms. "Balance and equity apply across the whole range of human life. The insights and lessons of spiritual discipline apply to and operate in all the mundane aspects of our human nature and daily life."[115]

There is no equivalent to Adam Smith's Invisible Hand, where individuals do not need to act morally but need only follow the exigencies of the market (self interest, profit). Western economics claims this Invisible Hand to be value-free, but on the contrary, it is based on the values selfishness and greed. All economic activity must be considered from the viewpoint of its moral dimension (individual acts), and ethical dimension (acceptable social behavior):

- Economic relations should be honest and fair to both parties in any transaction, in line with their rights and duties. Profit earned from trade is condoned, and the honest merchant is a role model. No exploitation is involved as production is small-scale and profit in trade is due to 'comparative advantage'.[116]
- While slavery is not proscribed in the Quran, there are many passages which call for freeing slaves and for their humane treatment. It was an institution which Muhammad could hardly be expected to abolish at once. In any case, most slaves were household servants, not the inhumanly exploited 'slave labor' of the imperialist slave trade from the fifteenth century (see endnote 172).
- Money must be used morally, which means not only no interest, but no investment in immoral activities such as gambling and alcohol.
- Altruism and kindness are (economic) acts which Islam encourages through zakat.[117] The five-times-a-day prayers and the month of fasting each year emphasize that economic activity should not take precedence over worship in society. Indeed, they are often coordinated, insofar as the payment of zakat follows the fast of Ramadan, and the animal sacrifice is not a 'burnt offering' for God, but to feed the poor.
- Use of Nature should be 'economical'. "Waste not by excess, for Allah loves not the wasters." (7:31)
- Conspicuous consumption and flaunting of wealth is frowned upon, though expenditure appropriate to one's station is permitted, avoiding a complete leveling of wealth that leads to the elimination of incentive. "If you conceal [acts of charity], and make them reach those (really) in need, that is best for you." (2:271)

The murder passage also shows how Islam deals with economic aspects of life. The murder of a family's breadwinner is not only a family tragedy, but a severe economic blow. Compensation in this situation could well be preferable to lopping off the offender's head.

Ibn Khaldun (1332–1406) is considered a father of modern economics. In *Muqaddima* (introduction, 1377), he attempted to formulate universal laws about the rise and decline of tribes, dynasties/ states, arguing that empires rise and fall according to their social cohesion (*asabiya*), with subjected tribes eventually gaining control as the center declines. The greater the social cohesion, the more complex the division of labor, and the greater the economic growth. He noted that forces of supply and demand determine the prices of goods, and that macroeconomic forces of population growth, human capital development and innovations affect development.[118]

The right of private property and the respect for trade at the heart of Islam led to the development of sophisticated merchant capital principles related to contracts, including bills of exchange, long-distance international trade, credit, debt, profit, loss, capital, capital accumulation, circulating capital, capital expenditure, revenue, checks, promissory notes, savings accounts, pawning, loaning, exchange rates, banking deposits, double-entry bookkeeping and lawsuits.

At the same time, early Islamic economic practice looks more like socialism:

- The state played an important regulatory and initiatory role in the economy.
- Islamic jurists have argued that privatization of essential resources that benefit the community as a whole, such as oil, gas, and other fire-producing fuels, agricultural land, and water, is forbidden.[119]
- In cases where the right to private ownership causes harm to the public interest, Maliki and Hanbali jurists allow the state to limit the amount an individual is allowed to own.[120]
- Price fixing is forbidden.[121]
- The principles of vicegerency and zakat lead directly to the concept of social welfare, pensions, a minimum income, guaranteed employment.
- The prohibition of interest and *gharar* requires sharing risk in cooperative economic activities. No class of elite bankers can develop within this framework.[122]

An "economy of poverty" prevailed in early Islam. "God's guidance made sure the flow of money and goods was 'purified' by being channeled from those who had much of it to those who had little" by encouraging zakat and discouraging *riba* on loans.[123]

The main institutions dealing with economic livelihood were *awqaf* (trusts, foundations, singular *waqf*), guilds, trade organizations, free markets, and small producers, though during the 11th–13th centuries, the Karimis, an early enterprise and business group controlled by entrepreneurs, came to dominate much of the Islamic world's economy. The group was controlled by about fifty Muslim merchants of Yemeni, Egyptian and Indian origins, each dominating a trade route along the Silk Road, Mediterranean and Red Seas and the Indian Ocean, and influencing politics through dealings with emirs, sultans, viziers and non-Muslim merchants. Large scale corporations exploiting unskilled wage labor, as developed later in the West, were not possible, as exploitation (profit derived from others' labor) was haram.

Economic life in each country was governed according to sharia, which controlled excesses associated with usury and ensured that zakat provided a safety net for those at the bottom. While there were ups and downs in quality of life according to the fairness of different leaders across the Muslim world and over time, and of course the vagaries of world politics, a hint of the essential difference in quality of life between Islam and western civilizations is found in Pickthall's memoirs of life in the late Ottoman Levant:

> When I read *The Arabian Nights* I see the daily life of
> Damascus, Jerusalem, Aleppo, Cairo, and the other cities as
> I found it in the early nineties of last century. What struck
> me, even in its decay and poverty, was the joyousness of that
> life compared with anything that I had seen in Europe. The
> people seemed quite independent of our cares of life, our
> anxious clutching after wealth, our fear of death.[124]

"'Work' is never fully differentiated from human action, including art in general and the ethical considerations contained in the sharia pertaining to the domain of human action as a whole."[125] Work is a sacred activity as much as prayer: "Work is prayer" and "God forgives one, upon repentance, what one owes Him, but not what one owes to God's other creatures." The former an Arab proverb, the latter a hadith.[126]

> The rhythm of traditional Islamic life has always been such
> that the hours of work are punctuated by prayer; this is also
> true of what is considered cultural activity or leisure today.
> The very architecture of the traditional city is such that
> spaces for worship, work, education, cultural activities and
> the rest are harmoniously interrelated and integrated into
> an organic unity as far as the relation of these spaces and
> their functions to each other are concerned. ... [There is] no
> emphasis in Islam upon the virtue of work for the sake of
> work, as one finds in certain forms of Protestantism. Work is
> considered a virtue in light of one's needs and the necessity
> of establishing equilibrium in one's individual and social
> life, a duty ... kept in check and prevented from becoming
> excessive by the emphasis that the Quran places upon the
> transience of life, the danger of greed and covetousness,
> and the importance of avoiding the excessive accumulation
> of wealth.[127]

It is better to pray or devote time to family or society than to accumulate money. In Medina, the Prophet emphasized that the members of the new religious community should devote a third of their day to work, a third to rest, and a third to prayer, leisure, family and social activities. Work should allow for friendly relations, discouraging the soulless work environment which became the hallmark of mass production. The use of modern technology "destroys the spiritual and qualitative relationship between the maker of things and objects produced, breaking the spiritual link that used to exist between members of a guild, once guilds were turned into labor unions."[128]

Early Relations between Europe and the Muslim World

The Christian world and the Muslim worlds were reading from different 'maps', so relations between them were plagued with resentment and misunderstanding from the start. This began with the sweep of Muslim 'armies' across Byzantine-held lands (from Syria to Egypt and across north Africa to Spain), six centuries after the time of Jesus when Christianity was already on the decline, riven by sectarianism—not just Catholicism vs eastern Orthodoxy, but Nestorian, Copt and other movements which arose largely over the question of the divinity of Jesus. Islam's map swept aside the differences among the Christian sects with its bold assertion that the 'People of the Book', the Jews and Christians, had lost their way, that their scriptures were distorted, that just as there is only one God, there is one superior way to acknowledge this truth (Islam), and that all who profess 'one God' are brothers despite their differences.

The conquerors were greeted as liberators from the heavy hand of the Byzantine church, which persecuted non-Orthodox 'heretics', just as the Catholic Church persecuted non-conformists[129] as enemies (along with the brash new Muslims). The Muslims, in contrast, left locals to worship in peace. The Egyptian Coptic monophysites and 'heretical' Christian sects such as the Nestorians preferred to live in the *dar al-islam* of the Muslim rulers than under their Christian brothers. When Europeans were herding Jews into ghettos and inciting pogroms against them to distract their oppressed peasants from the true perpetrators of their misery, Jews were serving as senior government officials under Abbasid, Ayyubid and Ottoman sultans in Baghdad, Cairo and Istanbul.

Western, i.e., Christian and now secular, views of Islam have ranged from the traditional bigoted misconception of Islam as idolatry of the Prophet Muhammad, hence "Mohammedanism", to disparagement of Islam as yet another Christian sect or heresy. Dante puts Muhammad in his ninth circle of Hell as a sower of religious discord, though the intent of Islam is to unite the monotheisms around a definitive revelation. One of the more sympathetic albeit inaccurate views of Islam popular in the West is that it is an adaptation of Christianity for Arabs, that Muhammad was the Arabs' prophet, though in fact Arabs were a minority in Islam within a few decades of Muhammad's death, and constitute only 18% of the world's Muslims today.[130]

The breathtaking military victories of the Islamic armies and proselytizing of the faithful convinced the vast majority of conquered peoples to adopt Islam, leading to their conversion from paganism, Buddhism, Christianity and Judaism as the new faith extended from the Atlantic to the Pacific. Islam proved to be a far more formidable force than these competitors because of its central tenet of the unity of the temporal and spiritual realms—one's life has no meaning without faith. At the same time, it was tolerant of other faiths. In the heart of temporal Islam—the Middle East—Christians, Jews and others continued to profess their faiths, enjoying a peaceful coexistence with Muslims.

The westward march of Islam was stopped in Spain and on the fringes of Byzantium by Emperor Charlemagne in the ninth century. The confrontation between Catholicism and Islam, however, continued, culminating in the horrific Crusades of the 11th–13th centuries and the later expulsion of Muslims from Spain and/or their conversion or slaughter, leaving a legacy of mutual hostility that still haunts us. While Pope John Paul II apologized to the Eastern Orthodox Church for the sack of Byzantium in the fourth Crusade,[131] he forgot to apologize to Muslims for *all four* Crusades. His successor Pope Benedictus XVI even condemned the supposed Islamic "command to spread by the sword the faith", quoting a Byzantine emperor and taking the relevant Quranic quote out of context.[132] While it was the Catholic Church that became the ideological mantle of the Roman Empire and later instigated the Crusades against the Muslim world, and the Christian empires from the sixteenth century on that made the world a battleground for conquest, the conventional wisdom in the West was and is that it is Islam that is inherently violent and intolerant.

Muslims were defined on the western 'map' by Orientalism, the tradition lying at the heart of western discourse about the Muslim world, which views Muslims as 'the other', oriental, a negative inversion of western culture, more sensual and less rational. It continues the tradition of hostile dismissal of Islam, which can be seen in *A True and Faithful Account of the Religion and Manners of the Mohammedans",* supposedly written by Joseph Pitts, a sailor who was captured by Algerian corsairs in 1678 and converted to Islam, finally escaping and returning to Exeter. Despite his many years reciting the Quran, he dismisses it as "a Legend of Falsities, and abominable Follies and Absurdities". Orientalism posits unreason, despotism, and backwardness as the fundamentals of the Orient, which in the nineteenth century, when it was explicitly formulated, included the Ottoman Caliphate and the Arab world, as well as India and China, implicitly projecting the new western civilization as the only valid modernity. Missionaries saw Islam as a Christian heresy, embedded in the lives of Muslims in a way that it is not for Christians or Jews, requiring "reforming" to make it compatible with the ways of the modern world. This mindset justified and still justifies the invasion and even colonization of Muslim lands in order to modernize them in line with the imperial agenda.

Relations with Orthodox Christians were better, and have remained so up to the present, for their map was more like the Muslim one. For many years, Muslims and Christians prayed together in the churches of Middle Eastern cities, notably, the Basilica of St. John in Damascus, where Christians and

Muslims worshipped together for 50 years before it was formally converted into the Umayyad Mosque. As late as 649, a Nestorian bishop wrote: "These Arabs fight not against our Christian religion; nay, rather they defend our faith, they revere our priests and saints, and they make gifts to our churches and monasteries." Indeed, the great theologian of the early church, St. John of Damascus (d. 749), who grew up in the Umayyad Arab court of Damascus, was convinced that Islam was at root not a new religion, but instead a new variation of Christianity.

But John was an Orthodox Christian, and in some ways Islam itself could be seen to have grown out of the largely Orthodox Christian environment of the late antique Levant (Syria, Lebanon, Jordan, Palestine). Its rituals are strikingly similar to those of the eastern Orthodox Christian. William Dalrymple describes how the bowing and prostrations of Muslim prayer are related to the older Syrian Orthodox tradition that is still practiced in pewless churches across the Levant.[133] The architecture of the earliest minarets, which are square rather than round, derives from the church towers of Byzantine Syria, while Ramadan, at first sight one of the most distinctive of Islamic practices, bears startling similarities to Lent, which in the eastern Christian churches still involves, as it once did in the Catholic Church as well, an all-day dry fast. If a monk from sixth century Byzantium were to come back today, he would find much more in common with a modern Muslim than he would with, say, a contemporary American Evangelical. Yet this simple truth has been lost by our tendency to think of Christianity as a thoroughly western religion rather than the oriental faith it is.

Moorish Spain was a model for ethnic and religious tolerance, where East and West met, and together, flourished. Originally a province of the Umayyad Caliphate (711–750), the Emirate of Cordoba (750–929), then the Caliphate of Cordoba (929–1031), which was finally reduced to only the Emirate of Granada in the south, Moorish Spain saw Muslims, Jews and Christians living in harmony, creating a prosperous, peaceful society, a highpoint in Spain's history. Under the Caliphate of Cordoba, Andalus became a beacon of learning, and the city of Cordoba became one of the leading cultural and economic centers in both the Mediterranean basin and the Islamic world.

By the late fifteenth century, the military and economic balance of power between the Islamic world and Christian Europe shifted. The Golden Age of Islamic civilization was receding even as it endured in the three great Muslim 'empires' of the 16th–19th centuries, centered in Constantinople, Isfahan and Delhi, still spreading across the African Sahel and the islands of southeast Asia. From that point on Europeans saw Islam and its civilization not as a dangerous rival, but as inferior, and a thin layer of Muslims concurred and started to adopt western technology, habits and outlook.

For nine centuries, Islamic civilization had outshone Christian civilization, and saved the Greek and Latin scientific and cultural heritage from destruction by Christendom. Many crucial elements in modern science, such as algebra, Arabic numerals, and the concept of the zero (vital to the advancement of mathematics) were transmitted to medieval Europe from Islam. Sophisticated instruments which were to make possible the European voyages of discovery were developed by Muslim scholars, including the astrolabe, the quadrant and accurate navigational maps. But by the eighteenth century, the West spurned Islamic culture, and only wanted raw materials from the Muslim world for their industrializing economies. What had happened?

The simple answer is: capitalism, a radically new 'map' of the world. Just why capitalism arose in Europe when it did, radically changing the relations between East and West, continues to confound economic historians, just as why it didn't arise in Islamic civilization. Hodgson suggests the Occident was as much a remote outpost as Japan or Korea, and developed relatively undisturbed by the devastation caused in Eurasia by the Mongols and Timurids, with fertile land and a good climate.[134] Robert Wright argues that cultural evolution is a process of developing relationships based on nonzero-sum interactions,[135] which trade epitomizes (both sides benefit through comparative advantage and economies of scale), that 14th–17th century Europe was a patchwork of small warring states, stimulating all kinds of nonzero-sum interactions. 'Barbarians' continually challenged ossifying societies and then quickly absorbed the most useful memes (units of cultural information), leading to a kind of hothouse of cultural evolution. Muslims societies were more spread out across Eurasia, and Islam dominated cultural life to a much greater extent than did the now increasingly sectarian, discredited Christian civilization in the West.

The standard explanation for Islam's subsequent lagging is that Islam did not experience a 'reformation' comparable to the Protestant Reformation. Islam was in fact the 'reformation' of Christianity, addressing the same decadence and pagan accretions that the iconoclastic movement in Orthodox Christianity did in the 8th–9th centuries *under the influence of Islam*. Similarly in the sixteenth century, Martin Luther famously rejected the priest as intermediary, and published the Bible in language accessible to the masses—both founding principles of Islam. Islamic civilization experienced several renaissances—under the Abbasids and again under Ulugbek in the fifteenth century in Central Asia, where medical, astronomical, mathematical, and cultural developments were far in advance of the West.

Nonetheless, while Christianity and Judaism adapted to the modern world of capitalism, Islam did not. Rather than 'adapted', however, developments within Christianity and Judaism actually *gave rise* to capitalism/ imperialism and secularism, providing the new social formation's ideological grounding, and then gave rise to Marxism and socialism as the logical real world 'end times'.

Both Judaism and Christianity had for long been associated with empire. Christianity provided the ideology of the late Roman Empire, which became the Holy Roman Empire in the Middle Ages. The constant wars between Wright's 'patchwork of warring states'—primarily Britain, France and Spain—only ceased temporarily to make way for the Crusades, and then, with the rise of new military and navigation technology, turned outward, as British, French and Spanish privateers turned their energies to conquering and pillaging less militarily advanced peoples further afield. This radical new development recapitulated the rape and pillage of the Roman Empire, whose memes were embedded in Christian Europe. This very ugly 'map' portrayed the 'other' as the enemy, to be conquered or decimated via war, unlike Islam's map of the world, which embraced the 'other' and sought to expand *dar al-islam*.

By the fourteenth century, Christian elites abandoned any remaining religious scruples about usury, and put banking—and the traditional usurers in Christendom, the Jews—at the center of their 'map'. Banks proved to be a revolutionary instrument in recycling the gold and silver stolen from newly discovered, relatively peaceful societies around the world. Jews made alliances with European monarchs, and were "responsible for the construction of some of the most powerful states of the Mediterranean and European worlds, including the Hapsburg, Hohenzollern, and Ottoman empires,"[136] the underlying reasoning being to wield financial resources at the national level and encourage the expansion of the nation state abroad in pursuit of profit—the logic of imperialism. In contrast, Islam stubbornly resisted the revolution in economic relations based on banking, and did not experience the accompanying political-military and social revolutions of the Christian world, preferring instead to peacefully expand through trade and assimilation with local societies.

The different fates of the West and Islamic civilization have much to do vicegerency. God created Nature in a balance (*mizan*) and mankind's responsibility is to maintain this fragile equilibrium through wise governance and sound personal conduct. The believing men and women are those who "walk on the Earth in humility." (25:63) This responsibility and even empathy for Nature contrasts with the Old Testament "Let them have dominion over the fish of the sea, and over the fowl of the air, and over the cattle, and over all the earth, and over every creeping thing that creepeth upon the earth."[137] This could be taken as a credo for the newly expanding western Christian empires, which seized defenseless non-European lands to exploit, in contrast to the tradition of Muslim traders around the world, who came in peace and traded fairly.

The Ascendancy of Rationalism and Capitalism in the West

From the sixteenth century on, "largely as a result of changes in the

Occident, the economic and cultural life of Muslim peoples was to be denatured and undermined."[138] Its social patterns stood in the way of industrialism and of the methodical exploitation of human material. "Machines require an egalitarian and fluid social structure, whereas men, left to their own devices, had found that quite a different kind of structure best served their needs."[139]

In the seventeenth century, Bacon's formulation of human progress—advancing the happiness of mankind by "the endowment of human life with new inventions and riches"[140]—became the implicit aim of the newly 'enlightened' western civilization. It is at about the time of Bacon's cheery formulation of the new materialist outlook that the Islamic scientific and philosophical outlook becomes sharply distinct from the West:

> The modern astronomy and physics of Galileo and Newton were based on an already secularized view of the cosmos, the reduction of Nature to pure quantity, and a complete separation between the knowing subject and the object to be known based on Cartesian dualism. A new science was born, one that discovered much in the realm of quantity, but at the price of losing the traditional worldview and neglecting the spiritual dimension and qualitative aspect of Nature.[141]

Nasr points out that the Enlightenment desacralized the cosmos:

> The rustling of the wind in the forest and the chant of the birds celebrating the rising of the sun can no longer be heard as the invocation of God's Blessed Names and as His Praise according to the Quranic verse, 'All things hymn the praise of God.' Rather, they become meaningless noise, at best pleasant but devoid of a spiritual message to be heard and understood. Nature hides her inner reality, seeming outwardly to confirm the view of that science that would deny the existence of this inner reality."[142]

This gave rise to "technocracy"[143] in the 18th–19th centuries, where 'progress' is based solely on increased efficiency of production.[144] The new social order of Europe and its colonies had a new economic basis: instead of relying upon a surplus of agricultural produce, it was founded on a technology and an investment of capital that enabled the West to reproduce its resources indefinitely, so that western society was no longer subject to the same constraints as an agrarian culture.[145] Tools were no longer just an extension of man, but became central to the world of culture, and even attacked the old culture (e.g., the printing press attacked oral traditions, the telescope attacked religious dogmas), moral values (revelation) increasingly were crowded out by intellectual values (reason).

In economic terms, this new system is capitalism, where everything, including the production process and technological innovation, is measured in terms of money and the quest for profit, not in terms of usefulness and service to society, let alone worship. By an easy sleight-of-hand, Bacon's 'human progress' becomes 'technological progress'. The narrative of the Bible becomes a quaint fairytale, Pilgrim's Progress is replaced by the narrative of Material Progress. The spiritual journey is essentially abandoned.

"Technopoly" takes technocracy to its logical conclusion: technology takes control of the evolution of society itself in the guise of the machine-tool (now microchip) industry. Machines now produce machines, we live in cities and work in factories organized on 'principles' of efficiency and profit maximization, thinking is best done by computers, and man's role is merely to facilitate this. [146] Our aim becomes not Bacon's nice 'to reduce ignorance and suffering', but 'to adapt to the requirements of new technologies' (which will solve all our problems and do all our thinking). We wake up (if at all) to the realization that we have lost our humanity in this swirl of gadgets and things. Alfred North Whitehead hit the nail on the head when he stated that the greatest invention of the nineteenth century was the idea of invention itself.

The 'belief' of society is now in principles which invention needs: objectivity, efficiency, expertise, standardization, measurement and economic growth. People are no longer children of God or even citizens but consumers. Society has no moral center; rather, the focus is on efficiency, interest, economic advance. The promise is of 'heaven on earth' through technological progress and material abundance, casting aside traditional narratives that stress frugality, stability and orderliness. Welcome to the material world, aka modernity.

It is certainly true that Islamic society 'lagged' behind western society in economic terms as it entered this war-obsessed industrial age. And as the West gained material strength (i.e., military strength), it moved against the relatively low-tech Islamic world and eventually conquered it and tried to impose its technocracy/ technopoly, though it has faced stubborn resistance ever since, even where it has had willing handmaidens, such as Turkey's Mustafa Kemal and Iran's Reza Shah Pahlavi.

How to explain this 'backwardness' when science has always played a central role on Islam's map of the world? The Quran repeatedly instructs man to use his powers of intelligence and observation, and to study all the aspects of God's creation: "(here) indeed are Signs for a people that are wise." (2:164) Within a few years of Muhammad's death, a great civilization and, later, universities were flourishing, for, "Seeking knowledge is an obligation for every Muslim."[147] The synthesis of eastern and western ideas and of new thought with old initially brought about great advances in medicine, mathematics, physics, astronomy, geography, architecture, art, literature, and history. But while science flourished until the sixteenth century, it was never directed solely at producing more goods or efficiency, and did not *shape* society, as it has done in the West ever since.

For Islam, humanity is part of Nature, not something apart or above. Thus, a 'science' which posits an outside subject manipulating soulless, alien matter did not develop in Islamic society. If a law is a law of Nature and we are a part of Nature, we are subject to the law rather than master of it, negating the Jewish-Christian notion of man as mapmaker, with 'dominion over Nature'.

Today's positivist science issues from this fallacy, is an intrinsic part of capitalism, and thus colludes in its goals. Only speculative astronomy has no direct 'productive' application, and interestingly it is there that recent advances have pointed to the fundamental materialist flaw in the rational-industrial worldview, calling for a 'Tao of physics', positing that the universe was created out of nothing. But this is a mere footnote to the obsession with monocultural economic growth, 'improving' the standard of living even for the richest people in the richest countries, come hell or high water. In contrast, Islam advocates a modest standard of living. Mohammad lived a simple life in a house without furniture; according to his wife Aisha, sewed his own clothes and helped with household chores.

The 'decline' of Muslim civilization—as was the case with hundreds of other cultures attacked by the restless, warlike imperialists—came with the post-Enlightenment confrontation between the West and all other regions, which involved war, exploitation, colonization and outright theft, bringing about the "development of underdevelopment"[148] in Muslim and third world lands, and turning Islamic thinkers against the entire modernist project.

In a final twist, the very act of trying to 'catch up' in the nineteenth century involved relying on the innovations which had facilitated capitalism's rapid expansion, especially usury and banks, exacerbating Islam's decline. Usurious loans were lavishly made in the nineteenth century to the Ottomans and their representatives in Tunis and Egypt, and then used as a pretext to invade to 'protect shareholders' and further exploit these countries as part of European empires. Also, by importing western technology wholesale (including engineers, all paid for by loans from foreign banks) in a colonial context, dependency was merely reinforced, rather than overcome.[149]

The warlike nature of imperial power, intent on destroying competition and monopolizing trade and production in the interests of profit, meant that this system fed on itself, accelerating both production and war on a world scale and the destruction and subjugation of the 'enemy', soon leaving the Muslim world 'behind'. It never had a chance. Its map led in a very different direction.

The quality of life in the Muslim world in the Middle Ages ebbed and flowed, and at times and in certain places, it flourished. Arguably most Muslims then lived a better life than their Christian counterparts did, or than most people do today, without the extremes of poverty and riches or the dehumanizing exploitation inherent in capitalism and the imperial order, which allows countries in the 'center' to have much higher standards of living than in the 'periphery',[150] while a tiny elite in the center enjoys a much higher standard of living than the remaining 99% of people living in the center. Turkestan in the 16th–17th centuries in the era of the Timurids is just one example of Islamic civilization as a much preferable alternative to western civilization at that time.

How Islamic science might have developed without the fateful interaction with the capitalist West is a moot point. The question now is how to create a new map—given the uncharted territory we face today—to develop an economic system and scientific tradition which avoids the glaring pitfalls that western secularism and technopoly has revealed.

Relations from the Sixteenth Century to 'Independence'

A warlike spirit of exploration in search of gold, accompanied by a new skeptical spirit of scientific inquiry freed of religious scruples and supported by the printing press, seized the West in the late Middle Ages. This development, like the signs of Nature, can also be seen as "Signs for a people that are wise". (2:164) Christendom was transformed into a qualitatively new socio-economic order, conquering and transforming the world in the process,[151] inaugurating the era of modern imperialism. Karen Armstrong calls this a second Axial Age—the secular one—which led to electoral democracy, pluralism, an emphasis on individual human rights, and secularism, features which were "dictated by the needs of the modern state".

Reconquista Christian Spain and Portugal became the first of the western empires, given a head start in their struggle to assert their own political power against their European rivals, by their use of innovations in the technology of sea-faring and fire-power. The Christian empires quickly seized the entire American hemisphere, killing those natives who resisted, stealing their gold, establishing colonies, and spreading Christianity by the sword where necessary. It was the very opposite of the way Islam was spreading at the very same time in Africa and southeast Asia.

The subsequent five centuries are now celebrated in the West as a triumph of man over Nature, a new era of prosperity, freedom and democracy, the pinnacle of human civilization. The reality is quite different. It was a period of genocides[152] and increasingly destructive wars—both civil and world. The global wars from the eighteenth century onward killed hundreds of millions.

Environmental destruction proceeded to such an extent that the very physical survival of humanity is now in question.

The Muslim umma lived mostly under (Christian) imperial occupation starting in the nineteenth century and ending at various times in the twentieth century according to circumstances. During this colonial period, the occupying powers intensively shaped the economic and political forces in their colonies to allow the maximum extraction of profit, with the intention of keeping them subservient indefinitely, despite repeated promises to eventually liberate them (US President Woodrow Wilson's Fourteen Points in 1918, and Roosevelt and Churchill's Atlantic Charter in 1941, asserting that self-determination was a right of all people). 'Independence' was finally achieved only after violent struggle, leaving the colonies with distorted economies, domestic political unrest, and conflicts with newly-defined neighbors, where borders were determined with no concern for the unity of ethnicities, let alone the umma, instead contriving a complex web of multi-ethnic states with a view to maintaining western geopolitical domination.

In much of the Muslim world, the imperial project was actually less destructive than elsewhere, delayed by the reluctance of the European empires to destroy the already weakened Ottoman Caliphate, as they were able to use it to pursue their own interests. However, in Africa hundreds of thousands of Muslims, up to 25% of African slaves, were sent into the new capitalist version of slavery, far more cruel than earlier forms,[153] *forcibly* converted to Christianity in the American colonies. Arab and Asian Muslims were more fortunate, and were not decimated and their lands entirely colonized, with the exception of Algeria by the French.[154] Their exploitation was more refined—through seducing and then bankrupting Muslim rulers (Ottomans, local sultans) or through rigged trade relations and taxation (India, southeast Asia). The colonial 'crusade' may have been less violent than the original ones of the 11th–13th centuries, but its impact was far more devastating. The map of the powerful Muslim world was reduced to a dependent patchwork of 'nation states' with artificial borders, and Muslim society has been gravely weakened through enforced modernization western-style, according to the western map of the world.

This new secular political order had no equivalent in Islamic history. Private corporations such as the British East India and Dutch East India Companies—privateers (pirates in the employ of the imperial state)—sailed around Africa and on to India and the far East, treating natives (especially Muslims) as the enemy, killing and enslaving them, and then fighting each other to try to gain monopoly control of previously peaceful open-to-all trade routes. As with the conquest of the Americas, this began with the Portuguese and Spanish, but soon the Dutch, British and French joined the fray.

Their methods, in contrast to their Muslim 'enemies' (who for centuries had been sharing the trade routes in a civilized way), were intrigue and deception or outright warfare. European imperialism presented the choice of resistance or submission; cooperation was not an option. Europe unleashed violence on a scale never before seen on those shores, as it did in the Americas. Muslims had been Asia's traders as early as the eighth century, when Arab merchants arrived and settled, assimilating and bringing Islamic culture peacefully to natives, many of whom willingly converted.[155] The trade by Muslims, Jews and Hindus in the Indian Ocean, the Arabian Sea and the Persian Gulf that had lasted 500 years ended over night, replaced by Portuguese hegemony, which lasted until the arrival of the Dutch and then the British and then the Americans.

The Turkic Ottoman Caliphate centered in Constantinople/ Istanbul,[156] the Safavids in Persia, and the Moghuls in India dominated the Muslim world from the 16th–19th centuries, but by the nineteenth century had been seriously compromised by the imperialists. The dynasties were left in place only because the new rulers couldn't agree on how to divvy up the spoils.

Britain proved to be the 'best' imperial strategist, leaving it in control of most of the colonial world by 1900, including India and Egypt (the latter nominally part of the by-now bankrupt Ottoman Caliphate), though it had to share the largely Muslim southeast Asia with the Dutch. Farsighted imperial strategist Halford Mackinder, aware that this system, based on brute force and controlling over 100 million subjected people, could not last forever, proposed a less formal empire to be called the British Commonwealth of Nations. The global Christian empire would have a Jewish-dominated Palestine, beholden to England for its tenuous survival, as the empire's linchpin, surrounded by a balkanized group of weak Arab states. Though wrapped in the romance of the Promised Land, the real British aim in establishing a Jewish state was purely secular—to meet the needs of empire in the unreconstructed Muslim heartland.

This capitalist empire was different than empires such as the Roman, Persian or Byzantine, or the Islamic caliphates, the non-Muslim ones based solely on military conquest and economic hegemony, the Muslim ones on providing a loose, peaceful administration over a multicultural federation. As capitalism advances, writes Hilferding, a steadily increasing proportion of capital in industry is controlled by international banks, "the banker is being transformed into an industrial capitalist", and bank capital becomes "finance capital".[157] Imperialism is the advanced stage of capitalism, characterized by banks and industrial monopolies relying on the export of capital and colonialism for increasing profits. "The exploitation of the periphery with the connivance of the center's working class is hidden behind the innocent-looking balance sheets of these faceless financial corporations."[158]

Until the eighteenth century, the **Ottoman Caliphate** outshone the up-and-coming European empires. At its height in the sixteenth century, it had magnanimously agreed to capitulations (legal immunity and trade privileges) for English and French merchants in Ottoman territories. These capitulations eventually contributed to undermining it, as they were used to allow western mass produced cheap manufactures to flood the Caliphate's markets in the nineteenth century, leaving local producers without customers and draining the Caliphate's monetary reserves. Aggressive Europeans increasingly abused their privileges, granting local Greek, Arab Christian and Jewish Ottoman merchants and clerks foreign citizenship/ protection, enriching them (and themselves), and a much weakened Ottoman sultan was now unable to cancel these privileges. From 15–33% of citizens were 'foreigners' in major cities (Jerusalem, Salonica, Izmir), undermining the intent of the new Tanzimat citizenship law, which granted equal citizenship rights to all ethnicities, and encouraging ethnic tensions and western-style nationalism.

Reforms, in an attempt to catch up with Europe, came from the top—with Tanzimat (literally "regulations", 1839–1876), begun by Sultan Mahmud II (r. 1808–1839) and continued by his son Abdulmecid I (r. 1839–1861), copying European economic and political institutions such as paper money, the postal system, commercial laws, a central bank, uniform citizenship and taxation (replacing the *jizya* payment by non-Muslim *dhimmi*), the abolition of slavery, modern public schools and universities, a press code. Mahmud II had dissolved (and then massacred) the professional soldier class of the Caliphate, the Janissaries, and started to build a western-style army. The Ottoman Caliphate was formally recognized as one of the European powers in the Congress of Paris in 1856. A movement of secularists, the westernized Young Turks, struggled to achieve a constitutional monarchy in the 1876 constitution.

The new Sultan Abdulhamid II (r. 1876–1909) suspended it, faced with intractable problems (virtual war with Europe, insurrection at home, huge waves of refugees from Europe). Russia especially had designs on the Ottoman Caliphate from the eighteenth century, coveting the largely Slavic Balkans and control of the Black Sea. Tsarina Catherine had annexed the Khanate of Crimea in 1783, obtaining a port on the Black Sea and right of passage into the Mediterranean, as well as the right to intervene on behalf of the Orthodox subjects of the sultan—yet more capitulations. Britain convinced the Ottomans to join it in the Crimean War (1853–1856) to forestall Russian plans to swallow up the entire Balkans and Istanbul itself, though the war was a disaster for both sides, with a half a million deaths, further bankrupting the Turks.[159]

Not skipping a beat, Russia declared war on the Ottomans in 1877, winning within a few months. Britain again positioned itself as an intermediary, but the Russians nonetheless achieved 'independence' for Romania, Serbia and Montenegro, and autonomy for Bulgaria, as well as other concessions from the Ottomans. Britain got strategic Cyprus as a bribe from the Ottomans to ensure future British aid against the Russians.

Britain did not need to invade the Caliphate: its 'generous' support for loans to the sultan (which he could never repay) gave it control over Ottoman spending, when a Public Debt Administration was forced on Abdulhamid in 1881, giving foreign creditors first crack at any state revenues. Britain and France were doing the same thing in Tunis and Egypt (adding the Sudan to the British Empire for good measure) at this time, allowing them to carve out crypto-colonies there, leaving only the pretense of Ottoman sovereignty. As a result of all this scheming, over a million Crimean Tatar and Turkish refugees had to flee the Christian aggressors,[160] arriving penniless in Anatolia, adding to Ottoman woes.

Tanzimat reforms weakened guilds, Sufi brotherhoods and Muslim identity. They allowed the European imperialists to weave increasingly complex webs of intrigue. Ottoman rule had not produced a strong landlord class that could invest its surplus in industry. The Ottomans were faced with an "entirely different type of civilization in the West", and compared with past enemies, the "Muslim world would find it far more difficult to meet the challenge."[161] To shore up his credibility, Abdulhamid increasingly appealed to his nominal subjects as Caliph,[162] and, despite his autocratic ways, inspired many reformers not interested in assimilation with the West, but in renewing Islam and preserving the Caliphate. He is remembered now for his principled resistance to offers from rich European Jews for financial aid in return for promising a Jewish homeland in Palestine.[163] This set the rising powerful banking and media elite in Europe against him too, who encouraged the Armenians and Balkan insurgents to rise up. The Committee for Unity and Progress (CUP), a liberal group formed in 1889, allied with the Young Turks in 1906, deposed Abdulhamid and achieved their coveted constitutional monarchy (1908), inspired by the revolutions in Russia (1905) and Persia (1906), which also demanded constitutional monarchies.

The collapse of the caliphate and the advent of 'independence', however, was only a matter of time, much like the collapse of the Soviet Union after its first and last president, Mikhail Gorbachev, opened up to the West in good faith in the 1980s. The West had no use for an alternative political order which was collectivist, rejected ethnic chauvinism and was based on moral tenets, which both the Ottoman Caliphate and the Soviet Union were, however flawed they might have been. Neither was compatible with the modern, centralized, ethnically homogenized capitalist states of Europe. The precious, truly multicultural mosaic of the caliphate[164] was shattered. With the descent into WWI, "four centuries of relative peace and dynamism was replaced by four miserable years of tyranny."[165]

The gradual consolidation of western imperialism after the fifteenth century meant the inevitable colonization of the Muslim world: India, Malaysia and Indonesia in the eighteenth century, and Egypt and north Africa by the mid-nineteenth century. Only with the total collapse of the Ottoman empire at the end of WWI, after it had allied with the least invasive of the new empires, Germany, was this process completed, with the Levant, Arabia and Mesopotamia (present-day Iraq), as well as Persia, becoming in effect western colonies. The history of the Muslim world in the past century and a half is a litany of heroic, if tragic and largely unsuccessful attempts, to resist invaders.

Egypt's Muhammad Ali (r. 1805–1849), an Ottoman officer who seized power and declared himself khedive (prince), attempted ambitious military, industrial and agricultural reforms along the lines of the Ottoman Tanzimat, including trade and industrial state monopolies, which this vigorous leader used to rapidly build up Egypt's economic potential. Ottoman Sultan Mahmud II had Muhammad Ali send his troops to Arabia to recapture Mecca and Medina from the Saud Bedouin tribe which he did decisively by 1819. By the late 1830s he had also seized Syria from the Caliph. He was popular and could well have founded an Arab caliphate (though himself of Albanian origins), prompting Britain to send troops in 1840 to Syria to force Muhammad Ali's troops out. In the Convention of London (1840) Britain recognized the Khedive's family as the hereditary rulers of Egypt and Sudan, but limited his army to 18,000, and forced him to disband the system of state monopolies financing his reform program (and keeping British goods out).

His grandson Khedive Ismail embarked on a program of investment in the 1860s to modernize Egypt, this time with British-French 'help' in the form of large bank loans at high interest rates, which of course landed him directly in their clutches. He had to sell Egypt's 'shares' in the Suez Canal to the British government in 1875 to meet his debts, and in 1876 the British and French forced him to submit to an international finance commission to manage Egypt's revenues. This made Egypt the second colony of the banking world—**Tunis** had suffered the same fate in 1869, when Italy, Britain and France forced it to let an international debt commission control its government revenues. (The Caliphate's turn came in 1881.)

Both Egypt and Tunis had to "suffer the indignity of having their laws flouted by foreigners" and to allow large-scale immigration of a new colonial administrative and capitalist class, the immigrants demanding that they be treated under "the terms of the sixteenth century capitulations treaties so they would not have to pay tariffs or be subject to local legal systems."[166] European governments forced both countries to set up a system of Mixed Courts, composed of local and European judges, to hear cases involving Europeans, where Europeans received preferential treatment. Britain finally invaded Egypt in 1882 and controlled Egypt as a *de facto* colony until the 1952 revolution.

The banks were the key to the new hands-off imperial strategy, which is still alive and well today. They were used to destroy the entire Ottoman Caliphate, starting with Egypt and Tunis. Evelyn Baring (later Lord Cromer) gave the following explanation of his mission when he came to Egypt in 1877 as "the British Commissioner of the Public Debt": "The origin of the Egyptian Question in its present phase was financial."[167] Cromer returned in 1883 as British Agent and Consul-General to advise the Khedive. This political maneuvering used usurious banking practice to provide a pretext to seize ('buy') the strategic Suez Canal, financed by international loans and built by Egyptian forced labor. It became a standard for later imperial moves involving the IMF as Egypt's current pawnbroker.

There was a strong liberal-landlord dominated nationalist movement in Egypt continuing Urabi's goal of complete independence, led after WWI by the liberal Wafd Party, culminating in the 1919 revolution, which forced Britain to grant Egypt some of the trappings of independence, unilaterally declaring it 'independent' in 1922, which led to it joining the (British-controlled) League of Nations in 1937. The Wafd Party consistently won the vast majority in elections, but was kept from exercising real power by the monarchy controlled by the British, and their dream of genuine independence was crushed, fatally weakening them in the lead-up to the 1952 revolution.

After WWI, rather than turning the Ottoman territories into fully fledged colonies, the British used the Egyptian model of supporting a friendly monarchy and co-opting local elites elsewhere. Yugoslavia was created in 1918 as a pro-British 'southern Slav' kingdom from the Serbian, Croatian and Slovenian kingdoms after the collapse of Habsburg Austria-Hungary, with the Ottoman Muslims deported to Turkey or incorporated into Yugoslavia's **Bosnia** and **Kosovo**. Pro-British monarchies similar to Egypt's were created in British-French "mandates" in **Jordan** and Iraq. Defiant **Syria** remained under more direct French control, as the French carved out tiny **Lebanon**, making it very useful as the only majority Christian 'state' in the Arab world. France gave a strategic Syrian coastal region to the Turks as a bribe in the run-up to WWII.

The Italians had invaded **Libya** in 1911 and the Ottomans ceded it to them in 1912. The Italian occupation was particularly brutal, followed by British occupation during and after WWII. Much earlier, in 1830, France had invaded **Algeria** with the intention of incorporating it directly into France, rather than leaving it as a colony. France faced a surprisingly able Islamic leader Abd al-Qadir (1808–1883), a Sufi sheikh, who led the resistance, but his insurgency was finally suppressed.[168] One million French *pieds noirs* settlers were encouraged to take the best agricultural land from the native Algerians, there being no intention of 'civilizing' the locals to the point where they could govern themselves without the occupiers. This overt colonization led to a horrific civil war as the moment of 'independence' approached after WWII.

Morocco has been a monarchy since the eighth century, reaching its greatest size under the sixteenth century Saadi dynasty which ruled most of northwest Africa, as well as large sections of Andalus. Following the *reconquista* of the Iberian Peninsula, Muslims and Jews were forced to seek refuge in Morocco. After the Saadi, the Alaouite dynasty (claiming descent from Ali) eventually gained control in the seventeenth century, though it was formally part of the Ottoman Caliphate. The Portuguese, French, Spanish and British all attacked Morocco from the fifteenth century on, establishing enclaves, eager to seize control of the strategic maritime nation.

This prompted Sultan Mohammed III to be the first sovereign to recognize the rebel United States as an independent nation in 1777, declaring that American merchant ships sailing the Barbary Coast would be under the protection of the sultanate. The Moroccan-American Treaty of Friendship stands as the US's oldest friendship treaty. The Spanish and then French finally invaded and occupied Morocco but left the popular monarchy in place. Morocco was considered part of the French sphere of influence. France made it a protectorate in 1912, and was awarded Morocco as a League of Nations mandate after WWI.

In **Africa,** Abyssinia (Eritrea, Ethiopia) has special importance for Muslims as the site of the first *hijra* in 614[169] and the oldest Muslim settlement in Africa (Negash). Many companions of Muhammad, including Bilal ibn Ribah, the first *muezzin* (caller to prayer), were from there. Abyssinia's Coptic Christian community lived peaceably with its Muslims.

Islam was the dominant religion in central Africa prior to the invasion by European powers. By the eleventh century Muslim merchants had traveled overland from Baghdad and were established in the kingdom of Takrur on the lower Senegal River, the kingdom of Ghana in the Sahel, Gao on the Niger River, Hausaland and Kanem, east of Lake Chad. The local rulers all willingly became Muslims by the twelfth century, as Islam granted them the 'international' legitimacy that they coveted. Caravans from north Africa and Egypt brought scholars, books, commercial credit, and sharia, which provided a just international legal system. Somalia was the home of sultanates which formed in the eighth century.

The Muslim kingdom of Mali dates from the thirteenth century. It expanded to become the Songhay empire. By the fifteenth century, Islam reached Sudan and Timbuktu, penetrating the countryside, and down the east coast of Africa.[170] There were 30 Muslim cities from Mogadishu to Sainsibar (Zanzibar) and Kilwa.

Morocco defeated the Songhay forces in 1591, after which the Bornu/ Kanem 'empire' (1380–1893, in today's Chad, Niger and Cameroon) was the most powerful state in black Africa. "By the seventeenth century, Muslim-ruled states formed a continuous line from the Atlantic to the Red Sea." This expansion of the umma came peacefully with merchants, first because of the advantages it gave to local rulers and merchants, and then as "the religion's themes of justice and righteousness were appropriated by rural groups."[171]

The Muslim economic systems were based on supplying slaves to Ottoman Egypt in exchange for guns, horses and armor. Prior to the sixteenth century, slaves were less important than gold and salt, were generally war captives and mostly women used as household servants or concubines. They were rarely sought to provide cheap labor for agriculture or industry. Most of the sultans were themselves children of concubines. The Egyptian Mamluk sultans were descended from slaves (*mamluk* means slave in Arabic).[172] After the arrival of the Portuguese, coastal societies now acquired advanced western technology (guns) and the Europeans voraciously bought slaves for genuine 'slave labor', providing the means (guns) and demand to increase their numbers from a few thousand per year to 70,000 by 1750, for a total of six million before the genocidal practice—carried out by Christian and Jewish merchants corrupting local Muslim potentates—was finally brought to an end in the nineteenth century.

As western imperialism came into conflict with Islam in Africa, Christianity was imposed along with colonialism on the animist natives, and Muslims were taken as slaves or otherwise treated as second-class citizens. Starting in 1498, the Portuguese (Vasco Da Gama the most famous) terrorized local Muslim populations in a religious crusade especially targeting them. The Portuguese privateers destroyed and looted the Muslim cities and established military bases on orders of the crown—the Dutch and British used 'chartered private companies'—on Indian Ocean routes.

Each imperial power was obsessed with monopolizing the new trade routes, turning the entire world into a militarized *dar al-harb*. Normal trade, formerly dominated by local Muslims, collapsed in their wake, and the quasi-monopoly trade established among the competing imperial powers meant that all profit went to the imperial centers, impoverishing local (Muslim) suppliers and destroying the formerly thriving local economies. This balkanized the once peaceful and prosperous Africa and Asia into starving 'third world countries' which today must beg rations from the current version of the Cromers and Portuguese conquerors and their banking officials.

The new-style slave trade with the Americas disrupted the entire central African west coast, once a densely populated, wealthy region, where Islam was the predominant religion alongside tribal animism. The formal occupation of Africa by the imperial powers got underway in earnest after 1870, when western Africa was divided into 15 colonies primarily by the French and British, who had already enslaved millions from the so-called Slave

Coast (Togo, Benin, Nigeria) as well as Guinea-Bissau, Gambia and Ghana. The French destroyed Hajj Umar's empire (present-day Guinea, Senegal, Mali) which had been corrupted by imperialism's hunger for slaves, as well as that of Samori Ture in Mali in 1898. The British penetrated the Niger River basin, present-day Ghana and Nigeria in equatorial and Sahel Africa. They incorporated Sudan into Egypt in 1899, destroying the Caliphate of Abd Allah ibn Muhammad (the Mahdi) in Sudan.

The Muslim merchants had no chance against this onslaught, as they relied on peaceful trade and generally integrated with the locals. There was resistance—apart from the first defensive jihad which was declared in southeast Asia by Aceh against the Portuguese in the sixteenth century, in Africa jihad was declared in 1725 in Fulbe in modern Guinea—but the more powerful and ruthless 'civilization' of the West inevitably triumphed.

Three of Africa's five jihadist movements against the imperialists are legendary. Caliphs governed 'caliphates' in Nigeria (Uthman dan Fodio), Libya (Grand Sanusi) and in Sudan (the Mahdi) in the 18th–19th centuries, and opposed the invaders. The most successful was that of Uthman dan Fodio (c. 1754–1817) in Hausaland. Fed up with the corrupt, ineffectual ruler and his court, Uthman formed a community in the Hausa Sultanate of Gobir and its environs dedicated to education and reform. He established a federation of sultanates which survived politically and prospered economically until the British conquest of 1903 and the creation of colonial Nigeria.[173]

Sudan's caliphate (1879–1898) under Muhammad Ahmad (the Mahdi) (d. 1885) won renown for driving out the British, killing the ex-governor general of Sudan, Major-General Charles Gordon, who was an evangelical Christian notorious for his hatred of Islam. The British of course

returned with superior firepower, decimating the rebels. Even arch-imperialist Winston Churchill, who was there as a reporter-soldier, was appalled at the massacre.

British and Italian occupation of Somalia was resisted by Muhammad ibn Abd Allah Hasan (1864–1920) who also declared himself the Mahdi but was scornfully called the Mad Mullah by the British,[174] who were defeated by him four times before British air strikes destroyed the Somali fighters. Only Togo was (briefly) German, and Guinea Bissau Portuguese. 'Independence' for Africa's Muslims came late, Ghana being the first to achieve it in 1957, after a long struggle.

During the colonial period, slaves, gold, rubber and other raw materials were exported and thousands of Christian missionaries came to convert the native peoples from animism and Islam. The horrors of African colonialism, well captured in Joseph Conrad's *Heart of Darkness* (1899), are hard to exaggerate and are more than enough to condemn the 'Enlightenment' enterprise and discredit both Christianity and Judaism as moral forces in modernity.

The Arab Peninsula became a nest of western intrigue during WWI, with T.E. Lawrence inciting the Bedouin to rise against the Ottomans, supporting the Hashemite Sharif Hussein bin Ali, who seized Mecca in 1916, only to lose it to the Saudis in 1924. The Saudis readily made peace with the imperialists, and, after putting down the 1927–1930 rebellion by their xenophobic *Ikhwan* (brothers),[175] achieved 'independence' as an absolute monarchy, in a state since 1932 known as **Saudi Arabia** (the only country in the world named after a tribe). Standard Oil of California (Chevron) became the Saudi link with the outside world in 1933 with the creation of the Arab-American oil company Aramco.

Distant **Oman** was occupied by the Portuguese (1508–1648). It then became part of the Ottoman Caliphate until 1741, when a Yemeni tribal chief, Ahmad ibn Said, took control, created and ruled an independent mini-'empire' along the African coast. This allowed continued penetration of the African continent by Islam[176] even as the European powers were waging war to monopolize all trade there. Unfortunately, the sultans were corrupted by the western slave trade, and their presence (and the arrival of European firearms) encouraged tribal wars. The strategically located Oman was finally incorporated into the British Empire in 1860.

The Qasimi tribe's raiding on the so-called Pirate Coast, which includes **Yemen,** was quelled by the British East India Company with Omani assent in 1819, and the strategic port of Aden was taken over from the Portuguese by the British in 1839.[177] The rest of the coast was absorbed into the British Empire as the Trucial Coast sheikhdoms (**United Arab Emirates, Bahrain, Qatar**). The British also moved into Omani-controlled east Africa (Zanzibar, Kenya). The French and Italians seized the predominantly Muslim Horn of Africa (Somalia, Ethiopia).

The British Mandate of Mesopotamia was carved out of three provinces of the Ottoman Caliphate in present-day **Iraq** by the League of Nations following WWI. Britain imposed the Hashemite[178] monarch Faisal I on Iraq in 1921, giving power to the Sunni over the Kurds (who wanted independence) and the Shia (who were the majority). British diplomat Gertrude Bell defended this decision "because otherwise we will have a theocratic state, which is the very devil." During the British occupation, the Shia and Kurds had fought together for independence, and were bombed into submission. 'Independence' was granted in 1932, when the British Mandate officially ended, but the Anglo-Iraq Treaty of 1930 guaranteed Britain the right to invade to protect its oil interests (the Iraqi Petroleum Corporation was majority-owned by British Petroleum and Shell.). In 1899, **Kuwait** had been carved out of Ottoman Mesopotamia and made a 'protectorate' by the British because of its strategic location (granted 'independence' in 1961).

As the Mongols swept across Eurasia in the thirteenth century, the Safaviya Sufi order spread in **Persia (Iran)** and its leader Ismail declared himself Shah in 1501, beginning the reign of the Safavid dynasty. To consolidate his power, Ismail forced the largely Sunni population to convert to Shiism, a process which took a century to consolidate.

The monarchy reached its zenith under Shah Abbas (r. 1587–1629), and by the eighteenth century, was in decline. An adviser to the Shah, an Afghan warlord from Qandahar besieged the Safavid capital of Esfahan in 1722. The Persians were saved by a military leader, Nadir Afshar, who proceeded to rule until 1747, but over a much reduced Persia, the empire now partitioned among the Ottomans, Afghans, and Russians.

In the nineteenth century, Persia was ruled by tribal chiefs with their own *ad hoc* armies and the rich landowning ulama. The Qajar shahs (1794–1925) were not strong and, unlike their Ottoman counterparts and Indian Muslims under direct British occupation, made no concerted attempt at modern reforms. Briefly, the uncorrupt, intelligent Amir Kabir was appointed prime minister (r. 1848–1851), and not only defended Qajar territorial integrity against both the Russian and Ottomans, but also systematized the collection of taxes, the state budget and administration of law, encouraging local production and trade, cutting princes' income and powers, modernizing the army and curtailing the influence of foreign embassies. Kabir initiated the development of Tehran, opened the first nationwide newspaper, and in 1851 established Dar al-Fonun as a modern polytechnic university. The young Shah Nasir al-Din (1848–1898) had him murdered in 1852. These reforming efforts, intent on creating an independent nation, were made in the face of not only a jealous aristocratic elite, but western and Ottoman rival powers.

In 1872 'Baron' Julius de Reuter (a naturalized British Jew, founder of Reuters news agency) was offered a contract to build and operate all of Persia's railways, and exploit the mineral resources for 70 years, as well as to create a national bank. Lord Curzon described it as "the most complete surrender of the entire resources of a kingdom into foreign hands that has ever been dreamed of, much less accomplished in history". Protests by Russia, Iran's neighbour and Britain's rival in the region, sank this particular arrangement. At least Reuter was promising to build some infrastructure. Shah Nasir al-Din was merrily selling these favors to Russians and British businessmen and bankers alike with no such advantages to the nation, and squandering the proceeds. Yet another concession was made in 1890 to yet another Brit for a 50-year monopoly on the production, sale and export of all tobacco. This straw broke the camel's back, sparking a nationwide boycott and forcing the Shah to cancel the monopoly. The Shah was assassinated by a follower of Afghani (see Chapter 2) in 1899. Dissatisfaction mounted and led to further uprisings, uniting the radicals with the ulama and merchants "in a protest that took on the dimensions of a national movement",[179] culminating in a constitutional revolution (1905–11).

The Shah closed down the Majlis (national assembly) in 1908, at the same time as the Russian Tsar did under similar pressures (even as the Ottoman liberals were pushing ahead with their constitutional revolution). When the incompetent Shah's rule threatened the nation with total collapse, the British and Russians allowed the Majlis to reconvene. The Majlis promptly invited an American economic delegation to help it organize the nation's finances,[180] and "the financial reforms proved to be so successful, the British and Russians feared Iran might attempt to become independent of them, and closed the Majlis in 1911."[181]

As a kind of endnote to this bizarre interlude in Iran's history, with the decline of the Iranian monarchy in the face of British-Russian invasions, there arose not one but two apocalyptic movements—the Babi, later the Bahai sect (based on the Hidden Imam, supported by the urban poor, professionals and later the peasantry) and the Aga Khan Ismailis.[182]

Britain retained the upper hand in the Anglo-Russian Convention of 1907, which divided Persia into spheres of influence, regardless of its nominal 'independence'. An Australian prospector discovered oil in 1908, prompting the British navy to press for the creation of what came to be known as the Anglo-Persian Oil Company in 1909. Winston Churchill personally managed negotiations to retain British government majority control of the newly named Anglo-Iranian Oil Company (now BP).

During WWI, the country was occupied by British and Russian forces but was essentially neutral. In 1919, after the Russian revolution and withdrawal, Britain attempted to establish a protectorate in Iran, which was unsuccessful. But an acceptable alternative was at hand. An ambitious officer, Reza Khan, carried out a coup in 1921 and crowned himself Shah, establishing the Pahlavi dynasty, putting 'independent' Persia in safe secular authoritarian hands, giving Britain control of the now vital new energy source in both Iraq and Persia.

Afghanistan only became a separate state in the mid-eighteenth century under the Safavid Shah Nadir's adviser, Ahmad Durrani (r. 1747–1772), who broke with the Persian dynasty after the Shah's death. After inflicting two wars (1839, 1878) in attempts to subdue Afghanistan in the nineteenth century and keep Russia at bay, the British forced the Afghan emir into exile and his successor to sign the 1879 treaty ceding Quetta, the Khyber Pass and other territories, and allowing the British to control Afghanistan's foreign affairs.

Under the influence of British-Russian intrigues, from the 1890s on, both Central Asia and Afghanistan modernized somewhat. Under Russian and subsequent Soviet rule, Central Asia got railways, established a modern education system, and developed large-scale farming.[183] Under British prompting, Afghan emirs and King Amanullah Khan attempted minimal reforms and improved relations with the West. The king faced fierce resistance, and he was deposed in 1929 by Nadir Khan (with British support), leaving Afghanistan largely untouched by western influence until the 1960s. This 'Great Game' left a trail of painful tribal and linguistic divisions, trade routes disrupted, local economies in decline, ruled by quisling local leaders tied to the center.

Timurid rule of **Central Asia** and Afghanistan in the fifteenth century produced an enlightened society which reached its zenith under Amir Timur's grandson Ulugbeg (r. 1411–1449), who was both an enlightened administrator and a brilliant astronomer. The successor states in the sixteenth century were the Uzbek khanate and the Safavids in Persia. The **Kazan** khanate (now Tatarstan) was incorporated into the Russian empire in 1552, the urbanized natives either killed or forcibly converted to Christianity. With the decline of the Safavid dynasty in Persia, Russia was able to easily move in and occupy **Azerbaijan, Dagestan**, the **Kazakh** steppe, and finally **Turkestan** (present-day Uzbekistan, Turkmenistan, Kyrgyzstan and Tajikistan) in the 18th–19th centuries. The **Caucasus** tribes were more resistant, and it was not till the mid-nineteenth century that they were quelled and incorporated into the empire, after defeating Shamil (d. 1871), a Naqshbandi sheikh, who held the armies of the Tsar at bay from 1834–1859.[184]

In **India,** the Delhi sultanate (13th–15th centuries), founded by Turkic Mamluks from Afghanistan, was a precursor to the Moghul 'empire' of the sixteenth century, founded by Babur, a descendant of Amir Timur, in 1512, invading India from Kabul.

The greatest Moghul leader was Akbar (r. 1560–1605), who continued to expand the 'empire'. Akbar began his reign as a pious follower of a Chishti (Sufi) saint. He was illiterate, but intelligent and enjoyed philosophical and theological discussion, including with Hindu, Jain, Zoroastrian, Catholic and Jewish scholars, and with the help of the Persian (Shia) Abu al-Fazl, developed a new Sufi order *din-i ilahi* (Divine Religion) with himself as "ideal ruler of *falsafah*",[185] a true philosopher-king, whose rule remains a model today.

In addition to the Taj Mahal, Akbar's grandson Shah Jahan (r. 1628–1658) is responsible for one of history's greatest economic projects: the transformation of eastern Bengal (present-day Bangladesh) into a major rice-growing region. Eastern Bengal was still forested. Shah Jahan had jungles cleared and, after eliminating piracy from the estuaries of the Ganges, began settling it. Agents of his son and successor Aurangzeb awarded tax-free grants of land to rice farmers, recruiting mostly animist peasants who readily converted to Islam, as the agents built mosques and appointed Chishti imams.

Bengal became renowned for rice, sugar cane, silk and cotton textiles, before the British arrived and dismantled the once-prosperous Moghul 'empire'.

The Moghuls' realm reached its greatest extent under Akbar's great-grandson Aurangzeb (r. 1658–1707), whose strict application of sharia caused friction with India's Hindus (which the British were quick to exploit). India developed a rich tradition of Sufism (Suhrawardi, Chishti, Qadiri, Naqshbandi), reflecting its long tradition of spirituality. The Sikh religion grew out of the tradition of Islamic monotheism, insisting on the unity and compatibility of Hinduism and Islam.[186]

In 1756, Robert Clive wrote to historian Robert Orme describing his methods in conquering the now thriving Bengal: "Fighting, tricks, chicanery, intrigues, politics and the Lord knows what; in short there will be a fine Field for you to display your genius in." After deposing the Nawob, securing first Bengal and then further territories for the East India Company and indirectly for the British government, Clive imposed a tax system on the natives to pay for the export of their textiles to England (essentially free of charge). The East India Company continued his policies of taxation and land registry, which had the same effect as the Enclosure Acts in Britain, and led to the collapse of agriculture.

In 1835 the colonial administration replaced Persian with English in schools and administration, and replaced sharia with civil courts. The East India Company had already fashioned an "Anglo-Muhammadan" legal system based on England's legal system, which was the most punitive in world by the eighteenth century.[187] All this was disastrous and led to the 1857 mutiny, which the British blamed on the Muslims. They enacted draconian restrictions on the practice of Islam, abolishing the pretense of Moghul rule, and in 1858 appointing a viceroy as the direct representative of the crown and a secretary of state for India in the British Cabinet.

From the start of India's travails at the hands of the imperialists, the Muslim Mappilas in southern Kerala, like the heroic Aceh natives in southeast Asia, became famous for resisting the Portuguese in the 16th–17th centuries. The British used the Mappilas' reputation for militancy to exacerbate Muslim-Hindu tensions in the south, at the very time they were repressing Islam in the north. Thus, paradoxically, the strong Muslim resistance contributed to the accelerated destruction of India's Muslim culture at the hands of the British.

By the late nineteenth century, all Indians were seeking greater control of their economy and political representation, leading to the founding of the moderate Hindu-Muslim Indian National Congress in 1885 by a sympathetic Englishman to act as a lobby group with British officials. Future founder of Pakistan Muhammad Ali Jinnah (1876–1948) joined in 1906, though reformer Sayyed Ahmad Khan opposed the Congress, worried that simple representative elections would leave Muslims without adequate representation (Muslims constituted 25–30% of the population). The Aga Khan (see endnote 182) lobbied for better treatment of Muslims, the All-India Muslim League was founded in 1906 with his support, and Jinnah joined, hedging his bets on the future.

The British fomented sectarianism and used divide-and-rule. In the 1871 census, Indian subjects were counted according to religion, and local democratic institutions were organized starting in 1909 with electorates created according to religion. The creation of a new 'Hindu' identity generated a similar demand by Muslims, Sikhs and others. The nationalist Hindu Mahasabha (RSS) was founded in 1921 which eventually became today's militant Hindu BJP. The British privileged Sikhs by recruiting them into the army after the 1857 mutiny, further exacerbating sectarian resentments.

At the same time, the wily British also cultivated elite Indian Muslims, promising them eventual 'independence'[188] if they stayed away from the increasingly militant anti-colonial National Congress. Their star, Jinnah, was a secularist who came from a Shia background, and whose Muslim League supported Britain during WWII when the Congress was pursuing its principled "Out of India" movement for immediate and genuine independence. When 'independence' came to the once prosperous Moghul 'empire' in 1947, it would bring unending war and tragedy for Muslim and non-Muslim alike.

Islam had come to **southeast Asia** as early as the ninth century with Muslim traders from the Red Sea, Persian Gulf and Indian coasts. In the fourteenth century Muslim refugees came from China. Because of the spice trade that flourished in the 14th–17th centuries, a surge of Arab merchants, artisans, Sufi and orthodox Muslim teachers came and settled, transforming the entire region, making it part of Islamic civilization. Islam for Malaysians offered "a new and more universal mysticism, and was taught as such by the heirs of the Indic gurus ... Civilization first came there, and was ultimately adopted from the life of its ports."[189] As in Africa, local leaders willingly converted and slowly the religion, with its appeal to social justice, spread among the people.

In 1600, the Dutch government chartered its privateers, the VOC— the equivalent of the British East India Company (1605). The 16th–18th centuries witnessed virtual war between Portuguese, British and Dutch traders, each determined to achieve a monopoly on the spice and later rubber trade in southeast Asia. Their combined policy of rape and pillage against the natives—as in Africa and India—especially targeted Muslims, who were the traditional traders in the islands that now constitute Indonesia and Malaysia. Because they resisted the privateers' quest for monopoly control of the routes, Muslim traders were treated as enemies, exacerbating the traditional hatred of Islam by 'Christian' empire-builders.

Through assimilation, Islam had supplanted Hinduism and Buddhism as the dominant religion of Java and Sumatra by the end of the sixteenth century, at the very moment the Europeans were beginning their conquests. The privateers terrorizing the once peaceful tropical islands prompted the first anti-imperialist uprising—in Aceh, which "from the 1520s into the mid-seventeenth century was a serious military threat to the Portuguese". During this period, the Muslim merchants managed to send their cargo ships to the Red Sea, avoiding the Portuguese-dominated Malabar Coast of west India.[190] The Aceh sultanate (today part of **Indonesia**) established direct contacts with the Hijaz and Egypt by the sixteenth century. The Ottoman Sultan Suleiman the Magnificent sent a mission in 1565 to support the Aceh sultan against the Portuguese threat to Malacca, and as a result the Portuguese were unable to establish their monopoly on the spice trade. These were diplomatic relations in the best sense of the word, resulting in spice ships sailing safely directly to the Red Sea, and scholars traveling back and forth to Cairo's Azhar University and the Hijaz. No need for monopoly and war.

Aceh was only conquered in the twentieth century, after Aceh's final appeal to a now weakened Ottoman Caliphate and their appeal even to the Americans went unheeded. Aceh's 30-year war against the Dutch (1873–1903), Sudan's defiance of the British, and Algeria's resistance to the French in the 19th–20th centuries are the most legendary of countless acts of resistance by the Muslim world against the imperialists. They inspired others, and led to the founding of the Islamic League in Java (1912), to counter local Chinese economic power in league with the Dutch. The League participated in a communist-led revolt against the Dutch in the mid-1920s, who suppressed both movements.

The discovery of tin in British **Malaysia** in the nineteenth century led to the immigration of tens of thousands of Chinese and Indian indentured laborers, and direct British control of (non-Dutch) territories through British "residents" in the sultans' courts. The sultans, caught between the Dutch and British, were forced to submit to one power and chose to become British protectorates. In contrast to direct colonial occupation, this British indirect rule through 'advisors' to local monarchs (as in Egypt, the Levant and Iraq) relying on its control of the oceans and finance, left the local Muslim culture (albeit much weakened) on the imperial 'map', skimming the profits from trade and the exploitation of local workers, and using military force only when necessary.

Though the British left the local Muslim sultans in place, they stirred up ethnic conflict by favoring Chinese merchants and Indian/ Chinese indentured labor, as in India with the Sikhs, who became famous as devoted soldiers of the Raj. This pattern of co-opting the traditional elites and playing off ethic groups against each other allowed the British to undermine Muslim rule and to govern their huge empire, but at a tremendous cost for all the locals in the long term.

Spain seized the **Philippines** in 1565. When the 'explorers' discovered the archipelago, it was well on the way to becoming Muslim. They became obsessed with converting the natives to Catholicism "and to extirpate Islam. In 1571, an expedition destroyed the Muslim sultanate at Manila and replaced it with a Spanish settlement."[191] By 1600, the coastal areas of the north and central 'Philippines' (named after the Spanish king) were under Spanish control. After the locals kicked out the Spanish in a war of independence in 1898, the US 'bought' it from Spain for $20 million and invaded, killing 200,000 and continuing the Christianization until finally ceding 'independence' in 1946, after 'liberating' it from the Japanese.

By the time of the outbreak of WWI, Britain controlled the Suez Canal, strategic ports in Kuwait, Oman, Bahrain, and both the Atlantic and Pacific oceans. The plan of conquest, which the 'war to end all wars' was supposed to realize, was to link the Rhodes-Rothschild South African gold fields northward, through a predominantly British (Christian) colonial Africa, through the Suez Canal to Mesopotamia, Kuwait, Persia, and the imperial crown jewel, India. With this solid imperial core—the Muslim heartland—the rest of the world would come into line either as friend or subordinate. British bases and colonies around the world were to ensure its control of trade, natural resources and labor power in its vast world colonial network. To some extent this was realized by 1919 when Britain presided over a new League of Nations.

But from the Muslim point of view, by the end of WWI, the entire umma, with the exception of Yemen, Afghanistan—isolated absolute monarchies—and to a lesser extent Turkey and Iran, were now effectively occupied by the non-Muslim imperialists or their agents, a source of great anguish for believers. The more strategic Afghanistan was in any case 'governed' by the 1921 Anglo-Afghan Treaty, giving Britain effective control over Afghan foreign affairs. Turkey and Iran were solidly in thrall to secularism, their leaders busy dismantling what was left of Islamic civilization. The British and subsequently the Americans were careful not to occupy the Hejaz (Mecca, Medina), though the Hashemite Kingdom of Hejaz (1916–1925) and the subsequent Saudi kingdom were effectively imperial protectorates.

Apart from the pervasive sense of shame and humiliation in the Muslim world, which greatly undermined Islamic civilization, the features on the imperial map that the future 'independent' states would inherit were mixed:

- There was some economic development (dams, canals, railroads built for exporting raw materials and cash crops).
- The transformation of agriculture from subsistence to cash-for-export was generally good for the landowning elite, but a disaster for the peasants, whose living standard in cash terms generally plummeted, and became subject to the vagaries of the international market.

- American crops were introduced in Eurasia which allowed cheaper subsistence (food staples such as potatoes and tomatoes), and higher quality raw materials and other foods (superior rubber from Brazil to Malaya and Sumatra, cocoa to Africa, and cotton to Central Asia).
- Slavery first was transformed into genocide in Africa by pious Christians and liberals, and then abolished by pious Christians and liberals, but even that development was generally a disaster, leaving newly freed Africans without land or a means of livelihood, resulting in squatters, violence, and further migration.
- Pre-imperial general illiteracy (and highly developed spirituality) slowly gave way to a push for mass secular education, though even this was in spite of imperial design. The British limited high school education of local Egyptians to less than 100 per year in Egypt in 1900, and delayed the founding of the Egyptian University till 1908. The minimum number of locals possible was trained (with the intent of co-opting them to the imperial agenda).

The imperialists were busy transforming the multiethnic, peaceful union of Muslims across Eurasia into rival, secular, chauvinistic 'nation states', a construct fashioned out of Europe's many bloody wars, and confirmed by the Peace of Westphalia in 1648, something peculiar to European history. They were imposed on the Middle East and North Africa after WWI, according to the Sykes-Picot Agreement between Britain, France and Russia precisely to divide and weaken the region. The Treaty of Lausanne in 1923, recognizing the republic of Turkey, now safely in secular, westernized hands, was followed by the abolition of the Caliphate in 1924. In one fell stroke, the Muslim world's map was erased completely. This was a severe blow to Muslims around the world, who now lived everywhere under the (Christian) imperial yoke. At least, prior to this, Muslims had had Muslim rulers. Islam appeared to be doomed.

WWII merely compounded the bitter humiliation. The by now tried-and-true 'nation' and 'secular state' political constructs were eventually forced on the entire Muslim world, after yet more League of Nations-style mandates were created by the new United Nations. The UN, a noble idea, was used from the start to promote cynical imperial policies. The whole world would be subjugated to the whims of the (imperialist) permanent members of the Security Council. Only the veto power of the anti-imperialist Soviet Union prevented the UN from becoming entirely the imperialist system's Trojan Horse—as Russia and China's, on occasion, still do.

European wars did not leave the distant colonies untouched. The Dutch used the wealth they extracted from Indonesia and Malaysia to defray the costs of the Napoleonic Wars—at the expense of the Javanese.[192] In WWI France sent 300,000 Africans to the front, the British—more than a million Indians. The

Russian Tsar demanded Muslim recruits from Turkestan, setting off a revolt and retaliation, resulting in as many as 500,000 deaths. The colonies were expected to help pay for these wars as well, contributing food, raw materials and labor. Of course, there was no talk of reparations to the fledging nations for the ravages of imperialism. The Arabs had a particularly poisonous dose of medicine, as they had a European Jewish colony thrust violently on them in most of Palestine, even as the British and French were resisting granting the Arab peoples meaningful independence.

In India the British stoked the growing Muslim-Hindu tensions with their wartime refusal to grant unconditional independence to India, and at the same time their courting of Indian Muslims, promising them an independent Muslim state after the war. It worked. In a masterful inversion of logic, it was Congress's "Quit India" campaign boycotting the war effort that was portrayed in the (British-controlled) media as treasonous. An "Indian National Army", sponsored by the Japanese, recruited and organized Indian nationalists out of Burma during the war. Its members were persecuted as traitors after the war, even as Muslim League leader Jinnah piously supported his British masters and reaped the rewards of colonial obedience. The world's first Muslim state would be stillborn, a plaything of the imperialists.

1492 and 1979 stand like bookends for the West's modernist civilization. 1492 marks the end of the Islamic civilization in Spain, with the fall of Granada and the forced emigration or conversion of Spanish Muslims and Jews. "The Strait of Gibraltar became a cultural barrier for the first time in history."[193] The transformation of Europe over the next three centuries resulted in Europe and its offspring, the US, taking control of the entire world, reducing the Muslim world to a collection of weak and squabbling colonial and neocolonial satraps. For a few years, Japan's shocking defeat of the Russian navy in 1905 gave all Asians heart, including Muslims—the imperialists could be defeated at their own game, Great Game I.

The period of 'independence' of the Muslim world, their participation in the neocolonial Great Game II, began at different dates depending on the circumstances of each 'nation', extending from 1918 to the 1970s, during which their leaders' attempts to transform their new states according to the imperial map bore their bitter fruit, under the guise of secular nationalism and pseudo-socialism.

Meanwhile, recalling the period of Mongol occupation in the 13th–14th centuries, Islam continued to flourish across southeast Asia, Africa and Eurasia despite the onslaught of the enemy. Muslims, even without a clear map, did not lose their way entirely. Islam is a deeply-rooted faith, and represented a powerful ideological challenge to both the Mongols and the new imperialists. Then and now, it promised a more just way of life based on the moral code laid down in the Quran and hadiths. Its sharia was universal and fair, in contrast to western legal systems, which privileged the rich and powerful. Fully aware of this, the wily imperialists moved quickly wherever they could to replace sharia courts with their own, restricting it to domestic issues.

But by the 1970s the contradictions of the neoimperialist system were showing, and Islam as an alternative was beginning to re-emerge. The revolution in Iran in 1979 exposed the bankruptcy of 'independence', changing everything in the Middle East and Central Asia, and combined with the enduring resistance in Palestine and the radical Islamists 'fresh' from Afghanistan, put Islam on the imperialists' 'map' around the world.

***

APPENDIX A
Philosophical Debates in Islam

The philosophical debates which have characterized Islamic thought through the ages mirror the sharia legal debate. They came to a head in the 8th–10th centuries in the disputes between the extreme rationalist Mutazilites ('withdrawers')—"highly critical of the luxury of the court and frequently politically active against the establishment"[194] (still associated with Shia rationalists) —and traditionalists. While jurists were debating whether or not they could use their God-given gift of reason (*ijtihad*) to interpret the revealed word, or whether they should just quote precedence (*taqlid*), rationalist and traditionalist philosophers were debating the philosophical version of *ijtihad* vs *taqlid*: the issues of 1. reason vs revelation, 2. free will and personal morality vs predestination, and 3. transcendence vs immanence.

The Quran provided ammunition for both camps:

1. **Reason**, "The worst of beasts in the sight of Allah are the deaf and the dumb—those who understand not." (8:22) vs **revelation**, "Say: 'We believe in Allah, and in what has been revealed to us and what was revealed to Abraham, Ishmael ...'" (3:84). Like the Shia, the Mutazilites declared that justice was of the essence of God: he could not enjoin anything contrary to reason.

2. **Free will**, "Verily never will God change the condition of a people until they change what is in themselves." (13:11) vs **predestination**, "God lets anyone He wishes go astray while He guides whomever He wishes." (35:8) The Mutazilites 'withdrew' from the debate, defending free will.

3. **Transcendence**, "Nothing is like him" (42:11) vs **immanence**, "Wherever you turn, there is God's face." (2:115).

Caliph Ma'mun's (r. 813–33) attempt to impose the Mutazilite beliefs was unpopular, as a religion relying on a predetermined fate (an immanent God) and simple belief is more accessible and more easily grasped than a religion emphasizing personal responsibility (a remote God) and reason. The popular traditionalist scholar Hanbal led the opposition, leading to his persecution. The debate was to some extent resolved in a compromise formulated by Abul Hasan al-Ashari (d. 935), an ex-Mutazilite who continued to advocate the use of reason in harmony with hadiths.

Striking a balance between Sufis and traditionalists on just how immanent (personal) God is, as opposed to being transcendent (remote), and whether reason or revelation hold the upper hand, Ashari argued that the divine *attributes* (knowledge, power, life, nature) are real but distinct from God's *essence* which is unknowable. We can never prove God's existence with reason, but must accept 'him' on faith as revealed by the prophets, relying on revelation to *experience* God.

The attributes-essence distinction also left room for man's free will to sin, which is not of God's *essence*. At the same time, the distinction did not "reduce God to a coherent but arid concept", too remote to inspire simple folk, as critics of the Mutazilites argued. Squaring the circle, "Ashari used reason and logic to show that God was beyond our understanding,"[195] and this position has dominated Islamic philosophy ever since. Seyyed Nasr criticizes the Sunni Asharite status quo for making knowledge completely subservient to faith.[196]

The Hanafi and Shafii legal schools owe a debt to the Mutazilites for their concern with social justice and rationality, though the Mutazilites are now more a footnote in Islamic history. A logical consequence of their strong advocacy of free will was that individuals have a duty to put God's rules into practice, to "enjoin good and forbid evil", a policy associated, ironically, with the ultraconservative Saudis with their volunteer morality brigades, the Committee for the Propagation of Virtue and the Prevention of Vice, swatting errant youth for public indecency, despite the fact that free will is not a central belief of the Hanbali school followed in Saudi Arabia, necessary to accuse the sinners of choosing to sin (and thus swatting them). This voluntarism resulted in "pious anarchy" and social tensions under Ma'mun, as it no doubt does in Saudi Arabia today, and is the exception to the rule in Muslim societies throughout history.

In Islam there is no mechanism for imposing dogmatic conformity. Thus, apart from the major Sunni-Shia division, the different Sunni legal schools predominate in different countries, although there is widespread consensus on most matters. There are several major Sufi orders, three Sunni theological schools. State enforcement of belief has been relatively rare: the Mutazilite-led persecution of rivals under Abbasid Caliph Mu'tasim and al-Wathiq (r. 833–848), the 16th century destruction of Iranian Sunnism under Safavids (more motivated by power politics in opposition to the Ottoman

Caliphate) and the 19th–20th century Saudi Wahhabism used by tribal chiefs turned national leaders. There have been no major sectarian wars in Islamic history, in sharp contrast to Christian history.

APPENDIX B
The 'Protestant' Ethic, the Rise of New Ageism and Fundamentalism

In contrast to the stability of Islamic belief over time, Christianity went through massive upheavals. Apart from the messianic movements such as the thirteenth century Albigensians, who were brutally suppressed, the sixteenth century Reformation fatally undermined Christendom. Protestantism began as a revolt against corruption and the priesthood as intermediary, and it went on to become the new religion of the growing cities where a wealthy merchant class was gaining ascendancy over the establishment, much as Islam itself represented a religious reform movement responding to a growing merchant class in Mecca, requiring a more individual ethic, free of tribalism. The Reformation itself took inspiration from Islam in ridding itself of pagan elements such as depictions of humans, music, alcohol, and gambling as sacrilegious, all of which were widespread in Catholic Europe.

The schism in the church led to a series of religious wars in Europe and the Catholic Counter-Reformation, countless martyred 'heretics', literalism in scriptural hermeneutics, and a confusing and ever-growing array of sects— Calvinism, Anglicanism, Puritanism and many more. The Protestant ethic and predestination came to justify material success as evidence of God's favor (regardless of the means by which the wealth was accumulated). Luther's main tenet was faith, as against reason, but the turmoil which he incited undermined belief, and the growing movement of Enlightenment rationalism ultimately did away with faith altogether, leaving only the mistakenly-named "Protestant ethic" and material success to console Christians.

But even this 'ethic', or rather lack of ethics, had little to do with Christianity, let alone Protestantism. Judaism's restless cultural and social alienation lies at the root of the West's philosophy of progress—alienation not only from a mythical 'promised land' but, in tandem with this, from oneself and nature. The wandering, usurious Jew, bent on revenge against a world that is in essence his enemy, is the most compelling and unsettling ethnic archetype ingrained in the modern human psyche. Judaism, like Christianity and Islam, forbids charging interest—except in the case of your enemy: "From him exact usury whom it would not be a crime to kill. (Deuteronomy 23:19) Hence, in European Christendom the 'dirty work' of money-lending fell to the Jews by default, confirming their status as outcast in Christendom.[197]

As globalization took hold from the fifteenth century on, with the emphasis on rationalism, technology, trade and conquest, the Christian attitude towards usury, and consequently, Jews, began to change. Instead of being despised, they became more and more the model for western civilization. The nations most open to Jews—Holland and England—were the first to develop banking, establish central banks and expand their commercial empires. As Jews integrated into society, their character traits, forged over a long and difficult history, took hold—patience, steadfast devotion to learning and work, and more subtly, acceptance and even love of usury, accumulation of capital (not flagrant displays of wealth, as the feudal rich indulged in), and the co-requisite treatment of the outside world (both people and Nature) as 'the enemy', to be exploited. The Jewish outlook fit the new system of capitalism like a glove, where humans and Nature itself became 'the other', to be conquered and exploited. The western world became Jewish, as Marx put it,[198] and adopted the Jewish idea of success.

In his study of the rise of capitalism in the late medieval period, Werner Sombart described the "struggle between two—Jewish and Christian— outlooks, between two radically differing—nay, opposite—views of economic life", the former intent on maximizing profit, the latter on just prices, "fair wages and fair profits", on observing "commercial etiquette". "To make profit was looked upon by most people throughout the period as improper, as 'unchristian'". Economic life was still tied together by "religious and ethical bonds". Sombart was inspired in his research by Max Weber's *The Protestant Ethic and the Spirit of Capitalism* (1905), but asks "whether all that Weber ascribes to Puritanism might not with equal justice be referred to Judaism, and probably in a greater degree; nay, it might well be suggested that that which is called Puritanism is in reality Judaism."[199]

The undermining of Christian belief proceeded apace with the concerted attack on the Trinity as a pagan accretion (as Islam had long claimed), with the new quantitative sciences discrediting the many literal holes in the Bible. The mystical duality of the transcendent/ immanent nature of God was lost. A shallow deism was adopted by the new rationalists (Newton, Descartes, Voltaire, Darwin) which appealed only to the intellect and quickly led to agnosticism and atheism in the 18th–19th centuries, when capitalism, science, and nationalism became the new organizing forces in society.

This disdain for the transcendent nature of the religious experience, which defies rational analysis, was most famously expressed by Baruch Spinoza (1632–1677) who argued that revealed religion was inferior to scientific knowledge of God. To him, the rites and symbols of the faith were for the masses who were incapable of scientific, rational thought. "For Spinoza, God is simply the principle of law, the sum of all eternal laws in existence." Spinoza was with good reason excommunicated by Amsterdam's chief rabbi. Diderot (1713–1784) quipped that once 'God' ceases to be a passionately subjective experience, 'he' does not exist, leaving only Nature.[200]

While Kant (1724–1804) admitted that you can't prove the existence of God, as he exists beyond space/ time, he too reduced religion to a convenience to help people live a moral life, a reflection of man's "practical reason", his moral conscience, the ideal limit that enables us to achieve a comprehensive idea of the world. The result was that "the center of religion was no longer the mystery of God but man himself."[201] In contrast to this intellectual ferment undermining traditional Christianity and Judaism, there was no corresponding move to secularism via deism in Islam. Maybe Afghani wanted this (see Chapter 3), but he was saved by his firm opposition to imperialism rooted in Islam.

Hegel provided a resolution of the revelation/ reason dilemma: "The Spirit was willing to suffer limitation and exile in order to achieve true spirituality and self-consciousness",[202] being dependent upon the world and upon human beings for its fulfillment. But Hegel's dialectic is purely intellectual, with no corresponding ritual practices which the practitioner can use to get beyond reality. All successful religions entail exacting rituals that help confirm belief, especially prayer and fasting, the bedrock of Islam as they once were for Christianity and Judaism. For the cynical Schopenhauer, lacking a God, only art, music and a discipline of renunciation and compassion can bring us a measure of serenity. Nietzsche's ever more powerful superman became God, as did the Marxian liberated communist man. Freud's neurotic patients were made to realize they were mistakenly clutching at a personalized god as a misplaced exalted father-figure promising justice and endless life. For all of them, religion had crashed and died on the shoals of rationalism.

The transcendent religious experience for Christians did not die with these elegant critiques. The process of secularization and the triumph of reason inevitably led to a reaction among the more passionate, resulting in a plethora of religious sects from the eighteenth century on. John Wesley (1703–1791), founder of Methodism, strove to follow a "religion of the heart" by being "born again", insisting that emotional experience was the only proof of genuine faith, a kind of backdoor mysticism. The Romantics saw rationalism as reductive, and argued that it "left out the imaginative and intuitive activities of the human spirit".[203] Only psychoanalyst Karl Jung among twentieth century 'scientists' held out in favor of the mystical, subjective religious experience as definitive and true.

Even as traditional Christianity declined in the West, there has been a growth of an opposite movement toward the rediscovery of spirituality through the New Age movements, which began in the late nineteenth century and flowered in the 1960s, characterized by a fascination with eastern mysticism, including Hinduism, Buddhism and Sufism. However, New Ageism includes the practice of witchcraft and demonic cults and the cultivation of psychic forces, "a perversion of traditional spirituality; Rene Guenon refers to this as the countertradition."[204]

Also in reaction to secularism and the breakdown of morality as capitalism penetrated social life in the nineteenth century, a crude Christian revival movement gathered momentum and came to be called fundamentalism, calling for a literal reading and observance of the Bible, despite its many inconsistencies. A sincere reading, assuming the inerrancy of the Biblical message, would inevitably lead to the deconstruction of texts which cannot be literally true and at the same time contradict other passages. Such a reading would not pretend to completely understand the mysteries of God as reflected in fallible human language.

This deconstruction has proceeded in the face of the literalists, as the new rationalist social scientists began applying literary critical analysis to the Bible, exposing, for example, the fact that four writers compiled the books of Moses centuries after he supposedly lived, that the Gospels have major differences in narrative sequence and the events in Jesus' life, etc. This 'tampering' with the holy texts was seen by fundamentalists (literalists) as anathema; they insisted on both a literal reading, while at the same time affirmed the inerrancy of the text, a case of having one's cake and eating it.

Judaism also has its fundamentalists/ literalists, the Haredim, as well as the secular Zionists who have refashioned Judaism, though Zionism is a negation of Judaism, rather than its continuation. Founder of Israel Ben Gurion dismissed Judaism as "the historical misfortune of the Jewish people and an obstacle to its transformation into a normal state."

There have been tentative attempts in Islam to deconstruct the Quranic text, generating similar anger among Islam's fundamentalists/ literalists. The big difference between Christianity/ Judaism and Islam is that in Islam the Quran is believed to be the unmediated text of the word of God, unlike Christian/ Jewish texts which are all secondary sources. To a neutral observer, the Quran is a marked improvement, appropriately vague on the creation story, astronomy, etc., making it difficult to discredit by rationalists. Furthermore, it is clear that many verses in the Quran which refer to literal historical events per force require a text/ context dialectical analysis, and that other verses were revealed to Muhammad as allegorical,[205] requiring interpretation. So this process of deconstruction is much less problematic. "In the realm of scientific thought generally, textual inerrancy has been easier to defend in the Quran than in the Bible."[206] Muslim literalists can be as exasperating as their Christian and Jewish counterparts, but the superiority of the Quran as a consistent text means there are fewer flat-earthers. The vast majority of Muslims are better understood as traditionalists, proud of the accumulated heritage of Islam and merely calling for social and economic reforms consistent with the tenets of Islam.

There are fewer al-Qaeda type militant fundamentalists among Christian fundamentalists (such as David Koresh), though many among the

Jewish ones, as the history of contemporary Israel confirms. In explanation of the apparent lack of violence among Christian fundamentalists, Seyyed Nasr argues that "Christian fundamentalism is by and large not violent or militaristic ... because it does not face continuous pressure by forces external to western society."[207]

Given the invasion of Muslim lands by nonbelievers, the rise of resistance, including what is labeled Islamic terrorism is hardly surprising, as jihad is permissible against invaders and in defense of religion, though the killing of civilians is not condoned by any serious Islamic scholars. It is in fact Christian and Jewish fundamentalists who are most responsible for what can only be called state terrorist acts today, supporting illegal US wars and extra-judicial assassinations, and Israeli violence against Palestinians. Terrorism by proxy is just as terrible as direct terrorism, and makes all western citizens—Christian fundamentalist included—guilty to the extent of their support.

The fundamentalists/ literalists in all the monotheisms are making a great deal of noise these days and killing thousands of innocent people. In Israel and many countries in Europe and North America, fundamentalists are wielding political power (US President George W Bush (r. 2001–2008) was 'born again' and Canadian Prime Minister Stephen Harper (r. 2007) is evangelical). The Islamic awakening emerging through today's Arab Spring frightens them, but they are the ones who have incited many Muslims to turn to their own militant fundamentalists/ literalists, in a sense, to fight fire with fire. The rise of Islamic fundamentalists is considered in Chapters 3–5. But they do not control the discourse in Islam as do their Christian and Jewish counterparts the discourse in Christianity and Judaism, and they cannot prevail for many reasons, and not because the US and Israel kill them with drones. On the contrary, this deadly reaction only incites the growth of their numbers.

The very stability of Islamic theology through the ages and the less problematic Quranic text has meant that it is the *traditionalists* who dominate the discourse and who will prevail, and to the extent that reforms are needed in Islam at all, traditionalists have a much healthier foundation on which to build their movement than do any of the monotheistic fundamentalists. Western media paints an upside-down version of this reality. It ignores the Christian/ Jewish fundamentalists for the most part, and blows the Muslim variety out of all proportions. It is the Christian and Jewish fundamentalists who are in reality the bigger problem, in the first place because they are the bellwethers of imperialism. Terrorism emanating from the Muslim world will recede when this project is dismantled.

In the West, there is still room for morality in politics, as is the intent of Islam. Though Christianity from the start was not strongly political in nature, the founders of the US, where the 'separation of church and state' was enshrined in the constitution, did not intend to prevent politicians from basing their political affairs on Christian morality. Even today, it is popular in the US for political leaders to mouth Christian/ Jewish beliefs.[208] The original intent, in the face of the explosion of Christian sects in the eighteenth century, was to make sure no one sect could gain a stranglehold on government. With the subsequent prominence of Catholics, Jews and agnostics, and the consolidation of capitalism as the (amoral) economic structure, the constitution was reinterpreted to reflect the new social forces and took on its current radically secular meaning, where all public manifestations of religion are frowned on, and the only laws of importance are ones issued by the secular state.

ENDNOTES

1   Khurram Murad, *Dawah among Non-Muslims in the West: Some Conceptual and Methodological Aspects*, London: Islamic Foundation, 1986, 18.

2   This most controversial of the tenets of Islam gave rise to the Mutazalite debate which still echoes in Islamic theology today. See Chapter 1 Appendix B.

3   Karl Jaspers, *The Origin and Goal of History*, USA: Yale University Press, 1953.

4   Karen Armstrong, *A History of God: The 4000-Year Quest of Judaism, Christianity and Islam*, New York: Alfred Knopf, 1994, 38. The resistance to imperialism beginning in the late nineteenth century throughout Asia looked to Confucianism, Buddhism and Hinduism as well as Islam. Armstrong includes rationalism in Greece, and though it is inappropriate to consider it as a revealed religion, it also inspired the secular anti-imperialism of Marx and Lenin, and was pursued with a passion and conviction similar to that inspired by religion.

5   This belief, popularized by the Perennialist School of the philosophy of religion, was expounded by al-Farabi (d. 950), and is reflected in Islam's perennial tolerance of other religious traditions which do not conflict with the fundamental beliefs if Islam.

6   Gai Eaton, *King of the Castle: Choice and Responsibility in the Modern World*, UK: Islamic Texts Society, 1977, 9.

7   Ibid., 190.

8   Who is not named in the Quran but simply referred to as Adam's companion, and is not from Adam's rib, but created in her own right.

9   Tim Winter, interviewed by John Cleary, Australian Broadcasting Corporation, 18 May 2004.

10   Karen Armstrong, *Islam: A short History*, Modern Library, 2000, 7, 133.

11   Muhammad's cousin Ubaydallah Ibn Jahsh, Muhammad's Christian adviser Waraqa Ibn Nawfal, and Zayd Ibn Amr, uncle of Umar Ibn al-Khattab who became Muhammad's companion and the second caliph, see Armstrong, *A History of God*, 136.

12   Abraham had a son Ismail by his servant Hagar, but when his formerly barren wife Sarah gave birth to Isaac, she feared that Ismail would overshadow Isaac, and Abraham took Hagar and Ismail to Mecca. Later Abraham returned to Mecca and built the Kaaba as the first shrine to the one true God.

13   Armstrong, *Islam*, 17.

14   Armstrong, *A History of God*, 136.

15   Muhammad Iqbal explained the role of Islam as the culmination of the Axial Age religious movements as follows: "The peak of non-concrete, symbolical rationalism had been reached in Plato and Aristotle, the human mind was finally ready to make the great leap to a full adequate, scientific way of think-

ing. [Islam introduced] the attitude of positive and open-ended yet still logical and systematic observation which made possible inductive science." Quoted in Marshall Hodgson, edited and introduction by Edmund Burk, *Rethinking World History: Essays on Europe, Islam and World History*, Cambridge University Press, 1993, 236-7.

16   "Allah will raise up, to [suitable] ranks and [degrees], those of you who believe and who have been granted knowledge." (58:11)

17   The Jewish texts were not recorded definitively until the third century BC, long after the 'events' recorded in them. The four canonical gospels (Matthew, Mark, Luke, John) were compiled beginning a generation after the death of Jesus, with Mark now considered the earliest Gospel (c.65–70). They were called the four "Pillars of the Church" by Irenaeus of Lyons (185), and confirmed at the Council of Rome (382). The earliest surviving complete copies of the gospels date to the fourth century. Thus, they correspond at best to the hadiths of Islam, there being no definitive text ascribed directly to divine revelations to Jesus.

18   Abraham, Moses, David, Jesus and Muhammad stand out in the Quran as "messenger" prophets who brought God's message in writing. The Quran mentions Jesus twenty-five times, more often, by name, than Muhammad, and Mary is mentioned more in the Quran than in the New Testament.

19   Armstrong, *Islam*, xi.

20   Hijra (emigration) Era, 622AD. See below.

21   The Islamic lunar calendar 'loses' a year every 35 years. To avoid confusion, *anno Domini* dates will be used here.

22   He left with Abu Bakr; others had gone on ahead earlier, leaving Mecca by twos and threes so that the departure would not be noticed and stopped.

23   Egypt's 1973 war against Israel was called Operation Badr or the Ramadan war.

24   Caliph means steward/ spiritual leader.

25   Hodgson, *Rethinking World History*, 105.

26   Under sharia law, *dhimmi* status was originally afforded to Jews, Christians, and Sabians. The protected religions later came to include Zoroastrians, Hindus and Buddhists. Eventually, the Hanafi school applied this term to all non-Muslims living in Islamic lands. As an example of the distinctions between Muslims and *dhimmis*, sharia law permits the consumption of pork and alcohol by non-Muslims living in Islamic countries, although they may not be openly displayed. Modern Hanafi scholars do not make any legal distinction between a *dhimmi* and a Muslim citizen.

27   Hodgson, *Rethinking World History*, 176.

28   Armstrong, *Islam*, 29–30.

29   The passages in the Quran which are highly critical of Jews must be read in the context of the betrayal of the Muslim community in Medina by local Jewish tribes, especially at the time of the battle of the Trench in 627. Jews held a privileged status in the caliphates as 'People of the Book' and because of their tradition of learning. Muslim anti-Jewish sentiment arose only as a reaction to Zionism, the creation of Israel and Israel's wars of expansion on traditional Arab lands.

30   Who believed Jesus had one nature, not two.

31   The rebellion following the massacre continued until finally quelled by a cousin of Muawiya, Marwan who briefly succeeded the dissolute Yazid as caliph, followed by the able Abd al-Malik (r. 685–705).

32   He calls it a "bourgeois revolution". Chris Harman, *A People's History of the World*, UK: Verso, 1999, 129.

33   Gai Eaton, *Islam and the Destiny of Man*, UK: Islamic Texts Society, 1994, 167.

34   A nephew of Hisham (see endnote 39 below).

35   A branch of Shiism, the 'seveners' who believed there were only seven Imams

after Muhammad. See the definition of Shiism below and endnote 42.

36   Eaton, *Islam and the Destiny of Man*, 173.

37   Hodgson, *Rethinking World History*, 118.

38   The term empire does not do justice to the federations established in the name of Islam, which were much looser and less invasive than either the Roman Empire or the empires based on capitalism that came later.

39   Muhammad's family tree originates in the Quraish tribe with Hashem, great-great-grandfather of Muhammad, and his twin brother Abd Shams:

              Abd Shams (-> Umayyads) and

              Hashem (-> Abd al-Muttalib -> **al-Abbas, Abu Talib** *(-> Ali)* and **Abdallah** -> *Muhammad (-> Fatima/Ali -> Hasan and Husayn -> Shia imams))*

40   Eaton, *Islam and the Destiny of Man*, 161.

41   Seyyed Hossein Nasr, *Islam in the Modern World: Challenged by the West, Threatened by fundamentalism, Keeping faith with Tradition*, USA: Harper One, 2010, 31–32.

42   The twelfth generation descendant of Muhammad, Imam Muhamm ibn al-Hasan al-Mahdi, disappeared (the Occultation) in 941, and these 'twelver' Shia believe his return will herald the triumph of the Islamic order on Earth.

43   Hodgson, *Rethinking World History*, 14., 135–136.

44   Sadakat Kadri, *Heaven on Earth: A Journey Through Sharia Law from the Deserts of Ancient Arabia to the Streets of the Modern Muslim World*, NY: Farrar, Straus and Giroux, 2012, 6.

45   Armstrong, *Islam*, 65.

46   Eaton, *Islam and the Destiny of Man*, 180.

47   John 4:14. This use of water as a metaphor is common to Christianity and Islam. In Islam, paradise is "Gardens beneath which Rivers flow, to dwell therein (forever)". 58:22.

48   3:104. See also 31:17.

49   Gai Eaton, *King of the Castle*, 185.

50   Steffen Stelzer "Ethics", in Tim Winter (ed.), *The Cambridge Companion to Classical Islamic Theology*, Cambridge University Press, 2008, 165.

51   Traditional empires allowed for the obliteration of conquered peoples without any 'international criminal court' to turn to. The US has no reason to abide by or participate in international conventions or nascent legal institutions like the ICC. Financial, economic and military power determine international 'law'; i.e., 'might still makes right'. That said, international laws and conventions can play a positive role, if only in embarrassing the empire and making the most egregious criminals liable to arrest in countries which sincerely attempt to implement human rights laws.

52   John Voll, "Revivalism and Social Transformation in Islamic History," *The Muslim World*, LXXVI (3–4): 168–180, in Sohrab Behdad and Farhad Nomani (eds), *Islam and the Everyday World: Public policy dilemmas*, New York: Routledge, 2006, 14.

53   E.g., alcohol is bad; therefore, all intoxicants are bad.

54   Nasr, *Islam in the Modern World*, 5.

55   Hadith reported by al-Tirmidhi and Abu Dawud.

56   Kadri, *Heaven on Earth*, 57.

57   Hanafi (45.5%), Maliki (15%), Shafii (28%), Hanbali (2%). In John Esposito, Ibrahim Kalin, Ed Marques, Usra Ghazi (eds), *The 500 Most Influential Muslims in the World*, Georgetown: Royal Islamic Strategic Studies Center and Prince Alwaleed bin Talal Center for Muslim-Christian Understanding, 2009.

58   Prevalent in north African and west African countries (Tunisia, Morocco, Algeria, Libya, Mali and Nigeria), as well as being the official legal science of Kuwait, Bahrain and the United Arab Emirates.

59   The Shafii scholar and chief qadi of Baghdad Abu al-Hasan al-Mawardi

(972–1058) wrote *The Ordnances* formulating the Sunni theory of government, including the doctrine *darura* (necessity) and *mukrih* (coercion).

60 This popular sound byte is attributed to a fatwa issued by al-Qaffal al-Kabir (904–976) of the Shafii school from Tashkent in Central Asia.

61 Winter, *The Cambridge Companion to Classical Islamic Theology*, 244.

62 See Chapter 2. Muhammad al-Ghazali (d. 1111) expressed the dominant view that even an unjust Muslim ruler should not be overthrown violently, in the interests of preserving the unity of the umma. In *Moderation in Religious Belief,* Ghazali argues that Muslims must submit to a sinful regime. A government should not be overthrown "so long as they uphold prayer among you". (hadith of al-Muslim) This anticipates Thomas Hobbes during English Civil War (and Henry Kissinger today), who argued that the common good demanded obedience because tyranny was better than anarchy.

63 Re Ibn Khaldun, see below in the section on economics. Ibn Rushd (1126–1198), known in the West as Averroes, was a Spanish master of Aristotelian philosophy, Islamic philosophy and theology, Maliki law, psychology, politics, music theory, medicine, astronomy, geography, mathematics, physics and celestial mechanics. Ibn Sina (980–1037), known in the West as Avicenna, was a Persian scientist and doctor whose *Book of Healing* and *Canon of Medicine* are still studied today.

64 Ogier Ghiselin de Busbecq, *Turkish Letters* (1555–1562), quoted in Hodgson, *Rethinking World History*, 158.

65 With the exception of Amir Timur, the fourteenth century descendant of the Mongols, who recapitulated the pre-Islamic Mongol conquest of Eurasia. The 1980 attack on Iran by (secular, US-backed) Iraqi Saddam Hussein, egged on by the US, was the most egregious exception to this 'law' of Islamic politics. Note that when the US invaded Iraq in 1991, Iraq sent its military planes to its erstwhile enemy, Iran.

66 Kadri, *Heaven on Earth,* 52–67.

67 Including, it should be stressed, the divine revelation concerning the obligation of zakat and provision of adequate sustenance for the poor. Umar Abd-Allah "Theological dimension of Islamic law", in Winter, *The Cambridge Companion to Classical Islamic Theology*, 242–243.

68 Yusuf al-Qaradawi, "Statement on Shiites", *www.usislam.org*, 2008. The more militant Salafi Sunnis consider Shia to be heretics.

69 Caliph Umar suspended the penalty altogether during a famine.

70 "By criminals and murderers who cause disorder in the settled and peaceful society or by armed forces who attempt to overthrow the Islamic State," Abul Ala Maududi, *The Meaning of the Qur'an,* <englishtafsir.com>.

71 "Tumult and oppression are worse than slaughter. Nor will they cease fighting you until they turn you back from their faith if they can. And if any of you turn back from their faith and die in unbelief, their works will bear no fruit in this life and in the Hereafter; they will be companions of the Fire and will abide therein." (2:217)

72 Kadri, *Heaven on Earth,* 28.

73 "He that blasphemeth the name of the Lord, he shall surely be put to death, and all the congregation shall certainly stone him." (Leviticus 24:16) If someone "entice thee secretly, saying, Let us go and serve other gods ... thou shalt surely kill him." Deuteronomy 13:6–9.

74 Mohamed Talib (Tunisia), "Religious Liberty: A Muslim Perspective", in Mehran Kamrava, (ed.), *The New Noices of Islam: Rethinking Politics and Modernity, A Reader,* LA: University of California Press, 2006, 113–114.

75 Reported by al-Bukhari. "Spy not, neither backbite one another. Would one of you like to eat the flesh of his dead brother? You would hate it (so hate backbiting)." (49:12)

76 Behdad, *Islam and the Everyday World,* 12. The Maliki school's al-Shatibi's

relied on the Quran for the 'rights of God' and *maslaha* for the 'rights of man'. Wahhab used *maslaha*, as did Abduh, and as do the Muslim Brotherhood.

77 Eaton, *King of the Castle* 195.

78 Though never formally declared a 'pillar', jihad has always been a popular element in Islamic discourse. Banna, Maududi and Qutb all wrote about jihad as a duty in the face of the invasion of Muslim lands by the nonbelievers. In *The Neglected Duty*, Egyptian Islamic Jihad's Muhammad al-Faraj explicitly calls jihad "the sixth pillar of Islam". See Chapter 4.

79 Tariq Ramadan, *In the Footsteps of the Prophet: Lessons from the Life of Muhammad*, UK: Oxford University Press, 2007, 52.

80 Hadith reported by Bayhaqi, though its authenticity is disputed. Ramadan, *In the Footsteps of the Prophet*, 179, 194.

81 The Quraish were preparing to attack the Muslims of Medina when this verse was revealed.

82 Ayesha Jalal, *Partisans of Allah: Jihad in South Asia*, USA: Harvard University Press, 2008, 7.

83 Kadri, *Heaven on Earth,* 150.

84 Nasr, *Islam in the Modern World,* 47.

85 Armstrong, *A History of God*, 160.

86 Nasr, *Islam in the Modern World*, 6.

87 Eaton, *Islam and the Destiny of Man*, 232.

88 In 922, on the 300th anniversary of the *hijra*, the beginning of the Islamic order.

89 Eaton, *Islam and the Destiny of Man*, 230. The other Sufi who must be mentioned here is the Andalusian Muhidin ibn Arab (d. 1240).

90 Hans Kung, *Islam: Past, Present and Future*, tr. John Bowden, UK: Oneworld 2004, 305.

91 Mawlawis were inspired by Jalal al-Din Rumi and are famous for the Whirling Dervishes; Sheikh Wali Allah was a Naqshbandi, reflecting their more activist orientation, involved in reform movements starting in the nineteenth century. Rumi held that all existence and all religions were one, all manifestations of the same divine reality. "Sufism, with its emphasis on love rather than judgment, represents the New Testament of Islam." William Dalrymple, "The Muslims in the Middle", *New York Times*, 16 August 2010.

92 Nasr, *Islam in the Modern World*, 75.

93 Hodgson, *Rethinking World History*, 188.

94 Egyptian Sufis even voted for Ahmed Shafiq, the candidate most associated with Mubarak in the 2012 presidential election. He claimed he was a Sufi himself (Egypt, Turkey and Persia are traditionally the great centers of Sufism), and the Sufis fear that a strict Muslim regime would restrict their worship at saints' shrines. At the same time, many more orthodox Muslims are directly inspired by Sufism to become more politically active and reform-minded.

95 An example of the subversive nature of Sufism is Abu Abdullah Muhammad al-Arabi al-Darqawi (1760–1823), a Moroccan Sufi leader who stressed non-involvement in worldly affairs but was nonetheless imprisoned for supporting revolts against the throne. The Darqawa *tariqa* became the most popular Moroccan Sufi order. In both Algeria and Morocco the Darqawiyya were involved in political activities. A branch of the Dawqawiyya called the Murabitun has established a foothold in the Mexican Chiapas. Another branch of the Darqawis, known as the Alawiya (not to be confused with the Syrian Alawis), has become prominent in the West.

96 Charles Haviland, "The roar of Rumi - 800 years on", *news.bbc.co.uk,* 30 September 2007. Quote from Armstrong, *Islam*, 101.

97 The periods when Christian society was governed as a theocracy were few and limited (the Vatican states, the Anabaptists under Munster, Geneva under Calvin).

98 Armstrong, *A History of God*, 159.

99   The penultimate Ottoman Sultan, Abdelhamid II, was a stern autocrat, intel-
          ligent, devout and uncorrupt, combining state power and religious inspiration
          as a unifying figure. He was deposed by secular-minded reformers in 1908 who
          put a puppet monarch in his place, accelerating the collapse of the caliphate.
100   Hadith narrated by Abu Dawood and Tirmidhi.
101   Jeong Chun Hai and Nor Fadzlina Nawi, *Principles of Public Administration: An
          Introduction*, Kuala Lumpur: Karisma Publications, 2007. The hadith narrated
          by Tirmidhi (4:2167), Ibn Majah (2:1303), Abu Dawood.
102   It was written when he was advising the new Pakistani government in the
          1950s, but the exigencies of post-WWII Pakistan made it impossible to carry
          out Asad's project. As an Austrian Jew who converted to Islam during his travels
          in the Middle East in the 1920s–1930s, he was well-versed in the pitfalls of
          European secular democracy and saw in Islam a convincing answer to how
          a community could be shaped "so that men could live rightly and in fullness",
          and "relationships arranged so that they might break through the loneliness
          which surrounded every man". Asad, *The Road to Mecca*, 69.
103   Muhammad Asad, *Principles of State and Government in Islam,* USA: University
          of California, 1961, 5. Unless otherwise endnoted, all quotes in this section
          are from this book.
104   As indeed are the principles of international law, so that they can serve as
          guidelines to a vastly diverse set of peoples and situations.
105   Asad was close to the Saudi King Abdulaziz (r. 1932–53) in the 1930s but
          broke with him over the creation of an absolute monarchy based on the Saud
          tribe.
106   Equity is used to stress the social aspect, equality within the accepted moral
          order. This is not absolute equality but according to the society's accepted
          roles. See the next section on economics.
107   Hadith of Abu Musa . "If you wish to rule, then you are unfit." Hadith by al-
          Bukhari.
108   Quote from Ibn Saad, *The Major Classes.* In Asad, *Principles of State and
          Government in Islam*, 92.
109   Eaton, *King of the Castle*, 97.
110   2:30 Meaning viceroy or viceregent.
111   Originally property referred primarily to land, and was defined by use, as in
          John Locke's natural rights theory. Capitalism redefined property to encompass
          all monetary wealth. Wealth as an individual's claim on the annual *income* of
          society is thus associated with exploitation of labor/ Nature and from trade,
          and has no limit, unlike property associated with land and use. Such 'wealth'
          actually *thrives* on destruction of private property in war (viz. the rapid recovery
          of Europe after the incredibly destructive WWI&II). The "stability and conserva-
          tion of property slow the machine down." Eaton, *King of the Castle*, 53.
112   "So protect yourself from Hell Fire, by giving in charity even half a date; and if
          he does not find it, then with a kind word." Hadith reported by al-Bukhari and
          al-Muslim.
113   See Tariq Ramadan, *Western Muslims and the Future of Islam*, UK: Oxford
          University Press, 2004, Chapter 8.
114   Rent is a problematic concept in Islam. It is acceptable in a restricted sense,
          but the concept of a rentier class living off rent is haram.
115   Ziauddin Sardar, *Reading the Qur'an: The Contemporary Relevance of the
          Sacred Text of Islam*, UK: Oxford University Press, 2011, 132–133.
116   Trade results in an overall increase in welfare for both buyer and seller due to
          lower opportunity costs of some producers/ countries compared to others.
117   Zakat as a religious obligation differs from modern income-tax, which is "de-
          signed on the one hand to transfer responsibilities from the individual, the family
          or the community to the State and, on the other, to alter relationships within
          society." Eaton, *King of the Castle,* 107. Just as important, zakat is specifically

directed towards assisting the poor (and a few other similarly moral concerns), and cannot be transferred into some other expense like building highways, etc. at the whim of some official.

118   Weiss, Dieter, "Ibn Khaldun on economic transformation," *International Journal of Middle Eastern Studies*, vol. 27, 1995, 29–37.

119   "All Muslims are partners in three things—in water, herbage and fire." Hadith reported by Abu Daud and Ibn Majah.

120   Farhad Nomani and Ali Rahnema, *Islamic Economic Systems*, New Jersey: Zed books, 1994, 7–9.

121   In Medina, a small group of merchants met agricultural producers outside the city and bought the entire date crop, thereby gaining a monopoly over the market. The produce was later sold at a higher price within the city. Muhammad condemned this practice since it caused injury both to the producers (forced to sell to a monopolist at a lower price) and the inhabitants (forced to buy from a monopolist at a higher price), and caused a maldistribution of income—a zero-sum transaction, as opposed to the desired positive-sum result of trade.

122   The perverse result of an interest-based economy controlled by private banks is revealed by the fact that "35% to 40% of everything we buy goes to interest." Ellen Brown, "It's the Interest, Stupid! Why Bankers Rule the World", *Global Research,* 8 November 2012.

123   Michael Bonner, "Poverty and Economics in the Qur'an", *Journal of Inter-disciplinary History*, xxxv:3, quoted in Winter, *The Cambridge Companion to Classical Islamic Theology*, 391–406.

124   Muhammad Mamduke Pickthall, *Oriental Encounters: Palestine and Syria,* UK: W. Collins Sons, 1918.

125   Nasr, *Islam in the Modern World*, 51.

126   Ibid., 52.

127   Ibid., 53–55.

128   Ibid., 60. This attitude towards work was prevalent in all traditional societies, which made sure that mundane tasks reflected/ embodied the spiritual/ ritual, "through which we make our way towards the central place". Eaton, *King of the Castle*, 195.

129   Apart from the official 6,000 heretics killed by the Inquisition, hundreds of thou-sands (possibly millions—there are no reliable statistics) died during religious wars and various 'crusades', not just against Muslims but for instance against the Albigensians in the thirteenth century. "Pinker tackles the Albigensian Crusade", *bedejournal.blogspot.ca*, 8 November 2011.

130   By the same token, Christianity is sometimes called 'Judaism adapted for the Roman Empire'.

131   In 2004, while Bartholomew I, Patriarch of Constantinople, was visiting the Vatican, John Paul II asked, "How can we not share, at a distance of eight centuries, the pain and disgust?"

132   Commemorating the fifth anniversary of 911, on 12 September 2006, while lecturing on "Faith, Reason and the University" at the University of Regens-burg, Pope Benedict quoted Byzantine Emperor Manuel II Palaiologos (r. 1391–1425), "Show me just what Muhammad brought that was new and there you will find things only evil and inhuman, such as his command to spread by the sword the faith he preached". The Pope made things worse by argu-ing that verse 2:256 stating "There is no compulsion in religion" was an early verse revealed when Mohamed was powerless in Mecca, though this verse was one of the later Medina verses revealed at a time when the Muslim state was powerful.

133   William Dalrymple, *From The Holy Mountain,* USA: Holt, 1999.

134   Hodgson, *Rethinking World History*, 217.

135   Robert Wright, *Nonzero: The Logic of Human Destiny*, USA: Vintage, 2001.

136   Benjamin Ginsberg, *The Fatal Embrace: Jews and the State,* Chicago: Uni-

versity of Chicago Press, 1993, 9.

137   Genesis 1:26, King James version.

138   Hodgson, *Rethinking World History*, 100.

139   Eaton, *King of the Castle*, 84.

140   Francis Bacon, *Novum Organum* (1620), #81, in Basil Montague, ed. and trans., *The Works*, 3 vols., Philadelphia: Parry and MacMillan, 1854, 3: 357.

141   Nasr, *Islam in the Modern World*, 191.

142   Ibid., 200.

143   Neil Postman, *Technopoly: The Surrender of Culture to Technology*, USA: Vintage, 1993.

144   R.H. Tawney's *Religion and the Rise of Capitalism* (1926) "bemoaned the division between commerce and social morality brought about by the Protestant Reformation, leading as it did to the subordination of Christian teaching to the pursuit of material wealth". Geoffrey Foote, *The Labour Party's Political Thought: A History*, London: Macmillan Press, 1997, 74.

145   Armstrong, *A History of God*, 142.

146   Postman, *Technopoly*, 70.

147   Ibn Majah hadith.

148   Andre Gunder Frank, *The Development of Underdevelopment*, USA: Monthly Review Press, 1966.

149   An eloquent soundbyte about banking and interest is found in a letter from Afghani (see Chapter 2) to Ayatollah Mirza Hassan Shirazi in Najaf in the 1890s: "What shall cause thee to understand what is the Bank? It means the complete handing over of the reins of government to the enemy of Islam, the enslaving of the people to that enemy, the surrendering of them and of all dominion and authority into the hands of the foreign foe." Quoted in Pankaj Mishra, "Why weren't they grateful?" *London Review of Books*, Vol. 34 No. 12, 21 June 2012.

150   'Center' referring to the imperial center, periphery to the colonies. See Eric Walberg, *Postmodern Imperialism: Geopolitics and the Great Games*, USA: Clarity Press, 2011.

151   Karen Armstrong, *The Battle for God: A History of Fundamentalism*, USA: Random House, 2000, 106.

152   The three recent genocides started with the extermination of almost all North American natives, reducing the population from as many as 100 million to 1.8 million (David Stannard, *American Holocaust: The Conquest of the New World*, UK: Oxford University Press, 1992.); the slave trade, involving the enslavement of 6 million Africans to man cotton and sugar plantations in the Americas; the extermination of millions of Jews and others considered subhuman or otherwise undesirable by the Nazis.

153   Perhaps as many as a million, from Hausaland and the tribes of the Senegal and Gambia rivers, which were Muslim or converting to Islam at the time. See Gwendolyn Zoharah Simmons, "African-American Islam", in Karin van Nieuwkerk (ed.), *Women Embracing Islam: Gender and Conversion in the West*, Austin, TX: University of Texas, 2006, 175.

154   The French attempt in Tunisia and the Italian attempt in Libya failed.

155   The Chinese Hui nation (10 million), who are today indistinguishable from the Han and live in the heart of Han China, are descendants of Arab and Turkic Silk Road merchants. There are approximately 20 million Muslims in China today.

156   It became Istanbul officially in 1930.

157   R. Hilferding, *Finance Capital*, Moscow, 1912 (in Russian), 338–339, quoted by V. Lenin, *Imperialism, the Highest Stage of Capitalism*, Peking: Foreign Languages Press, [1917] 1970, 52.

158   Walberg, *Postmodern Imperialism*, 31–33.

159   It was a smashing success for the bankers, as usual, increasing the debt of the British state, too.

160   European media headlines screamed about Ottoman atrocities, just as it did about Syria trying to hold together an ethnically diverse nation in 2011–2013 under foreign pressure.

161   Armstrong, *Islam*, 138.

162   His predecessor Abdulaziz II (r. 1861–1875) had revived the title of caliph in a desperate attempt to appeal to the world Muslim committee to rally around the Ottomans in their ongoing crises.

163   According to the head of the Zionist movement at the time, Theodore Herzl, the sultan told Herzl's emissary in 1896, "If Herzl is as much your friend as you are mine, then advise him not to take another step in this matter. I cannot sell even a square foot of land as it does not belong to me but belongs to my people."

164   In 1906 Istanbul was only 50% Muslim, 20% Greek Orthodox. Salonica in 1913 (after thousands of Jews and Muslims had fled) was still 40% Jewish, 30% Muslim, 25% Greek. Michelle Campos, *Ottoman Brothers: Muslims, Christians and Jews in early 20th century Palestine*, USA: Stanford, 2011.

165   The "tyranny" being WWI, into which the westernizing Turkish liberals pushed the Caliphate on Germany's side. They saw a bloody war as the way to stoke the flames of Turkish nationalism and complete the transformation of the Caliphate into a modern western-style state. Ironically, the West's multicultural groupings—the EU, Russian Federation and NAFTA—face the same perils today, with ethnic chauvinism easily whipped up, exposing the fragility of this secular 'neo-Ottomanism'.

166   Egger, *A History of the Muslim World since 1260*, 300.

167   Earl of Cromer, *Modern Egypt*, New York: Macmillan, 1908. Egypt's public debt had jumped from 3.2 million pounds in 1863 to 94 million pounds in 1876, 16 million for building the canal and most of rest to pay interest on debt to European financiers.

168   He was allowed to live out his life as a religious leader in Damascus, respected by the French for his humane treatment of French prisoners.

169   In 614, eleven male and five female converts sought refuge from Quraysh persecution in Mecca, in the Kingdom of Aksum (Abyssinia), ruled by a Christian King, Ashama ibn Abjar (King Negus), who according to Muslim tradition, later embraced Islam. The next year, 83 men and 18 women emigrated. They went to Medina after Muhammad and his followers made the *hijra* in 622.

170   Swahili vocabulary is derived from Arabic, the word Swahili referring to the geographical Sahel.

171   Egger, *A History of the Muslim World since 1260*, 133–134, 140–141.

172   "We are accustomed to thinking of slaves as being forced into the most menial and oppressive types of work, but this was not always the case in the Ottoman Empire. The recruits of the Ottoman devshirme remained slaves all their lives, and yet they joined the highest ranks of the administrators in the land. Many provincial governors were life-long slaves who wielded enormous powers." Egger, *A History of the Muslim World since 1260*, 74.

173   David Robinson, "The 'Islamic revolutions' of West Africa on the frontiers of the Islamic world", *yale.edu*, February 2008. For Nigerian Muslims, the Uthmanian reforms form the social charter of northern Nigeria today.

174   Egger, *A History of the Muslim World since 1260*, 358.

175   A tribal faction who wanted to cut all relations with the imperialists.

176   Immigrants from India and Omani scholars translated Islamic literature into Swahili.

177   Administered from Delhi until it was made a crown colony in 1937.

178   Claiming descent from the Prophet's uncle Abu Talib, chief of the Hashemites.

179   Egger, *A History of the Muslim World since 1260*, 337.

180   William Shuster was the Majlis Ministry of Finance adviser for a few months in 1911.

181   Egger, *A History of the Muslim World since 1260,* 338.
182   The governor of Kirman, Hasan Ali Shah, head of the Nizari Ismailis, the second largest branch of Shiism and spiritual descendant of the Fatimid Caliphate (909–1094), fled to Afghanistan and then Bombay, supported by the British, who protected and funded him.
183   The Soviet period showed how more rational development of the periphery could benefit the masses. By the mid-twentieth century, the standard of living in Soviet Central Asia was far higher than in Egypt, neighboring 'independent' Afghanistan and colonial India, and remains so today, despite its incorporation into the modern version of imperialism.
184   The Russian colonial style, like the French, imposed Russian culture as part of a multicultural mosaic, as opposed to the more reserved and disdainful British in India and Egypt, who kept the natives at arms length and fomented sectarianism. These differences account for the more enduring nature of center-periphery relations between Russia, France and their ex-colonies.
185   According to his official biography *Akbar-Namah.* Egger, *A History of the Muslim World since 1260,* 204.
186   Armstrong, *Islam,* 125.
187   Britain's laws included 200 capital offenses. Public hangings were numerous and used as mass entertainment.
188   Only 4% of the Indian umma supported independence in the 1937 elections.
189   Hodgson, *Rethinking World History,* 16.
190   Egger, *A History of the Muslim World since 1260,* 239.
191   Ibid., 240.
192   Ibid., 290.
193   Ibid., 108. It also, of course, marks Christopher Columbus's 'discovery' of America.
194   Armstrong, *A History of God,* 163.
195   Ibid., 166.
196   Ashari also argued there are no natural laws, that God is the cause of everything at every moment and can do as 'he' wills, which limits how much reason can be applied to reveal God's mysterious ways, a position which contributed to the helplessness of Islamic science in the face of the secular scientific and industrial revolutions of the 17th–19th centuries, despite the clear revelations in the Quran calling for the "need for intelligence in deciphering the 'signs' or 'messages' of God". Nasr, *Islam in the Modern World,* 143, 269.
197   Jewish money-lending activities extended into the Muslim world as well, though Islam developed ways of pooling funds to share risk and avoid the charging of interest. With the rise of capitalism the Muslim world was forced to bend the rule in dealings with the West, and became increasingly indebted, the pretext for Britain and France occupying Egypt and Tunis and even taking control of Ottoman finances.
198   Karl Marx, *On the Jewish Question* (1844).
199   Werner Sombart, *The Jews and Modern Capitalism,* Glencoe, USA: The Free Press [Leipzig, 1911] 1951, 192. For Marx the happy ending is the negation of this: "Emancipation from huckstering and money, consequently from practical, real Judaism, would be the self-emancipation of our time." But on the contrary, with the consolidation of capitalism and its world order, imperialism, "we are all Jews", at least for proponents of western civilization. Marx, *On the Jewish Question.*
200   Armstrong, *A History of God,* 312, 342.
201   Emanuel Kant, *The Critique of Practical Reason* (1788), in Armstrong, *A History of God,* 315.
202   Armstrong, *A History of God,* 352.
203   Ibid., 347.
204   Nasr, *Islam in the Modern World,* 98.

205   "He it is Who has sent down to you the Book: In it are verses basic or funda-
        mental (of established meaning); they are the foundation of the Book: others
        are allegorical. But those in whose hearts is perversity follow the part thereof
        that is allegorical, seeking discord, and searching for its hidden meanings,
        but no one knows its hidden meanings except God. And those who are firmly
        grounded in knowledge say: 'We believe in the Book; the whole of it is from
        our Lord:' and none will grasp the Message except men of understanding."
        (3:7)
206   Ruthven, *Fundamentalism,* 70.
207   Nasr, *Islam in the Modern World,* 265.
208   In the 1991 bill declaring Education and Sharing Day in honor of Lubovitcher
        Rabbi Menachem Schneerson, the Noahide laws—a version of Judaism for
        non-Jews—were described as the "ethical values and principles [that are] the
        basis of civilized society and upon which our great Nation was founded."

CHAPTER TWO

THE GENESIS OF RE-EMERGING ISLAMIC CIVILIZATION

Reform from within the Imperialist System

If the heyday of imperialism in the 18th–19th centuries was devastating for the Muslim world, its decline in the twentieth century was even more destructive. Full-scale occupation by the imperial powers soon ended, followed by the partition of India, the insertion of a mostly European Jewish colony in the heart of Palestine, and hard-fought wars of liberation in Algeria and elsewhere, resulting in the killing and displacement of millions of Muslims and their Christian and Jewish brothers, Arab and non-Arab alike, in an upheaval that rivaled the Mongol invasions of the thirteenth century.

Governments in the Muslim world were set up by hastily departing occupiers with the intent of maintaining their hegemony, confident that economic and political power was in the hands of accommodating assimilationist-minded officials, trained and vetted by the imperialists, who had been left with sophisticated 'maps' for the future conduct of their affairs— which colonial advisers would continue to interpret for them. Only Algeria started 'anew', after a devastating civil war that resulted in over a million deaths, and even its revolution—and mapmakers—were forged in the furnaces of the Enlightenment.

Iran's experience of 'independence' featured both foreign manipulation and yet a kernel of resistance by the conservative ulama, which was less vulnerable to pressure than was the religious establishment in Egypt and India, which were under direct British occupation. However, the dynamics of politics in all three followed a similar overall trajectory, where there was no room for popular democracy. For the imperialists bringing modernity and 'independence' to the periphery, it was possible to allow democracy only at the (rich) center, where the forces of capitalism were in control and the chances of revolution were small. It was absolutely necessary to prevent and—failing that—to shape and contain revolution at the periphery, to ensure post-'independence' continuity.

Thus the 'independence' which colonial Muslim subjects fought so hard for did not yet herald a return to Islamic civilization. The colonial administrations left behind carried on the imperial project in a new guise—neocolonialism. The project to fashion secular nation states in the Muslim world based on western economic and politic systems has been dubbed Kemalism, in recognition of the post-Caliphate Turkish leader. It spawned a number of policies, sometimes openly hostile to Islam, sometimes trying to use Islam to legitimize itself.

In opposition to it, reflecting the reason/ revelation dialectic, there arose a traditionalist opposition, adopting certain features of modernity at times and rejecting, or trying to, others. Whether a certain reformer or movement is genuinely grounded in Quranic beliefs (and not just using Islamic phrases to justify policies which undermine the tenets of Islam) is a judgment call.

The secular Kemalists by definition have no theory of economics apart from the capitalist/ socialist schools. They uniformly adopted western economic and legal systems, including interest and unlimited market penetration of society and/ or socialist policies of nationalization and planning, governed by secular theories. But even the social justice advocated by socialism, the secular antidote to soulless capitalism, fell victim to the materialism inherent in it, and eventually proved helpless in the face of neocolonialism abetted by its Middle East representative, Israel.

It fell to Muslims to 're-invert the materialist logic' of Hegel-Marx in practice—to give a meaningful place to spiritual life on their map. But it has meant that Islam must engage with history, that Muslims must meet the challenges of today with reason, i.e., *ijtihad*, and confront them actively, i.e., jihad, both personal (*fard ayn*) and collective (*fard kifaya*).

Perhaps ironically, all the movements for renewal in Islamic history have been traditionalist or 'revivalist' in some way, either literally (trying to imitate Muhammad and the early generations of Muslims) or metaphorically (trying to recapture their dynamism and spirituality). Just as Muhammad continued the great reformation process of monotheism, revealing the message and interpreting it in light of the reality he faced, so subsequent movements for renewal in Islam have been engaging with their politico-historical contexts.

The first restorative movement after the death of Muhammad was prompted by the disarray and decadence of the Umayyad and Abbasid courts in the 8th–9th centuries, leading to a renewed respect for hadiths/ sunna, establishing independent sharia courts, and creating a skilled ulama to preserve and develop Islamic scholarship. The second, responding to the Mongol invasions, inspired Ibn Taymiya to turn again to the Quran and hadiths, using *ijtihad* to advocate jihad to free the umma of the Mongol yoke and restore *dar al-islam*. Both were the sublimation of the reason/ revelation dialectic in their historical contexts.

The crisis in the world resulting from the rise of imperialism has required Islam to engage with reality in a new way, for the world is now effectively one *dar*—the Muslim and non-Muslim worlds are being forced through globalization to integrate. It is impossible to maintain a closed society given the reach of modern technology, and given the large-scale migrations that have taken place since the end of WWII. The challenge posed today is both *to* Islam and *by* Islam—to both 'modernize Islam' and 'Islamize modernity'.[1] Western 'modernity' is not the only modernity, and it is not universal. Islam is universal, but only if it engages with its temporal context meaningfully.

As in the West, there are the fundamentalists/ literalists[2] on *both* sides of the revelation/ reason divide. Their beliefs are in both cases dogmatic. That revelation is all there is to religion (Wahhab) is dogmatic, but so is the Kemalists' insistence on reason alone, which is just as dogmatic. Wahhabism ironically is a kind of "mirror image of Kemalism, with its attempt 'to shape individuals' beliefs and identities into a stifling uniformity".[3] Revelation ungrounded in reason and reason ungrounded in revelation are equally powerless to engage fully with reality to allow man to pursue his 'two journeys', both to give meaning to life and death, and achieve the positive goals (*maqasid*) of dignity, welfare, justice, and the common good.

On the revelation side, the strictly Salafi Saudi and Gulf monarchies, while rejecting some western-style domestic reforms and trying to revive the traditional way of life of the early (Bedouin) Muslims, use a literalist reading of the Quran, with the tacit approval of the imperialists. By accepting this unholy alliance, they have openly cooperated in pursuing goals which have nothing to do with re-establishing Islamic civilization—from destroying (anti-imperialist) socialist forces around the world to attacking traditionalist Muslims and Islamic reformers whose aims are contrary to both the imperial agenda and, by association, the Wahabbi premodern agenda. They are described here as **premodern accommodationists**.

On the reason side, those reformers who aim to adopt the western scenario of 'separation of religion and state', reducing the influence of Islam to a minor role in society, by association accept the western secular political and economic system—western modernity. They are unapologetic **assimilationists**, or at the very least, like their more 'devout' opponents, accommodationists,

> the 'Uncle Toms' of Islam. Their defence of Islam depended, they thought, on proving that it accorded perfectly with the moral and philosophical norms of European civilization. The idea that the civilization they admired so blindly might be open to radical criticism in terms of Islamic norms scarcely crossed their minds.[4]

Both extremes work within the imperialist-imposed order, accepting the implicit hegemony of the world market and financial system. Both are imitators—the former, slavishly copying the original seventh century lifestyle of the Arabian Peninsula, the latter, slavishly copying the secular lifestyle of the West. Both concentrate on appearances, which cannot hide their failure to produce vibrant societies imbued with Islam's ethical and moral principles, resulting in both cases in parodies of Islam in practice.

In their defense, we can pose the questions:

- 'Are the Saudis craven or farsighted?' They are against engaging meaningfully with the current global capitalist culture, only grudgingly complying with the minimal demands of western modernity domestically. Nonetheless, they passively condone and sometimes actively abet US strategies in the Middle East. But eventually, even their passivity provokes a counter reaction. Indeed they produced al-Qaeda, a violent modern movement that is a reaction to the unholy alliance. At the same time, al-Qaeda promotes the Saudi/ Wahabbi premodern version of Islam and has a not inconsiderable following among the faithful. Will this particular engagement with reality contribute to the long-run triumph of Islamic civilization? Can they suddenly unveil a new Islamic map and start following it?

- Similarly, we can ask: 'Are the Kemals or Nassers heretics or farsighted?' Kemal claimed he was freeing Islam from its compromising involvement in state affairs, though he in fact suppressed Islam ruthlessly. The forced secularism of these anti-Islamists raised literacy levels and laid the foundations for some kind of engagement with the modern world, but also led the way to revival of Islam and Islam-inspired reform of society. The secularism they promoted left a cruel and bitter legacy and, like their premodern counterparts, they laid the foundations of a long-term extremist current within Islam. No new map reflecting Islam's enduring essence has been fashioned by the existing nodes of organized power within Sunni Islam, but rather a perverse, apocalyptic one, drawn by angry rebels, fed up with the sorry state of the umma and its leaders.

Apart from these extremes, there are those who stepped back and formulated a more ambitious goal and a strategy that was more long-term, working outside the system, either to transform it or overthrow it to realize God's realm on earth. These real reformers, trying to capture the spirit of Islam in a modern context are sometimes called holistic modernists,[5] worthy successors to the great Islamic thinkers and doers of the past, such as Ghazali,

Ibn Rushd, Ibn Taymiya. But they could just as easily be called **traditionalists**, as Islam has within it the methodological principles and political tools for addressing evolving historical circumstances—*ijtihad* and jihad.

Different scholars use different terminology. Akbar Ahmed divides Muslim activists into three categories, using Indian experience—Ajmer[6] (Sufi), Deoband[7] (traditionalist/ orthodox), Aligarh[8] (liberal reformers). As a liberal himself, he is partial to the latter: "Whether they are devout or more secular Muslims, followers of Aligarh share the desire to engage with modern ideas while preserving what to them is essential to Islam."[9] These liberal reformers are also called "Islamic modernists", some calling for an Islamic Renaissance, others for an Islamic Reformation, hoping to modernize their societies to protect them from the onslaught of colonialism.[10]

Iranian-American scholar Seyyed Nasr reduces the categories to two, contrasting "traditional Islam" to the "modernist trend ... a whole series of so-called fundamentalist movements that speak of reviving Islam in opposition to modernism and western civilization".[11] His defense of Islamic tradition firmly rejects the unrelenting western and modernist disparagement of tradition as responsible for holding Islam back. He argues that Islam needs no 'reformation', that the recent reform calls have been a distraction from the real need to *strengthen* tradition, and have actually contributed to the cumulative crisis within Islam and in the world in general. From the eighteenth century, Islam weakened and an Islamic critique of western Enlightenment developments was not undertaken. Nasr's call for renewal begins there and is a reaction to the rise of the "Islamic modernist" (accommodationist) reformers, a kind of rally-the-troops call to traditionalists, calling for a renewal of tradition, a new-old Islamic education, incorporating much of secular western scientific method and technology, but within a moral and ethical worldview grounded in traditional Islam. [12]

Nasr's categories are more robust, but this view still begs the question: can a renewed Islamic civilization arise on the ruins of the western Enlightenment project? Is it enough to tweak the revelation-reason argument (supposedly settled on the side of revelation by Ashari in the tenth century), and accept that God too follows 'laws of nature' (albeit which he formulated) and which we can discern and then use (but responsibly)? Or does this end up leading inevitably to Newton's deism, God the Clockmaker, the Enlightenment slide to secularism and our current crisis? There is no explicit critique of capitalism as a radically new socio-economic formation to ground the analysis.

Underlying the current reform debates are the same opposing forces that fueled the first revivalist movement in Islam, when the traditionalists and Sufis opposed the rationalist Mutazilites in the 8th–10th centuries over the issues of determinism vs free will, immanence vs transcendence (see Chapter 1 Appendix A). If there is only revelation (no free will), if God governs every movement of every atom at each moment, there is no need for reason, and no possibility of changing our situation. At the same time, if we as humans have complete freedom in our actions and thoughts, if God is some remote, abstract concept with no affect on us, it is possible to argue there is no need for 'him'.

The latter (reason ungrounded in revelation) is the logic behind the Enlightenment and secularization of the West, which throws the baby out with the bath water, throws open 'the gates of *ijtihad*' in a negative way, allowing into our lives the amorality that characterizes the world today and is destroying it. The opposite (revelation ungrounded in reason), denying reform, 'closes the gates of *ijtihad*' and results in Islam becoming dogmatic, disconnected from the current reality, irrelevant except as Marx's "opium of the people", the world's "universal basis of consolation and justification".[13]

The different paths of reform fall between these extremes. Reform means both *tajdid* (renewal, referring to rereading the Quran) and *ijtihad*. We must engage with both text and context, merging "two levels of knowledge: that of the eternal principles of practice and ethics and that of the ever-changing realities of human societies [in a] dialectical relationship between text and context".[14] There are texts which deal with religious practice which are unchanging, but also texts which are allegorical/ adaptable/ in need of interpretation. There is God's law and man's law, *hadd* and *ta'zir*, ethical and moral principles which are eternal and laws which man must formulate to guarantee the translation of those principles into reality. In short, revelation and reason.

We should not condemn any particular individual or group here—there are sincere reformers among liberals as well as orthodox and Sufis. What is important is to identify reformers who demand more than just "adaptation reform" to the present western world system; rather, who critique it, putting on the agenda "transformation reform".[15] This leaves out most well-meaning reformers who consider themselves liberals (Ahmed's Aligarhs), just as it does the Sufi mystics who abjure any political involvement in defense of the purity of religious beliefs and practices, as well as fundamentalists who resist any reforms based on *ijtihad* within Islam, who are happy to let imperialism pursue its unethical strategies and goals.

Ahmed's categories lump Wahhabis, Salafis, Shia revolutionaries and Muslim Brothers together as Deoband, and Kemal and less categorical secularists like Khan together as Aligarhs. These tripartite categories are useful but need qualification (see Appendix B). Given the inherent tradition of reform in Islamic history, it is wrong to narrowly define only the 'Deobandis' as followers of the legendary fourteenth century reformer Ibn Taymiya, as Ahmed does. All sincere Muslims are heirs to Ibn Taymiya and recognize the need for *ijtihad*/jihad in the face of invasion be it imperialist or the more subtle neocolonialist variant. Unless a clear break is made with the imperialist order, there can be no re-emergence of Islamic civilization.

The Wahhabis and Salafis of the Gulf are not really traditionalists (and have nothing in common with Iran's Shia), but an aberration which the imperialists have promoted as a useful ally in controlling the rest of the Muslim world, and who have spawned al-Qaeda types as a manifestation of resentment among Muslims, especially rebellious Saudis. Nasr clinches this vital point by calling the terrorists emanating from the Muslim world **neo-Wahhabis**.

With this in mind, my analysis slots the various reform movements within the Islamic political world into those whose programs leave the system of imperialism intact (accommodationists, assimilationists, liberals), vs those whose programs confront imperialism (and who can simply be called traditionalists). These are by no means air-tight categories, as some who advocate accommodation later rejected this strategy (and vice versa), nor are there clear-cut good guys (though there are bad guys). The accommodationists by definition are working within the 'system' using imperial 'maps', the genuine reformers at least until recently—outside it, drawing their own maps. The best way to fight imperialism changes with the context, requiring *ijtihad* and jihad from Muslims and non-Muslims alike.

Wali Allah/ Wahhab/ Afghani/ Abduh

The eighteenth century was a watershed for the Muslim world. Prior to the eighteenth century, Arabic and Persia were the *lingua franca* of a truly world Islamic civilization, with cultural and economic coherence among hundreds of different ethnic groups. An Arab merchant could operate with confidence in Nigeria or Aceh (in present day Indonesia), knowing his presence would be welcomed, that he could be understood wherever he went, that all legal matters would be decided fairly by sharia. Post-eighteenth century, English (for a while, also Dutch and French) replaced Arabic and Persian in international commerce, imperial law replaced sharia, and local languages and European culture filled the void created as the West cut the delicate strings that held the Muslim umma together. This recapitulated in a more radical way what took place in Christendom with the declining use of Latin a few centuries earlier, though the decline of the Christian order was more from internal contradictions, while the last caliphate and the other Muslim 'empires' disintegrated more due to external pressures and ultimately occupation, abolishing *dar al-islam,* precipitating the upheavals of today.

In response to this, preceding all the other reformers are two contrasting figures—the remarkable Indian **Shah Wali Allah** (1703–1762), a Naqshbandi Sufi, and the Arab Muhammad ibn Abd al-Wahhab (1703–1791) born in the same year, but inspired in very different ways by the state of Islam they witnessed.

Shah Wali Allah worked to overcome divisions among the four schools of Islamic law, and bridge the chasm between both mystics and ulama,

Sunni and Shia. Responding to the British as they grabbed the reins of power from the faltering Moghul dynasty, he defied the ulama and translated the Quran into Persian, and his son—into Urdu, *a la* Martin Luther. What was needed was an educated umma, versed in both the Quran and real world science, armed with their own mapmaking skills. Any improvement of the situation of Muslims in the face of a newly aggressive West armed with always advancing technology, Wali Allah determined, must start here. Only an educated umma can practice effective *ijtihad*. Beginning with Wali Allah, education became the priority of all reformers. All India's major Islamic movements today, the Deoband, Ahli Hadith and Aligarh, claim to be following Wali Allah, the first more Sufi in rituals, the second closer to the Wahhabis, [16] the third liberal.

Much as Wahhab is painted black in the western media and Islamic reform literature, writes Muhammad Asad, "All the renaissance movements in modern Islam— the Ahli Hadith movement in India, the Sanusi movement in north Africa, the work of Jamal al-Din al-Afghani and the Egyptian Muhammad Abduh—can be directly traced back to the spiritual impetus set in motion in the eighteenth century by **Muhammad ibn Abd al-Wahhab.**"[17]

Wahhab was the son of a qadi and grandson of a mufti, a strict believer in revelation vs reason, a literalist, a follower of Hanbal and Ibn Taymiya.

He disapproved of the Sufi practice of praying at the tombs of 'saints', their revering of Muhammad as a 'perfect man' and of natural wonders (miracles), and their use of amulets and spells to ward off evil. Even the Prophet was just an ordinary man—his grave should not be revered nor can he intercede on someone's behalf with God. While Wali Allah sought to educate fellow Muslims to explain that such rituals were not sanctioned by the Quran or the hadiths, the impatient Wahhab "called anyone who engaged in those acts a polytheist, a valid target of jihad."[18]

Wahhab himself used *ijtihad* to justify

rebellion against the Ottoman sultan by appealing to passages from Ibn Taymiya, the great *mujtahid (*practitioner of *ijtihad*) of the Mamluk era. "Ibn Taymiya argued that war by the Mamluks against the Mongol Il-khanid regime of Ghazan (r. 1295–1304) was an obligatory jihad on the grounds that the Il-khanid were infidels."[19] Though Ghazan claimed to have converted, Ibn Taymiya asserted he continued to adhere to Mongol customary law. Similarly, the weak Ottomans were not following sharia law to the letter ('Where,' Wahhab queried, 'were the beheadings and amputations?'), and were adopting western customs as western empires eclipsed the Muslim world. The Muslim world would become strong again only by adhering to the purified Islam, minus the decadent accretions of the westernizers and Sufis (not to mention the 'innovator' Shias).

Though his followers over the next two centuries adhered to the radically austere practices which Wahhab called for, *ijtihad* came to an end when his version of Islam was adopted by the Saud tribe that took over the Arabian Peninsula and established an absolute monarchy in alliance with imperialism.[20]

Wali Allah's concern with education to mobilize the umma against imperialism and Wahhab's more revolutionary spirit came together in the nineteenth century's most notable reform figure **Jamal al-Din al-Afghani** (1838–1897), a rather mysterious figure, both ardent Muslim and Mason, Sufi and rationalist,[21] "a certain wildman of genius".[22] Afghani's ambiguity

about modernity has meant he is sometimes embraced by both liberal accommodationists and traditionalists. He saw the weakness in Islamic practice to be the absence of justice and *shura* (consultation), and the need to broaden *shura* to include the umma through a constitution and elections. Islamic society had hardened into autocracy after the first Caliphate, when monarchy became the norm. His political aspirations have represented the dominant themes of modern Islamic politics ever since: Islamic unity, reform through the use of *ijtihad*, science and education, and resistance to foreign domination and the un-Islamic rulers who collaborate with it, reviving the spirit of Islam of the time of the Prophet.

All of Ahmed's archetypes—Sufi, Deoband, Aligarh—were present in Afghani, in equal parts Wahhab and Wali Allah. As a Sufi, he conceived of God as a force for transformation at a deep level that would help in the transition to modernity. Though Iranian, he presented himself as an Afghan Sunni (hence, 'al-Afghani') to Sunnis, at times a revolutionary, a religious philosopher, a rationalist. He did not make a show of great piety (he reportedly used the Shia *mut'a* temporary marriage custom to facilitate love affairs and did not have a traditional family life); he did not urge a literalist return to the Quran and hadiths. At the same time, he was not a proponent of parliamentary democracy, though he headed a secret Egyptian Masonic lodge.[23]

Rather he saw in Islam a rational and powerful force to strengthen and unify the Muslim world, which could fight Muslim rulers' decadence and corruption, and by using the West's technology, resist occupation by the new, aggressive European empires. To promote his goal, he was happy to adopt whatever guise best suited his purpose at the moment. He soon discarded his plan to overthrow the decadent Ottoman, Qajar and other Muslim rulers, realizing they were necessary to his plans, and instead used his brilliance and charisma to open doors to the Ottoman Sultan Abdulhamit II and the Persian Shah Naser al-Din, advocating a caliph presiding over a pan-Islamic society. He saw clearly the threat that western imperialism posed to the umma.

Afghani taught briefly at Azhar University in Cairo where he founded his school of thought with the Egyptian, Muhammad Abduh. He was feted by liberal intellectuals in Europe, and urged Muslim leaders to adopt reforms to avoid complete loss of political, economic and spiritual sovereignty. He was expelled from Egypt in 1879 by the British, and went to Paris to found the reformist journal *The Indissoluble Bond* with Abduh. He was also expelled from Istanbul and later Persia when the rulers he was advising understood what he was up to.[24]

Enraged by Sayyid Ahmed Khan's deferential attitude toward the British (see below) Afghani attacked him (in Arabic, and thus unlikely to be read by Europeans) in "The Refutation of the Materialists" (1881) his most famous essay. However, with western politicians, Afghani criticized Islam, arguing it was a good way for social control, but inimical to science. Two years after his attack on Khan, Afghani wrote a reply to Ernst Renan (in French, and thus unlikely to be read by Muslims) where he argued that all religions are hostile to philosophy and science:

> Whenever religion will have the upper hand, it will eliminate philosophy; and the contrary happens when it is philosophy that reigns. So long as humanity exists, the struggle will not cease between dogma and free investigation, between religion and philosophy.

He was pessimistic about the outcome because "the masses dislike reason" but also—intentionally ambiguous—because "humanity thirsts for the ideal".[25] Afghani epitomized the contradictions of the West for the Islamic world, portraying it as a threat but also a source of technology, philosophy, and the education necessary to repel it.

Muhammad Abduh (1849–1905) was a disciple of Afghani, famous for saying: "I went to the West and saw Islam, but no Muslims; I got back to the East and saw Muslims, but not Islam." He studied with Afghani while at Azhar and was exiled from Egypt in 1882 for six years for supporting the Urabi Revolt against the British. In 1884 he joined Afghani in Paris to publish *The Indissoluble Bond*. When he returned to Egypt in 1888, the brilliant and now more subdued Abduh was appointed judge in the Courts of First Instance of the Native Tribunals and later the Court of Appeal. He reformed the Egyptian sharia courts and founded a college

for qadis. In 1898 he founded the journal *al-Manar* (lighthouse, minaret), and in 1899 was appointed Chief Mufti of Egypt, added sciences to Azhar's curriculum, and began a massive commentary on the Quran. He distanced himself from his former mentor Afghani, and appeared to move towards the accommodationist camp, being "a trusted and admired advisor to the British High Commissioner of Egypt" in his final years.[26]

Abduh believed that the ulama had no religious authority except as a source of general guidance, that the Quran should be read above all as an ethical guide, that it was necessary to "graft modern legal and constitutional innovations on to traditional Islamic ideas that the people could understand: a society in which people cannot, becomes in effect a country without law."[27] He was convinced Islam was a "religion of progress that was compatible with the adoption of modern technology and organizational methods."[28] He was dedicated to promoting literacy and mass education, and sought harmony between Sunnis and Shia, and with Judaism and Christianity.

Wahhab and Afghani were the revolutionary outsiders of these early figures, though only Afghani had a clear understanding of modern imperialism. The Wahhabi movement was oblivious to the new imperial order and was thus easily co-opted. Abduh's work "despite his intentions, might logically issue in a relegation of Islam to an essentially private nicety ... denatured as a form of social organization."[29] Wali Allah, Afghani and Abduh all advocated reopening the gates of *ijtihad* by a newly educated umma, argued that the limiting of reasoning in Islam to at most a few scholars was merely the result of fear of disunity among Muslims in a period of political instability, and that intellectual stagnation must be overcome. They all inspired a broad range of reformers, some using pious quotes from the Quran to hide a very un-Islamic agenda, others well-meaning but duped or pressured into following a course which undermined Islam rather than strengthening or at least preserving it. Only a few avoided the pitfall of accommodating the new world order ranged against the umma.

Three points must be made in surveying subsequent figures of 19th–20th century reform:

1. Theorists of Islamic reform, like their counterparts on the left, cannot be neatly separated from their activities in promoting their agenda. By the nineteenth century, Marx had correctly observed: "The philosophers have only interpreted the world, in various ways; the point is to change it."[30] The founder of the Muslim Brotherhood, Hassan al-Banna, was both theorist and activist, head of a powerful mass movement, much like Vladimir Lenin in Russia. Leftists call this melding of theory and practice praxis, and most of the notable theorists were active politically. The Islamists' Trotsky is arguably Qutb or Bin Laden, pursuing a permanent revolution.

2. Theorists such as Iqbal, Rida and Qutb (see Chapter 3) developed their thought and changed it over time, their strategic thinking responding to historical developments of their particular era (the rise of Saudi accommodationism, the 1967 Israeli victory) and under varying personal circumstances (i.e., prison). However, the main themes of the reformers can be laid out, even if certain writers 'switched sides' at some point. The change in views represented an honest response to history for those who remained devout, an example of self-reflective *ijtihad*.

3. Islamic reform differs from Jewish reform (secular Zionism) or Christian reform (deism/ atheism) because of the enduring balance of revelation and reason in Islam, and the historicity of Muhammad and the Quran. Genuine reform is *always* a 'return to basics' with varying degrees of reason/ revelation, *ijtihad/ taqlid*.

Thus dividing up the many Islamic thinker-activists is tricky. There are no outstanding theorists who directly advocate accommodation in line with either of the West's twentieth century projects—capitalism or socialism—though there are, of course, plenty of western non-Muslim advocates of accommodation. Many intend genuine Islamic reform but devise policies which nonetheless lead to assimilation. Others may have originally worked towards a new Islamic politics but changed their minds for whatever reasons (Soroush). Furthermore, the effects of reformers can be very different than what they had intended, or can be undermined.

Political Nationalism/ Economic Nationalism (Socialism): Constructing a Secular State Independent of the West

None of these early Muslim reformers were advocates of nationalism. Nationalism itself is a product of imperialism. In the 'center', it developed as the imperialists "impose Imperialism upon the masses under the attractive guise of sensational patriotism."[31] In the 'periphery' it both developed as a *reaction* to the occupiers via a national-liberation movement, and later was co-opted by the imperialists or Soviet advisers to encourage local elites opposed to an Islamic order. There is no nationalism in the Quran or Islamic civilization, since all people are one under God.

So there were no rigid lines on the umma's (geographic) map dividing Muslims into 'nations'. State boundaries were imposed by imperialism as a way of divvying up the spoils but also to balkanize/ dismember/ disempower. The promotion of western-style nationalism by post-'independence' leaders thus paved the way for post-'independence' assimilationist policies by secularlists, undermining the Islamic project.

The Muslim world witnessed the rise of various nationalisms as a response to western modernity. As part of Tanzimat, the nineteenth century sultans and Young Ottomans (see below) encouraged an equivalent to nationalism which was called Ottomanism, trying to inculcate a sense of pride, regardless of ethnicity or religion, in belonging to the Caliphate. There was nothing backing this policy, and western powers easily whipped up ethnic nationalisms within the Caliphate, imitating the growing nationalisms of Europe. As Ottomanism flopped, Zionism and Slavic and Armenian separatism increased. There was no Arab nationalist movement of importance, as ethnic solidarity was less important for Arabs than religious solidarity.

There were 12 million Orthodox Christians in the Caliphate, who had coexisted more or less in peace with their Muslim neighbors before western interference. France, Britain and Russia demanded and got the right to 'protect' their coreligionists as part of the capitulations ceded by the Ottomans in the sixteenth century. This meant that the beneficiaries of the Tanzimat reforms were in the first place Christians, as well as Jews with European links, who made use of the old capitulations in the more open context to expand their trade and investments virtually outside Ottoman control.

In order to pursue his western-oriented bourgeois vision, complete with Turkish nationalism, Kemal Ataturk abolished the Caliphate in 1924, a fatal blow to the world umma, which led in turn to the rise of secular nationalist movements in all the Muslim-majority colonies around world. Turkish (and Iranian) nationalism was closer to the ethnic nationalism which arose in Europe in the nineteenth century and attracted liberal reformers as a force to replace Islam as the binding agent in society.

Iranian and Turkish nationalism followed different paths, but were both based on the primacy of cultural and ethnic identity, not Islam. Arab nationalism, however, sought to nationalize Islam itself, considering Islam and its civilization to be primarily the fruit of what some Arab theoreticians of Arab nationalism have called 'the Arab genius' ... Arabs came to identify 'Arab identity' not with the whole of Islam, now nationalized, but with Sunnism. The Arab Shia, whether in Iraq, Lebanon, Yemen, the Persian Gulf, or Saudi Arabia itself, were more or less marginalized, especially politically. The reassertion of the reality of Shiism outside of Iran and within the Arab world itself has posed an existential challenge to the modern 'Arab self-identity' forged to some extent by Arab nationalism.[32]

Arab thinkers in a sense 'nationalized' Islam, even Christian ones such as the Syrian Christian and founder of the Baath Party, Michel Aflaq, who exhorted, "Muhammad was all the Arabs. Let all the Arabs today be Muhammad."[33] Arab nationalism is thus more complex than Turkish or Iranian nationalism, arising first out of the failure of Ottomanism in the late Caliphate, searching for its *raison d'etre* in Islam as a specifically Arab phenomenon, "with all the dangers that such an act implies for the universal teachings of Islam, [where] the love of one's nation comes from faith."[34]

All new 'national' governments set up by the departing foreign rulers continued the assimilationist trend through treaties of independence granting former imperial powers privileges to control their local economies—a kind of neo-capitulations. The key element for the successful operation of the imperialist strategy of passing on power to existing administrations was establishing a version of electoral democracy that would leave the fledgling elites in place. However, the western-style parliamentary system was "not designed to accommodate the dynamics of tribal-based societies or the politics of religious communalism".[35] In fact it was designed to thwart the emergence of some kind of genuine democracy which could meet the needs of the umma.

In virtually all cases the adoption of western-style electoral democracy resulted in dictatorships in Muslim countries,[36] which the imperialists vetted and often helped install in coups (Husni al-Zaim in Syria, Saddam Hussein in Iraq, even Muammar al-Gaddafi in Libya). They were supported as long as they followed the 'rules of the game'. Some, the imperialists found tolerable (Tunisia, Yemen, initially Libya and Iraq), and their corruption and repression was overlooked. Others became the target of western wrath as they sought to promote domestic interests.

Pan-Arabists blamed the Ottoman Turks, Islam, and imperialism in varying degrees for their weakness, which meant that they were more likely to opt for socialism, attempting to wrest control from the imperialists by 'nationalizing' the economic system. Though devout Muslims were by definition anti-Soviet because of the militant atheism of the Soviet Union, they were forced after WWII to turn to the Soviet Union for support when faced by a new enemy; European Jews with imperial support were now colonizing Palestine, and Arab socialism, sometimes flavored with a taste of Islam, became the order of the day. Egypt's Gamal Abdel-Nasser's Arab Socialist Union and the Syrian and Iraqi Baath (renaissance) Parties, with ambitious socialist programs, relied on a mix of social justice and nationalism to attract support. But, headed by inexperienced and poorly educated leaders, they degenerated into dictatorships, however well-intentioned, and repressed the traditional repositories of wisdom—the ulama, Sufis and Muslim traditionalists—ultimately making accommodation with the West, including the Soviet Union, necessary to maintain power.

The failure of post-'independence' governments reveals the weakness of the neocolonial secular model, which encouraged tribal divisions similar to pre-Islamic times in Arabia which the Prophet had opposed. From the Arab and Muslim perspective, WWI was a vicious European civil war based on greed and tribalism. Islam's promise, not just as a private belief *a la* post-Enlightenment Christianity, but as a time-tested program for a peaceful just society, became an increasingly powerful magnet. Islamic religious leaders were at the forefront of national liberation movements resisting colonialism, though they were bypassed when the imperialists withdrew, handing over power to the secular liberals, who continued the repression of Islam to shore up their own rickety position.

The problem of what constitutes a nation was at the heart of the matter. Islamic polities were traditionally organized communally rather than territorially. However, the imperialists hastily drew up boundaries (more as red lines to keep out rival neighboring imperialists), and undertook the process of nation-building based on these boundaries after WWII, 'assisted' by the World Bank and International Monetary Fund, which gave financial control of national governments to new national elites. This was a direct continuation of the policy of international bankers in the nineteenth century whereby they took effective control of indebted weak governments.

Western military pacts were set up (MEDO/ CENTO/ SEATO/ ASEAN);[37] the new governments were pressured to join; and they became indebted by buying weapons to protect themselves against neighboring neocolonies, which they now fought over the artificial borders left behind at independence. Some leaders gave a nod to Islam, such as Indonesia's Sukarno, who incorporated Islam into the otherwise secular constitution at independence through the Pancasila five principles—moral and ethical norms derived from Islam acceptable to the nation's Christian, Buddhist and Hindu minorities.

Militantly secular governments (Tunisia's Bourguiba) actively undermined the role of Islam. Such

> states were informed by a narrow, and often distorted, conception of secularism [which did] not entail the ideological neutrality of the state [but] promoted their own discourses as substitutes for religion … instead of using Islam as a source of legislation in a manner that was congruent with the people's customs and sensibilities.[38]

This suppression of Islam was an important cause of the rise of Islamic fundamentalism, and worked to undermine the legitimacy of the secular state, exposing it as a fraud "promoting alien ideologies". As noted by Marx, the imperialist secular state project "needed to be free from the social forces that religion represented" (the traditional landowning and ulama elites, as well as the morality of the Quran). Marx applauded the secular French state in "The Civil War in France": the state was freed from "all manner of medieval rubbish, seigniorial rights" but he recognized that the new state was serving the clear political-economic agenda of capitalism.

Similarly, in Muslim society, there was "medieval rubbish" to clear away, but the secularists were more interested in discarding Islam itself, which was and still is the big stumbling block for the West.[39]

> The nationalisms in the Middle East, Arabic, Persian, Turkish, are now more or less [over], they are ending one way or the other. That is, they're showing their bankruptcy … Arab Nationalism began with a thesis … that the Islamic civilization began to go down when the Arab hegemony over Islamic civilization came to an end, that is with the Abbasids.[40]

This nationalism dismisses 700 years of Islamic civilization and undermines the attempt to build an alternative social order based on this rich history. "How can you revive a patient that has been dead for that long a time?"[41]

Relations between Europe and the Muslim World from 'Independence' to Independence

For local leaders in Muslim majority countries who followed the colonial/neocolonial maps bequeathed to them in the wake of the collapse of the

Caliphate, the goal was at best to attain a privileged position on imperialism's map. This was to be won by accepting the new and now dominant world order and the occupiers' civil law codes forbidding sharia and all religious influence in politics and the economy. The occupiers generally promised the locals (e.g., in Egypt the growing educated middle class who joined the landlord/merchant-dominated Wafd Party) limited 'independence' at some future date, after the 'civilizing mission' of the occupiers was completed. With the writing on the wall for the imperialists, the British and French spent the decades of the 1920s–1950s planning the hand-over of power in their colonies, training and entrusting the complex task of running a nation's life to hand-picked locals, which gave the assimilationists a head start at 'independence'. (True, the final date was much sooner than expected; the Dutch in southeast Asia and the British in India and Egypt were the most stubborn.)

This was the post-WWII scenario—Great Game II—where the former colonies and their colonial masters would operate under the sole remaining empire—the US—against the 'Godless communists'. [42] The reality of this vision of the future soon came into focus, with the colonial system ensuring a passable life in the former centers, but for the periphery, leading to mass poverty and ecological degradation (governed by the global market), and war (the result of arbitrary new borders and the alien concept of 'nation states'). The alternative was for the former colonies to ally with the 'Godless communists', which made them the target of unremitting subversion by the West (leading to the same 'mass poverty etc.'). Imperialism has no happy ending.

The silver lining for a few lucky Arab nations was the discovery of massive oil deposits, just as the US in particular was running out of its own. The premodern Bedouin of the Arab peninsula were able to strike an unholy pact with the imperialists, allowing them to enforce the austere, now rigidified Wahhabi version of Islam, keeping the imperialists at arms length through accommodation. Their 'backwardness' could even be used by the 'enlightened' imperialists as a textbook case demonstrating the undesirability of Islamic governments as an alternative to the empire's 'tough love'. At the same time as the tribal monarchs stifled any flowering of culture and innovation at home, they used their vast oil revenues to import western technology and provide enough welfare to keep their people from demanding the positive features of western political life—civil society, democracy, freedom of thought. What emerged was a kind of premodern accommodationism that the West could tolerate, indeed use to its own advantage, absorbing the 'petrodollars' with western goods while keeping Islam out of the imperial equation.

The seeds of **Turkey**'s radical secularism were visible by the early twentieth century. Freemasons had (illegal) lodges in all Ottoman cities, engaged in tapping into the local social and business networks, promoting secular education, philanthropy, and mutual aid. After the secularist Young Turks and Committee for Unity and Progress (CUP) reinstated the constitution in 1908, Masons suddenly became part of the ruling elite, a legitimate and institutionalized part of the new order. They played an important role in integrating the Muslim business elite into western capitalism.[43] CUP won a two-thirds majority in the 1912 elections but war broke out in the Balkans (instigated by the British) which ushered in WWI. The liberals were able to push Ottoman Turkey into the war (against Russia, which meant on Germany's side), arguing it was a way to unite Turkic peoples from the Balkans to China, and cynically demanded the sultan proclaim it a jihad. They victimized the Armenians, trying to regain the half of Armenian territory ceded to Russia in 1878, leading to the infamous slaughter that has plagued Turkish relations ever since, a slaughter carried out in the name of *liberalism*, something that had never happened in the centuries of Ottoman rule.[44]

The Ottoman Caliphate territories were seized and divvied up by the 'victors' after WWI. The last sultan, Mehmed VI, signed the humiliating Treaty of Sevres in 1920, forcing large concessions on territories of the Caliphate in favor of Greece, Italy, Britain and France. Islam itself became the target for the Young Turks, who defied the sultan, re-organized the army under the brilliant renegade officer Mustafa Kemal, and saved the Turkish Anatolian heartland from dismemberment by the victorious Allies. Kemal consolidated power from a village, Ankara, in the Anatolian highlands, and against all odds, drove out the British and their Greek allies, who had already declared Anatolian coastal areas to be part of a greater Greece. The allies were forced to restore territory in Anatolia and Thrace in the Treaty of Lausanne in 1923.

The openly apostate Kemal's prestige as the savior of what was left of the Caliphate allowed him to move quickly against the Muslim establishment and to accelerate the process of fashioning the new Turkey as a western secular state. Calling himself Ataturk (father of the Turks), he declared a Turkish Republic and formally abolished the Caliphate in 1924. As president, Kemal (r. 1924–1938) abolished Sufi orders, nationalized the religious foundations, made religion a purely private affair, closed madrasas and severely restricted religious education. He

- replaced sharia with the Swiss civil code and Italian penal code,
- replaced the Arabic script with a new Latin-based script (expunging Arabic words with their Islamic overtones),
- replaced Friday with Sunday as the 'seventh day of rest' holiday,
- gave women complete legal equality with men,
- closed many mosques, turning the great ones of Istanbul into museums for western tourists, much like the churches in the Soviet Union, though he was also solidly anti-communist.

The authoritarian Kemal intended to emulate European electoral democracy, even setting up an opposition party (the Liberal Republican Party) in 1930, but when it quickly became the vehicle of Islamists opposed to his radical secularism, he had it shut down. Turkey remained neutral during WWII. In March 1949, it became the first Muslim nation to recognize Israel[45] and maintained close diplomatic, economic and military relations with Israel throughout the Cold War. Turkey joined NATO in 1952, but this decision hardly reflected the 'will of the people'. Kemal reportedly quipped, "For the people, despite the people!"[46]

When the political reins were loosened, Kemal's Republican People's Party immediately lost in 1950 to the Democratic Party allied with Islamist Said Nursi's Followers of Light on a platform of relaxing militant secularism and state control.

Islam immediately began to re-emerge. Religious instruction and the wearing of traditional dress were allowed, Sufi orders were legalized, and Islamic studies reintroduced at universities. Then, as in Pakistan, Turkey's military staged coups—in 1960,[47] 1971 and 1980—to stop moves towards promoting more religious practice, though the 1980 coup changed the nature of the 'game', as happened throughout the region, including Pakistan.[48] Turkey had modernized, but never broke through the barrier that separated the western center from periphery to become a part of Europe.

The British attitude towards 'independence' for **Egypt** and its other Muslim colonies is revealed in the words of Lord Cromer, consul general in Egypt from 1883–1907 and architect of Britain's policy in the Arab world:

> It is absurd to suppose that Europe will look on as a passive spectator whilst a retrograde government based on purely Muhammadan principles and oriental ideas, is established in Egypt. The material interests at stake are too important. The new generation of Egyptians has to be persuaded or forced into imbibing the true spirit of Western civilization.[49]

Egypt was granted 'independence' in 1922, but only after a long, hard struggle. After the 1919 liberal revolution, faced with demands from Egyptian leaders for genuine independence as promised by US President Woodrow Wilson in his Fourteen Points, the British finally issued a unilateral declaration recognizing Egypt as "an independent sovereign State" but subject to considerations of the "security of communications of the British Empire in Egypt", foreign interests and minorities, and Sudan. The British allowed Egyptian landlords, merchants and liberal intelligentsia to participate in elections after that, and even—briefly—to form governments under a tightly controlled monarchy.

Egyptians thus educated by their colonial mentors naturally advocated policies which facilitated the functioning of the reigning secular political-economic system, using western concepts to reinterpret Islam to meet the requirements of the system. Even so, the occupiers still saw Egyptian secular liberals as hostile, given their demands for genuine independence, at times imprisoning and even exiling them (Zaghloul). These patriots were and are revered as heroes of the independence struggle, regardless of their policies. They emerged from colonialism and helped their 'nations' develop, thereby helping their peoples. Egypt's most well known early reformers include:

Rifaa al-Tahtawi (1801–1873), who was sent by Muhammad Ali as the imam for the Egyptian delegation to Paris in 1826 to study. The young imam

noted in *A Paris Profile* "the dearth of chastity among many of their women, and the lack of jealousy among their men ... how adultery for them is a vice and a shame but not a primary sin. [Paris] is charged with abominations, innovations, and perdition, although the city of Paris is the wisest city of the entire world and the home of world-based science." One of the "Islamic modernists", he wanted to borrow what was not in conflict with sharia, and argued that there were western ideas (liberal and socialist) that were indeed consistent with sharia—the demand for justice, welfare and education.[50] His primary concern was adopting western mass education *a la* Wali Allah in India.

Qasim Amin (1863–1908), a judge who wrote *The Emancipation of Women* (1899), arguing that the current status of women did not reflect the intent of the Quran but rather customs and mores of the times. He advocated education for women, and an end to veiling and polygamy. Amin went on to become one of the founders of the Egyptian National Movement, as well as of Cairo University.

Saad Zaghloul (1859–1927), who in 1918 led an official Egyptian delegation (*wafd*) to the Paris Peace Conference demanding that the United Kingdom formally recognize the independence and unity of Egypt and Sudan (which had been united under Muhammad Ali). Britain refused to recognize the delegation and exiled him to Malta, and later to the Seychelles.[51] Zaghloul's exile precipitated the 1919 revolution. Elections in 1924 gave the Wafd Party an overwhelming majority, and two weeks later, Zaghloul formed the first Wafd government, but resigned within months, and never exercised meaningful authority. Suffrage was limited and the movement was dominated by the landlord and merchant classes.

Taha Hussein (1889–1973), who was a figurehead for the 'Arab Renaissance' and the modernist movement in the Arab World. Despite being blind from the age of three, he became a noted writer, professor and in 1950 minister of knowledge, trying to implement free universal education, which was carried out later under Nasser. He transformed many of the Quranic schools into primary schools and established several universities. He argued that Egypt was a 'Mediterranean culture', emphasizing its Roman/ Greek heritage (vs Islamic/ African).[52]

Ali Abd al-Raziq (1888-1966), who like Abduh was an Azhar sheikh and judge, but who is now regarded as the intellectual father of 'Islamic secularism'. His *Islam and the Foundations of Governance* (1925), published a year after Mustafa Kemal abolished the caliphate, argued for western-style separation of state and religion, though not the 'secularization' of society. It triggered an intellectual and political battle in Egypt, leading to his dismissal from Azhar (he was reinstated in the 1940s). Raziq argued that the Quran and the sunna do not require the rule of a caliph or imam, that Islam's importance is only as moral revelation. He served as minister of endowments. A later liberal reformer, Nasr Abu Zayd praised Taha Hussein, Abduh and Raziq, who "contextualized social and political issues within religious discourse, attacking the thoughtless imitation of the past as a way to move Islamic culture forward."[53]

Ahmad Amin (1886–1954), who was an important figure in the rise of nationalism, and argued that ethics was based on reason and intuition, not solely on religion and customs. He vaunted Egypt's "Pharaonic core" (as Iranian nationalists did ancient Persia's cultural heritage) and interpreted the ninth century Fatimid Caliphate in Egypt and the later Mamluks as an early assertion of Egyptian 'independence'.

The nationalists and liberals were 'ready' to take power by 1882 and most certainly by 1919, but were stymied by Egypt's colonial master. Egypt was the center of the British Empire's geopolitical strategy, with its Suez Canal the gateway to Asia, the linchpin in its empire, with a large population of 15 million (80% extremely poor peasants with a growing colonial administrative class).

As the traditional heart of Islam for centuries, crowned by Azhar University, Egypt experienced a strong movement seeking to return to its Islamic roots rather than just to join the imperial order as an underling. However, even as the liberals and nationalists were being both nurtured and stymied by the British, Islamists were faced with a hostile ulama that frowned on political protest. As the liberals were increasingly discredited over time, the Muslim Brotherhood (MB), like the Wahhabis in the Arabian Peninsula, began as an insurgent movement independent of the traditional ulama against what were viewed as illegitimate rulers: in the case of the MB, the British and the secular Egyptian monarchy (a non-Egyptian legacy of the Ottomans), in the case of the Wahhabis, the Ottomans.

But unlike the case in what would become Saudi Arabia, Islamists in Egypt did not have the luxury of overthrowing a distant caliph, and establishing a state in what was then the nonstrategic desert wastelands of Arabia, home to Islam's inviolable cities, Mecca and Medina. Unwilling to remain passive in the face of social decline and disintegration of the umma, they established their own reform movement, focusing on moral/ social reform, educational/ social welfare projects, hospitals, mosques, schools, cottage industries and social clubs, in preparation for a future post-colonial Islamic state. This remarkable exercise in *ijtihad,* in reaction to both the continued occupation *and* the new nationalism, gave rise to a movement of revolutionary Islamic activism across the Muslim world, combining religion with social activism in a revivalist ideology through mass organizations.

Egypt's long transition—from (capitalist) 'independence' (1922) to (socialist) 'independence' (1952) (and later back to capitalist 'independence' in 1972)—during which the MB played a vital insurgent role, makes Egypt unique. The various forces of change contending with each other—liberalism, nationalism, socialism, Islamism—have been battling it out for almost a century now. The theory behind the MB's program is the focus of Chapters 3 and its later surge and triumph in 2011–2012 is the subject of Chapter 4.

As the MB rapidly grew during the 1930s, it—rather than the liberals and socialists became the focus of anti-colonial resistance. By 1949, the MB had 2,000 branches and 500,000 members. Meanwhile, the secular anti-imperial forces as represented by the Wafd Party were fighting the British from inside colonial administration offices. The British had to play a delicate balancing game.

Yielding to popular will to ensure Egyptian help in WWII, Britain allied briefly with the Wafd Party against King Farouq, forcing him to appoint the Wafd head, Mustafa Nahas, as prime minister. The Wafd used this opportunity to try to implement its own reform program, making Arabic compulsory for official correspondence and expanding mass education. Farouq was forced to dismiss Prime Minister Nahas in 1944 when he refused to declare war on Germany, and his British-installed successor, Ahmed Maher, was promptly assassinated. Egypt was paralyzed by a wave of strikes in 1946 supported by the MB, communists and Wafd, demanding that British troops leave and Egypt be granted meaningful independence.

For the devout, WWII and the post-WWII environment, even more than the pre-war environment, was a morass of corruption and crass materialism, making it impossible to follow the sharia. The enormous hardships of the war imposed by the British, who stationed tens of thousands of contemptuous, drunken soldiers in Egypt, gave way to repression and further hardship after the war. Hopes for real independence were quickly dashed, even as Anglo-American complicity with the Zionists gave birth to an independent Jewish state, a ruthless, expansionist colonial regime, next door in Palestine. Israel immediately launched wars and undermined Egyptian society by recruiting Egyptian Jews to undertake terrorist acts against British and American targets, as well as in public places, injuring innocent civilians, the most notorious case being the Lavon affair in 1954.[54]

The beleaguered British were unwilling to end the empire one minute too soon *or* to allow an Islamist Egypt, which would have been the result of an honest election. Instead, they continued to enrage all Egyptians. The camel's back broke when the British killing of 50 Egyptian police in Ismailia on 25 January 1952 which led to the Free Officers coup that July. This army coup was tolerated by the British insofar as the alternative was Islamist, and they quickly moved to co-opt the military regime, offering arms to the desperate Egyptians, faced with the implacable and formidable (British spawned) Jewish foe in what was now Israel.

The army coup in 1952 was carried out by a committed anti-Zionist and a hero of the 1948 war against Israel, Colonel Gamal Abdel-Nasser (r. 1954–1970). The MB naturally supported the coup as a genuine declaration of independence from Britain, and it was briefly legalized in 1952–1954. However, there was no room for an Islamic solution to Egypt's crises in the Free Officers' plans, and an assassination attempt on Nasser by a devout hot-headed veterinary student led to the MB being banned and all leading members arrested. This time, it was Egyptian nationalists doing the repressing. The MB was virtually wiped out—for the duration of Nasser's rule.

A soldier from a poor family, Nasser had a limited education. He was a charismatic revolutionary, and while he studied the Quran and considered himself a practicing Muslim all his life, his early influences were nationalists such as Mustafa Kamel (1874–1908), founder of the Egyptian National Party. He made an abrupt break with the old order in 1952, abolishing the monarchy and later expelling the foreign nationals dominating the economy. Nasser's shining hour was his nationalization of the Suez Canal in 1956. The British-French-Israeli attack on Egypt to recover the canal was thwarted by the US, eager to take over from the bankrupt European imperialists in the Middle East. It gave Nasser the prestige, mandate and hard currency to pursue his dream of a secular, socialist Egypt, without the need to integrate the powerful Islamist MB, with its considerable social infrastructure based on social justice (which could have ensured the success of his anti-imperial experiment). Nasser tricked not only the Islamists, the British and French, but the Americans, by proceeding along a socialist path, eventually turning to the Soviet Union for support, in the face of American support for Israel.

Though largely secular, Nasser and other pan-Arab nationalists/ socialists inspired by Nasserism in Algeria, Iraq, Syria, Yemen, Libya and among oppositionist groups across the Middle East, tried to use the language of Islam to respond to popular pressure. Nasser founded the journal *Minbar al-islam* (pulpit of Islam), but at the same time abolished autonomous sharia courts in 1955 to unify the judicial system,[55] brought all mosques and *awqaf* under the control of the Ministry of Religious Endowments, and nationalized Azhar in 1961, pressuring it to issue fatwas in favor of socialism.

In his *Philosophy of the Revolution* (1955), he described Islam as one of the three geographic historical circles to which Egypt belonged:

> Arab, African, Islamic. The third circle is our brothers in faith who together face one direction—the qibla—and one prayer, that can have the positive outcome of uniting our efforts. When I went to Saudi Arabia to give condolences to the king and stopped in front of the Kaaba, I realized that all Muslims around the world were facing this one direction. I said to myself, it is necessary to change our view, not to think of the hajj as only a ticket to heaven or a way to ask forgiveness. We must see the hajj as an immense political event. It is necessary that media not present the hajj as only a ritual, but as a huge international conference every year of all Muslim countries and peoples, to encourage Muslims to unite and help each other. The king told me this is the wisdom of the hajj, and I can't believe there is any other truth than this to the hajj. We have huge numbers and huge abilities if we work together.[56]

Nasser is considered the Arab world's greatest leader in the twentieth century, despite his failed experiment and tragic end. To call him an accommodationist is perhaps startling, but from an Islamic point of view, his top-down adoption of the Soviet model of development (he was a recipient of the Hero of the Soviet Union title) and suppression of Islamists was intended to put Egypt at the center of the new socialist world map then seemingly emerging in the Arab and African world. Islam was window-dressing, a means to a secular socialist end, rather than the source of a renewed Islamic civilization, to be achieved by living an Islamic way of life under an Islamic government.

He fashioned a system that was reasonably just, but never achieved the enthusiastic response that one based on Islam would have had. Over time, he realized this shortcoming, and made a pilgrimage to Mecca, insisting his socialist vision represented the true meaning of Islam, even as thousands of Islamists languished in his jails.

The poet Nizar Kabbani described Nasser as "the last prophet", and the scale of popular veneration for him today in Egypt and the wider Arab world, is "arguably greater than that of any other political leader since the Prophet Muhammad".[57] This mix of socialism and nationalism with a sprig of Islam was a heady brew, but came crashing down with the humiliating defeat by Egypt and its allies in the war with Israel in 1967, bringing to an end the dreams of both nationalists and socialists across the Arab world. Tawfiq al-Hakim described Nasser as a "confused Sultan" who pursued grand but ultimately empty dreams—a man of stirring rhetoric, but no real plan of action. His relationship with the Egyptian people "rendered intermediary organizations and individuals unnecessary", [58] and his failure to create durable institutions meant that after his death at the age of 52, Egypt returned to the unstable political state it was in before his coup, leaving the road open for the imperialists to return. Built on Nasser's charisma, Egypt's social system unraveled after his death.

One of Nasser's influences was Khalid Muhammad Khalid (1920–1996), whose *From Here We Start* advocated a secular socialism. At first, Khalid opposed the Muslim Brotherhood, but by the 1960s his disenchantment with the failed economic policies of Nasser's dictatorship gradually led Khalid to join the Islamic revivalist movement. His *The State in Islam* (1981) and *Islam and the State* (1989) defend the political role of Islam, describing it as a religion, a political system, a culture and a civilization.

Nasserist socialism was exposed as only skin-deep when Nasser's trusted comrade and vice president, Anwar Sadat (r. 1970–1981) took power, followed by Hosni Mubarak (r. 1981–2011). They lost no time in dismantling Nasser's severe but just system and adopting an openly assimilationist program with the West, accepting US-Israeli regional hegemony and the western neoliberal agenda. Initially Sadat freed the imprisoned Islamists, virtually legalizing the MB (though not for participation in elections), welcoming the Islamists back from exile in Saudi Arabia and Europe. But this was merely part of their common interest in undoing Nasser's powerful legacy, and it soon came to haunt both the assimilationists and the MB. When Egyptians woke up to the fact that they no longer had either their threadbare socialism or religious freedom, and that they had been robbed of their wealth by a new corrupt elite, the result was a return to the civil unrest and violence that sparked the 1952 'revolution'.

The result of Egypt's failed experiments in both capitalism and socialism is that, according to Hani Shukrallah and Hosny Guindy writing in 2000, "Half the country ... is at war with Abdel-Nasser, half with Anwar el-Sadat."[59]

However, Nasserism—a combination of nationalism and socialism with a touch of Islam—continues to inspire many today throughout the Arab world. Despite Nasser's dictatorial methods and many crudities in economic policies, the period was very successful in raising living standards for all Egyptians (apart from the former elite) and creating a healthy industrial sector with a low foreign debt. Corruption was almost non-existent. The anti-imperialist Nasser managed to get large amounts of aid from both the US and Soviet Union, which was used responsibly. Sadat and Mubarak undid all this.

Saddam Hussein (r. 1976–2003) in Iraq, Muammar al-Gaddafi (r. 1969–2011) in Libya, Jamal al-Nimeiri (r. 1969–1985) and Omar al-Bashir (r. 1989) in Sudan were/are staunch anti-imperialists, and like Nasser, preside(d) over self-serving dictatorships. They all claimed to be socialist (though in actuality were closer to being rentier socialists, depending heavily on the bonanza of oil) and at the same time look(ed) for support from the religious establishment and/or pressured it to approve their policies. They all were attacked by the imperialists when they got out of line, and whatever vision they had for their countries lies in ruins. Iraq's version of Nasserism was obliterated by multiple US invasions, facilitated by Saddam Hussein's recklessness. The death throes of Nasserism continue in Syria as this book goes to press, with the Baath Party's grip on power finally being shaken.

With the demise of the Soviet Union, both liberals and socialists were forced to seek accommodation with the western secular order. But the imperialists became choosy; for them, there was no longer any room for a Nasser, even a contrite Saddam Hussein or Gaddafi, leaving the political playing field open to Islamists by default.[60]

In the **Levant**, the last French troops withdrew from newly independent **Syria** and **Lebanon** in 1946. While still under French control, Syria held presidential elections in 1943, following which an elected government (based on universal male suffrage), led by the liberal-landlord dominated National Bloc's Shukri al-Quwatly, came to power. It soon split along regional/ tribal lines into the National Party (Quwatly, Damascus group) vs the People's Party (Aleppo, Homs). The Syrian Muslim Brotherhood (1937) led by scholar-activist Mustafa al-Sibai, author of *Islamic Socialism*, garnered 3 seats in Syria's first elections after independence in 1947, approving the 1949 secular constitution calling for an "end to dependence upon foreign powers, to feudalism and to the domination of the upper class elite".[61]

In March 1949, the US organized a coup d'état against Quwatly's government to install military rule, presided over by Colonel Husni al-Zaim. Zaim effectively recognized Israel by signing an armistice, and ratified the TAPLINE (Trans-Arabian Pipeline Company) project, allowing Aramco (Arabian-American Oil Company) to pipe Saudi oil across Syria to the Mediterranean. The Syrian parliament had earlier rejected both these demands due to western and US support for Israel during the 1948 Arab-Israeli War. Between 1949, when Quwatly's democratic government was dislodged, and 1955, five more coups were organized.[62]

The engine of pan-Arab nationalism was the Baath Party, which had sprung up as the mouthpiece of pan-Arabism after WWII. The Syrian chapter merged with Nasser's Arab Socialist Party in 1954, supported by young leftist Syrian officers. Syria even joined Egypt in the United Arab Republic (UAR, 1958–61). Syria's political dynamics were similar to Egypt's, though western meddling was more blatant, weakening the social fabric and leading to a more rigid military rule. Baathist military officers consolidated their control of the Baath Party in the 1963 coup. Anti-communist Islamists staged the siege of the Hama Sultan mosque in 1964, resulting in up to 100 deaths. Reflecting their pan-Arabism, the Syrian and Iraqi Baathists were united in one party, despite the very different dynamics imposed on them by their colonial heritage. They finally split in 1966 when a coup overthrew the civilian leadership of the Syrian party. The Alawi Hafez al-Assad established himself as Syria's president-dictator in 1971 and suppressed another Islamist uprising in Hama in 1981–1982, killing as many as 10,000.

France had carved out **Lebanon** as a majority Christian (both Maronite and Orthodox) 'nation', granted 'independence' in 1946, but its demographics shifted in favor of Muslims, especially with the massive Palestinian refugee presence after 1948. Wedged between Syria and Israel, its toxic ethnic mix (toxic only as a result of western meddling) erupted in full-scale civil war in 1975.

Jordan was granted 'independence' from Britain in 1946 as an absolute monarchy under the Hashemites, who also ruled Iraq, promoting a British-friendly Arab nationalism. Jordan's Muslim Brotherhood (1942) was under the Egyptian MB until the latter was outlawed in 1954. The Jordanian MB was not banned, and though not allowed to run in elections, it grudgingly supported King Hussein against nationalists and communists, much like the Egyptian MB prior to WWII and before Nasser's coup in 1952.

Resistance in the British Mandate for **Palestine** to British plans to carve a Jewish state out of Palestine peaked in the late 1930s with a general strike demanding an end to Jewish immigration, which was brutally suppressed by the British. Though there was no justification for taking Palestinian lands and giving them to European Jews[63] the UN approved the creation of a Jewish state alongside a Palestinian Arab one, ignoring the confusion of ethnicity and religion. The British made no effort to prepare the Palestinians to form a government after the occupier's hurried departure.

Said Ramadan, Banna's son-in-law, came to the region in 1945 and recruited fighters for the MB in the impending war against the Zionist state. By 1947, there were 25 branches of the Brotherhood in Palestine, with between 12,000 and 20,000 members. The Arab Liberation Army was hastily put together in 1948 by the fledgling Arab states, with Brotherhood members fighting alongside. Untrained, without proper weapons, it was routed by the Zionists, forcing hundreds of thousands of Palestinians into exile in refugee camps.

The Palestinian MB was not militant. Focused on social and religious activity, it lost popularity to militant national resistance groups and Hizb ut-Tahrir (Party of Liberation, see Chapter 3). Palestinians remained without a unifying nationalist political organization until Fatah (victory) was founded in the late 1950s and the Palestinian Liberation Organization (PLO) was sponsored by Egypt in 1964.

PLO head Yasser Arafat was recognized as the *de facto* leader of Palestine, which gained observer status at the UN in 1974. The Brotherhood was strengthened by the creation of the Islamic Center in 1973 by Shaykh Ahmad Yassin, and became politicized by the 1979 Islamic Revolution in Iran as disillusionment with the secularist and increasingly accommodationist PLO set in.

The new prominence of the PLO had been important to legitimizing the Palestinian cause in the West, but from the start, for accommodationist Arab regimes intent on maintaining their neocolonial power and intimidated by the power of world Zionism, the PLO was more about finding a way "to co-opt and restrain the Palestinian resistance movement" to prevent it from drawing Arab states inadvertently into war. Only the Soviet Union—after Stalin had recognized his fatal misjudgment in recognizing Israel in 1948—was a firm supporter of the Palestinian cause, but it too was ineffectual, concerned in the first place with its own survival in the face of the overwhelming economic and military might of the US empire.

The history of Palestine is one of war and exile, but also of the return of Islam to a central place in the lives of all Muslims, mobilized in defense of al-Quds (Jerusalem), which is as holy to Muslims as it is to Christians and Jews (and was at peace under Muslim rule for over a millennium). The exile of millions of Palestinians and their plight as refugees has sparked interest in Islam among non-Muslims, much like the persecution and expulsion of Muslim traders in the 16th–19th centuries in southeast Asia contributed to the growth of the umma there as a reaction to the injustices of imperialism.

The British protectorate of **Libya**, taken over from Italy in 1943, achieved 'independence' in 1951 after a brutal occupation by both. The British ceded power to 'King' Idris, chief of the Senussi Sufi order, who was a weak leader and acquiesced to continued British domination. Muammar al-Gaddafi came to power in a coup in 1969, soon betraying his CIA backers, and following Nasser, declared his own version of socialism and Islam, nationalizing the oil industry and supporting the Palestinian struggle. He focused on African and Arab unity, remaining aloof from the Soviet Union, and persecuting traditional Islamists, forcing Libyans to rally around his cult of personality and his own 'modernized' version of Islam.

The French ceded **Tunisia** to the solidly secular, anticommunist President Habib Bourguiba in 1956, who served as president-dictator for 32 years. Bourguiba repressed Islam, but had some domestic credibility as an active leader of the independence movement against the French. He converted the Zaytuna mosque into a western-style university, eliminated sharia courts, and alienated Muslims by maligning the hijab and appearing on daytime TV during Ramadan drinking orange juice. In 1981, Bourguiba arrested over 3,000 Islamists for gathering at a mosque without authorization. One of the arrested Islamists, Rashid al-Ghannouchi—leader of Tunisia's largest Islamic movement—received a life prison sentence.

Algeria achieved genuine independence from France in 1962 after a million Algerians died in the liberation struggle, dominated by the socialists and nationalists. From 1865–1945, France had pursued an extreme assimilation policy, eventually promising Algerians quasi-French citizenship (naturalization) if they renounced their Muslim civil status and accepted French law. Only 2,000 requested naturalization. Determined to wipe out Islam as a cultural force, the French nationalized the religious endowments, strictly controlling the sheikhs, paying them as civil servants and taking responsibility for building mosques. Ironically this made the demand for the separation of religion and the state a radically *pro*-Islamic one—to free the mosques from the clutches of the secular state. Instead, the French set up the *Association Culturelle Musulman*, the "worst of both worlds", as it no longer handed out official perks and still had the stigma of being co-opted attached to it.[64] This situation finally exploded as reformist ulama seized mosques, and in 1957 the now beleaguered French authorities closed down all reformist organizations, effectively handing the underground, secular independence movement the reins of power. After the revolution, "the Algerian state appeared astonishingly similar to the Pahlavi state, strongly secular … omnipresent in social, cultural, economic spheres, conducting agrarian reform that antagonized Islamic groups."[65]

Contrary to US fears, Algeria did not come under Soviet influence. Crippled by the long struggle for independence and the departure of French colons who had largely run the economy, and now dominated by secular, socialist leaders (who were just as much a product of the French left as the rightwing Bourguiba was of the French right), it was not to play a major role in regional politics, and the Islamist movement remained more or less underground. Algeria's new anti-imperialist elite was nonetheless westernized and secular, and the ulama insular and conservative, severely weakened and compromised by a century and a half of heavy-handed French secular rule.

The new very secular President Ahmed Ben Bella (r. 1962–1965) tried to co-opt Islam, hammering home Islam's socialistic message, much like Nasser in Egypt. Muhammad's companion Abu Dharr was billed as the "father of socialism", the revolution was the "revolution of the poor against the rich",[66] but the state's overall message was secularism. In 1964, protests against an increasingly autocratic Ben Bella led to a military coup by Houari Boumedienne (r. 1965–1979), who continued the secular, state socialist policies of Ben Bella. Again, in 1970, Boumedienne tried to co-opt the Islamists (as Sadat was doing at the same time in Egypt), but land reforms provoked Islamist opposition similar to what had occurred in Iran in 1964 (see below). The new dictator came full circle to experience the isolation of Ben Bella, as there just wasn't a secular mass movement supporting socialism imposed by fiat. By the late 1970s, events elsewhere would overtake this secularist-led revolution that had run out of steam.

Morocco experienced a form of apartheid under the French, who built *villes,* French quarters where Moroccans were banned. Sultan Mohammed V (r. 1927–1961) was deposed by the French in 1953 for siding with the nationalists, but returned triumphantly as king in 1955. Morocco extricated itself from French and Spanish clutches in 1956, but as a conservative pro-western kingdom. The monarchy had pre-colonial credibility, and Islamists were initially allowed some room to organize, as was the case in Jordan. Morocco became famous as the playground for decadent westerners, including writers such as Paul Bowles and William Burroughs.

The reign of the next king, Hassan II (r. 1961–1999), was bleak. He brought in Morocco's first constitution in 1963, affirming multi-party politics, but gave himself the real power, provoking widespread protest and leading him to dissolve parliament. The 1960s–1980s were labeled the "years of lead", during which tens of thousands of Islamists and leftists were tortured, killed, exiled or forcibly disappeared under the watchful eye of the CIA, which organized Morocco's security forces in the 1960s. When elections were later held, they were rigged. Hassan survived two assassination attempts in the early 1970s.

As in colonial times, the African umma suffered even more than its Arab and Asian counterparts. It was forced into hastily declared secular states, based on imperial-era borders, in the 1950s–1960s. **Sudan**'s post-colonial 'liberation' was doomed from the start. The British delayed independence for Sudan until the last moment in 1956, determined it would not unite with Nasser's Egypt. Already civil war, between the Muslim Arabized north and the south—animist and increasing Catholic-Protestant Christian, thanks to western missionaries—ensured it would be a dysfunctional state. The process of conversion to Islam had been arrested by the imperialists a century previously, who brought a meek, apolitical Christianity (with European Islamophobic baggage) along with their occupation, leaving a legacy of conflict for the future. Their imported concept of a 'nation state' was completely alien to the dozens of tribes, many nomadic, who eked out a precarious existence on the edge of the desert. The only shreds of unity beyond the level of the tribe were the conflicting religious bonds and the growing secular communist and Nasserist movements.

Always close to Egypt, Sudan has had a Muslim Brotherhood presence since 1949, and the MB proved to be an ally for post-'independence' leaders against the powerful communists/ Nasserists, supporting the ban on communists (the largest communist party in Africa) in 1965. An offshoot of the MB, the Islamic Charter Front led by Hassan al-Turabi (b.1932), joined the government of military dictator Jamal al-Nimeiri (r. 1969–1985), who finally established a truce in the civil war in 1972.

The British occupied all of present-day **Somalia** in 1941 and ceded 'independence' in 1960. Major General Siad Barre (r. 1969–1991) seized power and imposed an extreme, Maoist-style secular dictatorship which at first allied with the Soviet Union. Barre started the Ogaden war to seize territory from a now socialist Ethiopia, and when the Soviets tried to mediate, Barre turned to the US. His 'scientific socialism' in shambles, civil war broke out and he was overthrown, leaving a power vacuum which no central government could fill. Somaliland and Puntland emerged in the north as unrecognized independent 'nations'.

Ethiopia, approximately one-third Muslim, was ruled by Emperor Haile Selassie (r. 1916–1936) until invaded by Italy and then occupied by Britain in 1941. It was granted 'independence' in 1944, and Selassie continued to rule (r. 1941–1974), annexing Eritrea in 1952, which led to an insurgency. He was overthrown in a leftist coup in 1974 led by Mengistu Haile Mariam, the unrest due to the massive hike in oil prices, primarily by Saudi Arabia. As elsewhere, the socialist version of 'independence' proved deadly for both Somalia and Ethiopia.

Sahel Africa had been transformed radically by imperialism. The mass dislocation of peoples resulting from the slave trade and the colonial invasions disrupted the traditional way of life and left a legacy of conflict and poverty. What could have become a Muslim-majority, peaceful united continent without imperialism became an unending scene of horror before and after 'independence'. The west African 'nations' where Islam was becoming the dominant religion before the imperialists arrived are now loosely federated as the Economic Community of West African States (ECOWAS, 1974).

	Colony	Independence	Muslim
Togo	German/ French	1960	20%
Benin	French	1960	25%
Burkina Faso	French	1960	60%
Chad	French	1960	54%
Ivory Coast	French	1960	40%
Guinea	French	1958	85%
Mali	French	1960	90%
Niger	French	1960	90%
Senegal	French	1960	94%
Nigeria	British	1960	51%
Gambia	British	1965	90%
Ghana	British	1957	16%
Sierra Leone	British	1961	60%
Guinea-Bissau	Portuguese	1973	50%
Liberia	US	1847	12%

The period of 'independence' from 1957–1970s was a particularly cruel one, characterized by corrupt dictators continuing colonial exploitation in conjunction with the imperial powers and their international banking and development agencies. The Soviet Union provided its own version of development aid based on secular socialism, though it had no choice but to work with the post-colonial regimes, however unpalatable. Both the imperialists and Soviets competed for influence with the new local elites, who sometimes turned sincerely or cynically to socialism to buttress their popularity, even while cooperating with their former colonial centers. Both the West and the socialist bloc trained hundreds of thousands of Africans, and both East and West provided experts in agriculture, industry and arms.

On the whole the secular experiment was a disappointment, sometimes a disaster. After 'independence', Nigeria, the largest nation and home to Africa's largest Muslim community, suffered military dictatorships from 1966–1999. Its oil wealth (in the Christianized south) led to extreme corruption, and benefited only the elite.

The return of Islam to a central role in Africans' lives continues. The umma in Sudan, northern Nigeria and Mali are struggling with how to end western meddling, and reinstitute Islamic institutions such as sharia to meet contemporary needs. The huge inroad made by British missionaries in Nigeria and Sudan, and the fusion of the animist/ Christian south and the Muslim north in both 'countries' in an unworkable union, leaves the specter of civil war hanging over both,[67] recalling the Nigerian Biafra tragedy of the 1967–1970, and the Sudanese civil war (1955–1972), when Christianized regions declared independence, counting on western support.

The **Saud** tribe adopted the Wahhabi doctrine and captured Mecca from 1803–1818, again in 1908 and for good in 1924 in the name of jihad, making them a legend in the Muslim world, though not a benign one. They were known for their thorough plundering and merciless killings, the raids being "deadlier than traditional Bedouin raids, which usually avoided killing for fear of triggering a blood feud."[68] Through a 'happy' confluence of events, the tribe took possession of most of the Arabian Peninsula by 1924, and its 'independence' was recognized by Britain. The peninsula was remote and poor, and the imperialists understood that unbelievers occupying the holy cities was not such a good idea from their point of view.

Leopold Weiss (Muhammed Asad), an Austrian Jewish convert to Islam who travelled extensively in the Hejaz (the southwestern Arabian Peninsula, which includes Mecca and Medina) and wilds of Arabia in the 1930s, was a personal friend and adviser to King Abd al-Aziz ibn Saud (r. 1932–1953). He hailed "the spiritual impetus" set in motion in the eighteenth century by Wahhab.[69] However, the form of Islam that became dominant in Saudi Arabia has its defects, Asad continued, the narrowing of religious endeavors to a "literal observation of injunctions, overlooking the need for penetrating to their spiritual content", and "the Arab's zealotic, self-righteous orientation of feeling, peculiar to the true Semite". He became disillusioned with the compromises the king made with the West and the Wahhabi doctrines, which Asad saw as undermining Islam. He was soon barred from returning to Arabia and his books were banned. His *Road to Mecca* (1954) is a superb evocation of the state of Islam in the 1920s–1950s.

After WWII, the Saudi kingdom, with its newly discovered massive oil wealth and tiny, tribal population was able to establish a *modus vivendi* with the new American empire, allowing this reactionary Islam concerned with appearances to be enforced locally, and leaving economic development and foreign policy to Washington and American oil companies, working in isolation from the local population. Where imperialism was able to establish a firm foothold, and in an urbanized context (Egypt, India and southeast Asia), Wahhabis were not able to promote their desert austerity with much success.

Like the liberal assimilationists promoting Arab nationalism, the Saudis and Gulf monarchies have also promoted unthreatening pan-Islamic organizations originally founded with the approval of the imperialists to fight communism, such as the Islamic World Congress (1949), Muslim World League (1962),[70] the Organization for Islamic Cooperation (1969), among others, and finally began to support the PLO after 1967, though Saudi King Faisal's goal was to move allegiance in the Arab world away from the pan-Arab movement towards a pan-Islam controlled by Saudi Arabia.

'Islamic civilization in the past has witnessed invasions and other empires rise and fall, as Islam held its own and then expanded in the wake of the empires.' This is no doubt how a Saudi 'prince' rationalizes accommodation with the West (though it would surely have appalled Wahhab), as he performs the hajj, and promotes *dawa* (proselytizing) and pan-Islamism in preparation for the triumph of Islam in the distant future. But such reasoning cannot hide the fact that these quietist fundamentalists operate within the system of imperialism, either in alliance (Saudis, Gulf) or, along with their adherents around the world, piously refusing to dirty their hands in politics, leaving this to the corrupt secular politicians by default.

As custodians of the holy cities, the Saudis took the idea of 'nationalizing Islam' to the extreme. In the process, their creed rejected 1,200 years of Islamic civilization, and removed the spark of genius from their citizens. In building their modern infrastructure from scratch on windfall oil revenues from the 1950s on, the Saudis did not try to revive the ecologically and psychologically beneficial urban technology of traditional Islam, and create a modern Islamic utopia based on the Quran. Neither they nor their liberal accommodationist counterparts showed any concern for the accumulated artistic and scientific wealth of traditional Islamic civilization. Preserving the artistic legacy of Islam from the onslaught of modernity was, ironically, largely the result of the devotion of a tiny handful of western traditionalist scholars such as Louis Massignon, who convinced the French governor of Morocco in 1902 not to destroy the old medinas such as Fes, but to build modern colonial *villes* adjacent to them.[71] On the contrary, the Saudis have been busy destroying 95% of the Islamic heritage in Medina and Mecca (see Chapter 4 endnote 92).

Bahrain, **Qatar**, **Oman** and the sheikhdoms comprising the **United Arab Emirates** were British protectorates and bases until they were granted nominal independence in 1970–1972, when the US took over guaranteeing their security within the western camp. In 1971, majority-Shia Bahrain became 'independent' and in 1973, the first elections (men only) were held to elect the thirty members of the National Assembly, which immediately demanded the eviction of the US Navy base (the US military presence in Bahrain dates to 1949). The ruling Sunni al-Khalifas dissolved the assembly in 1975. Sitting on huge oil and gas reserves, these tiny 'nations' have followed the Saudi Wahhabi accommodationist lead.

Yemen became Britain's main military outpost in the region after Nasser nationalized the Suez Canal in 1956. Present-day Yemen was formed from a collection of British protectorates patched together in 1963 to form the Federation and Protectorate of South Arabia, with a British promise of total independence in 1968. Inspired by Egypt's Nasser, nationalist groups immediately began an armed struggle. With the temporary closure of the Suez Canal in 1967, the British forces were cut off and southern Yemen declared itself the People's Republic of South Yemen, and in 1970, the People's Democratic Republic of Yemen. This was the closest the Soviets ever came to having a reliable ally in the Middle East, but secular socialism was not a strong enough social bond, and socialist Yemen unraveled in 1990 along with its distant Russian sponsor, and was forced to join the north.

Iraq achieved 'independence' in 1932 at the same time as Saudi Arabia, but British influence ended only in 1958 when Brigadier Abd al-Karim Qasim overthrew the British-installed Hashemite monarchy, and annulled the British-US sponsored military alliance, the Baghdad Pact (MEDO, Middle East Defense Organization). Iraq started down the then popular secular socialist path of Nasser in Egypt.

In 1963, the Iraqi Baath Party took power in a coup allegedly supported by the CIA (Qasim had allied with the Communist Party), and after a period of instability an army officer, Saddam Hussein,[72] became *de facto* leader of Iraq in 1976 and president in 1979. He severely repressed not only Islamists,[73] but, like Nasser in Egypt, his erstwhile communist supporters. Though he created the most advanced Arab nation and managed to become an important geopolitical player, his fatal misjudgments—the war against Iran in 1980 and the invasion of Kuwait in 1990[74]—led to his isolation and the destruction of his secular dream. "God is great" was hastily inserted on the Iraqi flag in January 1991 as the US prepared to 'liberate' Kuwait, though it is claimed that even that was spoiled by the holy words being in Saddam Hussein's handwriting.[75]

Much the same process as took place in post-WWI Turkey came about under the new Pahlavi dynasty in **Iran**, though Reza Shah Pahlavi (r. 1925–1941, b. Reza Khan) was not so aggressively anti-Islam as 'Ataturk' and left the still powerful ulama in Qom alone. He had wanted to be 'crowned' president, as he fancied himself Persia's Ataturk (he paid a state visit to Turkey

Ataturk and Reza Shah Pahlavi

in 1934), but was convinced by the British to declare himself 'Shah' despite his plebian origins, as the ulama, much more powerful in Shia Persia than in Sunni Turkey, were more likely to accept a monarchy than a republic and had to be kept onside. He proceeded to transform Iran (renamed in the 1930s, reflecting the Shah's pro-Aryan sympathies) along Kemalist lines, ordering women to discard the veil, modernizing fashions, building infrastructure.

As WWII went into high gear, the British, along with their allies of convenience, the Soviets, occupied Iran and deposed the Shah, as he had started to show signs of incipient genuine independence.[76] installing his more pliant 22-year-old son Mohammad Reza Shah Pahlavi (r. 1941–1979). The unofficial occupation of 'independent' Iran proceeded apace, as the young Shah continued the Kemalist reforms of his father. At the end of WWII, Soviet and British troops were still occupying Iran. While the British were happy to withdraw, leaving Iran now in safe hands, pro-Soviet elements tried to seize power in the Soviet-occupied north. The Soviet Union hoped that this movement would spread and bring Iran into the anti-colonial camp. The Azerbaijan People's Government and the Republic of Kurdistan were declared in late 1945 but collapsed when the Soviet forces retreated in 1946.

Just how independent these people's republics might have become under Stalin's stern guidance is a moot point. The Iranians had had enough of imperial and other intrigues. The communists (Tudeh Party) were killed, but a genuine patriotic National Front Prime Minister Mohammad Mossadeq (1882–1967) took a leaf from their book and nationalized the Anglo-Iranian Oil Company in 1951. He was overthrown in 1953 in a coup baldly orchestrated by the British and the CIA, and grudgingly supported by the conservative ulama, who disapproved of nationalism and anything that smacked of socialism. The US and Britain re-installed the now thoroughly discredited Shah junior, who dutifully continued the secularization process begun by his father, and proceeded to run Iran as an obedient, secular neocolony of the US, abandoning his father's attempt to retain a modicum of independence by playing off the imperial powers against each other.

The Shah's forced secularization culminated in the White Revolution of 1963, which proposed ambitious capitalist land reforms, using the growing oil wealth to buy land from large landowners and sell it to landless peasants. That, plus state-funded industrial development, privatization, women's suffrage and a mass literacy campaign, was intended to both sap the popularity of the ulama and undercut the Shah's leftist critics. Instead, cynicism and corruption prevailed. The land reform was mostly still-born, benefiting village chiefs, other officials and the landlords themselves. There was little trickle-down effect in terms of private investment in industry, but the reforms did succeed in radicalizing just about everyone, including the ulama, landlords, still landless peasants and a growing urban underclass, in addition to the middle class.

The respected Ayatollah Khomeini was reading from a very different map of the world, and didn't like where Iran was headed. He threw down the gauntlet, calling the Shah illegitimate, and demanding his overthrow. Demonstrations led to Khomeini's exile in Turkey and then Iraq. This explains the remarkable Islamo-socialist Third-worldism that sprang up in the 1960s, led by Ali Shariati (see Chapter 3). The open hostility of the powerful ulama to the Shah by the 1960s and this alliance of leftists and Islamists were the keys to the success of the 1979 revolution. The coincidence of the interests of the conservative ulama from 1963 on with the liberal and leftist anti-monarchists had created a momentum that even the oil revenues following the 1973 oil embargo couldn't stop. Both the pro-1906 Constitution secularists and the anti-1906 Constitution ulama joined forces against the unpopular monarch. The 'peacock' prince took his megalomania to an extreme, changing the Islamic calendar to a Persian imperial one and in 1971 celebrating 2,500 years of empire in a Disney Persepolis, with hundreds of western gliterati imported to drink champagne at government expense, a few years before his fantasy world would come crashing down, a dramatic moment that was like a clarion call to Muslims around the world: the era of secular accommodationism was coming to an end.

Afghanistan was formally recognized as 'independent' by Britain in 1919, 13 years before Saudi Arabia. The irony of this Machiavellian move by the West to 'recognize' premodern absolute monarchies while carefully continuing to keep the other more advanced Muslim nations subservient should not be lost. The Soviet Union also recognized these monarchies (Afghanistan in 1919 and Saudi Arabia in 1924), but with the intention of weaning them from reliance on the imperialists (and, of course, Islam). Afghans educated in the Soviet Union, who marveled at the comparatively high standard of living of their Uzbek and Tajik cousins across the border, and the considerable Soviet aid to Afghanistan from the 1950s on, created an enthusiastic movement to overthrow the monarchy and establish socialism.

At the same time, Islam in Afghanistan was becoming politicized and militantly anticommunist under the influence of the Muslim Brotherhood and Pakistan's Jamaat i-Islami (Islamic society). Among the leaders in the 1960s were Burhanuddin Rabbani and Gulbuddin Hikmatyar. After King Zahir Shah's cousin Daoud, with the help of communists, toppled the king and established a republic in 1973, the CIA stepped up its subversion working together with Pakistan, first under Zulfikar Bhutto, later under General Zia, and with the Shah of Iran, to try to control the new Afghan government. According to Soviet archives, "Beginning in 1974, the Shah of Iran launched a determined effort to draw Kabul into the security sphere embracing India, Pakistan and Persian Gulf states" actively encouraged by the US. "SAVAK [the Shah's secret police] and the CIA worked hand-in-hand with Afghan fundamentalists, who were linked with the Brothers and the Muslim World League, while Pakistan's Inter-Services Intelligence (ISI) helped coordinate raids on Afghanistan."[77] Now Afghanistan's President Daoud, under pressure from the US, Iran and Pakistan, began to tilt to the right, met the Shah and Bhutto, and started installing rightwing officers in key posts. His power base was reduced to a small ultraconservative clique, with the real power behind the scene wielded by SAVAK, the Brotherhood, and the World Muslim League.

The situation became critical, and as Daoud moved closer to the US, in April 1978, Nur Muhammad Taraki (r. 1978–1979) staged a leftwing coup and appealed to the Soviet Union for support. Following the coup (reluctantly supported by a Soviet Union now pursuing detente with the US), it became the only socialist state in the Muslim world (apart from south Yemen). This proved to be a tragedy for all concerned—except the US.

Zbegniew Brzezinski told *La Nouvel Observateur* in 1998 that US arms began flowing to the Islamist opposition by July 1979. But the Islamists were supported by Pakistan's ISI, the Shah and the CIA through the Safari Club much earlier, US geopolitical strategists seeing a window of opportunity where the Afghan government led by Daoud was weak and not widely supported. Events moved rapidly, as the Pakistani ISI and the US set up, trained, armed and funded a private international army which came to be called mujahideen (though there were no religious qualifications required), and launched an all-out campaign of terror, assassinating hundreds of teachers and civil servants, both Afghan and Soviet, in complete violation of Islam.

Despite the fact that the superpowers were engaging in a policy of détente and that it was in the rational interests of both sides to keep Afghanistan on a secular road of development as opposed to a militant Islamic one, the US was locked in its zero-sum game strategy against communism. It would eventually bring together communist China, Islamic Iran, Iranophobes Saudi Arabia and Egypt, and many more incongruous 'allies'. Afghanistan descended into over 30 years of brutal war which began with an alliance made in Hell, and which at the same time helped to usher in a new world political dynamic, where Islam now was center stage.

By the beginning of the twentieth century, Afghani and Abduh's reform efforts reached the Russian-occupied Muslim umma in **Crimea, the Caucasus, central Russia** and **Central Asia**, in the form of Jadidism (renewal), focusing on education. After the 1917 revolution, the Russian empire's Turkic Muslims were initially lured by the Turkish military officer Enver Pasha (1881–1922) who put forward a pan-Turkic vision,[78] though, like the Bolsheviks, he was promoting a secular vision—at best Jinnah's Muslim nationalism—that had little resonance with pious Muslims in this region, whose ties with the Turks' Ottoman Caliphate were in any case remote. The Muslim tribal leaders tentatively accepted the assurances of the communists that Islam would be allowed, despite their professed atheism (the tribal leaders had little choice), but soon Russia's Muslims were forced to assimilate into the new secular communist order. They were divided up into 'nationalities' in autonomous republics within the Soviet Union, with artificial new borders and national histories written to order, not unlike the imperialists' efforts. At least after the Stalinist repressions, they, along with the other Muslim majority 'republics' Azerbaijan and Tatarstan, became prosperous and reasonably contented members of the stern secular Soviet 'caliphate' until its collapse. The militant atheism of the Soviet Union largely dissipated, leaving Islam surviving in homes and the handful of madrasas and mosques allowed to function.

India produced important figures of Islamic thought, both liberal and traditionalist, as the umma struggled for independence along with other subject populations in the British Raj. In the footsteps of Wali Allah (see above) came the liberal Sir Sayyid Ahmed Khan (1817–1898), an employee of East India Company until the 1857 revolt, which prompted him to write *The Causes of the Indian Mutiny*—a daring critique of British policies that he blamed for causing the revolt. He continued Wali Allah's goal of educating the Indian umma; after visiting Europe in 1869, he returned to India to found the Muhammedan Anglo-Oriental College, later called the Aligarh Muslim University, modeled on Cambridge University curricula, to promote the social and economic development of Indian Muslims. Indian Muslims were soon leaders in translating the Quran into English, which now is an acceptable practice even to the strictest of Salafis.[79] He freely admitted Indian backwardness and believed that it was in the Indians' best interest to learn from the British as a pupil would from a tutor.[80]

Sayyid Khan was suspicious of the Indian independence movement and called upon Muslims to loyally serve the British Raj. He denounced secular nationalist organizations such as the Indian National Congress, instead concentrating on promoting Muslim unity, albeit a unity acceptable to the British. In Pakistan, he is hailed as the father of the Two Nations Theory and one of the founding fathers of Pakistan along with Muhammad Iqbal and Muhammad Ali Jinnah. His philosophy guided the creation of the All-India Muslim League in 1906, as a political party separate from the Congress.

The Deoband reform movement started in 1866 near Delhi, with both Sufi and orthodox influences, and began to build new madrasas studying not only Hanafi *fiqh,* but—in the new reform tradition—the Quran, hadiths and logic, eventually opening 10,000 affiliates, rivaling Azhar. The Tablighi Jamat (1926, invitation society) is associated with them but focused only on *dawa,* combining "traditional Sufi values with radical social implications. Social egalitarianism is a major value."[81] It was weakened by the 1947 partition, which it opposed,[82] and the subsequent state of war between India and Pakistan, though it is still a major force in both countries, as well as in Bangladesh, Malaysia, South Africa and the UK. Barelvis are, like the Deobandi, orthodox Sunni.

Ubaidullah Sindhi (1872–1944) was born into a Sikh family and converted to Islam early in life and enrolled in the Darul Uloom Deoband. He was involved in the pan-Islamic movement and during WWI left India to seek support of the Central Powers for a pan-Islamic revolution in India. Sindhi rallied Afghan Amir Habibullah Khan to the cause. At the end of the war, he left for Communist Russia, Turkey and finally Saudi Arabia, where he spent 14 years, considering himself a follower of Shah Wali Allah. His pan-Islamism gave way to Indian nationalism and socialism, looking to reconcile with the victors in WWII in order to allow India to advance rapidly after the war without facing active hostility by the West, calling for economic reforms to ban interest, limit property accumulation, allow small-holders, encourage cooperatives, and to promote an Asian confederation to confront imperialism. Muhammad Iqbal In contrast to Sindhi, Muhammad Iqbal (1877–1938), a Sufi poet turned political activist, began as a liberal, supporting the Indian

nationalist movement under Congress, intent on reforming Islam within a future united India, but by working with the imperialists to bring this about, counting on democracy to liberate India and allow a vigorous Islam to flower. In a tongue-in-cheek reference, he quipped, "Democracy is one aspect of our own political ideal that is being worked out in the British Empire, the greatest Muhammadan Empire in the world."[83] He also wrote in admiration of Karl Marx, Lenin and the Russian revolution: "The time of sovereignty of the masses has arrived/ Wipes away all traces of ancient law and customs."[84]

As his disappointment with British schemes grew and he realized his vision was flawed, placing him in the camp with assimilationists, Iqbal went from Indian nationalist to pan-Islamist. "The West had elevated progress at the expense of continuity; its secular individualism separated the notion of personality from God and made it idolatrous and potentially demonic."[85] At the Pakistan Conference in 1931, he stated: "The biggest blunder made by Europe was the separation of Church and State. This deprived their culture of moral soul and diverted it to atheistic materialism."[86] He realized that secularism and nationalism in an imperial world order would only lead to militarism and war.

Although Iqbal was a founder along with Jinnah of the Muslim League, he was not impressed with Jinnah's secular vision of a future Pakistan. In a speech to the Muslim League in 1930, he called only for the "creation of a Muslim India within India".[87] He came to see Europe as a collection of mutually intolerant democracies whose sole function was to exploit the poor in the interest of the rich.

> Europe today is the greatest hindrance in the way of man's
> ethical advancement. The Muslim, on the other hand, is in
> possession of these ultimate ideas on the basis of a revelation,
> which, speaking from the inmost depths of life, internalizes
> its own apparent externality … Early Muslims emerging
> out of the spiritual slavery of pre-Islamic Asia were not in
> a position to realize the true significance of this basic idea.
> Let the Muslim of today appreciate his position, reconstruct
> his social life in the light of ultimate principles, and evolve,

> out of the hitherto partially revealed purpose of Islam, that spiritual democracy which is the ultimate aim of Islam. ... Eventually the community that is more truly divinely rooted must take over again and restore balance in the development. Islam is the enduring resource of an evolving historical community, constantly to be worked out anew in detail, yet retaining its integrity in richly historical terms.[88]

Some form of caliphate was essential to unite the world's Muslims, but it would require Islamic states based on a thoroughly reformed and dynamic sharia, since every generation has to rethink Islamic law to fit its changing circumstances. He was disillusioned by the religious scholars whom he described as "absolutely incapable of receiving any fresh inspiration from modern thought and experience."[89]

The imperialists decided that partition and 'independent' Muslim- and Hindu-based states in the Raj best served their interests. The British handed power to the secular Muslim League leader Jinnah, seeing the Muslims as conservative and less likely in the post-WWII era to side with the Soviet Union because of its atheism. A united socialist India, next door to the Soviet Union and communist China, was a terrifying prospect to the British and Americans.

Just as the support for the Saudi Wahhabis and attempts to manipulate Islamists against leftists (see below) was a wild gamble by the imperialists, this support by the imperialists for the creation of a state whose sole justification lay in religion, Islam, was equally fateful. The sympathy of British leaders for the Muslim League parallels their sympathy for the Zionists, who loudly supported the British in WWII, eager to snatch a Jewish state from the British mandate of Palestine. The Arabs—like Congress in India—were hostile towards their imperial master, and both the Arabs and Hindu nationalists (and many devout Muslim Indians) to some extent supported Germany as the 'lesser of two evils'. Both the (secular) 'Muslim nationalists' in India and the (secular) 'Jewish nationalists' in Palestine and Europe used a desperate British imperialism on its last legs to get their otherwise unattainable goals, goals which conveniently served the long term imperial interests, but had little to do with reviving Islamic civilization or genuine Judaism.

The partition of India left up to 2 million dead and 11 million refugees, transforming the once peaceful, united South Asian subcontinent into a weak, divided one plagued by unending ethnic and religious conflict. The Muslim population in India fell from 30% to 14%, and the majority of those who stayed more or less joined the untouchables (Dalits) at the bottom of the economic hierarchy. Effectively, the project divided the largest community of the world umma, and fatally weakened the movement of Islamic revival in the Indian subcontinent.

Abul Kalam Azad (1888–1958) was a political leader of the Indian independence movement, the most prominent Muslim leader who opposed the partition of India, because he thought Muslims would be more powerful in a united India. He established an Urdu weekly newspaper in 1912, *Al-Hilal* (soon banned), and openly attacked British policies, encouraging young Muslims to fight for independence and Hindu-Muslim unity. His work helped improve the relationship between Hindus and Muslims in Bengal, which had soured due to the controversy surrounding the British partition of Bengal and the issue of separate communal electorates. He was imprisoned until 1920, and became leader of the Khilafat movement, allied with Gandhi, supporting Gandhi's nonviolent civil disobedience and policy of promoting small-scale indigenous production. In 1923, at an age of 35, he became president of the Indian National Congress, promoting Hindu-Muslim unity, secularism and socialism. Azad served as Congress president from 1940–1945, during which the Quit India rebellion was launched, and he was imprisoned again along with the entire Congress leadership for three years. After independence, he served as India's education minister and was responsible for a rapid expansion of literacy and higher education.

Pakistan was founded by the avowed secularist Muhammad Ali Jinnah (r. 1947–1948),[90] who was noted for his love of western suits and lack of religious fervor. A weak, westernized Pakistan was manipulated by both

the departing British and arriving Americans, encouraged to pursue the Kemalist strategy of top-down secular reforms and integration into the western global economy. Pakistan wouldn't have survived its early years without US financial and food aid. The horrific partition and ethnic tensions among uprooted peoples from the start did not allow the formation of a Muslim Brotherhood-type organization which could unite the country around a program of Islamic social justice. Pakistan's Muslims are a highly pluralist mix of Sunni and Shia, with large communities of Ahmadi, Bahai and others.

Though Pakistan's founder was a secularist Shia, and the largely Sunni Indian ulama were against creating a Muslim nation, the country was nonetheless billed as founded on Islam, and Islamic forces soon accepted this as a *fait accompli*; particularly, the remarkable traditionalist Islamic scholar-activist Maulana Maududi. His Jamaat i-Islami (1941, Islamic society) became the most important traditionalist Muslim organization, with a counterpart in the now hostile India, where serious Muslims increasingly suffered from the state of war between the two countries over Kashmir (see Chapter 3).

There were considerable tensions caused by Sunni-Shia differences, the deviations by Bahais and Ahmadis from standard Sunni practice, and the fact that the newly-dubbed 'Pakistanis' were thrown together under traumatic conditions and now lived for the most part in extreme poverty. The largest sect is the Ahmadi, which considers its nineteenth century founder Mirza Ghulam Ahmad (1835–1908) to be the real 'last prophet', a reincarnation of Jesus. Hundreds of its members were killed in a virtual pogrom in 1953, the subject of Judge Muhammad Munir's report on the Lahore riots that year against the Ahmadis, which tried to define apostasy[91] and how an Islamic state should be structured.[92] The report advised that given the inability of the ulama to agree on what constitutes apostasy, and the dangers of religious sectarianism, "it would be a mistake for religion and the state to mix."[93]

Nonetheless, Pakistan became an 'Islamic state' according to its 1956 constitution. Just as in Turkey in 1960, the secularist army in Pakistan (fresh from 'the playing-fields of Eton') under Field Marshal Muhammad Ayub Khan moved in 1958 to stop the drift towards Islamization. Ayub Khan's 1958 coup ushered in the first of three military juntas[94]—marginalizing the ulama, following a Kemalist strategy of secular nationalism, and promoting liberal lay Islamic scholars such as Fazlur Rahman.[95] The goal was a secular Islamic state, i.e., acceptable to both Pakistan's US sponsor and Pakistanis, who after all had sacrificed their lives in the quixotic founding of a nation state based on their Muslim identities (Pakistan being the most heterodox Muslim nation in the world).

Under this haphazard Kemalism, compounded by ethnic chauvinism, Pakistan descended into civil war in 1971, resulting in another million deaths— this time of Muslims by Muslims. Eight million Bangladeshis fled to India and 20 million were displaced.[96] This prompted India to intervene in east Pakistan, trounce the Pakistani army, and usher in a new state, Bangladesh, leaving an even more bitter legacy for what was left of Jinnah's dream state, now a humiliated pariah, with its eastern half allied with India. Animosity between India and Pakistan reached new heights over the unsolvable problem of Kashmir, a useful stand-off for the imperialists to keep socialist India off-balance and Pakistan in the imperial fold.

In a mild replay of Nasser in Egypt, Prime Minister Zulfikar Ali Bhutto (r. 1971–1977) rode the wave of secular anti-imperialism of the 1960s–1970s, marking Pakistan's most hopeful period. The civil war was mercifully over, and Bhutto moved quickly to emulate India in a more truly independent policy of economic nationalism. Land reform, nuclear energy, and economic development, with broad international help, including from the Soviet Union, gave the impression that Pakistan was coming of age. Like Jinnah, Bhutto was Shia, but carefully nonsectarian, introducing legislation to make Islam broadly the inspiration of the legal system. He probably would have patched up relations with India.

The coup against him and his execution by General Zia ul-Haq (r. 1977–1988), riding the wave of Islamic revival of the 1970s–1980s, could not have been done without US connivance. The US was not happy with the independent socialist Bhutto. Despite his professed anti-communism, he was developing peaceful relations with and taking aid from the Soviet Union. Like Nasser before him, he was too smart for his own good.

The whole chaotic history of 'independent' Pakistan left the country (now, count*ries*) a failed state, though both Pakistan/ Bangladesh and India have continued to produce Muslim intellectuals and activists, and a substantial diaspora of Asian Muslims in the West, who have their own role to play in the ongoing re-emergence of Islamic civilization around the world (see Chapter 3).

As elsewhere, the imperialists handed power over to secularists in **southeast Asia** after WWII. Indonesia and Malaysia were granted independence in the 1950s after bitter wars of liberation in which the Islamist forces played a much more important role than in north Africa and Persia, there being far less filtering of western secularism into their societies. During the **Indonesia**n war of independence, the Nahdlatul Ulama (1923, NU, renaissance scholars) declared that the fight against the Dutch colonial forces was a holy war, obligatory for all Muslims. Among the guerrilla groups fighting for independence were Hizbullah (Party of God) and Sabillilah (Path of God), which were led by the NU. The NU called for an Islamic state and sharia, and like the MB, is dedicated to helping peasants and the marginalized urban population, funding schools, hospitals, and organizing local communities (*kampungs*) into more coherent groups in order to help combat poverty. It soon became the largest Muslim organization in Indonesia (with 30 million followers today). Another traditionalist, MB-type organization, Muhammadiya, in Java (1912), focuses on Islamic education, health and zakat (with 29 million followers today).

After Indonesia was granted 'independence', NU members served in a number of cabinet posts. In 1955, Indonesia held its first parliamentary elections in which the NU was third as part of the coalition Masyumi, behind Sukarno's Indonesian National Party. In 1958, some Masyumi members joined a rebellion against Sukarno, and, along with the Socialist Party, Masyumi was banned in 1960. After Suharto's coup deposing Sukarno in 1965, swept up in the anti-communist hysteria of the times, both NU and Muhammadiyah joined other Muslim groups to declare that the extermination of the "Gestapu/PKI" (the 30 September Movement and the Indonesian Communist Party) constituted holy war, and Muslim militants joined the killing spree of leftists unleashed by Suharto, a prelude to Afghanistan 1979.[97]

During Suharto's 33-year dictatorship, he tried to control and co-opt the Islamists, forcing all Islamic parties to unite under one government-supervised Islamist party, the Partai Persatuan Pembangunan (1971, Party for Unity and Development). In turning to the Islamists in his campaign to destroy his socialist enemies in the 1960s and then uniting his Islamist opponents, Indonesian General Suharto laid the foundations for a rapid revival of Islam.

In **Malaysia**, there were several Islamic journals modeled on Abduh's *al-Manar,* and by 1923, students at Azhar University in Egypt founded the Indonesia-Malaya Convention. The imperialists were more worried about the communists, who conducted a strong insurgency leading up to independence in 1957, when the British handed over power to the United Malaysia National Organization (UMNO), the main political party in the National Front (a coalition of three parties representing Malays, Chinese, Indians), which has governed Malaysia ever since. UMNO from the start represented the interests of the Malays and Muslims.

Malaysia, traditionally ruled by Muslim sultans (there are nine sultanates in the federation), was particularly affected by the Dutch/ British imperial policy of importing non-Muslim Indian and Chinese labor. By 1940 in British/ Dutch-controlled Malay territories only 50% of the population was Malay, with 38% Chinese, 11% Indian. The plight of the Malays, who were becoming a minority in their own country led to ethnic/ religious tensions (a Malay is defined in the constitution as a Muslim) which exploded in riots in 1969. This pushed the government to introduce policies to protect the Malays' slim majority. The New Economic Policy of the National Front, where Muslims played the leading role, instituted reforms which increased the share of the national wealth held by Malays from 2% (Chinese 25%, foreigners 73%) to 20% (1990). This both worked against the rise of militant Islam and at the same time contributed to the revival of Islam within the system as a defining element in Malay identity.

The **Philippines** was in the processing of becoming Muslim when the Spanish seized it in the sixteenth century and converted most natives forcibly to Christianity. The remote Mindanao natives in the south (10% of the population, 9 million) were not so easily cowed, but the US occupiers (1900–1946), and governments after 'independence' in 1946, paid Christians from the north to settle in Mindanao, providing land and services to them alone, leading to the rise of a separatist movement, the Moro National Liberation Front (MNLF).

The imperialist occupations of the Muslim world, from Morocco and Algeria, to Egypt, India and on to southeast Asia, did their level best to bury Islam, but they were in fact directly responsible for the rise of vigorous Islamic movements, whether traditionalist or militant, intent on wresting back real sovereignty—based on Islam.

***

APPENDIX A
Calls for an Islamic Reformation

Analysts talk of the ongoing reform process as an Islamic Reformation, conjuring up the specter of Martin Luther, contending that:

- Islam needs both a Reformation and an Enlightenment, "a great leap from the Middle Ages into postmodernity".[98]
- "Islam is being reconstituted as profoundly as western Christianity was during the Protestant Reformation. ... The Reformation triggered a period of religious violence among Christians that lasted for two centuries until the secular forces of the Enlightenment ushered in the age of religious toleration that the West takes for granted today."[99]
- "The latter half of the twentieth century was a time of change as profound for the Muslim world as the Protestant Reformation was for Christendom. Like the printing press in the sixteenth century, the combination of mass education and mass communications is transforming this world."[100]

Such a comparison is misleading—superficial at best, or at worst, wrong, as it implies not a dialogue with modernity, but a monologue by modernity addressed to Islam, that it is Islam that is the problem rather than modernity. Islam was in fact the 'reformation' of Christianity. (See Chapter 1 Early relations between Europe and the Muslim world) The call for a reformation today is really intended to send Islam down the road that Luther's movement *led* to: western-style secularism. Certainly, the advantages of western modernity, especially mass literacy and much of the technology, must and will be incorporated into Islamic civilization. Sharia must meet the goals (*maqasid*) of contemporary Islamic society.

The Protestant Reformation was to end priestly intercession with God. Islam already rejected such a notion. Right from the start, the Sunni and Shia variants of religious experience provided the two religious approaches—direct communion with God (Sunni) vs priestly intercession via the imams and ulama (Shia), though without the pretenses of Catholicism and papal infallibility. Protestant reformers were in fact intolerant and even fanatical, enforcing narrow puritanical views: no working on the Sabbath, no dancing or music, no theater or art.

If there is any comparison, it is between the early Protestants and the Wahhabis, with their rejection of "the authority of clerics and their ancient institutions in favor of direct access to religious texts, and a vigilant and self-policing community of true believers"[101] and their fixation on pietism and quietism, separated from the Medinan message of the activist role of Islam in the world. The concern with appearances—maintaining formal religious practice while stripping it and religious discourse of the deeper dimensions of its meaning—lends itself to ignoring the more important message in the Quran about morality.

The Islamic traditionalists of today are similar to the Catholics of the Middle Ages but without an authoritarian worldly hierarchy and the mind-numbing theology of the Trinity, or the flagrant corruption of the religious establishment in the Middle Ages which provoked the Reformation. And the Islamic establishment includes the vital Sufi movement concerned with the transcendent, mystical inner experience, absent or repressed for the most part in Christianity, both Catholic and Protestant.

Council on Foreign Relations member Vali Nasr hits the nail: "What the West really wants is not Islamic Protestantism but the kind of liberal rethinking that swept the Catholic world in the latter part of the twentieth century, producing Christian Democratic parties and the agenda of the Second Vatican Council."[102] Vatican II was Catholicism's reply to modernity and accommodated Catholicism, presided over by Popes John Paul II and Benedict XVI, to the imperialist order.

In order to understand the very different path that Islam has taken and will no doubt continue to take, it is necessary to distinguish between the spiritual and mundane, where Sufis, Wahhabis and academics remain aloof from the 'real world', and more politically-committed Muslims focus on social activism as their path to realizing Islam, which after all is a way-of-life religion.[103] Islamic activists seek to adapt the Islamic program to the current historical context, but do not deny or pretend to substitute their work for the beauty of the religious experience, which remains the 'same' as it was throughout Islam's history, a timeless experience, which nonetheless requires a social reality which is conducive to it.

Ultimately, the pursuit of this higher level of religious experience is what Islamic civilization is all about, and it is for the benefit all humanity. The degradation of this inner religious experience is the bitter fruit of western domination of the Muslim world. But then that goes for the inner spiritual experience of Muslims and non-Muslims alike in the age of empire.

The term "Islamic renaissance" is less transparent, as nahda (renaissance) is used by the Muslim Brotherhood in both Tunisia and Egypt and by other traditionalist figures to conjure up the idea of rebirth of Islamic civilization, which does not necessarily imply caving in to the western agenda, but on the contrary, forging a contemporary Islam based on scholarship and politico-economic activism. Comparison with the European Renaissance is misguided as this was actually "a rebirth of the paganism which Christianity had supplanted, and it was the source of that very 'decadence' which Muslims perceive in western life and thought." It ultimately undermined Christianity, and "forces and ideologies which destroyed one religion may as easily destroy another."[104]

APPENDIX B
Contemporary Secularists/ Nationalists and Islam

The second half of the twentieth century witnessed both the continued decline of the ulama and the emergence of secular Muslim intellectuals who dared to practice *ijtihad*, critiquing the Quran, dismissing some or all hadiths. There are many Arab nationals at European and American universities, who earn their daily bread by advocating assimilationist ideology based on western Enlightenment thinking, working alongside western Orientalist scholars.

Hans Kung (b. 1928), a noted European theologian and revisionist Catholic, clearly inspired by the post-911 anti-Muslim hysteria, addressed the issue of reform of Islam in his ambitious *Islam: Past, Present and Future* (2004). He is confident that

> Islamic law should and would change in the future to meet the challenge of human rights, gender equality, and the rights of minorities, by developing a new ethical framework of rights and responsibilities ... Muslim politics will acquire 'secularity' without totally embracing secularism, and Islamic economics, including the banking system, will evolve further as a major system of commerce based on ethical principles.[105]

His "postmodern polycentric paradigm" sees today's world as one of "political, economic and cultural understanding, co-operation and integration laid down in the UN Charter and at its most advanced in the framework of the European Union. In the long run, peace and freedom can be built up only on the basis of constitutional states, tolerance, human rights, and ethical standards."[106]

This confuses what *should be* with what *is*. An appropriate paradigm for today's world is not "political, economic and cultural understanding, co-operation and integration" but, at best, a secular socio-political life governed by capitalism, with religion playing a subservient, nonessential role *a la* Christianity/ Judaism. At worst, a terminal 'clash of civilizations'. Kung leaves no room for Islam's sacralization of history, claiming that the differences between Islam and the West are more apparent than real, and that the religious divide between Islam and the other two Abrahamic faiths can be readily bridged: all religions are "in transition from the crisis of modernity into a 'postmodernity' of some kind and exposed to the same kind of structural problems."[107]

Kung provides a sympathetic overview of Islamic history and thought, and recognizes both imperialism and Christianity, as compromised by its association with imperialism, as problematic: the West is confronted by Islam as the heir to Christianity, "which as a consequence of its compromise with colonialism and imperialism and the social development towards individualism and secularism, has lost its credibility in southern lands." This is responsible for the "re-Islamization of Muslim states, the intensification of the Muslim mission in Africa and Asia, and migration and activation of Muslim minorities in West".[108]

He rejects the notion of "value-free science, where there is growing awareness of social morality and constructive revaluation of religion as a social force". He admits that

> the price that the West had to pay for the differentiation of society and the epoch-making change in values and norms in the society of late modernity associated with it was a high one: the other spheres of life were left with no religious and indeed largely also with no moral basis and ultimate horizon of meaning.[109]

He acknowledges that "human dignity includes both rights and responsibilities,"[110] that we lost our pre-Enlightenment commitment to human obligations to God/ ruler/ parents, when 'human rights' became an Enlightenment fetish for political theorists and an instrument of US foreign policy. Moreover, he admits that "Islamic renewal is attempting to create a new basis for economics, culture and science through belief in the one God (*tawhid*) in submission (*islam*) to his will by observing his commandments." As a revisionist Catholic, he approves of the fact that there is no infallibility of a semi-divine pope, and realizes that the push for sharia law, for example in northern Nigeria, was perfectly logical for the locals, as the alternative western-inspired legal system favored the powerful and rich, and as such was fundamentally unjust, that sharia, universal law for rich and poor, was more just. All this sounds like the words of a 'revert'.[111]

Yet Kung rejects the notion that Islam's claims in this regard make it different than Judaism or Christianity, that perhaps it is Islam's role today to bring all this about. He effectively calls for the Muslim world to bow down to Enlightenment thought (and imperialism)—the real 'paradigm'—in the naïve hope that the imperialists will also embrace his rosy worldview and start acting responsibly towards the periphery and to Nature. While Kung does not directly call for assimilation (no one does who wishes to be taken seriously), his recommendations would result in the Islamic world joining the West in a junior role, given the hegemony of western imperialism.

Akbar Ahmed (b. 1941) has written extensively about Islamic reform from a liberal perspective. Originally from Pakistan, he is a professor at American University and fellow at the Brookings Institute's Saban Center for Middle East Policy, which is funded by Haim Saban, a Zionist Israeli originally from Egypt. He is regularly interviewed by CNN, CBS, BBC, and Fox News, called "America's most celebrated and leading Islamic scholar" and "the greatest scholar of Islam in America and the world."[112] He is a solid liberal, seeing no contradiction between complete economic integration within imperialism and keeping true to Islam. His popular classification of Muslims as (Sufi) Ajmer, (traditionalist) Deoband and (liberal) Aligarh is critiqued above.

Ahmed traveled across the Muslim world following 911, surveying Muslim world opinion, and was shocked to find that everywhere, his traditionalist Deobandis were now the most popular movement, even among liberal Aligarh students in India, that they had been radicalized by the Islamophobia they face in a largely Hindu India, and looked favorably at Islamist militancy. He came to respect the Deobandis due to their "assertive action in defending, preserving and transmitting Islamic tradition and identity".

However, apart from the confusion of lumping Bin Laden together with Egypt's President Mohamed Morsi as Deobandis, it's not possible to slot reformers into one or the other of his category. Abduh and the Iranian Shahs, "genuine democrats and military dictators" are night and day. Ahmed exposes the weakness of his slots when he calls Tariq Ramadan "a Deoband in Aligarh clothes" and Yusuf Islam (Cat Stevens) an "Ajmer in Deoband clothes". But any vigorous intellect encompasses all three aspects of Islam to some degree. Hence, many reformers have moved from being more liberal to more traditionalist as a result of experience, and many traditionalist political activists (e.g., Banna) have Sufi origins, since a selfless, heightened sense of spirituality is a necessary trait of someone willing to devote his life to realizing his vision of Islam. And changing one's views over time, in light of experience and personal growth, does not necessarily indicate cravenness, but can show courage and wisdom.

Ahmed recognizes as much when he argues that Ghazali and others "have sought to reconcile the three models ... Their works offering a balance between mysticism, faith, and rationality. Iqbal expressed admiration for the thirteenth century Rumi but his poems embody the Deoband worldview."

> The Prophet's popularity reflects both the paradox and strength of Islam: the Ajmer mystics will sing songs of love for the Prophet and trace their spiritual lineage directly to him; the orthodox Deoband will hold him up as their ultimate exemplar, imitating him; the Aligarh modernist will cite him proudly as the original revolutionary of history, who gave rights to women, minorities and the disenfranchised.[113]

Yet, rather than following Ghazali's lead, the Saban Institute scholar concludes that the Ajmer model embodies "pluralism and acceptance of others, perhaps the only one that can lead Muslims out of the ethnic, religious, and political conflicts that globalization has thrust on them and that they continue to ignore at their peril."[114]

Among Iranian émigrés, the best know liberal Islamic scholar is **Abdolkarim Soroush** (b. 1945), listed among the Council on Foreign Relations *Foreign Policy* magazine's top ten world intellectuals. He is probably the most influential critic of the Iranian revolution today. He has come a long way. Before the revolution, he was a dissident. After the revolution, Soroush returned to Iran and was appointed by Khomeini to the Cultural Revolution Institute which, during the 1980–1983 cultural revolution, presided over the Islamization of universities. In 1983, he became a researcher at the Institute for Cultural Research and Studies. In the 1990s, he became critical of the political role played by the Iranian clergy, calling for the separation of religion and politics and founding the journal *Kiyan* which was shut down in 1998. He then moved to the US to teach at Harvard and Yale.

Soroush now argues that "religion need not be changed, but rather the human understanding of it."[115] Although he speaks of "religious democracy", he is associated with the concept of "postmodern Islam" (elsewhere, simply post-Islam) which rejects the "notion of Islamic methods of governance" insisting on representative electoral government as the only one compatible with Islam. "There should be general consent of the governed behind even the sharia law."[116]

Much as Afghani saw Islam as a means of social control, Soroush argues that political Islam becomes an ideology (a "social and political instrument used to determine and direct public behavior"),[117] and that "to transform religion into an ideology is to cast it in a definitive, unchanging mold." "The permanence of religion is now ascribed to the religious ideology" and undermines the "imperative of political struggle given changing historical conditions" crippling pursuit of knowledge and the development of *fiqh* through *ijtihad*. The guiding criterion for governance must be human rights and public opinion, not the enforcing of a particular conception of religion in the first place.[118] The role of Islam in politics should be limited to advice on how to make the legal code congruent with *fiqh*. He wants to reduce the size and role of the professional ulama and cut off state support for the study of religion, warning the clerical establishment to embrace change or suffer the fate of the Catholic Church.

While accountability and some form of electoral democracy is all well and good, there is no reason why ideology can't change to meet historical changes or that religion should not have an ideological role in society. Asad argues that this is in fact Islam's strength, that Islam was the first open, ideological society, in contrast to the closed, racially or geographically limited societies of the past. And Soroush's "religious democracy" must in any case by definition be founded on concrete religious institutions.[119] Soroush's emphasis on rights and his criticism of duties as a feudal concept is resisted by critics who point out that the Enlightenment shift to rights over duties leads to secularism, that Muslims have higher duties and rights than adherents of other faiths (i.e., vicegerency, zakat, prayer, hajj).

Iran remains today the centre of debate about the future of Islam and politics. Iran's pre-eminent dissident Akbar Ganji (since 2006 living in Europe) says, "Ideologizing religion opens the way for a totalitarian system, and by its tendency toward violence, war-mongering, and restricting freedoms, it inevitably encourages secularism and apostasy."[120] There are indeed indications that this top-down Islamic state creates disillusionment, with reported mosque attendance low (Iran 30% vs Egypt and Turkey 40% and Pakistan 75%).[121] But then this is the fate of all revolutions, which eventually are worn down by outside hostility or routine.

In Britain, **Aziz al-Azmeh** (b. 1947) is a leading Arab political theorist, author of "Islamic secularism" (1993) and *Islam and Modernities* (2009). Like Kung, he defends the western Enlightenment against critics who trace the mess of today's intellectual and politic reality to that very Enlightenment. This is no surprise, as Azmeh is a secularist and Marxist, both trends solidly rooted in the Enlightenment. He argues that

> The tropes and notions of political and social thought available today [belong to] a universal repertoire ... which, though of western origin, has in the last century and a half become a universal patrimony beyond which political and social thought is inconceivable, [having] filtered through modern state structures, forms of discourse and communication, educational and legal systems, terms of political life and much more, which have become globalized, native not only to their points of origin, but worldwide.[122]

We are condemned to our brave new world and must make the best of it. Communism once provided an alternative reality to the western project but is no more. For Azmeh, the quixotic Islamist project as epitomized in Osama bin Laden types is doomed, and rightly so.

Azmeh dismisses the hypostatization or fetishism of reason, "construed as life, which is at once subject and object of knowledge" which characterizes western scholarship, but denounces the equal if opposite process of hypostatizing revelation among militant Islamists, who rightly identify the West's plans as inimical to Islam, but indulge in a "politics of nostalgia", pining for an "unsullied reality prior to the corruption of the present". True, it is impossible to return to some Golden Age that can be recaptured for all eternity. There is only the past, complex and contradictory, that can serve as a fund, a common heritage, which can be mined and built upon.

He argues that the tensions in relations between the Muslim and western worlds are the legacy of imperialism, which, like the stand-off with the communist world, is a logical consequence of the reaction to imperialism, "the offspring of modernity rather than of tradition". Further, he sees the West's liberal "multiculturalism" as the latest version of the West's policy of destroying pre-capitalist societies, which were formerly dismissed as un-cultures. Now, with large-scale immigration by former colonial subjects to the center as a reserve of cheap labor, these can be tolerated since their wings have been clipped and the notion of culture is reduced to spicy food, exotic music and clothes, and a religion which accepts the secular, neoimperial order. "Race became ethnicity, then culture; normative hierarchy and inequality gave way to representation in terms of difference; and xenophobia was in many circles replaced by xenophilia."[123]

His Marxist critique of modernity is compelling. Capitalism undermines the non-capitalist communal cultures during its imperial phase, and replaces them with secular culture centered on rationalism and commoditization. Immigrants must blend into the now multicultural culture, which, say in the case of Britain, means supporting Chelsea or United, absorbing imperial history and acknowledging the civilizing mission of the British Empire.

Azmeh laments the collapse of the socialist opposition to imperialism, arguing that the Soviet Union did not collapse, but was rather destroyed by 76 years of western subversion and attack, just as Arab attempts at socialism were attacked, with Islamists effectively operating in league with their supposed imperialist enemies. Islamic hardliners and terrorists—used to destroy the Soviet Union and publicized to give Islam a bad name—continue to be used by the imperialists today. Azmeh describes a "vicious circle of complicity" of the three protagonists he attacks, embodied in New Labour, the British National Party and Islamist ideologues. In the case of France "Jean-Marie Le Pen is an ally of Islamic fundamentalism."[124]

This critique is sound. Islamists have indeed been used by the imperialists, with the Wahhabi-inspired Saudis in first place. But ironically, it is the very separation of religion from social realities, which lies at the heart of the secular western tradition (which Azmeh recognizes as sterile in its present postmodern phase), that has allowed militant Islamists, disgusted by western materialism, to promote their utopian Golden Age social order without having to sully themselves by taking into account history and the current reality. Being excluded from politics, they can spin their fantasies, denigrating the real world to the point of blowing themselves and others up.

Azmeh is firm in his belief that Islam has no place in resolving the dilemmas posed by imperialism. He scoffs at the idea of deriving a concrete program for today's society from the Quran. He condemns attempts to find inspiration in Islam to counter the "universal project", which he labels "primitivist withdrawal to concentrate on the specific as opposed to the universal, or to cling to the idea that we might be a nation different from other nations, our essence defined wholly or partially by religion". He leaves no alternative but to submit, albeit grumbling, to the now "universal" *diktat* of western discourse, bankrupt though he argues it is. Just as bad are "former militants of the Arab left, nationalists who are disenchanted, sincere or naive, or who think they are being wily" for "giving credence to the Islamist discourse".[125] He clearly pines for his own Golden Age of socialism, though that is arguably more utopian than the dreams of Islamists.

ENDNOTES

1 Ramadan is accused of the former by traditionalist Muslims, of the latter—by western critics. See Tariq Ramadan, *Radical Reform: Islamic Ethics and Liberation*, UK: Oxford University Press, 2009, 143.

2 See Chapter 1 Appendix B: The 'Protestant' ethic, the rise of New Ageism and fundamentalism.

3 Or for that matter of communism, which also ignores the spiritual dimension. See Vali Nasr, *Forces of Fortune: The Rise of the New Muslim Middle Class and What It will Mean for Our World*, USA: Free Press, 2009, 152.

4 Gai Eaton, *Islam and the Destiny of Man*, UK: Islamic Texts Society, 1994, 25.

5 See John Esposito, *Islam and Politics*, USA: Syracuse University Press, 1984.

6 Named after the home of the Sufi Moinuddin Chishti (1141–1230).

7 Named after the reform movement founded in India in 1866. See below.

8 Named after the reform movement founded by Khan in India in the 1870s. See below.

9 Akbar Ahmed, *Journey into Islam: The Crisis of Globalization*, Washington DC: Brookings Institution Press, 2007, 37.

10 See Appendix B for a critique of Akbar Ahmed.

11 Seyyed Hossein Nasr, *Islam in the Modern World: Challenged by the West, Threatened by fundamentalism, Keeping faith with Tradition*, USA: Harper One, 2010, 2.

12 Although there were still scientific institutions such as hospitals and observatories, the artisan guilds with their transmission of morality declined, and the madrassas mostly stopped teaching *aql* sciences (rationalism, mathematics), focusing on *naql* (the transmitted, religious sciences). Seyyed Nasr criticizes the fact that in the 19th–20th centuries, the Ottoman, Qajar and Moghul 'empires' and their successors—in fact, the Muslim world as a whole—turned wholesale to western education to try to 'catch up' under pressure from colonial occupations which were reshaping their colonies to fit into the western imperial-capitalist order.

13 Karl Marx, *Introduction to a Contribution to the Critique of Hegel's Philosophy of Right* (1843).

14 Ramadan, *Radical Reform*, 23.

15 Ibid., 33.

16 The Barelvi movement was founded by **Ahmed Raza Khan Fazil-e-Barelvi** (1856–1921), who opposed labeling then-British held India *dar al-harb*, thus opposing jihad in contrast to the Deobandi who wished to begin jihad. From a quarter to a third of Pakistanis and Indians consider themselves Barelvi as opposed to Deobandi, though

Saudi funding has gone to both (in addition to the more Wahhabi Ahli Hadith) in an attempt to bring south Asian Muslims under Wahhabi influence. The Ahli Hadith reject the teachings of the Hanafi school, acknowledging only the Koran and the Sunna. The Deobandis founded Tablighi Jamaat, the largest Islamic movement in the world with headquarters in India. In the course of the Afghan wars (1979+) the Saudis recognized that the Deobandis were more influential and had a far larger presence than the Ahli Hadith in both Pakistan as well as Afghanistan. Consequently, much Saudi funding began making its way to Deobandi madrasas in Pakistan.

Syed Ahmad Shaheed (of Rae Bareli) (1786–1831), also called Syed Ahmed Barelvi, is considered the most outstanding immediate follower of Wali Allah, remembered for his jihad against the Sikhs in the Punjab. Syed Ahmad and his army were decimated in Balakot in 1831. His defeat ended the dream of establishing an Islamic state in Peshawar, now Pakistan. These orthodox followers of Wali Allah, unlike Saudi Wahhabis, accepted Sufism and features of mystical Islam such as the belief in the intercession of the saints. Syed Ahmad anticipated modern Islamists in his waging of jihad and attempt to create an Islamic state with strict enforcement of Islamic law.

17 Muhammad Asad, *The Road to Mecca*, NY: [Simon and Schuster 1954] Fons Vitae 2000, 160.

18 Vernon Egger, *A History of the Muslim World since 1260: The Making of a Global Community*, New Jersey: Pearson, 2008, 273.

19 Ibid., 275.

20 Thus it would be accurate to call the Saudis Salafis. Similarly, the Bin Ladens, though clearly a reaction to the Saudi pact with empire, might be better called Qutbians (see Chapter 3 endnote 125.). To avoid obscurity and confusion, the terms Wahhabis and neo-Wahhabis are used here.

21 "Al-Afghani was an adept of the Ishraqi mysticism of Suhrawardi at the same time as he was a passionate advocate of modernization." Karen Armstrong, *A History of God: The 4000-Year Quest of Judaism, Christianity and Islam*, New York: Alfred Knopf, 1994, 363.

22 Wilfrid Blunt, *Secret History of the English Occupation of Egypt*, A Knopf, 1922, 76.

23 Hanna Abi Rashid, *Dairat al-maarif al-Masoniyya*, Beirut, 1961.

24 Afghani is credited with instigating the tobacco boycott protesting western concessions sold by the Shah who squandered the money, forcing the Shah to rescind the concession. One of his disciples assassinated the Shah. He is also considered a liberal influence who inspired the first constitution in 1906. He is revered in both Afghanistan (he died in Istanbul and his remains were interred at the University of Kabul in a mausoleum in 1944) and Iran, where Asad Abadi Square in Tehran is named after him.

25 Egger, *A History of the Muslim World since 1260*, 345.

26 Ibid., 353.

27 Quoted in Karen Armstrong, *Islam: A Short History*, Modern Library, 2000, 153.

28 Egger, *A History of the Muslim World since 1260*, 381.

29 Marshall Hodgson, editor and introduction Edmund Burk, *Rethinking World History: Essays on Europe, Islam and World History*, Cambridge University Press, 1993, 235.

30 Karl Marx, *Theses On Feuerbach* (1888).

31 J.A. Hobson, *Imperialism: A Study*, 3d ed., London: Allen and Unwin, [1902] 1938, 361.

32 Nasr, *Islam in the Modern World*, 85–86.

33 In 1943 available at <albaath.online.fr/English/Aflaq-040on%20heritage.htm>.

34 Nasr, *Islam in the Modern World*, 33.

35 Egger, *A History of the Muslim World since 1260*, 432.

36 "The western equation *secularization = freedom = religious pluralism = democracy* has no equivalent in Muslim-majority societies where, through the historical experiences of the past century, the equation has tended to associate other representations that would rather sound like: *secularization = colonialism = de-Islamization = dictatorship*." Ramadan, *Radical Reform*, 265.

37 Eric Walberg, *Postmodern Imperialism: Geopolitics and the Great Games*, USA:

Clarity Press, 2011, 73.

38   M. Moaddel, *Islamic Modernism, Nationalism and Fundamentalism: Episode and Discourse,* USA: University of Chicago Press, 2005, 339.

39   Ibid., 341.

40   Seyyed Hossein Nasr, "Islam and Modern Science", Georgetown University lecture.

41   Ibid.

42   See Walberg, *Postmodern Imperialism.*

43   30–40% of members were Muslim; Jews and Christians the majority members.

44   Armenians in Istanbul and other cities prospered; those living in traditional Armenian lands suffered (alongside the settled Muslim population) raids by nomadic Kurdish tribes. In 1839, the situation improved with the Tanzimat reforms. However, Sultan Abdulhamid II instigated a brutal crackdown in 1895 after a failed Armenian attempt to assassinate him.

45   Iran did so a year later.

46   Vali Nasr, *Forces of Fortune,* 242.

47   Prime Minister Adnan Menderes was executed for treason the next year.

48   Islam had suddenly become fashionable in Washington.

49   Amstrong, *A History of God,* 360. In his 24 years governing Egypt, Cromer never learned to read or speak Arabic. This colonial racism has been inculcated by many Egyptians. Mubarak's Prime Minister Nazif told US Ambassador Scobey in 2010 that the problem with instituting democracy in Egypt was the fact that the opposition didn't understand English.

50   Azzam Tamini, "The Origins of Islamic Secularism", in John Esposito, *Islam and Secularism in the Middle East,* USA: NYU Press, 2000, 18.

51   They had employed a similar tactic against Egyptian nationalist leader Ahmed Urabi in 1882, whom they exiled to Ceylon.

52   Moaddel, *Islamic Modernism, Nationalism and Fundamentalism,* 209.

53   Mehran Kamrava (ed.), *The New Voices of Islam: Rethinking Politics and Modernity, A Reader,* LA: University of California Press, 2006, 168. Re Zayd, see Chapter 5 endnote 32.

54   See Walberg, *Postmodern Imperialism,* endnote 91, 225.

55   The British introduced Mixed Courts in 1876 for foreign interests and then National Courts 1883 with jurisdiction over civilian and criminal cases involving Egyptians, restricting sharia courts to personal status matters, such as marriage, divorce, inheritance.

56   Gamal Abdel-Nasser, *Filsafa al-thawra (Philosophy of the Revolution),* Cairo: Madbouli, [1955] 2005, 80–82.

57   Tarek Osman, *Egypt on the Brink,* USA: Yale University Press, 2010, 42.

58   Ibid., 44, 64.

59   Hani Shukrallah and Hosny Guindy, "Liberating Nasser's legacy", *Al-Ahram Weekly.* 4 November 2000.

60   This is starkly shown in Syria today, where a post-Assad government will be dominated by Islamists, despite the role of the West in supporting the opposition. Ethnic Alawi Hafez al-Assad (r. 1971–1990) followed by his son Bashar do not have the backing of the broad Arab population, and from the start of the Assad reign, have been opposed by a complex combination of Islamists, secular Arabs and Kurds, now openly backed by the West.

61   Alison Pargeter, *Muslim Brotherhood, 2010: The burden of tradition,* London: Saqi, 2010, 65.

62   See Irfan Ahmad, "How the West de-democratised the Middle East", *informationclearinghouse.info,* 2012.

63   It was, after all, the nominally Christian Europeans who had persecuted the Jews, and the plan to establish Israel had nothing to do with religion in any case, as explained in Chapter 1.

64   The French openly allowed Israelis to train with French Algerian troops in the 1950s. This led to a deterioration of the situation of Algerian Jews, whose ancestors had

fought beside their Muslim brothers in the army of Abd al-Qadir against the French in the nineteenth century.

65 Moaddel, *Islamic Modernism, Nationalism and Fundamentalism,* 268, 272.

66 Ibid., 276.

67 Predominantly Christian South Sudan became an independent state in 2011, but armed conflict between north and south, and within north and within south, continues.

68 Egger, *A History of the Muslim World since 1260,* 274.

69 Asad, *The Road to Mecca,* 160.

70 Charles Freeman, a veteran US foreign service officer and ambassador to Saudi Arabia, stated, "Faisal made a deliberate decision that Islam was the antidote to Nasser."

71 See Nasr, *Islam in the Modern World.*

72 Whose role model was Stalin.

73 His worst act of murder was of the great Shia thinker Mohammad Baqir al-Sadr.

74 Hussein violated the imperial map—literally.

75 That said, he conducted himself with dignity during his trial, and died honorably as a Muslim with the Kalima (There is no god but God, and Muhammad is his messenger) as his last words, irrespective of those who taunted him as he died. Saddam Hussein's situation tragically epitomized the ideological clash between Islam and Arab nationalism.

76 Reza Shah Pahlavi had demanded a bigger share from the British-owned Anglo-Iranian Oil Company revenues, and by 1939, 50% of Iran's trade was with Germany.

77 Diego Cordovez and Selig Harrison, *Out of Afghanistan: The Inside Story of the Soviet Withdrawal,* Oxford: Oxford University Press, 1995, 16, 19, 23.

78 One of CUP secular Turks, Enver Pasha went to Moscow after the war and convinced Lenin to let him unite the Turkic peoples of the new communist Russia. When it became clear to the Bolsheviks that the wily Turk was hoping the Bolsheviks would fall and leave the Turkic peoples to the new Turkey, they killed him.

79 In the introduction to his 1912 translation, the first into English by a Muslim, Mirza Dehlawi writes he was motivated consciously by a desire to give "a complete and exhaustive reply to the manifold criticisms of the Koran by various Christian authors such as Drs Sale, Rodwell, and Sir W. Muir." See Eric Walberg, "The Quran in translation: Reading Islam's holy book", *Al-Ahram Weekly,* 20 September 2007.

80 Egger, *A History of the Muslim World since 1260,* 343. Traditionalist Deobandis, Ahli-Hadith and Barelvis all bitterly criticize 'Sir' Khan for working so closely with the British.

81 Ibid., 399.

82 No doubt envisioning an eventual revival of Islam across the subcontinent to replace the British Empire.

83 Available at <http://ikdasar.tripod.com/sa_2000/renaissance/Iqbal/esposito.htm>.

84 Sohrab Behdad and Farhad Nomani (eds), *Islam and the Everyday World: Public policy dilemmas,* New York: Routledge, 2006, 16.

85 Armstrong, *Islam,* 155.

86 Muhammad Munawwar, "Iqbal—Man of Faith and Vision", *allamaiqbal.com,* October 1982. available at <http://www.allamaiqbal.com/publications/journals/review/oct82/1.htm>.

87 Egger, *A History of the Muslim World since 1260,* 388.

88 Muhammad Iqbal, *Reconstruction of Religious Thought in Islam,* 1930.

89 Ibid., 16.

90 He was appointed governor general by the departing British.

91 The ulama could not agree on a definition but were unanimous in agreeing that it should be punished by death.

92 They couldn't agree on that either, despite an impressive Quranic exegesis on politics prepared for the new state by Muhammad Asad (See Chapter 1).

93 Egger, *A History of the Muslim World since 1260,* 435. The Ahmadi were declared to not even be officially Muslim by (secular) Prime Minister Zulfikar Bhutto in the 1973 constitution, barred from serving in the army or government and not allowed to

perform the hajj in 1975.

94   The departing British in 1947 bequeathed the two Pakistans half the large Indian Army, giving 'independent' India the other half.

95   He was condemned by the ulama and went into exile at the University of Chicago in 1969.

96   Egger, *A History of the Muslim World since 1260,* 435.

97   A Truth and Reconciliation Commission set up by the parliament after the fall of Suharto was struck down by the High Court, and textbooks introduced in 2004 which dealt with the massacre were withdrawn after complaints by the military and Muslim leaders in 2006.

98   Hans Kung, *Islam: Past, Present and Future,* UK: Oneworld, 2004, 575.

99   Egger, *A History of the Muslim World since 1260,* 496-497.

100   Dale Eickelman, "Inside the Islamic reformation", in Mehran Kamrava, *The New Voices of Islam,* 21.

101   Vali Nasr, *Forces of Fortune,* 185.

102   Ibid., 185.

103   In contrast, there are few Catholic activists who struggle to make Catholicism relevant to western society, and even fewer Protestant ones, except for the fundamentalists.

104   Gai Eaton, *Islam and the Destiny of Man,* UK: Islamic Texts Society, 1994, 25.

105   Available at <http://thebrowser.com/interviews/ziauddin-sardar-on-future-islam>.

106   Kung, *Islam,* 541, xxv.

107   Ibid., 22.

108   Ibid., 542.

109   Ibid., 649–650.

110   Ibid., 575.

111   Muslims consider all people are born Muslim and that people of other faiths who convert to Islam are thus reverting to their original faith.

112   The former by BBC, the latter by American Professor Stanley Wolpert.

113   Ibid., 38–39.

114   Ibid., 40.

115   Esposito, *Makers of Contemporary Islam,* 153.

116   Abdolkarim Soroush and Charles Butterworth, "Islam and Democracy", Middle East Institute, 21 November 2000. <www.drsoroush.com>.

117   Esposito, *Makers of Contemporary Islam,* 156.

118   Ibid., 161.

119   Ibid., 163.

120   Ibid., 87.

121   World Value Surveys, *worldvaluesurveys.org,* 2003.

122   Aziz Azmeh, *Islam and Modernities,* UK: Verso [1996] 2009, 33.

123   Ibid., 5.

124   Ibid., 75.

125   Ibid., 76.

CHAPTER THREE

THE THEORY OF
ISLAMIC RENEWAL

The main threat—and stimulus—to a renewed Islamic civilization came and continues to come from outside. The geopolitical 'games' that were played out in the Middle East meant that both the imperialist West and the communist East were hostile towards Islam and either dismissed it as a reactionary force or tried to tame it and manipulate Islamists to further their own ends. The post-communist game now being played—Great Game III[1]—continues this strategy with some important differences.[2]

But for Muslims looking to Islam as the structuring principle for their societies (as opposed to secular capitalism or socialism) the enemy has come from within as well:

1. From accommodationists and nationalists who were happy to set aside or even dump Islam, accepting a system where a comprador elite is nurtured and carries out the empire's wishes once-removed, unaware of the implications of close cooperation with the imperialists. The "Islamic modernists" or Aligarhs in Chapter 2 were easy prey to the incessant pressure of assimilation during the colonial occupation. Thinkers such as Iqbal and Rida came to rue their early infatuation with reform and adjusted their policy prescriptions. Yet it is unfair to unilaterally condemn westernizers in the Muslim world, as they often are playing their own 'game' in pursuit of independence for their nations, appealing to the *de facto* rulers in order to gain power for themselves. Just how they use that power is another matter. Not all were/are Mubaraks.[3]

2. From the conservative ulama, which had retreated into *taqlid* when confronted with the secularism of western imperialism. Thinkers

from accommodationists to revolutionaries, from Qasim Amin and Raziq to Sayyid Qutb, were dismissed from Azhar or their works proscribed. Saudi Arabia's Wahhabis have compromised Islam as a religion, both directly through collaboration, and indirectly through the creation of a sterile culture unable to go beyond the imperial order.

> Rather than being a genuine revival of Islam, they are in reality the other side of the coin of modernism, but of a much more dangerous kind than the earlier forms of puritanical reformism, because these new forms of 'fundamentalism' make use of the language and certain popular symbols of the Islamic religion while adopting some of the most negative and spiritually devastating aspects of the modern West ... They close the door to all intellectual efforts ... and adopt an exclusivism opposed to other religions at a time when accord between religions is so much needed.[4]

Islam's traditional tolerance is replaced by intolerance.

3. From the 1970s, terrorists—neo-Wahhabis—who use violence to provoke the imperialists in the hope of sparking revolutionary war. The bitter fruits (for us all) of the imperial games were/are reaped in the War on Terror, which has directly targeted Islamists, lumping them with terrorists[5] who, in the case of al-Qaeda, had been enthusiastically promoted, trained and armed by the US and others in pursuit of the destruction of the Soviet Union, and who serve the empire as a negative example.

The main battle now is "between traditional Islam and various countertraditional ideologies parading as Islam ... The central problem will be the subversion of Islam from within by forces claiming to speak in its name."[6] Both the accommodationists and neo-Wahhabis treat Islam as just another ideology useful for achieving power and regulating society, rather than as a way of life that encompasses both means and ends.

In this context, the "political spirituality" which infused the Arab Spring quickly made it an Islamic awakening, as Muslims began to shake off their comprador nationalist elites and challenge both their western political masters and timid conservative ulama, putting the question of how to put Islam into action at the top of the agenda. A more literate population, armed with the internet, has allowed greater discussion and sharing of history and new ideas. The possibility that Muslims can supplement the orthodox ulama with a literate popular discussion of how to bring Islam back to the center of political and economic life is now becoming a reality.

Though on the one hand inspiring accommodationists, who sought to reduce Islam to a means of social control, Afghani and Abduh also inspired others who aim to find and preserve the true core of Islam, to reconstruct the Islamic map to guide the world towards a peaceful, socially just society based on the Quran. To undertake the journey from postmodernism to postsecularism requires using *maqasid* theory to begin *ijtihad*, to determine which aspects of modernity are compatible with the Quran and how to proceed to build an alternative world.

There are reformers on the left, such as Shariati and Hassan Hanafi; and on the right, the Muslim Brotherhoods, Iran's Fadaian-e Islam and Pakistan's Jamaat i-Islami. But left/ right are not so useful: Qutb started out advocating an Islamic socialism but turned against Nasser's personal version of socialism toward the overthrow of the existing (socialist) order with a highly utopian vision of his own. On the 'right', Maududi believed that "the Islamic Movement ... has to change the whole pattern of living: it has to change the politics, ethics, economics and the civilization of the world."[7]

The major twentieth century reform thinkers considered here (Banna, Rida, Qutb, Maududi, Khomeini among others) all were motivated by a deep anger at the ravages of colonialism, the apparent success of the Zionist colonial project, and anger over the suppression of Islam by Kemalist/ colonial governments. In one way or another, they advocated the revival of sharia law and creation of an Islamic state in response to the modern secular laws and nation states imposed on them. Like the earlier notion of the caliphate, the modern Islamic state is modeled after the rule of Muhammad and rooted in Islamic law.

But the twentieth century experience of 'Islamic states' and attempts to return to the sharia traditions prior to imperialism have been disappointing, and this shibboleth requires reconsideration in light of twentieth century experience. Turkey's militant secularism, enforced by military coups and disruption of civilian rule since 1960, convinced the Islamists to soft-pedal their demands. Egypt's MB has denied any interest in declaring Egypt an Islamic state. Among governments in power, only the Saudis and Iranians seriously persist in adhering to their understanding of an Islamic state and strict sharia, and the results are very different. Al-Qaeda-type revolutionaries occasionally declare enclaves as Islamic emirates governed by sharia alone.

Traditionalists as Holistic Modernists
Turkey, Egypt, Levant, north Africa, Iran, Pakistan, southeast Asia, the West

Both **Turkey** and Egypt began their accommodation with capitalism in the nineteenth century. Under Kemal in Turkey and under the British occupation in Egypt (1920s–1950s), the Islamists became the main opposition, and the deep-seated faith of the people and their own long-suffering patience in the face of oppression ensured that popular respect for them increased. In both Turkey and Egypt, their return to prominence in their countries' social, political and economic life now has the air of triumphant inevitability despite the forces ranged against them.

The ideology of the godfather of Turkish Islamism, **Necmeddin Erbakan** (1926–2011), is set forth in a manifesto, "Milli Gorus" (1969, national vision). "National" refers not to Turkish ethnicity, but to the umma, a sharp departure from Kemalist western-style nationalism. His aims were to further Turkey's relations with the Arab 'nations', downgrade relations with Israel and the EU, create a neo-caliphate D-8 or the Developing Eight (Turkey, Iran, Malaysia, Indonesia, Egypt, Bangladesh, Pakistan and Nigeria, constituting 14% of the world's population (800 million people)), and institute a broad economic welfare program.

Erbakan was Turkey's first Islamist prime minister (1996–1997), turning secularism against the Kemalists, arguing that true secularism meant "not only state autonomy but religious autonomy".[8] He shattered the secular aura that Kemal had built in Turkey, and insisted that people should have "the right to live in accordance with their religious beliefs". Erbakan's patient defense of people's right to exercise their religious beliefs paved the way for the return of Islam to the center of Turkish life. By subordinating religion to the political realm, Kemalism had ironically "promoted the politicization of Islam and the struggle for the control of the state".[9]

Fethullah Gulen (b. 1941) founded the Gulen movement for a renewal of Turkish Islam, more open to pluralism and dialogue, inspired by Said Nursi and the Followers of Light movement, which began in the late 1920s and supported the first post-Kemal government in 1950. Gulen began his rise in the 1980s, moving to the US in 1998 under pressure from the secular establishment. The movement has Sufi origins, focusing on interfaith dialogue and education, though former Turkish intelligence official Osman Gundes claims its international schools have been used as a cover for CIA agents abroad.

Recep Tayyip Erdogan (b. 1954) founded the Justice and Development Party (AKP) in 2001, and advocated a compromise politics, reaffirming Turkey's EU membership aspirations, and cultivating an alliance with the Turkish liberal elite. His forceful pragmatism allowed him to stare down the generals, win an absolute majority in the 2002 elections, thus beginning a new era for Turkey and Islam, implementing the "Turkish model of Islamist-led democratic capitalism".[10] He told Egyptians in the first ever televised interview with a Turkish prime minister, "Management of people, management of science and management of money. If you do those three, you will accomplish your goal."[11] Turkey remains a secular nation, but is no longer avowedly assimilationist. Instead, it is playing a complex game as a NATO member[12] and at the same time as a Middle East regional power which can only be described as neo-Ottoman, intent on recreating Islamic civilization where Turks and Arabs can reaffirm their common culture and build an economic community which has a spiritual foundation. Encapsulating the philosophy of the AKP, Finance Minister Mehmet Simsek said: "In issues such as family we are conservative. In economy and relations with the world we are liberal. And in social justice and poverty we are socialist."[13]

The renewal of Islam in Turkey has come about as a result of political struggle, where activists such as Erbakan and Erdogan came from outside the system, relying on political instinct and a deep religiosity to turn back the secular westernizing tide. The new intellectual currents supporting this transformation are represented by the AKP Foreign Minister **Ahmet Davutoglu** (b. 1959), who was plucked out of the university milieu and catapulted into the senior cabinet position based on his vision of Turkish foreign relations set out in *Strategic Depth* (2001). His *Alternative Paradigms* (1993) explains the rise and fall of civilizations as due to their worldview, reminiscent of Ibn Khaldun's theory based on tribal solidarity, though "the motive behind the Muslim civilization is not sociology but psychology." He explains this Hegelian position based on the fact that, unlike in Christianity, "there is ontological hierarchy in Islam", as Allah is transcendent, beyond nature/ man, which translates into a *lack* of "social hierarchy in Islamic civilization". He sees Islam civilization as unique.

Christianity led to "the particularization of the divinity of knowledge, the secularization of knowledge" and the current high tech secular society in the West. Davutoglu compares the interaction between western and Islamic civilizations to

> the confrontation in the era of Alexander the Great between the philosophic traditions of Socrates, Plato and Aristotle on the one hand and of Buddha and Confucius on the other. A similar blending took place during the spread of Christianity. But then the era of nineteenth century colonialism came and it led to the spread of another self-perception in this region. This obviously resulted in a clash ... Today, the western paradigm has already reached the limits of its fertility. This is a cyclical pattern that we observe in all civilizations. This was also true of the Muslim civilization.[14]

He compares Hegel to twelfth century Ghazali when Islamic civilization reached an apogee in its self-awareness. "So, by the nineteenth century, western self-perception was consolidated as a civilizational paradigm and was translated into a political paradigm", where the modern state became the apogee of the "divine march of history",[15] which is now in decline.

Francis Fukuyama's myopic claim that history has ended is reminiscent of "the Ottomans' claim to have an 'eternal state'. ... This was, of course, the end of dynamism. ... It is not the end of history. On the contrary, history will now flow at a greater pace." Davutoglu is confident that the present era of globalization will return Islam to its rightful place at the center of world culture, as the western paradigm is replaced by one which reaffirms the truth of the Islamic worldview, though he is "not speaking about re-emergence of an Islamic identity" but of a "new synthesis".[16]

The renewal of Islam and its renewed presence on the political map today will, he feels, recapitulate earlier eras when Islam inspired the world, with the current intellectual ferment "translated into a political paradigm". Today, where globalization has taken place within the nation-state system, this means "the core issue for Islamic polity" is "to reinterpret its political tradition and theory as an alternative world-system rather than merely as a program for the Islamization of nation-states."[17] The future will be "a chaotic era, both ecologically and ontologically. Chaos will produce crises and crises will provide us a new zone of ethics in which we will need to make an intellectual leap. The traditional ethics do not provide for the new challenges of life. We need new biological ethics, new ecological ethics." This is in line with Tariq Ramadan's demand for transformation reform as opposed to mere adaptation reform.

The civilizational interaction will evolve because of the

> existence of Muslims and other eastern ethnicities in the heartland of Europe. This existence is a natural result of western hegemony over Muslim and eastern countries in the last two centuries. This is a historical process. At some time after a dominating center rules over a periphery, the periphery starts to pour into the center ... A new self-perception is formed and that is followed by a new political order.

This happened to the Ottoman system, which benefited from the interaction of center and periphery. It is happening today in the West including the US. "The US no longer needs a Caesar from Texas but a Marcus Aurelius from Boston ... [who] incorporates the newcomers into the system and provides the civilizational flexibility for their contribution. ... Barack Obama is both the Marcus Aurelius of Rome and the Sokullu Mehmet Pasha of the Ottomans."

Davutoglu sees Turkey as "the litmus test of globalization. Our success by means of the east-west, north-south relationship and by means of socio-cultural and economic crises will provide for the success of globalization. Our failure will drag globalization into a fault zone that may trigger a deep clash." [18] Turkey's transformation from secularism to postsecularism without declaring an 'Islamic state' is a blueprint for Europe, an "inoculation". He predicts that an ecumenical Christianity will also experience a renewal which is more open to dialogue with Islam. "Today certain European countries are resisting minarets. Why? The reason is the strong and rigid western self-perception. But a city with different cultural artifacts in its silhouette produces more and more pluralistic citizens."

Such historical thinking lies behind Turkey's radical foreign policy shifts in the past decade. Turkish migration to Europe is not just a process of assimilation into western secularism, but a kind of positive 'fifth column of religiosity', of Islamic civilization, into Europe. Europe and America need spiritual renewal and can learn from the East, just as Turkey in the past two centuries has learned a great deal from the West. Genuine multiculturalism was nurtured by the Ottomans without any dumbing down, as has been the case in today's globalization. This wealth of social experience of Islam is a treasure to be rediscovered by the West as the emptiness of its materialism is exposed.

A neo-caliphate will arise between the Muslim nations, Davutoglu contends, as the only way to end the horrors of war and ecological degradation in the region, directly the result of two centuries of imperial onslaught, fueled by the West's obsession with oil. Turkey's 'zero-problems' moves with its neighhbors to restore its influence throughout the region, from Armenia and Afghanistan to Iran, Libya and Syria, even while formally toeing the NATO line, must be seen in terms of this long-range perspective, reflecting the early relations with the umma's neighbors as the community established itself and grew.[19]

The focus of Islamic reform in the 19th–early 20th centuries was **Egypt**, the outstanding figure being Abduh. Another important figure was **Rashid Rida** (1865–1935), the Syrian biographer of Abduh, and co-editor of the Islamic journal *al-Manar* in the 1920–1930s. He soon bccame disillusioned with the liberals and shifted to a traditionalist position. He was "one of the first Muslims to advocate the establishment of a fully modernized but fully Islamic state, based on the reformed sharia" through the study of western sciences and *fiqh*,[20] as the repository of spiritual authority in earthly matters.[21] He blamed the Islamic world's weakness on Sufi excesses and the stagnation of the ulama, who compromised their integrity and the integrity of sharia by associating with worldly corrupt powers.[22] He called for a return to an Islam "purged of the historical accretions, and the use of *ijtihad* to meet modern realities."[23] Towards the end of his life, Rida became a staunch defender of the Saudi regime and an advocate of Wahhabism, saluting Wahhab as the "renewer of the twelfth century [of the Hijra]".[24] At the end, Rida promoted a restoration of the Caliphate for Islamic unity and as a counterweight to the western nation states, which would include "democratic consultation on the part of the government".[25]

MB founder **Hassan al-Banna** (1906–1949) (left) sought to infuse his grassroots organization "with some of the spiritual values of Sufism without

its devotional excesses". When he was twelve years old, he became involved in a Sufi order, and became a fully initiated member in 1922. At the age of thirteen, he participated in demonstrations during the revolution of 1919 against British rule. As leader of the MB, he called himself *murshid* (guide), a title usually reserved for the leaders of Sufi orders. "His favorite reading, Ghazali's *Revitalization of the Religious Sciences*, is strongly informed by Sufi mysticism."[26]

Banna clearly took inspiration from Ibn Taymiya's *ijtihad* allowing jihad against non-Muslim rulers, though he was faithful to the original meaning of jihad as, before all else, a struggle to enlighten via the Quran. The basic theory and strategy of Banna's organization is deceptively simple: to work within and beyond the secular framework of the nation through grassroots organizations to gradually create a new society based on Islamic principles, transforming a secular nation-state into an Islamic social order. Social activism, using the pen, tongue and heart rather than sword. A rousing slogan associated with the MB, but which in fact boils down to the same thing, captures its aim: "God is our objective; the Quran is our constitution, the Prophet is our leader, Jihad is our way, and death for the sake of God is the highest of our aspirations."

The Brotherhood's English language website *ikhwanweb.com* describes the principles of the Muslim Brotherhood as including firstly the introduction of sharia as "the basis controlling the affairs of state and society", and secondly, working to unify "Islamic countries and states, mainly among the Arab states, and liberating them from foreign imperialism". "We believe that political reform is the true and natural gateway for all other kinds of reform. We have announced our acceptance of democracy that acknowledges political pluralism, the peaceful rotation of power, the fact that the nation is the source of all powers, the freedom of the press, freedom of criticism and thought, freedom of peaceful demonstrations, freedom of assembly, and the independence of the judiciary."

Banna proved to be a master organizer, establishing an array of administrative structures in the 1930s which mobilized peasants, workers and professionals. Outreach was both local and abroad, relying on the revolutionary new telegraph and telephone. British state-of-the-art financial and administrative methods were turned against the occupiers. Banna relied on pre-existing social networks, in particular those built around mosques, Islamic welfare associations, and neighborhood groups. This weaving of traditional ties into a distinctively modern structure was at the root of his success. Directly attached to the Brotherhood, and feeding its expansion, were numerous businesses, clinics, and schools. Members were affiliated to the movement through a series of cells called *usar* (families, singular: *usra*). The money nexus had eroded traditional allegiances, leaving Muslims humiliated and alienated, and the MB quickly became a new family, based on the unshakable ties of Islam.

Rooted in Islam, Banna's message tackled issues including colonialism, public health, educational policy, natural resource management, social inequalities, Arab nationalism, the weakness of the Islamic world on the international scene, and the conflict in Palestine. By emphasizing concerns that appealed to a variety of constituencies, Banna was able to recruit from among a cross-section of Egyptian society, though modern-educated civil servants, office employees, and professionals remained dominant among the organization's activists and decision-makers. Incipient nationalists found an articulate and principled foe of imperialism, but without the chauvinism that characterized European nationalism in the 1930s–1940s.

Charity work and *dawa* included social welfare activism, which substituted for ineffective or nonexistent government services. All this required creative *ijtihad* by what were layman scholar-activists, reinforcing the Muslim duty to create balance (*mizan*) and justice (*adl, qist*), in sharp contrast to the occupiers' racism, cruelty, injustice, and their Christian missionaries advocating apostasy and accommodation with imperialism.

Banna is accused by critics of secretly planning to overthrow the monarchy by using the MB's Special Organization, which had been set up in the late 1930s to provide military assistance to the Palestinians. Like any organization intending to replace the existing order—whether by evolution or revolution—as the MB became more powerful, it was increasingly impossible to control, and in an atmosphere of anticolonial unrest and violence in Egypt and Palestine in the 1930s–1940s, officials were killed—the most famous being Prime Minister Ahmed Maher whom the British installed in 1945 to ensure that Egypt finally declared war against Germany. In November 1948 the government arrested 32 MB leaders, and in December the British-installed Prime Minister Mahmud Nokrashi ordered the dissolution of the MB, only to be assassinated by one of its members, veterinary student Abdel Meguid Ahmed Hassan. A month and a half later Banna himself was murdered by government agents.

Banna tried over his lifetime to achieve a peaceful transition to Islamic rule. He announced he would run in the 1941 elections in Alexandria, but King Farouq pressured him to withdraw, promising to ease restrictions on the MB, an empty promise as it turned out. Banna ran in a blatantly rigged elections in

1945. The MB sent troops to fight the war against the new state of Israel, while the local comprador elite and British occupiers were providing rusty guns for a ragtag volunteer army. The subsequent assassination of Nokrashi, a quisling prime minister, by a 'lone gunman' MBer was not, in fact, an indication that this was a policy favored by the MB. Despite the subsequent brutal suppression of the MB under Nasser, the organization never advanced a strategy of violent revenge or overthrow of that regime either.

Like the Wafd Party (and unlike the ineffectual communists), the MB did not have a clear plan for ending colonialism. There was no plan to overthrow the monarchy, kick out the British, and institute an Islamic state. The following suggest the MB orientation:

- Jihad is one of the Pillars of the Covenant of the MB (which include understanding, sincerity, action, jihad, sacrifice, obedience, perseverance, resoluteness, brotherhood and trust). Its weakest degree is "the heart's abhorrence of evil and its highest degree is fighting in the Way of Allah. Between these two degrees are numerous forms of Jihad, including struggling with the tongue, pen, or hand, and speaking a word of truth to a tyrannical ruler. This call (to Islam) cannot survive without Jihad. The price required to support it is huge, but the reward given to its upholders is more generous. 'And strive in His cause as you ought to strive.' (22: 78) By this, dear brothers, you know the meaning of your slogan 'Jihad is our way'."[27]
- "Allah did not ordain Jihad for the Muslims so that it may be used as a tool of oppression or tyranny or so that it may be used by some to further their personal gains. Rather Jihad is used to safeguard the mission of spreading Islam."[28]
- The love of wealth, the misappropriation of the benefits of war and striving to conquer through unjust methods are all forbidden. Only one intention was possible and that was "the offering of sacrifice and the taking of pains for the guidance of mankind".[29] [So] Be like trees among the people: They strike you with stones, and you shower them with blessings.[30]
- While recognizing that the School of Social Service "serves the missionaries and imperialists" cadres enrolled there are instructed that "its scientific and practical progress facilitates training of the Brothers in social welfare works."[31]
- "Chiefs, leaders, and men of rank and authority will hate you, all governments will rise as one against you, and every government will try to set limits to your activities."[32]

MB leaders have consistently disowned violence, as seen in the grassroots social justice focus of the organization from the start.

> It is forbidden to slay women, children, and old people,
> to kill the wounded, or to disturb monks, hermits, and the
> peaceful who offer no resistance. Contrast this mercy with
> the murderous warfare of the 'civilized' people and their
> terrible atrocities! Compare their international law alongside
> this all-embracing, divinely ordained justice![33]

The MB follows traditional Muslim discourse. Consultation and community consensus are important, but the will of the people remains subordinate to the Divine Will (the goal being the realization of God's realm on earth). In the context of electoral democracy this means creating a top-down hierarchy much like the democratic centralism of communist parties (where the will of party members was subordinated to the goal of revolution). This intensely collectivist ideology, with the MB hierarchy submitting to God, perhaps accounts for the lack of charismatic leaders within the movement. It is the antithesis of western-style political movements and thus paradoxically frightens people inured to politics characterized by personal charisma, messy campaigns and hyped upheavals, where alternative parties take power to basically tweak a system which is off-bounds to any genuine reformers.

From the late 1970s on, Islam eclipsed secular ideologies as the primary source of political activism.[34] 'Islam is the solution—not capitalism or socialism' captures the supra-class nature of the MB's appeal, attracting youth much like western youth were attracted to communism in the secular West, but more so. At a time when Vaclav Havel was feted in the West as Czechoslovakia's great dissident who was "living within the truth", thousands of MBers in Egypt were actually doing this under much worse conditions, without any western support. Their "project of moral and social renewal is a constructive and life-affirming one ... not just against the status quo but for a better alternative."[35]

Cultural restraint is integral to Islamic culture in general, which is more explicitly focused on worship and obedience (to God) than western culture. For Islamists, in the first place the MB, the main threat from the West is cultural rather than political/ economic. Protecting traditional duties and roles of women and men has always been seen as key to Islam's survival.[36] By the 1950s this conviction was reinforced by the secular culture of Arab nationalism and the allure of the rising consumerism in the West, which threatened traditional conservative religious values. This threat by the rapidly liberalizing western lifestyle, and its adoption by westernized urban elites in Egypt was most evident in women's issues, including education, work, dress and family planning.

The leading female activist in the MB, **Zainab al-Ghazali** (1917–2005), founded the Muslim Women's Association in 1937, and is considered the female counterpart to Banna. Islam offers women everything—freedom, economic rights, political rights, social rights, public and private rights ... Islam does not forbid a woman to actively participate in public life. It does not prevent her from working, entering politics, and expressing her opinion, or from being anything, as long as that does not interfere with her first duty as a mother, the one who first trains her children in the Islamic call.[37]

Ghazali was opposed to MB co-operation with the Free Officers and her network served as a liaison between the MB and the outside world after 1954. She was arrested in 1965 and sentenced to death, then life imprisonment, and released by Sadat in 1971.

This message of conservative Islam continues to appeal even to upper class women under western pressure to abandon traditional sex roles. Many women see the veil as allowing "freedom from being seen as sexual objects" in the public arena, providing anonymity as a "form of liberation and a way of achieving morality and piety". Western observers interpret the veil and separation of sexes as more a question of "a rejection of western mores and a shield against the invasion of western-bred corruption and immorality".[38] But it is more than that. These norms enable men to be brothers to one another, and women to be sisters, as they are not in a constant state of competition with each other, enabling normal physical affection between men /men and women/ women, creating greater social warmth. They protect and nurture the family, and children in particular, establishing the basis for collectivist, non-competitive social thought. Muslims are encouraged to compete only in doing good works.

The US Treasury Dept Terrorist Finance Unit stated in 2004 that the MB is "a political movement, an economic cadre and in some cases terrorist supporters ... They have one foot in our world and one foot in a world hostile to us. How to decipher what is good, bad or suspect is a severe complication." Such western views fail to see that Muslims in general have different worldview. To the MB, *capitalism and/or communism = materialism* is the problem, prioritizing the individual over the community, individual freedoms over spiritual duties/ responsibilities/ public morality.

A sociological interpretation of the rise of MB Islamic discourse, seeing it as a limited one, is presented by Asef Bayat.[39] Islamism emerged "as the language of self-assertion to mobilize those (largely middle-class high achievers) who felt marginalized by the dominant economic, political or cultural processes in their societies, those for whom the perceived failure of both capitalist modernity and socialist utopia made the language of morality, through religion, a substitute for politics." The movement grew, starting in the 1970s against the backdrop of Cold War politics and is clearly a historical phenomenon. Two simultaneous but contradictory processes pushed Islamism toward its hegemonic position: opportunity and suppression. The opportunity for massive education expansion, economic development, an abundance of wealth (oil money), and social mobility went hand in hand with continued political repression. Marginalization, a sense of humiliation, and growing inequality.[40]

In the 1950s, there were 10 universities in Arab world, but by 2003 more than 200. A highly educated but still marginalized middle class directs moral outrage at its own elites and governments allied with western powers, which has used "Islamic opposition as a bulwark against both communism and secular nationalism". In other words, political Islamism is a direct result of imperialism. A reaction to it, just as communism was a reaction to imperialism, but one which will burn itself out given time, Bayat contends.

It is different from Latin American liberation theology, which attacks a church hierarchy and directly borrows socialist concern for the poor to achieve social justice. Throughout the twentieth century, Islamism had the goal of establishing an Islamic state, implementing Islamic laws and moral codes, driven by white-collar professionals, confident that problem of poverty will be solved once God's law is implemented. This is the strata who formerly put their hopes in nationalism, Nasserism, Baathism, and socialism.

Bayat recognizes that this Islamization of Egyptian society was a natural result of the dilemma Egypt and Egyptians found themselves in, but looks hopefully to "post-Islamism" as emphasizing "rights instead of

duties, plurality in place of a singular authoritative voice, historicity rather than fixed scripture, and the future instead of the past."[41] Note that this was written before the Arab Spring.

The best-known MB theorist (or rather, ex-MB, as he and his writings were publicly disowned when he was hanged for treason in 1966) was **Sayyid Qutb** (1906–1966),who established the theoretical basis for militant Islam in the Muslim world both Sunni and Shia. He studied in the US in 1948, and intensely disapproved of what he saw as a society obsessed with materialism, violence and sex. He wrote *Social Justice in Islam* (1949), rejecting western capitalism and calling Islam a global civilization based on a law that "consists of mercy, love, help and mutual responsibility between Muslims in particular and all human beings in general".[42] Parliamentary government and democracy were manipulated by modern elites in cooperation with landlords to control the masses, allowing a concentration of political power, wealth and resources, economic exploitation, corruption and social injustice under a veil of democratic legitimacy. The cult of materialism undermines religion, morality and the family.

He began as a proponent of Islamic socialism, supporting Nasser's coup, espousing a "just dictatorship" that would "grant political liberties to the virtuous alone."[43] While in prison under Nasser from 1954–1964, he wrote *Milestones* (1964), borrowing from Maududi (see below) and the Ibn Taymiya doctrine of offensive jihad. The success of the Wahhabis in overthrowing their Ottoman rulers, and Afghani's frustration with both the Ottoman/Qajar monarchs and the imperialist occupiers, inspired both Qutb and Maududi. This trend towards revolution in Islamic renewal had finally found an articulate, even charismatic, spokesman in Qutb.

Milestones prompted his re-arrest and execution/martyrdom in 1966. Here he rejected both capitalist and socialist systems, and Marxism, of which he wrote:

> This theory conflicts with man's nature and its needs. This ideology prospers only in a degenerate society or in a society which has become cowed as a result of some form of prolonged dictatorship. But now, even under these circumstances, its materialistic economic system is failing, although this was the only foundation on which its structure was based. Russia, which is the leader of the communist countries, is itself suffering from shortages of food. The main reason for this is the failure of the system of collective farming, the failure of a system which is against human nature.[44]

The problem with socialism was that it asserted that society was fundamentally based on class, and that the working class was the repository of truth. However, truth lies not with a class but in the Quran, which would overcome class differences without violent revolution of one class against another. Islam in the seventh century had provided answers to the sectarian strife and rising economic disparities without resorting to class.[45]

Qutb emphasizes the importance of instituting sharia, a complete system extending into all aspects of life, which when instituted would, as was the communist or anarchist promise, require no government at all, allowing the 'withering away of the state'. "Assemblies of men which have absolute power to legislate laws" [46] or even a 'just dictatorship' is un-Islamic, where the laws are not made based on Islam. Secular regimes such as Nasser's were illegitimate as they were based on human (and thus corrupt) authority, rather than divine authority. Like Asad, Maududi and Baqir al-Sadr, Qutb tried to answer the question: how can we construct a government with divine guidance but which can legislate based on popular will?

The way to bring about this freedom was for a revolutionary vanguard to fight *jahiliya* (the state of ignorance) with a twofold approach: preaching, and undermining the organizations and authorities of the *jahili* system by "physical power and jihad". The vanguard movement would grow through preaching and jihad until it formed a truly Islamic community, then spread throughout the Islamic homeland and finally throughout the entire world, attaining leadership of humanity. "Jihad against the polytheists by fighting and against the hypocrites by preaching and argument."[47]

Though rejecting the Enlightenment, nonetheless this new Islamic radicalism derives from Rousseau ('force people to be free'), Marx (alienation and exploitation under capitalism/ imperialism), and Lenin (advocating the overthrow of the system by a small band of revolutionaries). His writings and death at the hands of the secular state prepared the way for a new movement of renewal and reaction to imperialism using this Enlightenment political strategy—and its weapons, inspiring Egypt's Islamic Jihad in the 1970s, and al-Qaeda in the 1980s–2010s.

Reformist Muslims questioned his understanding of sharia, and his increasing dismissal, in line with the Wahhabis, of not only all non-Muslim culture, but much of Muslim culture following the period of the first four caliphs.[48] Fundamentalist (Wahhabi) critics condemned Qutb's reformist ideas such as social justice and redistributive economics as western *bid'a* (innovation). They condemn him for using *ijtihad* and for redefining *ijma* (consensus) so that it takes in the entire umma, rather than just the ulama (his stateless society would run on consensus, without exploitative representative government).[49]

Alongside Afghani, Banna, Maududi, and Khomeini, Qutb is one of the most influential Muslim thinker-activists of the modern reform era, not only for his ideas but his life work and how he died. *Milestones* fuses "together the core elements of modern Islamism: the Kharijites' *takfir* (charge of unbelief), Ibn Taymiya's fatwas and policy prescriptions, Rashid Rida's Salafism, Maududi's concept of the contemporary *jahiliya* and Banna's political activism",[50] and like Vladimir Lenin's pamphlet *What Is To Be Done?*, remains a snapshot of its times, hinting at the revolutionary energy that social changes and the struggle against imperialism had unleashed. Qutb's journey from the MB's evolutionary social Islam to revolutionary offensive jihad aiming at a stateless Islamic society, governed only by sharia, must be put in its context—

the era of world communist revolution against capitalism—which had just planted a Jewish colony in the heart of Islam. But twentieth century urban Egypt had no place for Qutb's vision of revolution.

Shortly after his death, the ulama of Azhar University took the unusual step of putting Qutb on their index of heresy, declaring him a deviant (*munharif*). MB Murshid Hassan al-Hodeibi, under house arrest in 1969, disowned Qutb and wrote *Preachers Not Judges,* arguing it was not the state of ignorance (*jahiliya*) but ignorance (*juhl*) that needed to be fought—via *dawa.* A transformed people, having built Islamic institutions, would eventually transform the state. This evolutionary path would bring about an Islamic society, not violent civil war. The MB was biding its time until the Nasserites and these revolutionary Islamists burned themselves out.

Though not associated with the MB, an important traditionalist figure was Sheikh **Mahmoud Shaltut** (1893–1963), a disciple of Abduh and Rida, was appointed Grand Mufti and Rector of Azhar in 1958. Nasser tried to use Azhar to integrate education into a unified system, and convinced Shaltut to enact a policy of modernization of curricula with a broader public-service function for Azhar. Shaltut strongly supported the use of sharia law arguing it was not an obstacle to modern society, but rather a guide to making the changes modern society demands. Shaltut was successful in expanding Azhar's curricula to include western science and engineering, improving job opportunities for students, and producing modern scholars better able to serve the Muslim community. Though criticized for his support of Nasser, he was able to ensure that sharia remained the inspiration of Egypt's legal system. He spoke regularly on radio and TV about issues affecting contemporary Muslim society such as family law, private property, birth control, and polygamy (which he defended). He supported *ijtihad* and, like Abduh, saw overcoming the Sunni-Shia divide as vital to the umma, going so far as to issue a fatwa which essentially declared that worship according to the Twelver Shia doctrine is valid, and that there is nothing objectionable about a follower of one school referring to the judgments of another school, including the Shia Jafari school of *fiqh*.

Said Ramadan (1926–1995) was the Brotherhood's chief international organizer and son-in-law of Hassan al-Banna. Ramadan founded MB branches in Palestine and Jordan starting in 1945. In 1949 and 1951 he traveled to Pakistan, taking part in the meetings of the World Muslim Congress in Karachi—the first transnational body connecting the world's Islamist movements.[51] Ramadan also worked with Arab fundamentalists, especially Palestinians and Jordanians, to found Hizb ut-Tahrir (1953, Party of Liberation), advocating the revival of the caliphate, which was supported by Saudi Arabia and became popular especially in Central Asia after the collapse of the Soviet Union, with headquarters in London.

In 1954 he was stripped of his Egyptian citizenship by Nasser. Ramadan fled to Munich and settled in Geneva. There, in 1961, he founded the Islamic Center, which would serve for decades as the organizational headquarters for the Muslim Brotherhood in Europe.

Rather than allying itself with Nasser's brand of Arab nationalism, the US chose to make common cause with Saudi Arabia and the Islamist opposition to Nasserists. Starting in the 1950s, Washington encouraged the kingdom to create a network of Islamist organizations to support right-wing Islamic states. Ramadan's Islamic Center was a major beneficiary of the policy. In 2005, the *Wall Street Journal* reported that Ramadan worked with the CIA, using a Jordanian diplomatic passport secured for him by the CIA, and that Ramadan worked closely with the CIA's American Committee for Liberation from Bolshevism, which ran Radio Free Europe and Radio Liberty in the 1950s–1960s, on a "joint propaganda effort against the Soviet Union".

In 1962 Ramadan helped found the World Muslim League, which the Saudis used to fund *dawa*, the distribution of free Islamic literature, and the building of Wahhabi-oriented mosques and Islamic associations in Europe and the Muslim world. In 1971, he returned to Egypt at the head of a Brotherhood delegation financed by Saudi Arabia to broker a deal with Sadat to allow the Muslim Brotherhood to organize openly, 17 years after it had been outlawed. By the 1980s, coinciding with Khomeini's regime in Iran, Zia ul-Haq's Islamist dictatorship in Pakistan and the US-backed Afghan anti-Soviet jihad, the MB once again became a serious force in Egypt, Syria, Palestine, and elsewhere. In 1995, Ramadan's son, Hani, took over the reins of the Islamic Center. His son Tariq became a noted Islamic reform theorist.

The troubled relationship of the empire and the MB is a long one, with Ramadan at its heart. Both the British and Americans have used Islamists as part of their imperial strategies, only to turn against them when they come close to power. Some US officials see the Brotherhood as "important potential allies in the war on terrorism". Reuel Marc Gerecht, a former CIA officer and fellow at the neoconservative American Enterprise Institute, argues that even if the Brotherhood were to seize power in Egypt and suppress democracy, "the United States would still be better off with this alternative than with [the current] secular dictatorship."[52]

Yusuf al-Qaradawi (b. 1926) is the mostly widely known Egyptian sheikh, living in exile until 2011 in Qatar where he is head of the Faculty of Sharia and Islamic Studies and the Center for Sunnah and Sirah at the University of Qatar, a regular commentator on Al-Jazeera ("Shariah and Life"), chief religious scholar on *IslamOnline*, head of the European Council for Fatwa and Research and of the International Union for Muslim Scholars, and a trustee of the Oxford Center for Islamic Studies. He has long had a prominent role within the intellectual leadership of the Muslim Brotherhood. He twice turned down offers to be their leader—in 1976 and 2004, and was jailed three times for his relationship with them and subsequently stripped of his Egyptian citizenship in the 1970s—driving him to seek exile in Qatar.

He has spoken out against terrorism but defends the resistance to US occupation in Iraq and Israeli occupation of Palestine. His 2004 fatwa called for the boycott of American and Israeli products: "If we cannot strengthen the brothers, we have a duty to make the enemy weak."[53] He is not averse to "pious" Sufism, but is an outspoken critic of Shiism and Iran's political system.[54] After Egypt's revolution, which the Gulf states and Saudi Arabia disapproved of, his relations with the absolute monarchies have frayed, the Dubai police chief threatening him with arrest for his criticism of the Emirate's deportation of MB protesters.

Qaradawi represents an important new development among the ulama—even in Saudi Arabia, scholars are becoming satellite TV and internet media stars. Others include the Indian Zakir Naik (b. 1965),[55] Egyptians Amr Khalid (b. 1967) and Moez Masoud (b. 1978), the Turk Fethullah Gulen (see above), and the Saudi Ahmad al-Shugairi (b. 1973).

Hassan Hanafi (b. 1935), currently head of the Philosophy Department at Cairo University, was briefly associated with the MB but broke away due to the MB's condemnation of socialism, and is practically the only member remaining of the 'Islamic left'. He was exiled from 1979–1982 for his outspoken support for the Iranian revolution. He is a strong proponent of *ijtihad* and the *maqsid maslaha mursala* (public interest), a disciple of Iqbal, and a Sufi, known for his philosophical soundbytes: "Decolonization will not be completed except after the liberation of the object to become subject and the transformation of the observed to an observer."[56] Hanafi provides a postmodern critique of western civilization from a nonwestern standpoint—"There is no One Culture but only multiple cultures", leading to a new "world scientific consciousness".[57]

In **Palestine,** Sheik **Ahmed Yassin** (1937–2004) founded Hamas (1987, "enthusiasm", an acronym of "Islamic Resistance Movement"), a branch of the MB, during the first Intifada, to liberate Palestine from Israeli occupation and to establish an Islamic state in the area that is now Israel, the West Bank, and the Gaza Strip. Yassin was a quadriplegic and almost blind, but became a charismatic leader leading the opposition to the 1990s Oslo peace process, and was assassinated in an Israeli air strike. Labelled a terrorist organization by the EU and the US (but not by Russia and Turkey), Hamas won parliamentary elections in 2006 and has governed Gaza since June 2007. In 2009, Khaled Meshal, Hamas's Damascus-based political bureau chief, said the organization was willing to cooperate on "a resolution to the Arab-Israeli conflict which included a Palestinian state based on 1967 borders" provided that Palestinian refugees hold the right to return to Israel and that East Jerusalem be the new nation's capital. The military wing Izz ad-Din al-Qassam Brigades (1992) was named in commemoration of Sheikh **Izz ad-Din al-Qassam** (1882–1935), who led the fight against British, French, and Zionist organizations in the Levant in the 1920s–1930s and was killed by the British.

All of **north Africa** witnessed an intense process of assimilation in the twentieth century under French, Italian and British occupation, and then under the secularist regimes from the 1950s on. Islamist movements were underground and there was no opportunity for intellectual debates about reform. Islamic thinkers gravitated to Paris. The Arab Spring witnessed the return of many. The best-known thinker-activist is the head of the Tunisian MB, **Rashid al-Ghannouchi** (b. 1941), co-founder of al-Nahda (1981, also Ennahda, renaissance), currently the largest party in Tunisia, and aligned with the MB.

Ghannouchi began as a leftist nationalist, but during his studies in Europe realized that Arab nationalism was, at bottom, a western-inspired ideology which operates beyond the authenticating framework of the Islamic heritage. In 1966, he made his "final decision to move from the universe of Nasserism and Arab nationalism to that of Islam", and set about self-consciously re-learning the prayers and religious culture of his youth which acted "at the interior" of his soul.[58] This 'reversion' to a politically committed Islam by western-educated elites is a significant phenomenon, to a lesser extent seen in Judaism with the rise of Zionism, but virtually unknown in Christianity.

Ghannouchi sees western society as human-centered in outlook and values, celebrating man as master of the universe, while Muslim societies are God-centered, where the reference point is not human desire, but Divine Will, the purpose of which is not just to test humankind, but to guide people to success in this world *and* the next—the Islamic interpretation of 'success'. It is necessary to use *ijtihad, ijma* and *shura* to interpret the Quran and sunna in the context of today's world. "Modern pluralism is the constitutional mechanism for promoting consultation to express popular sovereignty." It is possible to use western liberal experience such as parliaments, councils, plebiscites. Rulers have a "contract with the community". Any secular democratic state where religious freedom exists is *dar al-islam* not *dar al-harb*.

Dictators in the Muslim world have suppressed civil society and it is necessary to "reconstruct civil society" via education, reforms of social services, legal and economic institutions (Islamic banks), professional organizations outside of government control (or where government acts as coordinator rather than dictator). He critiques north African governments' attempts to co-opt religion to try to monopolize the right to interpret and implement Islam (the result of north Africa's French heritage which leads to the "marginalization of religion and desacralization of the world"), preferring "the Anglo-Saxon notion of secularism" [59] where religion and civil society are not necessarily in conflict.

Tunisia's westernized elite had become so corrupt that they ended up having a relationship to the masses very similar to the one that existed between the ruling white minority and the black majority in South Africa, where the state was transformed into a machine of total repression, and people increasingly moved toward Islam to reassert their identity and shield themselves from the state. The "Islamic contribution is primarily in the form of a code of ethics, a transcendent morality that seems to have no place in today's democratic practice, a set of values for self-discipline and for the refinement of human conduct and a set of restrictions to combat monopoly and a set of safeguards to protect public opinion."[60] He criticizes the

> total stripping of the state from religion [which] would turn the state into a mafia, and the world economic system into an exercise in plundering, and politics into deception and hypocrisy ... This is exactly what happened in the western experience, despite there being some positive aspects. International politics became the preserve of a few financial brokers owning the biggest share of capital and by extension the media, through which they ultimately control politicians.[61]

Ensuring a well-educated electorate and open discussion is the only way to ensure that political life is conducted in such a way to ensure 'God's rule'. Islamic rule must be popular; it cannot just be handed down from a professional religious elite. "Islam since its inception, has always combined religion with politics, religion and state. The Prophet was the founder of the religion as well as the state, a political imam who arbitrated people's disputes, lead armies, and signed various accords and treaties." The state founded in Medina reflected a civilizational transformation and not simply a transfer of power. Turning this vision into a viable reality today is the challenge.[62]

Like Muhammad Asad, Tariq Ramadan and other critical thinkers, Ghannouchi is not welcome in Saudi Arabia. The relative openness of the postmodern West has allowed room for genuine Islamic reformers to develop, culminating in the Arab Spring—ironically, considering the role of imperialism in disrupting Islamic civilization and destroying it. Saudi and Gulf discomfort with the new openness in Islamic thinking reflects their own fears of domestic change and exposure of their unholy pact with empire.

Malek Bennabi (1905–1973) is an Algerian, who was director of higher education in Algeria from 1963–1967. His *Qur'anic Phenomenon* (1946) called for a radical revision of education in order to resolve the crisis of faith that confronted Muslim youth trained in Cartesian modes of thought and forced to depend on western Orientalists for an appreciation of Islam. Bennabi strove for a methodology of exegesis that would benefit from new fields of science, such as astrophysics, psychology and archaeology. In *The Conditions of the Renaissance* (1948) and *Vocation de l'Islam* (1954), he developed Ibn Khaldun's notion of social cycles. Muslim society developed in three stages: the first, at its most sublime, based on the living force of the Quran; the second being the flowering of Muslim civilization; the third, the period of stagnation. In *The Muslim in the World of Economics* (1972) he presents a program of renewal that draws its inspiration from the Quranic concepts of justice and dignity.[63]

An early **Iran**ian reformer was the socialist **Jalal Ali Ahmad** (1923–1969), who coined the anti-imperialist term *gharbzadegi* (westoxification/occidentosis). By the 1960s he was advocating a return to Islam as unifying principle. In "Concerning the Service and Betrayal of the Intellectuals" he predicted either an end to westoxification (and a revival of Islam) or a continuation leading to assimilation. He translated Sartre, Gide and Dostoyevsky, and even went to Israel to learn "how to deal with the West", admiring Israelis' use of the "spiritual power of mass martyrdom". He was critical of Arab accommodationists, especially the oil sheikhs, "rotten scales on the stem of the old but strong tree of Islam", predicting that Israel would "blow them away and rid [us] of the tyranny of the puppet regimes installed by the oil companies".[64]

The most revered public figure in the Shia world[65] is Ayatollah **Ali al-Sistani** (b. 1930), born in Iran and now the most senior ayatollah in Iraq (Najaf). He issued a fatwa in 2003 after the US invasion calling on all followers, both men and women, to vote, and advising the clergy to be engaged in politics to help Iraqis make "clearer decisions" and to fight "media propaganda". He exerted pressure on the US occupiers to proceed quickly with elections according to the principle of majority rule, accountability and representative government, to reflect and protect Shia identity. He has also repeatedly exhorted Shia not to respond to the continued violence targeting them in the aftermath of the invasion. The 2005 constitution showed Sistani's imprint and that of the Iranian 1906 constitution, calling for representative government but asserting that no law should contradict "the tenets of Islam's jurisprudence". Sistani is seen as being against both confrontation with the empire and ulama control of the political process, unlike Khomeini.

Ali Shariati (1933–1977) is called the "ideologue of the Iranian Revolution",[66] who sought to translate socialist ideas into cultural symbols of Shiism that Iranians could relate to, attracting many young Muslims who had been alienated both from the traditional clergy and from western culture. Shiism has a clear "worldview, ideology, philosophy of history, vision of the future, social base, leadership and experience with organization and activism" going back to the early days of the faith and preserved through the centuries by "high clerics, valiant warriors, orators, poets, and even petty preachers."[67] The current struggle recaps that of Abel vs Cain, where the religion of classless society is that of Abel vs the polytheism of class society, and Shiism is the religion of liberation, not the stale dogma it became by the twentieth century.[68] Shia should not merely await the return of the twelfth Imam but should actively work to hasten his return by fighting for social justice, "even to the point of embracing martyrdom—every day is Ashoura, every place is Karbala."[69]

He noted that Abduh had come to the conclusion that, while "Europe abandoned religion and made progress, we abandoned religion and went backward," requiring a radical reassessment of the way forward. He translated Fanon, who was anti-religious until Shariati convinced him that religion can enlighten to the same revolutionary ends (anticipating Foucault). Shariati referred to his brand of Shiism as 'red' or Alid Shiism, which leads logically to a monotheistic, classless society, which he contrasted with clerical-dominated, unrevolutionary "black Shiism" or Safavid Shiism. Khomeini's appreciation of both Ahmad and Shariati was because he was forced to ally with the Alid leftists against the rest of the ulama who still supported the Shah. Shariati rode the wave of religious revival, counterattacking liberals and Marxists while refashioning a new theory from them.[70]

Ruhollah Khomeini (1902–1989) became the most influential leader of the opposition to the Shah after the death of Ali Shariati in 1977, and became Supreme Leader or Guardian after the 1979 Iranian Revolution—a position created in the 1980 constitution as the highest ranking political and religious authority of the nation. In 1963, when the Shah announced the White Revolution, Khomeini, though no admirer of the Saudi monarchs, took his cue from Wahhab (and Qutb),[71] openly declared war against the Shah as a kafir leader, and was exiled to Turkey and then Iraq.

Khomeini represented the conservative Shia ulama in his concept of reform. In *Islamic Government* (1970) he expounded the Shia *Usuli*[72] theory of *velayat-e faqih* (guardianship by jurists) in the absence of the Hidden Imam, i.e., society's laws are God's laws, implying theocratic political rule by *mujtahideen* (Islamic jurists). All those holding government posts should have knowledge of sharia, and the country's ruler should be a *faqih* who "surpasses all others in knowledge" of Islamic law and justice. Though he originally approved of the 1906 constitution, by the time he wrote *Islamic Government,* he was condemning both constitutional rule and monarchy as enemies of Islam. Government does not legislate, because sharia is all the legislation necessary. Rather it functions to execute sharia via planning agencies using technicians and specialists.[73] This principle was incorporated in the new Iranian constitution in 1980.

Khomeini made statements at different times indicating both support and opposition to democracy, where popular elections take precedence, emphasizing instead issues Muslims agreed upon—Islamic revival, the fight against Zionism and imperialism—and downplaying issues that would divide Shia from Sunni, a style of leadership which Mahmoud Ahmedinejad has continued as president (r. 2006).

Khomeini believed in reunifying the Sunni-Shia umma in solidarity with third world revolutionaries, from the Sandinistas to the African National Congress and the Irish Republican Army, distancing himself from the premodern Saudi/ Gulf monarchies. He shifted his opinions in power from populist to conservative, and after approving the closing of newspapers during the writing of the constitution in 1979, angrily chastised the intellectuals: "Yes, we are reactionaries, and you are enlightened intellectuals: You want freedom for everything, freedom that will corrupt our youth, freedom that will pave the way for the oppressor, freedom that will drag our nation to the bottom."[74]

The leading Shia theorist of politics and economics, the **Iraqi** Arab Ayatollah **Mohammad Baqir al-Sadr** (1935–1980), was a co-founder of the Dawa Party which led the insurgency against Saddam Hussein (see Chapter 4). He was assassinated despite formally distancing himself from the party as it became more militant. He is renowned for his political and economic writings. His political program—*Wilayat al-umma* (Governance of the people)—proposes a modern day Islamic state where *khilafa* (governance) is "a right given to the whole of humanity", an obligation given by God to the human race, the vicegerents of Allah, to "tend the globe and administer human affairs".[75] He is closer to the Sunni traditionalists in that the legitimacy of a government in an Islamic state comes from the people, and not from the clerics, as argued by Khomeini, although the Imams and then the clerics did inherit the role of *shahada* (witness, martyrdom, here—supervision) from the time of the Prophets.[76]

In the absence of the twelfth Imam, the practical application of the *khilafa* required the establishment of a democratic system whereby the people regularly elect their representatives in government: "Islamic theory rejects monarchy as well as the various forms of dictatorial government; it also rejects the aristocratic regimes, and proposes a form of government which contains all the positive aspects of the democratic system."[77] The jurist holding religious authority represents Islam. By confirming legislative and executive actions, he gives them legality. Al-Sadr's son Jaafar al-Sadr[78] believes that a "civil state" in Iraq does not contradict religion but on the contrary "a fair and just regime should be able to earn the blessing of religions."

In *Our Economy*, Sadr rejected capitalism's notion that private property is justified in its own right, arguing instead that both private and public property originate from God, and that the rights and obligations of both private individuals and rulers are therefore dictated by Islam. He also rejects the conclusion that this makes Islamic economics a mixture between capitalism and socialism, arguing that capitalism and socialism each come about as the natural conclusion of certain ideologies, while Islamic economics comes about as the natural conclusion of Islamic ideology. Islamic limits on private property rights lead to creation of public and state property, which are used for maintaining a "social balance".

Sadr's point is that although private charity may mitigate acute economic inequality, an Islamic state may not rely solely on individual altruism and must take an active part in eradication of poverty and inequality and maintaining an acceptable social balance. He believes that everyone in society benefits from a socially acceptable standard of living for all, with variations only accounted for, within reason, by differences in individuals' drive and capacity. In modern capitalism, with advanced tools of production, the state must intervene in the market place to harness the rapid accumulation of wealth and capital. The resulting imbalance endangers social balance, and the state must mitigate this by

1. owning and operating those enterprises that require a high degree of concentration of capital, since individuals cannot/ should not possess such a large mass of capital; and
2. engaging in the market to appropriate excessive accumulation.

Sadr's vision of an Islamic economy is one in which small farmers, merchants, and craft workers live under a large interventionist state maintaining the necessary social balance. This vision was the first Islamic theory of government to address the special nature of capitalism, and was

the source of a heated debate in post-revolutionary Iran between the proponents of "traditional jurisprudence" and "dynamic jurisprudence".

In **Pakistan, Abul Ala Maududi** (1903–1979) is, along with Iqbal, Asad, Banna, Qutb, Khomeini and Baqir al-Sadr, the most important of the twentieth century traditionalist thinkers and activists. He clearly saw the devastation that imperialism had wrought on the Muslim world. In "Jihad for Islam" (1927) he attacks the western image of

Islam as a religion of the sword [which] started gaining prominence from the moment the dragon of western expansionism began devouring the weak and infirm nations of the world. In self-denial about its tyrannical acts... [it] had succeeded in shifting the blame to Islam because western dominance extended to controlling the production of knowledge. ... Asia, Africa, Europe, and America – which portion of this planet has been spared from bloodbath resulting from their unholy war?[79]

He attributed the demise of the Ottoman caliphate to the narrow calculations of Turkish and Arab nationalists. As Jinnah's Muslim League was pro-British and secular, Maududi founded Jamaat i-Islami (Islamic society) in 1941 in British India as a religious political movement to promote Islamic values and practices. Maududi was against the creation of Pakistan, but presented with a *fait accompli* after the partition of India, he was forced to redefine Jamaat i-Islami in 1947 to support an Islamic state in Pakistan, and headed the organization until 1972.

He was both scholar and advocate for implementing sharia law within an Islamic state. His writings—religious, political and economic—continue to be more widely read than those of any other Islamic reformer. His commentary on the Quran is popular and available online. In *The Islamic Law and Constitution* (1941) he coined and popularized the terms 'Islamic state' and 'Islamic revolution'. The state would be a "theo-democracy" based on tawhid, *risala* (prophethood) and *khilafa* (caliphate). "By creating a state based on God's law, man is freed from the servitude and exploitation that is entailed by being subject to laws made by men."[80] Qutb borrowed his assertion that *jahiliya* can apply to all societies except the first four caliphs (632–661), as well as the need for an Islamist revolutionary vanguard movement to achieve an Islamic state through jihad, which, like Banna, he called the sixth pillar of Islam, via preaching and resistance to the nonbeliever occupiers of Muslim lands.

He was admired in the Shia world as well. Ayatollah Khomeini met him in 1963. His concept of Islamic democracy informs both the Iranian and more recent Egyptian Islamic constitutions, as it "accepted the consensus of the community as opposed to one restricted to the ulama ... but qualified by an insistence on leaving interpretations of the sharia to the state, which would receive advice from ulama knowledgeable in Arabic and the juristic literature." He interpreted Islam as "a worldly ideology capable of mobilizing Muslims to submit themselves actively to God. Only an Islamic society and polity could guarantee the believer's piety and salvation."[81]

Maududi's brilliance as a scholarly popularizer of Islamic thought was compromised by his political activism after making his peace with the secular Jinnah, who was content to turn Pakistan into a secular, British/ US neocolony hostile to Indian socialism. Maududi was a foe to both imperialism and nationalism, but was forced to accept Jinnah's pact with the (British) devil, intending to build a militant Islamic movement to transform Pakistan into an Islamic state in the distant future.

At the same time, he insisted that jihad in Kashmir logically required breaking diplomatic relations with India, as jihad can only be declared by the political leader of the Muslim umma, who in the absence of the caliph, was the Pakistani leader. This radical but logical policy and his support for the campaign against Ahmadis (which led to the 1953 Lahore riots) was a danger to the survival of the new and very fragile secular state. He was sentenced to death for sedition in 1953, though pardoned and freed in 1955 due to international pressure in light of his renown as a scholar. At the same time, *both* Deobandis and Ahli-Hadith issued fatwas declaring him an infidel.

Fanned by Pakistan's greatest scholar, sectarianism and intolerance blossomed after 1974, the bitter legacy of 'Muslim nationalism'. His civil disobedience campaign against the 'socialist' Bhutto and support for Zia's coup in 1997, and his insistence on Deobandi Sunnism as the sole acceptable form of Islam, inspired Bin Laden in his more ambitious, narrowly defined path of Islamic revolution. In the end, he embraced the western-backed 'jihad' against the Soviet Union in 1979—yet another Pakistani pact with the devil (this time dressed as Uncle Sam), which made him an unwitting ally of the US.

The result has been a mixed political legacy. As popularizer of the concept of an Islamic state, he inspired both Khomeini and Banna, as well as Qutb and Bin Laden. At 'home', he is remembered for supporting Zia's Islamization (Hekmatyar was an admirer of Maududi), while Jamaat i-Islami has never played a major political role in either Pakistan or Afghanistan, overshadowed by Deobandi parties and madrassas in the North-West Frontier Province (where Taliban such as Mullah Omar studied). It split into separate organizations in India (1948), Kashmir and Bangladesh (1975).

Khurshid Ahmad (b. 1932) is a Pakistani economist depicting Islam as an alternative to capitalism, concerned with the rights of labor and the poor, and calling for Islamization of politics, law, economics and education. He was Jamaat i-Islami vice president and federal minister of planning, development and statistics in Zia ul-Haq's regime. "God has revealed only broad principles and has endowed man with the freedom to apply them in every age in a way suited to the spirit and conditions of that age. It is through the *ijtihad* that people of every age try to implement and apply divine guidance to the problems of their time."[82]

Muhammad Ilyas Kandhalvi (1885–1944) founded Tablighi Jamaat in **India** in 1926, the Deobandi grassroots *dawa* organization premised on the idea that personal transformation will lead to religious revival and eventually the formation of an Islamic state. It expanded its activities in 1946, and within two decades the group had a strong presence throughout southwest and southeast Asia, Africa, Europe, and North America. Tabligh Jamaat's aversion to politics helped it operate in societies, especially western countries, where politically active religious groups faced severe restrictions. Its European headquarters is in the UK and it is now considered the largest Muslim organization in the world.

Syed al-Naquib al-Attas (b. 1931) was a founder in 1970 of the National University of **Malaysia** (NUM), which aimed to replace English with Malay in higher education. He founded and directed the Institute of Malay Language, Literature, and Culture (IBKKM) at the NUM in 1973. His philosophy and methodology of education have the goal of Islamization of the mind, body and soul and to improve the personal and collective life of Muslims as well as others, and including the spiritual and non-human environment. In 1987, he founded and directed the International Institute of Islamic Thought and Civilization (ISTAC) in Kuala Lumpur.

A Sufi, Attas maintains that modern science sees the world as mere things, that it has reduced the study of the phenomenal world to an end in itself and has an uncontrollable propensity to destroy nature itself. To use nature without a higher spiritual end has brought mankind to the state of thinking that men are gods: "Devoid of real purpose, the pursuit of knowledge becomes a deviation from the truth, which necessarily puts into question the validity of such knowledge."

> We do affirm that religion is in harmony with science. But not with modern scientific methodology and philosophy of science. Since there is no science that is free of value, we must investigate the values and judgments inherent in the presuppositions and interpretations of modern science, understanding its implications and testing the validity of values that go along with the theory. The natural world is a book with knowledge; but that knowledge is not evident merely from the physical phenomena; they are nothing but signs, the meaning of which can be understood by those who are equipped with proper knowledge, wisdom and spiritual discernment. Some natural phenomena are obvious as to their meaning, while other natural things are ambiguous; similarly there are clear verses (*muhkamat*) of the Quran, while other verses are ambiguous (*mutashabihat*). [83]

Chandra Muzaffar (b. 1947), Professor of Global Studies at the University of Science of Malaysia in Penang, is head of the International Movement for a Just World (JUST), and was born into a Hindu family.

He argues that western powers try to maintain the 'secular state vs Islamic opposition' scenario to keep the umma divided, weak, at their mercy, with Muslim ruling elites "wallowing in vulgar opulence and indulging in crude extravagance—helped by their oil wealth ... They have kept huge segments of their people poor and ignorant while they feed their fantasies with all that money can buy." The global capitalist system is prejudiced against Muslims and its interests are inimical to Islamic notions of human dignity and social justice. "The world today is a whole system of political, economic and cultural relationships which have grown out of the 200 years of western domination of the planet." [84] *Tawhid* is emerging as the unifying worldview of the whole of humanity: including the belief in a common spiritual origin, mission and destiny, belief in the organic unity of existence, acknowledgment of humanity as God's vicgerent, universal moral values, and universal rights and responsibilities, in roles and relationships which nurture a holistic way of life. Like Iqbal, he believes that Muslims "would alter the pattern of world politics. The meaning and role of Islam lies in the inevitable march of history towards world unity."[85] Islam's proven ability to ensure justice has led to its phenomenal growth from the early seventh century onwards.

The West

Iranian émigré **Seyyed Hossein Nasr** (b. 1933), a political ecologist and professor of Islamic Studies at George Washington University, disputes the need for any radical reform in Islam, calling for a better contemporary application of the ideational wealth of Islamic civilization of the past, and argues for an ecology-based ecumenism that would seek unity among the faiths by concentrating on their common respect for life as a Creation. Huntington ironically "re-introduced the concept of culture to the study of foreign policy and international relations and underscored the notion that nation-states are no longer the sole source of identity in politics."[86] Huntingdon was rooting for western consumerism, but in the post-WWII US, the war of civilizations was a double-edged sword. With the defeat of 1967, Arab secularists were discredited, and *ijtihad* and *tajdid* developed as activist programs of Islamic reform and social transformation.

Feisal Abdul Rauf (b. 1948) is an American Sufi imam-activist based in New York, born in Kuwait, son of Egyptian Imam and Sunni scholar Muhammad Abdul Rauf (1917–2004), who in turn was actively involved in the American civil rights movement with Malcolm X. Feisal has written several books on Islam and its place in contemporary western society, including *What's Right with Islam Is What's Right with America* (2005) and founded two non-profit organizations whose stated missions are to enhance the discourse on Islam in society. He condemned the 9/11 attacks as un-Islamic, called on the

US government to reduce the threat of terrorism by altering its Middle Eastern foreign policies, and has advised the FBI and State Department on matters related to Islam and the US.[87]

In 2003, Rauf founded the Cordoba Initiative with offices in both New York and Kuala Lumpur, Malaysia. He opened Cordoba House at 45 Park Place in 2009, two blocks from Ground Zero in lower Manhattan as a Sufi Islamic Community Center with support of 9/11 families and Council on American-Islam Relations leaders, though it was denounced loudly in the media. The Muslim prayer room accommodating 1,000 nonetheless opened in September 2011.

Ziauddin Sardar (b. 1951) is a London-based Indian author, founder of *Critical Muslim*, and maker of BBC documentaries, including "Encounters With Islam" (1983), "Islamic Conversations" (Channel 4 1995), "Battle for Islam" (2005), and "The Life of Muhammad" (2011). He writes: "Muslims have been on the verge of physical, cultural and intellectual extinction simply because they have allowed parochialism and traditionalism to rule their minds."[88] "I am not against secularism—I believe that the state should be fair and just to all and neutral in matters of religion. But I am against secularism as an ideology—religion has an important part to play in the public sphere—in shaping civic society, in debating issues of ethics and morality, in promoting social justice and in holding corrupt politicians and decision-makers accountable."[89] "Sovereignty belongs to God in cosmic terms, but when it comes down to earthly sovereignty, it belongs to those who can make earthly decisions. The trust of responsibility and accountability for earthly decision belongs to all humanity ... through mutual consultation."[90]

Bashir Musa Mohammed Nafi (b. 1953) is an Egyptian who teaches history and Islamic studies at London's Birkbeck College. He critiques post-Enlightenment culture, as "imbued with a Darwinian view of the world: the belief in the sheer value of power, domination and the superiority of western civilization".

> Why should the Germans be asked to detach themselves, on every possible level, from their Nazi past, while the French, the British, the Dutch, the Americans, have made no effort to purify their souls of their imperialist past? Imperialism inflicted profound damage, not only on the cultural, economic and social life of the colonised peoples but also, more so, on the moral well-being of the colonizers themselves.[91]

Nafi sees Muslim self-confidence as being restored, though this is a long process involving "painful self-examination and renewal ... a continuation of the process of decolonization". In the non-western world, "western practices, with some variations, are largely hegemonic, exploitative, non-democratic and rarely responsive to the wishes of the peoples, especially when these wishes are in contradiction with western interests."

Tariq Ramadan (b. 1962) is a Swiss academic, whose Egyptian father Said Ramadan was the MB's chief international organizer (see above) and whose mother was Banna's eldest daughter. He writes about Islamic reform from a European Muslim's point of view, rejecting the assimilationist position that Islam must adapt to modernity. He believes that western Muslims must create a "western Islam" just as there is a separate "Asian Islam" and an "African Islam", which take into account cultural differences.

By this he means that European Muslims must re-examine not only the fundamental texts of Islam (primarily the Quran) and interpret them in light of their own cultural context, but also proposes the concept of "two books" as texts—the Quran and "the universe", "the world, nature, and the human and exact sciences". The universe consists of "Signs for a people that are wise" (2:164), on which Allah exhorts us to observe and reflect. This is the work of "context specialists", no longer only Quranic text specialists, who can "formulate judgments, stages, and action strategies according to the requirements and modalities of moral faithfulness and coherence in modern times". This does not just mean "relativizing the universal principles of Islam in order to give the impression that we are integrating ourselves into the rational order." [92] Muslims must critique modernity, develop a moral and ethical alternative inspired by Islam.

Ramadan brings together both the Wali Allah and Wahhabi aspects of reform. Only a highly literate umma, able to reason and think for themselves, can be a suitable vehicle for radical reform, not just of Islam, but of modernity. Being true to Islam's eternal truth paradoxically requires constant rereading and interpreting. Being true to the text means interpreting it in the context. He criticizes all other reformers for their failings, the assimilationists for their naiveté about imperialism, Hizb ut-Tahrir for their desire to 'Islamize modernity' by imposing "an 'Islamic system' purified of western failings", a caliphate. The Turkish AKP and the MBs are "more sophisticated and less dualistic" but have "determined a relationship to the texts and to political power based on analyses that date back to the early or mid-twentieth century; they find it difficult to evolve and make a comprehensive reassessment." [93]

Ramadan's use of the Sufi concept of 'two books' (the Quran and the actual signs around us), [94] his prescription for western Muslims to integrate [95] (Qaradawi advocates the more conservative "loyal resident alienage"), his concept of "Islam*s*" and his critique of the MB make him a particularly controversial figure among contemporary reformers.

There are important western intellectuals who have **converted** to Islam, providing powerful proof of its universality. They are invariably traditionalists, versed in Islamic history and Sufism, turning to Islam in revulsion against western modernity.

Sir Wilfrid Blunt (1840–1922) was remarkable as one of the early western anti-imperialists, who befriended and studied with Abduh, and who tried valiantly to reform the imperial center at the same time as he acted as an enlightened guide for the Muslim world under the imperial onslaught. He never converted formally, but his sympathy for Islam and disdain for British imperial culture is evident in his life and work. His *The Future of Islam (*1882) was published in the heat of the French invasion of Tunis and the 1882 uprising by Egyptian nationalists under Urabi, whom he urged the supposedly anti-imperial British Prime Minister Palmerston to support. However, the Foreign Office was more interested in securing the Suez Canal in perpetuity; Britain proceeded to occupy Egypt and helped overthrow the rebels. The "suppression of liberty in Egypt ... the struggle of 1882 will appear to [Egyptians] in its true light as the beginning of their national life."[96]

Blunt, writing in the third person, "predicted for the Mohammedan great political misfortunes in the immediate future ... a necessary stop in the process of their spiritual development", but he had "supreme confidence in Islam, not only as a spiritual, but as a temporal system, the heritage and gift of the Arabian race and capable of satisfying their most civilized wants and he believes in the hour of their political resurgence." The French and British invasions "precipitated the Mohammedan movement in North Africa" but "better days shall come ... The revival taking place in the Mohammedan world is indeed worthy of every Englishman's attention."[97] The changes are "analogous to those which Christendom underwent 400 years ago ... Though civilization presents itself to [Arabia] only as an enemy, [some Muslims are] capable, not only of understanding the better thought of Europe, but of sympathizing with it as akin to her [Islam's] own."[98] The "day of religious hatred between Moslem and Christian, I hope, is nearly at an end [as Christianity had] abandoned the hopeless task of converting Islam, as Islam has hers to conquering Europe. Moral sympathy should unite" the two great faiths. "Europe will never obtain sure colonial footing south of the Atlas." [99]

Like T.E. Laurence, he was an Arabophile and was eager to see the collapse of the Ottoman Caliphate as an artificial Turkish imposition on the Arab world. He criticized Ottomans as lazy, for not knowing Arabic and having "lax moral practice", and predicted their top-down imposition of Tanzimat reforms was doomed as it made no attempt to reconcile with the Quran. He lauded "Arabian thought" and wanted Mecca as the seat of the future caliphate, criticizing the Wahhabis as a puritanical aberration. His hope was that the British would occupy the bulk of the Ottoman world, preserving it as one umma "without further aggression from Europe" and allow the umma to reform as a unified community allied to Britain, governed through the "spiritual inheritance of Africa and Southern Asia".[100] Britain should nurture such leaders as Abduh to usher in reforms which would preserve Islam but meet the demands of modernity.

Blunt's 'blunt' critique of British imperial strategy and utopian vision didn't have a chance given imperial logic and British-French-German rivalry. He touchingly warned the imperial chauvinists that "the characteristics of the coloured people were of such intrinsic value that they must never be diluted by Anglo-Saxon rule with its debased industrialism, its crude cookery, and its flavourless religious creed,"[101] foreshadowing the later critique of postmodernity outlined here by Eaton from the right and Foucault from the left.

Marmaduke Pickthall (1875–1936), the son of a middle class Anglican parson, traveled to Egypt at age 18 in 1894[102] and, at the height of WWI in 1917, devastated by the war blessed on both sides by the Christian churches, he converted to Islam, announcing his decision after delivering a talk "Islam and Progress" to the Muslim Literary Society in London. Unlike Blunt, he considered the abolition of the Caliphate a great tragedy for Islam, moved to India to teach and translate the Quran, and became a close associate of Gandhi, supporting the ulama's rejection of both violent resistance to British rule and partition of India into Hindu and Muslim states. He was a revivalist favoring the caliphate pre-capitalist lifestyle of simplicity and peace. He represents a growing trend from the nineteenth century on, as imperialism invaded the Muslim world, and educated western youth became attracted to

the sincerity and purity of Islam, reacting to the hypocrisy of western consumerism and materialism, devoting themselves to *dawa* and fighting anti-Muslim prejudice.

René Guénon (1886–1951) was a French author and mystic who went to Egypt in 1930, converted to Islam and became a disciple of Sheikh Salama Hassan al-Radi, founder of the Hamidiya Shadhiliya Sufi order. He later establish a French Masonic lodge, *La Grande Triade,* founded on traditional Sufi ideals, which is still active today. He is a proponent of the Perennialist School, based on the belief that all the world's great religions share the same origin and are, at root, based on the same metaphysical principles, rejecting post-Enlightenment modernity: "The rational, material and secular worldview of modern science threatens to overwhelm the traditional human quest for the metaphysical and spiritual realities that underlie the grand design of the natural world."[103] He was devoted to reviving the "Primordial Tradition" which predates the monotheisms, and saw Sufism as providing a window into this tradition, which otherwise survived only in part in the oldest religious tradition extant—Hinduism. Describing

imperialism in the aftermath of WWI in "East and West" (1924), he wrote, "It is as if an organism with its head cut off were to go on living a life which was both intense and disordered."[104]

Muhammad Asad (Leopold Weiss, 1900–1992),[105] came from a long line of Austrian rabbis, and, like Pickthall, traveled to the Middle East as a young man, going to stay with a Zionist uncle in Jerusalem in 1922. But he was not impressed with the Jewish plans to create a state. Instead of becoming a Zionist, he was struck by how Islam infused Muslims' everyday lives with existential meaning, spiritual strength and inner peace, though he was disappointed in the corruption of Muslim society. In contrast to Islam, he wrote, Judaism

> tended to make God appear not as the creator and sustainer of all mankind but, rather, as a tribal deity adjusting all creation to the requirements of a 'chosen people'... Viewed against these fundamental shortcomings, even the ethical fervour of the later Prophets, like Isaiah and Jeremiah, seemed to be barren of a universal message ... Islam appears to me like a perfect work of architecture. All its parts are harmoniously conceived to complement and support each other; nothing is superfluous and nothing lacking; and the result is a structure of absolute balance and solid composure. [106]

His travels and sojourns through Egypt, Saudi Arabia, Iran, Afghanistan and the southern Soviet 'republics' were viewed with great suspicion by the colonial powers, as he took a close interest in the many liberation movements that were active at this time with the aim of freeing Muslim lands from colonial rule. In 1932 he met Muhammad Iqbal who persuaded Asad to stay on in British India and help the Muslims of India establish their separate Muslim state. His parents were murdered by the Nazis, even as Asad was interned by the British in India as an enemy alien. He was granted full citizenship by Pakistan after the war and appointed director of the Department of Islamic Reconstruction, later head of the Foreign Affairs Middle East Division to strengthen Pakistan's ties with the Muslim world, and Pakistan's minister plenipotentiary to the UN in 1952. In *This Law of Ours* (1980) he rejects the notion of *taqlid*, or strict judicial precedent, calling for *ijtihad*, rationalism and plurality in Islamic law, the true legacy of the Salafi or earliest generations of Muslims.

In *Islam at the Crossroads* (1954), he warns that by accepting western values and morality, the Muslim world will compromise its religion and culture, and at best be a poor imitation of the West. Education imbued with the values of Islam is a must to achieve a vibrant Islamic democracy. "After our own cultural decadence and centuries-old stagnation of Muslim thought, the West opposes attempts to renew Muslim thought and politics. Reactionary elements in Muslim society" are the "principle weapon in this campaign to discredit Islam." Western schools also lead to the situation where "distrust of Islam as a social doctrine is being systematically planted in the minds of younger generations of Muslim men and women," which leads to the discrediting of sharia. "Sharia can't just continue using *fiqh* traditions. There are many schools, contradictory, out-of-date, second hand. One can't impose these laws on a non-Muslim minority." [107] Asad proposed to harmonize existing *fiqh*, establishing a panel of scholars from all schools of *fiqh* to draft a sharia code. This codification and adoption of sharia would be "a basis for our communal life" which alone can prevent the "ultimate dissolution of our culture". Muslims must make clear to themselves and the world that "Islam is a practical proposition for all times, and therefore for our time as well." [108]

His son **Talal Asad** (b. 1933) is an anthropologist at City University of New York. He abandoned Islam in his 20s–30s, but disillusioned with western secularism, came back to a religious viewpoint after the 1967 war, [109] and developed the "anthropology of secularism", based on Neitzsche and Foucault. Secularism is not merely the division between public and private realms that allows religious diversity to flourish in the latter. It defines religion narrowly to give secularism hegemony in social and hence, personal life, actively excluding religion from public life (barring religious symbols and rituals in public) and losing touch with the ways in which embodied practices of conduct help to constitute culture. Muslims in the West are treated as a minority either to be tolerated (the liberal orientation) or restricted (the national orientation), depending on the politics of the day.

The Swiss **Frithjof Schuon** (1907–1998), like Guenon and Eaton, was first attracted to Hinduism before converting to Islam in Algeria in 1932 under the Sufi Sheikh Ahmad al-Alawi. He lived with and wrote about the

Plains Indians in the US, emphasizing the commonalities between native religions and Islam. Schuon likens the role of Muhammad in Islam to that of Mary: "Mary gave birth to Jesus without passing on to him any taint of earthly sin, and Muhammad acted as a channel for the Word without lending it any taint of merely human wisdom." For Christians, Jesus is "the Word made flesh," whereas for Muslims, the Word "took earthly shape in the form of a book."[110]

Martin Lings (1909–2005), an English convert and follower of Guenon and Schuon, is best known for *Muhammad: His Life Based on the Earliest Sources* (1983). A recent edition of Lings' books on Shakespeare includes a foreword by Prince Charles.

Charles Le Gai Eaton (1921–2010) was born in Switzerland and raised as an agnostic. He worked as a teacher and journalist in Jamaica and Egypt before joining the British diplomatic service, converting to Islam in 1951, and retiring to work at the Islamic Cultural Centre in London. Like Seyyed Nasr and Lings, he was a follower of Schuon. For Eaton, Islam—like all the great religions—is above all a path of inner transformation, the cultivation of virtue, but requiring recognition of the centrality of religion to all facets of life, so that this path can be followed by all. Eaton was especially concerned with reconciling Christianity and Islam. In *Islam and the Destiny of Man* he explains that "The rivalry between the two Faiths, the two cultures, resurfaced, as it was bound to do sooner or later since Islam claims a universal mission as does western civilization."[111] But he is confident that mutual understanding is possible: "It is time for the Muslims in Britain to settle down, to find their own way, to form a real community and to discover a specifically British way of living Islam ... This is no curry-island."

Maryam Jameelah (1934–2012) is a follower of Maududi, an American Jew who converted to Islam, emigrated to Pakistan, married and had a family, and then wrote several attacks on liberal Islamic reform movements. She denounced "our indigenous modernists who want to force Islam into the rigid mold of modern secularism and materialism in alliance with the Christian missions and foreign imperialisms. Indeed, they are the most effective agents for accomplishing their work."[112] She especially condemns Abduh, and the "new idolatry— contemporary deities of Change, Modernization, Development, and Progress".[113] "Imperialist powers set about the task of deculturizing us in a methodical, scientific manner to ensure that we should not ever be able to recover and reorganize ourselves into a vital force. A liberal elite was created who regarded their own faith, historical and cultural heritage with indifference which quickly developed into unconcealed contempt."[114] "Cultural slavery" is inseparable from "political slavery".[115]

Karen Armstrong (b. 1944) is a former nun who writes on Judaism, Christianity, Islam and Buddhism, now calling herself a "freelance monotheist".

She has advanced the theory that fundamentalist religion is a response to and product of modern culture, and has been influential in conveying sympathetically the meaning of Islam to a wide readership in Europe and North America.

Singer/composer **Cat Stevens** (b. 1948) cut his singing career short to become Yusuf Islam in 1977 and has been a high-profile spokesman for the British Muslim community.

Hamza Yusuf (Mark Hanson, b. 1958), is an American Islamic scholar, co-founder of Zaytuna College in Berkeley, California, according to Esposito, "the western world's most influential Islamic scholar",[116] dedicated to the revival of traditional study methods and the sciences of Islam. "Many people in the West do not realise how oppressive some Muslim states are—both for men and for women. This is a cultural issue, not an Islamic one. I would rather live as a Muslim in the West than in most of the Muslim countries, because I think the way Muslims are allowed to live in the West is closer to the Muslim way. A lot of Muslim immigrants feel the same way, which is why they are here."[117] Following the murder of the US ambassador to Libya first billed in the media as in retaliation for the internet film "Innocence of Muslims", Yusuf broadcast a Friday *khutba* on Youtube "Stop practicing Islam, or stop pretending" (27 September 2012) calling on Muslims to follow Muhammad's example in the face of insults— patience and *taqwa* (piety), to "answer a bad deed with a good deed, since bad is the absence of good, and we must fill the vacuum with good so there is no room for bad. This is part of striving to transcend our human nature, to transform our nature (*taqwa*)." [118]

Abdal Hakim Murad, (Tim Winter, b. 1960) is lecturer in Islamic studies in the Faculty of Divinity at Cambridge University. He foresees the "re-Islamization of Europe" when Turkey becomes part of the EU and relations with Russia develop.

> Islam, once we have become familiar with it, and settled into it comfortably, is the most suitable faith for the British. Its values are our values. Its moderate, undemonstrative style of piety, its insistence on modesty and a certain reserve, and its insistence on common sense and on pragmatism, combine to furnish the most natural and easy religious option for our people ... It is generous and inclusive. It allows us to celebrate our particularity, within, rather than in tension with, the greater and more lasting fellowship of faith."[119]

One notable feature uniting many reformers, including Rida in Egypt, Iqbal and Maududi in Pakistan, Jalal Ali Ahmad in Iran, Muhammad Asad's scholar son Talal and others in the West, and even Qutb and other extremists, is their shift towards a more traditionalist position over time, as a result of both the course of world events but also as a result of their own spiritual journeys and their realization of the aridity of a secular society built on technology and reason alone. Especially following 1967, this shift in worldview has been experienced by leading leftists in the Arab world, such as Mustafa Mahmoud, who refers to "my trip from doubt to faith",[120] and in Turkey by such as poet-philosopher Ismet Ozel, whose *Three Problems: Technology, Civilization and Alienation* (1978) argues that the alienation resulting from destructive technology and the artificial division of man and nature can only be healed by the enlightened principles of Islam which emphasize the synthesis of the sacred and the profane.

The ideas of Islamic revival and reform in the twentieth century have survived the war on Islam which followed the Cold War against the Soviet Union (itself, 'won' at the end in Afghanistan largely thanks to Islamists). The

> new geography of Muslim politics precludes a 'West versus the Rest' mentality because of the dissolution of prior notions of distance and frontier. There is a significant and continually growing Muslim voice in the 'West' itself [which means that] western and Muslim societies are now on the threshold of new understandings of one another,[121]

recapitulating the relationship between Japan and the US after WWII, which unwittingly led to the 'invasion' by Buddhism and eastern philosophy into the US.

Premodern Revivalists: from Wahhabi to Neo-Wahhabi

The Kharijites who murdered Muhammad's cousin Ali have from the start represented "a powerful current of puritanism which has, since their time, surfaced again and again in the history of Islam, calling for a return to the 'true values' of Islam, as they were practiced in Medina in the lifetime of the Prophet."[122] They believed that

> history had come to an end after the revelation to the Last Prophet. ... They developed a narrow and fixed, ahistoric interpretation of what it means to be a Muslim—to be in a perfect state of soul. Someone in that state cannot commit a sin and engage in any wrongdoing. Sin, therefore was a contradiction for a true Muslim—it nullified the believer and demonstrated that inwardly he was an apostate who had turned against Islam and could be put to death.[123]

Today's incarnation of these premodern revivalists, dubbed **neo-Wahhabis** by Seyyed Nasr, have their roots in the nineteenth century. Their equivalent in secular Europe were certain anarchists, who saw targeted acts of violence as a strategy to bring down the entire imperialist system, either by discrediting it, causing popular uprisings, or by inciting wars where the imperialists would destroy themselves. This scenario for revolution was adopted wholesale by the neo-Wahhabis.

Both the Wahhabis and their neo-Wahhabi al-Qaeda offshoots are fundamentalists (as opposed to traditionalists, see Chapter 1 Appendix B). While literalists in reading the Quran and rejection of western attire in favor of traditional dress, they inherently accept the Enlightenment, use secular science unthinkingly, and practice politics and economics which are far removed from the *maqasid* of the Quran, except for the formal banning of interest and a rigid adherence to their version of sharia. Wahhab's depiction of the Ottomans as the new Mongols, pseudo-Muslim leaders who could be overthrown as kufar, provided the justification for the Saud tribe's seizure of the holy cities, and eventually the establishment of the Saudi state. The 'gates of *ijtihad* closed' for the Wahhabis after that, and the new behind-the-scenes ruler of the world, America, was befriended and accommodated.

But the spirit of Wahhab lived on. The Saud tribal leader Ibn Saud had to quell his *Ikhwan* rebels, who wanted no truck with the imperialists.[124] Qutb refashioned 1960s secular anti-imperialist revolutionary thought in strictly religious terms. This movement became popular throughout the Middle East, attracting Muslim youth disillusioned with their secular accommodationist leaders, including Nasser, especially after the 1967 defeat, as Qutb correctly identified the real enemy of Islam as the imperialists, and by association, their Wahhabi allies in Saudi Arabia and the Gulf. Thus, it would be more accurate to call the terrorism emanating from the Muslim world "Qutbian terrorism",[125] and the suicide bombers as Islamo-anarchists, followers of "a western tradition of individual and pessimistic revolt for an elusive ideal world" rather than imbued with the Quranic concept of martyrdom.[126]

The catalysts that turned a conservative movement to revive Islam as the guiding force in society into a revolutionary jihad came together in the 1970s:

1. Sadat's open accommodation with Israel in 1979. The clause in the 1981 treaty promising a Palestinian state within five years was mere window-dressing, with the treaty seen by Muslims as Egypt abandoning the struggle to free Palestine in exchange for the return of Sinai and billions of dollars of 'aid' from the US.
2. Sadat's *infitah* (opening), an early application of Reaganomics and Thatcherism, the empire's new neoliberal ideology promoting privatization, deregulation and the dismantling of social welfare. No

longer would the Muslim states promise to fulfill even minimally the obligations in the Quran for social welfare, as the local elites became super-wealthy through corruption and accommodation with the West, and their economies stagnated.

3. Nasser and Sadat's persecution of the MB, which drove hundreds of articulate, well-educated, activist Islamists to seek refuge in Saudi Arabia, where they taught in schools and universities, educating a generation of Saudis into Banna's and Qutb's world of anti-imperialist, anti-communist jihad. They included Banna's son-in-law Said Ramadan (see above), Abdullah Azzam (see below), Omar Abdel Rahman (see Chapter 5 "Jihad vs Terrorism"), and Qutb's brother Muhammad, who wrote several textbooks for the Saudi school curriculum.[127]

4. The Islamic revolution in Iran in 1979, suggesting that politicization of Muslims could lead to the overthrow of their pro-western leaders.

5. The Soviet Union's occupation of Afghanistan in support of a secular socialist revolution in 1979. Communism's militant atheism made it a more egregious foe to Muslims than capitalism, and suddenly the 'lesser of the two evils' was providing a blank cheque to fund the destruction of the 'greater evil'.

Enemy countries (*dar al-harb*) that are at war with Muslims but are not attacking them personally demand 'collective duty' jihad. If a Muslim has the misfortune of living in *dar al-harb* where it is impossible to follow sharia law, Ibn Taymiya affirms, then they must emigrate, emulating the early Muslims' *hijra*.[128] In the early 1970s, the Egyptian Takfir wa al-hijra (unbelief and emigration) was organized, advocating that religious persons withdraw from the world because so many sinful Muslims had abandoned their faith. But this smacked of Christian monasticism, which was explicitly forbidden in the Quran. In any case, genuine *hijra* was no longer possible under imperialism, where the entire Muslim world was under the rule of kufar. Sadat's Egypt was at peace with Israel even as it was killing and dispossessing Palestinians in violation of sharia, making Egyptian politicians the enemy as well. What was a good Muslim to do?

The Wahhabi argument for armed jihad against kufar leaders, updated by Qutb, attracted those fed up with their worsening situation.[129] Distant Iran responded at the time to the Iranian version of these problems (the Shah had long been a tacit supporter of Israel, and US economic policy was the order of the day) with a full-fledged Islamic revolution. However, the Arab world was much better incorporated into the neocolonial order and jihad was in the air. The Soviets became the target that everyone could agree on, bringing all into a common effort—Wahhabis, Salafis, neo-Wahhabis, accommodationists, traditionalists, backed initially by the US, Saudi Arabia and Egypt, and soon joined by China, Israel and the newly Islamic Iran, concerned about the Shia Hazaris in Afghanistan. The US managed to deflect the pent-up frustrations of the Muslim world, projecting them onto its own sworn enemy.

The neo-Wahhabi mujahideen/ terrorists/ what-have-you were suddenly the heroes of the day, feted by Reagan in the White House,[130] and found their charismatic Qutb in the guise of Saudi millionaire ex-business administration student **Osama Bin Laden** (1957–2011), who established al-Qaeda in 1987, threw scholarly caution to the winds and began to issue fatwas, using videos and later the internet.

A young Egyptian electrician, **Muhammad Faraj** (1954–1982), wrote a manual on jihad "The Neglected Duty", describing jihad not just a collective or even individual duty, but as the "defining characteristic of Islam",[131] Banna/ Maududi's "sixth pillar". Faraj quotes Ibn Taymiya that, "It is a well-established rule of Islamic Law that the punishment of an apostate will be heavier than the punishment of someone who is by origin an infidel."[132] Based on this, his comrade in the Egyptian Islamic Jihad, the Egyptian medical doctor **Ayman al-Zawahiri** (b. 1951), demanded that they first target the 'near enemy' (pseudo-Muslim leaders) for violent overthrow as a prelude to overthrowing the 'far enemy' (Israel and the US),[133] though only Khalid Islambouli 'succeeded' in assassinating Sadat in 1981: "I have killed Pharaoh and I do not fear death!"

Palestinian **Abdullah Azzam** (1941–1989), founder of both the Office of Services along with Bin Laden and Hamas, took the plan of total war against the kufar to its logical conclusion, demanding armed struggle to free all lands with Muslims (in his case Palestine), arguing that whatever travails local Muslims experience would serve to mobilize the Muslim masses, and that any who die in the process would find their reward for martyrdom in Heaven.[134] Al-Qaeda member **Mamdouh Mahmud Salim** (b. 1958) 'reasoned' that it is even acceptable to kill innocent Muslims in the struggle to expel US invaders (if they are guilty of aiding the kufar or even if totally innocent they will at least still go to heaven) and Bin Laden/ Zawahiri jointly issued their "International Islamic Front for Jihad Against Jews and Crusaders" fatwa of February 1998:

> To kill the Americans and their allies—civilians and military—is an individual duty for every Muslim who can do it in any country in which it is possible, in order to liberate the al-Aqsa Mosque and the holy mosque [Mecca] from their grip, and in order for their armies to move out of all the lands of Islam, defeated and unable to threaten any Muslim[135]

This stretches the law of equity in the Quran ("An eye for an eye") to: let

America "taste some of what we are tasting".[136] But then the Bush-Obama practice of assassinating whoever the US government decides is a terrorist, including US citizens and unavoidably involving 'collateral damage', is exactly the sense of these fatwas, once again showing how much a product of Enlightenment thinking the current 'war on terror' is, *for both sides*. No court indictment is necessary for US president, since any evidence is 'top secret', giving him *carte blanche* to kill whoever, wherever he pleases.

Gaza-based **Abu Muhammad al-Maqdisi** (1959–2012), spiritual mentor of Iraq's al-Qaeda leader Zarqawi, used the Wahhabi doctrine that Muslims showing loyalty to polytheists become like them and are thus kufar to denounce the Saudi rulers who had invited the 543,000 US troops onto the sacred Arabian lands in 1990 to attack another Muslim nation, Iraq.[137] This reasoning, which is hard to argue with, made both Saudi leaders and US troops fair game for elimination (though not innocent civilians, for which there is no justification in Islam).

Bin Laden's rationale behind his one-man declaration of anything-goes against the mighty empire—though a very risky one—was that all the upheaval and suffering will force the empire to increase its military expenditures to the point of bankruptcy, and they would then have to abandon their Muslim comprador leaders to the forces of al-Qaeda. "If they defeated America, they thought, Arab governments would fall into their hands."[138]

Thus the 1998 fatwa was more intended to sabotage Egypt's Nonviolence Initiative to release thousands of imprisoned suspected radicals in return for their formal disavowal of violent activity, and to justify the Zawahiri-inspired killing of 58 tourists and four locals in Luxor in November 1997. That is, to keep the fires of revolution ablaze.

It is one thing to kill a leader (Sadat) who is seen as betraying Islam, in a one-off popular enactment of divine justice, but to make it part of an ongoing campaign of terror, without a realistic strategy—including the requisite mass support to overthrow the regime and replace it with something else—was both foolish and criminal, especially given imperialism's proven track-record of infiltrating rebel groups and carrying out false-flag acts of terrorism attributable to imperialism's enemies.[139]

The debate raging around whether 911 was just such a false-flag act continues with good reason. Immediately after 911, Bin Laden issued a statement denying involvement and saying "nor do I consider the killing of innocent women, children, and other humans as an appreciable act. Islam strictly forbids causing harm to innocent women, children, and other people". Disputed video pronouncements by him since claim credit for 911. But his earlier involvement in the 'jihad' in Afghanistan, and his co-authorship of the infamous fatwa "Jihad Against Jews and Crusaders", tacitly approved the Luxor killings in 1997 and the August 1998 bombings of US embassies in

Tanzania and Kenya, in which 224 mostly innocent bystanders were killed, contradicting his pious self image.[140]

The weakness of this exercise in *ijtihad* is clear. Does killing Americans "in any country"—effectively, killing imperialism's messengers, however lowly—help defeat America the empire? Or rather, does it merely increases repression against Muslims locally and make American foreign policy towards Muslims even more ruthless? The alternative—attacking the "far enemy" directly through an act of terrorism—similarly will harm far more Muslims in the long run than nonbelievers.

In armed jihad, Muhammad explicitly forbade killing children, women, slaves, and prisoners of war, restricting killing to enemy soldiers. "You shall not be treacherous, you shall not deceive, you shall not mutilate, you shall not kill children nor their inhabitants of hermitages."[141] So the indiscriminate violence theorized by such as Faraj and Zawahiri, and supposedly carried out by Egyptian Islamic Jihad and the various al-Qaeda affiliates are clearly in contradiction to the Quran, and as such are unacceptable as an exercise in *ijtihad*.

The extra-legal premoderns, with their dubious exercises in *ijtihad* (all Wahhab, no Wali Allah), are a direct result of the imperial policies of the twentieth century—occupation of Muslim lands and support of corrupt comprador leaders, and creation and support of a Jewish state, populated largely by European and American Jews, in the spiritual heartland of the Muslim world. These strategies, combined with the low level of intellectual life in the oil-rich, pampered Wahhabi-dominated states, produced a fertile breeding ground for the funding and propagation of this perversion of jihad, inspiring not only genuine terrorists of all stripes, but also providing cover for false-flag operations by the empire, intended to weaken Iraq (now Iran and Syria) and blacken Islam everywhere. [142]

It is just not possible that the US government watched this scenario unfold without tacit approval, since it was US petrodollars that have been paying for it all along. From 1997–2000, Saudi Arabia, the UAE and Pakistan—all US allies—recognized and aided the Taliban, and accepted Bin Laden's presence there. Clearly the Saudi leadership feared/ respected/ encouraged Bin Laden in his self-styled jihad as long as he left the them alone, as he was merely doing what they should have been doing as followers of Wahhab. Even the CIA realizes and admits this openly.[143]

These premoderns waged wars in Afghanistan in the 1980s–1990s, in Bosnia and Kosovo in the 1990s, in Libya and in Syria in 2011.They established 'caliphates', however short-lived, in parts of Yemen and Mali,[144] and continue to inspire terrorist acts, though targeting Muslims collaborators more often than forces of the empire. In military conflicts in each of these countries, al-Qaeda (or one of its associates) and the US have been on the same side, using local grievances to promote their intertwined agendas of defeating those holding local power. Their common (collaborative) slogan: 'regime change for those in the empire, regime change for all those *inconvenient to* the empire.'

ENDNOTES

1   See Eric Walberg, *Postmodern Imperialism: Geopolitics and the Great Games.*

2   Religion is now respected throughout the former socialist bloc, and Islam in the Russia Federation is playing an increasingly prominent role in society.

3   Even Egypt's ex-president Hosni Mubarak had enough of the anti-MB chaos caused by his followers and other secularists, calling out in March 2013 against violent protests and for Egyptians to "rally around their elected president", according to his lawyer Farid el-Deeb. "Mubarak wants Egyptians to rally around Morsi for peace", *Saudi Gazette*, 12 March 2013.

4   Seyyed Hossein Nasr, *Islam in the Modern World: Challenged by the West, Threatened by fundamentalism, Keeping faith with Tradition*, USA: Harper One, 2010, 267.

5   As does Akbar Ahmed, calling them Deobandis. See Chapter 2.

6   Nasr, *Islam in the Modern World,* 276.

7   Sohrab Behdad and Farhad Nomani (eds), *Islam and the Everyday World: Public policy dilemmas*, New York: Routledge, 2006, 19. His support of Zia al-Haq's cynical embrace of Islamic appearances while acting as a willing handmaiden to Reagan's 'jihad' against the Soviet Union was a sorry way to end his work to realize Islamic civilization.

8   John Esposito, *Islam and Secularism in the Middle East*, USA: NYU Press, 2000, 4–5.

9   Hakam Yavuz, "Political Islam and the Welfare Party in Turkey", *Comparative Politics*, vol. 30, no. 1 (October 1997), 65.

10   David Kirkpatrick, "Turkey's Erdogan nurtures new role in the Middle East", *New York Times*, 13 September 2011.

11   David Kirkpatrick, "Premier of Turkey takes role in region", *New York Times*, 12 September 2011.

12   Barack Obama made Turkey his first overseas bilateral meeting in 2009: "Turkey and the US can build a model partnership in which a predominantly Christian nation [and] a predominantly Muslim nation can create a modern international community that is respectful, that is secure, that is prosperous, that there are not inevitable tensions between cultures."

13   "Turkish Finmin says EU needs Turkey to retain importance", *europeanunion-platform.org*, 19 September 2011.

14   Quotes here from Kerim Balci, "Philosophical depth: A scholarly talk with the Turkish foreign minister", *turkishreview.org*, 1 November 2010.

15   Ahmet Davutoglu, "Philosophical and institutional dimensions of secularization: A comparative analysis", in John Esposito, *Islam and Secularism in the Middle East*, 184. Capitalism and socialism were "different forms of the same philosophical background ... The downfall of communism was not a victory of the West but the first step to the end of European domination of the world to be followed by the collapse of western capitalism." Ahmet Davutoglu, *Civilizational Transformation and the Muslim World,* USA: Quill, 1994, 64.

16   The limited globalization of Alexander the Great gave birth to three Hellenic trends: Stoicism, the Cynic School and the Epicurean School. Stoicism looked for a new order that sought a mechanical system that would rule over both Greece and Babel. Cynicism was born as a response to this mechanical order. Diogenes' "Stand out of my sunlight!" revolt against Alexander is in fact a symbolic expression of a resistance to the new mechanical order. The

Epicurean School created a new expectation from the new reality: Let's all seek our pleasures under the new mechanical order! The current globalization has produced three very similar trends. The new Stoics are those who speak of a "new world order". The modern Cynics are the postmodernists: Let everyone be happy in his own world and leave aside the quest for an absolute truth. The Epicureanist response to the recent globalization is the culture of consumption: I can drink my coke and be happy; why should I think about other systemic issues?

17   Ahmet Davutoglu, *Alternative Paradigms: The Impact of Islamic and Western Weltanschauungs on the Political Theory,* USA: University Press of America, 1993, 202.

18   He downplays the 'clash of civilizations' theory, insisting that "encounters between the Islamic and western civilizations" are fruitful, though his postmodern western critics disagree. See Svante Cornell, "What Drives Turkish Foreign Policy?", *Middle East Quarterly,* Vol. XIX: No. 1, Winter 2012.

19   Putting this policy into practice has proved not so easy. Turkey's embrace of the NATO/ Gulf-backed Syrian insurgency and its increased tensions with Israel, Armenia, Iran, Iraq and its own Kurds have so far created more enemies than friends.

20   Karen Armstrong, *Islam: A Short History*, Modern Library, 2000, 154.

21   Dale Eickelman and James Piscatori, *Muslim Politics,* USA: Princeton University Press, 1996, 28–32.

22   Muhammad Rashid, *The caliphate or the great imamate*, Cairo: Matbaat al-Manar bi-Misr, 1934, 57–65.

23   Emmanuel Sivan, *Radical Islam: Medieval Theology and Modern Politics*, USA: Yale University Press, 1990, 101

24   Ana Belén Soage, "Rashid Rida's Legacy", *The Muslim World,* 98/1, 2008, 57–65.

25   Cyril Glasse, *The New Encyclopedia of Islam*, USA: Altamira Press, 2001, 384.

26   Malise Ruthven, *Fundamentalism: The Search for Meaning*, UK: Oxford University Press, 2003, 174.

27   Hassan al-Banna, "The Message of the Teachings", Appendix in Qutb, *Milestones*, 250.

28   Hassan al-Banna, "Kitab al-jihad", 236.

29   Ibid.

30   Attributed to Banna. In James Traub, "Islamic Democrats", *New York Times*, 29 April 2007.

31   M. Moaddel, *Islamic Modernism, Nationalism and Fundamentalism: Episode and Discourse*, USA: University of Chicago Press, 2005, 211.

32   *Five Tracts of Hassan al-Banna* (1906–1949), tr. Charles Wendell, USA: Berkeley, University of California Press, 1978, 34.

33   Hassan al-Banna, "Kitab al-jihad", 239.

34   Carrie Wickham, *Mobilizing Islam: Religion, Activism and Political Change in Egypt*, USA: Columbia UP, 2003, 1.

35   Ibid., xi–xii.

36   John Esposito, *Islam: the straight path*, UK: Oxford University Press, [1988] 1998, 147.

37   Ibid., 148.

38   Ibid., 142, 158.

39   Asef Bayat, *Making Islam Democratic: Social Movements and the Post-Islamist Turn,* USA: Stanford University Press, 2007.

40   Ibid., 6.

41   Ibid., 11.

42   Quoted in John Calvert, *Sayyid Qutb and the Origins of Radical Islamism,* USA: Columbia University Press, 2010.

43   Writing in *Al-Akhbar*, 8 August 1952.

44 Sayyid Qutb, *Milestones*, Birmingham UK: Maktaba [1964] 2006, 23.
45 But then, that was before capitalism, with its corporations and assembly lines.
46 Qutb, *Milestones*, 93.
47 Ibid., 64.
48 Abou el-Fadl, *The Great Theft*, Canada: Harper Collins, 2005, and Abdelwahab Meddeb, *Malady of Islam*, USA: Basic Books, 2003, 104.
49 "Reformer Sayyid Qutb exposes his socialistic ideals" <http://www.hizmetbooks.org/Religion_Reformers_in_Islam/ref-51.htm>, Ahmad S. Moussalli, Radical Islamic *Fundamentalism: the Ideological and Political Discourse of Sayyid Qutb,* Lebanon: American University of Beirut, 1992, 223.
50 Daniel Benjamin and Steven Simon, *The Age of Sacred Terror*, USA: Random House, 2002, 62.
51 It traces its origins in the 1926 conference sponsored by the newly installed Saudi monarchy in Mecca and the 1931 conference in al-Quds (Jerusalem).
52 Reuel Marc Gerecht, *The Islamic Paradox*, USA: Aei Press, 2004, quoted in Richard Dreyfuss, "Cold War Holy Warrior", *motherjones.com*, January 2006.
53 *IslamOnline.net*, 22 February 2011.
54 See Chapter 1 endnote 58. He told *IslamOnline* that he advocates "a civil state with a religious background ... [but is] totally against theocracy. We are not a state for mullahs." The Iranian Press Agency has described Qaradawi as "a spokesman for "international Freemasonry and rabbis".
55 His Islamic Research Foundation owns the Peace TV channel in Dubai.
56 Hassan Hanafi, *Islam in the Modern World, vol. II Tradition, Revolution and Culture*, Cairo: Anglo-Egyptian Bookshop, 1995, 354–355, 364. Quoted in John Esposito and John Voll, *Makers of Contemporary Islam*, UK: Oxford University Press, 2001, 110.
57 Ibid., 89.
58 Francois Burgat, *The Islamic Movement in North Africa,* Center for Middle Eastern Studies, USA: University of Texas Press, 1997, 62.
59 Esposito, *Makers of Contemporary Islam*, 114–117.
60 Ibid., 205, 222.
61 Full Transcript of Rached Ghannouchi's lecture on Secularism, 2 March 2012.
62 Ibid.
63 Asma Rashid, "Malik Bennabi: his life and times", *islamicencyclopedia.org*.
64 Moaddel, *Islamic Modernism, Nationalism and Fundamentalism,* 253.
65 The 2007 World Public Opinion Poll of Iranians found Sistani had an approval rating of 70%, higher than any Shia leader, religious or secular, Iranian or non-Iranian. In Vali Nasr, *The Shia Revival: How Conflicts within Islam Will Shape the Future*, New York: W.W. Norton & Company, 2006, 166.
66 Ervand Abrahamian, "Ali Shariati: Ideologue of the Iranian revolution", MERIP Reports 102, January 1982, 25.
67 Ali Shariati, *Shiah*, Tehran: Ilham, 1983, 16, 114–115, quoted in Nasr, *Islam in the Modern World,* 130.
68 Ali Shariati, *On the Sociology of Islam*, USA: Mixan Press, 1979, 98.
69 Vali Nasr, *The Shia Revival*, USA: Norton, 2006, 128–129.
70 Moaddel, *Islamic Modernism, Nationalism and Fundamentalism*, 255–256.
71 The Fadaian-e Islam group in the 1950s–1960s modeled their work on the Brotherhood, and Qutb's *Milestones* was the most important political work widely read by Shia Islamists, including Ayatollah Khomeini who downplayed Shia-Sunni differences in his own writings. Olga Davidson and Mohammad Mahallati, "Iran, Egypt and the Ikhwan", *bitterlemons-international.org*, 4 March 2007.
72 During the reign of Shah Abbas (r. 1587–1629) a movement among the ulama *Akhbaris* (reporters) challenged the monopoly on religious judgments by the *mujtahids,* arguing that individual religious scholars make rulings based strictly on a literal interpretation of the hadiths, not just their reasoning powers. The

Usulis (founders) supported the more elitist role of the *mujtahids* and eventually asserted control. This elitist strain in Shia thought led to the highest *Usulis* being called *ayat-allah* (signs of God). Because of the difficulty of performing the hajj for Shia, there was a tradition of visiting the shrines of imams (mostly in Iraq) and ayatollahs. This is the background to Iran's theocracy.

73   This vision of perfect government is derived from the neo-Platonic Sufi Farabi's *The Virtuous City*, where he argues rigorous intellectual training will allow a *mujtahid* to acquire the perfect knowledge and authority necessary to rule the ideal city.

74   Speech at Feyziyeh Theological School, 24 August 1979, reproduced in Barry Rubin and Judith Colp Rubin, *Anti-American Terrorism and the Middle East: A Documentary Reader*, UK: Oxford University Press, 2002, 34.

75   Mohammed Baqir Al-Sadr, *Islamic Political System,* Qum, 1975, and *Islam Governs Life*, Qum, 1979.

76   Mohammed Baqir Al-Sadr, *Islam Governs Life*, 132.

77   Mohammed Baqir Al-Sadr, *Lamha fiqhiya*, 20.

78   Cousin and brother-in-law of Muqtada al-Sadr. He is a leading member of the Dawa Party.

79   Ayesha Jalal, *Partisans of Allah: Jihad in South Asia*, USA: Harvard University Press, 2008, 244–246.

80   Sayyid Qutb, *On Jihad* (1930) quoted in Vernon Egger, *A History of the Muslim World since 1260: The Making of a Global Community*, New Jersey: Pearson, 2008, 397.

81   Jalal, *Partisans of Allah*, 255, 258.

82   Mehran Kamrava (ed.), *The New Voices of Islam: Rethinking Politics and Modernity, A Reader*, I A· University of California Press, 2006, 16.

83   Syed al-Naquib al Attas, *Islam and Secularism*, Malaysia, ISTAC, 36.

84   Chandra Muzaffar, "Islam, Justice, and Politics", in Kamrava, *The New Voices of Islam,* 223.

85   Ibid., 228.

86   Eickelman, *Muslim Politics,*162.

87   There can be little progress in western-Islamic relations until the US president gives an "American Culpa" speech to the Muslim world, because there are "an endless supply of angry young Muslim rebels prepared to die for their cause and there [is] no sign of the attacks ending unless there [is] a fundamental change in the world."

88   Ziauddin Sardar, "Reformist Ideas and Muslim Intellectuals: The demands of the Real World", in Abdullah Omar Naseef (ed.), *Today's Problems, Tomorrow's Solutions: Future Thoughts on the Structure of Muslim Society*, London: Mansell, 1988.

89   Ziauddin Sardar, interviewed by Mustafa Nazir Ahmad, *The News on Sunday*, in *The Reformist*, Karachi, 23 November 2008.

90   Ziauddin Sardar, *Reading the Qur'an: The Contemporary Relevance of the Sacred Text of Islam*, UK: Oxford University Press, 2011, 301.

91   Bashir Nafi, Interview by Omayma Abdel-Latif, "The forces of convergence", *Al-Ahram Weekly*, 14 January 1999. All quotes here are from this interview.

92   Ibid., 36–37, and Tariq Ramadan, *Western Muslims and the Future of Islam*, UK: Oxford University Press, 2004, 5. Seyyed Nasr outlines Mulla Sadra's philosophy of education, where "Men and women are created in such a way that the Active Intellect appears at once, before their *nafs* (soul), and can be attained as the fruit of the perfection of the *nafs*. Through a process of education, which results in this perfection, they realize that they are the complete book containing all the signs of God manifested in His creation." Nasr, *Islam in the Modern World*, 161.

93   Ibid., 286.

94   Ayat means both sign and verse in Arabic, and the Quran exhorts us to observe

and understand Nature's "Signs for a people that are wise" (2:164) much as we can find understanding in the verses of the Quran. Our spiritual journey in life must interpret the signs of Nature in accordance with the Quran. "They are 'like' the Quran, illustrations inserted between the pages of the Book." (Eaton, *Islam and the Destiny of Man*, 91, 101.) This is the sense of referring to 'two books', though for purists, there can be only one book.

95   He argues that the secular state notion was brought into existence by Protestants and Jews in order to make space for themselves in face of the power of the Catholic Church, and that therefore in western societies, multicultural secularism protects freedom of religion of Muslims. Acceptance by western Muslims of living under the rule of the secular state does not mean that they should seek invisibility in the society, but rather participate in it actively, and contribute to its improvement as Muslims, demonstrating the value of Islam. Tariq Ramadan, Lecture, Islamic Institute of Toronto, December 2012 <http://youtube.com/watch?v=XoDTuB2BEf4>. But mightn't this just mean assimilation given the hegemony of western 'culture'?

96   Wilfrid Blunt, *Secret History of the English Occupation of Egypt*, USA: A Knopf, 1922, 363.

97   Wilfrid Blunt, *The Future of Islam,* London: Kegan Paul, Trench and Co, 1882, v, ix, 2.

98   Ibid., 159.

99   Ibid., 172, 177.

100   Ibid., 204, 214.

101   Quoted in Elizabeth Longford, *A Pilgrimage of Passion: The Life of Wilfrid Scawen Blunt*, New York: Knopf, 1980. 425.

102   See excerpt from his travelogue in Chapter 1, endnote 124.

103   Rene Guenon, *Insights into Islamic Esoterism and Taoism,* Sophia Perennis, 2003, ix.

104   Ibid., xviii.

105   Photo in Chapter 2.

106   Muhammad Asad, *The Road to Mecca*, New York: [Simon and Schuster, 1954] Fons Vitae 2000, 55-56.

107   Muhammad Asad, *Principles of State and Government in Islam,* USA: University of COlifornnia, 1961, 98.

108   Ibid., 106–107.

109   "Conversations with History - Talat Asad". <http://www.youtube.com/watch?v=kfAGnxKfwOg>.

110   Attribution in Gai Eaton, *Islam and the Destiny of Man*, UK: Islamic Texts Society, 1994, 80.

111   Eaton, *Islam and the Destiny of Man*, 1.

112   Maryam Jameelah, *Islam and Modernism*, Lahore: Muhammad Yusuf Khan, 1971, 59.

113   Maryam Jameelah, *Islam and Western Society*, New Delhi: Adam Publishers, 1982, xi.

114   Ibid., 46.

115   Maryam Jameelah, *Westernization versus Muslims*, Lahore: Muhammad Yusuf Khan, 1978, 5.

116   John Esposito and Ibrahim Kalin, *The 500 Most Influential Muslims in the World*, Georgetown USA, 2009.

117   Jack O'Sullivan, "If you hate the West, emigrate to a Muslim country", *Guardian,* 8 October 2001.

118   The Benghazi office was in fact a CIA operation, complete with illegal secret holding cells for militants, according to Paula Broadwell ex-lover of ex-CIA chief David Petraeus. This underlines the importance of context in determining what level of jihad a situation demands: patience in the face of insult, yes, but active resistance to *hiraba*.

119   Interview 11 May 2011, available at <http://pathtopeace.hostoi.com/2011/05/timothy-john-tim-winter-abdal-hakim-murad />.

120   Esposito, *Makers of Contemporary Islam*, 21.

121   Eickelman, *Muslim Politics,* 162.

122   Gai Eaton, *Islam and the Destiny of Man*, UK: Islamic Texts Society, 1994, 156.

123   Ziauddin Sardar, Interview by Mustafa Nazir Ahmad, *The News on Sunday*, in *The Reformist*, Karachi, 23 November 2008.

124   Surviving *Ikhwan* leaders ironically surrendered to the hated British in Kuwait in 1930.

125   Karen Armstrong, "The Label of Catholic Terror was never used about the IRA", *Guardian*, 11 July 2005.

126   Olivier Roy *Globalised Islam: The Search for a New Ummah,* London: Hurst, 2004, 44.

127   Trevor Stanley, "Understanding the Origins of Wahhabism and Salafism", *Terrorism Monitor* Volume 3 Issue 14, *jamestown.org,* 15 July 2005.

128   The first *hijra* was to Abyssinia, later to Medina.

129   This reasoning ironically convinced many Muslims that it was fine to emigrate to the Christian/Jewish West in search of a higher standard of living, as the Muslim world was occupied by the West in any case. As the war against Islam ramped up, this put them on the front line and resulted in some turning to terrorism, others to greater efforts to assimilate under heightened Islamophobia.

130   Walberg, *Postmodern Imperialism*, 89.

131   Egger, *A History of the Muslim World since 1260,* 478.

132   Abd al-Salam Faraj, "The Neglected Duty", ibid., 478.

133   Recall Afghani's more astute decision to work with existing Muslim regimes against imperialism rather than inciting their Muslim subjects to overthrow their leaders, weakening the already weak Muslim states, which accords with the eleventh century Ghazali's argument for enduring an unjust regime.

134   Azzam ironically was caught between the fractious Hekmatyar, Bin Laden and the Massoud factions in Afghanistan when the Soviets withdrew in 1989, and was blown up by one of them (or Mossad) while trying to mediate between Islamists and Afghan factions in Peshawar. Bin Laden used the opportunity to transform the Office of Services into al-Qaeda, and transformed Azzam's focus on freeing Muslim lands into a nihilist strategy of almost random violence anywhere, using Muslim lands as a spring-board.

135   Kadri, *Heaven on Earth,* 171–173.

136   This is a quote from a purported Bin Laden tape of 2004. Whether or not he actually said it, this is the simple logic of revenge which has nothing to do with Islam.

137   Wahhabi scholar Sulayman bin Abdallah al-Shaykh (1785–1818) argued this to attack the Egyptian occupation of the holy cities in the 1830s. Joas Wagemakers, "The Enduring Legacy of the Second Saudi State", *IJMES* 44:1, February 2012, 95.

138   Nasr, *Forces of Fortune,* 164.

139   There is ample evidence that, besides fighting the Soviets in Afghanistan, these neo-Wahhabis are repeatedly used by the imperialists, even as the imperialists solemnly pledge to fight them; for example, against the Shia-dominated political order in Iran and Iraq, and more recently against the secular anti-American order in Libya and Syria. This cynical use of Islamists by the imperialists began in the nineteenth century, and is not surprising given the lack of regard for human life witnessed in imperial wars in the twentieth century. See Walberg, *Postmodern Imperialism*, 137–139.

140   The date of the embassy bombings marked the eighth anniversary of the arrival of American forces in Saudi Arabia. The attacks were linked to the Egyptian Islamic Jihad, brought Bin Laden and Zawahiri to the attention of the American

public for the first time, and resulted in the FBI placing Bin Laden on its Ten Most Wanted Fugitives list and Bin Laden's indictment for "conspiracy to attack defense utilities of the United States". Bin Laden was never indicted in relation to 911.

141   Hadith reported by Ibn Hanbal, quoted in Ramadan, *In the Footsteps of the Prophet: Lessons from the Life of Muhammad*, UK: Oxford University Press, 2007.

.142   When extrajudicial killings and indiscriminate bombings in Iraq peaked in 2006, this was blamed by the US on insurgents, and torture was blamed on rogue elements in the Interior Ministry. The impression created was of senseless violence initiated by the Iraqis themselves, but the "sectarian violence" that engulfed Iraq "was not an unintended consequence of the US invasion and occupation, but an integral part of it" to target Iraqis who rejected the illegal invasion and occupation of their country. See Walberg, *Postmodern Imperialism*, 138.

143   Steve Coll *Ghost Wars: The Secret History of the CIA, Afghanistan, and Bin Laden, from the Soviet Invasion to September 10, 2001*, New York: Penguin, 2004, 511. Cofer Black, chief of the CIA Counterterroist Center said they "had to maintain contact with [anti-Taliban Afghan leader] Massoud to prepare for the day—a virtual certainty—when al-Qaeda pulled off a major attack against the US ... preparing the battlefield for WWIII." Ibid., 518.

144   Not so bizarre, considering the nineteenth century Oman-Yemen emirate and African jihadi movements of reformist Sufi orders which resulted in Islamic states in the 18th–19th centuries in northern Nigeria, Morocco, Libya, Sudan. See Chapter 1.

CHAPTER FOUR

20TH-21ST CENTURY EXPERIENCE OF ISLAM IN PRACTICE

The period of imperialist occupation and 'independence' up to the 1970s is touted by western historians as one of 'progress', though any outsider would be struck most of all by the century's horrendous world wars leadings to deaths in the millions, unceasing armed conflict, and rising mass poverty. In the West, Islam registers as a shibboleth, if at all. What has been the 20th–21st century experience of Islam in Turkey, Egypt, Levant, Africa, Saudi Arabia, the Gulf, Iran, Afghanistan, Central Asia, Pakistan/ India/ Bangladesh, southeast Asia, the West?

Until the 1980s, Islam had little impact on world politics, and the Islamic world was, relatively speaking, an island of peace, though an unhappy one—occupied and manipulated, weak and divided. The imposition of the imperial 'map' sidetracked the Muslim world's spiritual journey. The new post-'independence' governments mostly became secular dictatorial cliques, generally devoted to enriching themselves, though a few uncorrupt leaders made genuine attempts to move along a socialist path and to find strength and dignity by following pan-Arab dreams. Nasser in Egypt was famously disinterested in amassing wealth for himself and his family, dying virtually penniless. Saddam Hussein never had any outside wealth, as the cluster of opportunistic lawyers who swarmed his family to take on his trial defense discovered to their dismay.

However, when the pan-Arab hopes, too, were shattered in 1967, the overwhelming sense among Muslims was that they had strayed from the "straight path" under their secular regimes. Thinkers in the Muslim world began to reconsider how to use the truths of Islam to right the wrongs of today's society: zakat means that the poor have rightful claims to a share of the wealth of society; the proscription on usury should put financial capital under the strict control of society; exhortations to treat other humans and Nature with respect should inspire one's every economic step, just to scratch the surface. These are not just platitudes where they are deeply-felt social norms and religious duties and acted on accordingly, so argue the Islamists. Islam is not an "opium", but rather an inspiration for society which requires a clear political mechanism in order to be realized.

The year 1967 witnessed the beginning of a revival of Islam everywhere, though at different rates subject to circumstances. The Wahhabi influence especially increased around the world, as well-padded Saudi-backed pan-Islamism, with a green light from the US, replaced pan-Arabism, reflecting an identity crisis brought on by Israel, and disillusionment with the West and western-inspired secular governments. The war against Israel in 1973, the oil embargo, the return of Sinai to Egypt, and the 1979 Iranian revolution were new, hopeful signs to Muslims, also interpreted as "a series of events that God was using to call Muslims to reverse their abandonment of Islam" and to begin actively promoting the true faith.[1] The oil boycott and new wealth gave a boost to the confidence of the Arabs "who had considered themselves to be mere pawns in the Cold War",[2] and showed the Muslim world that it was possible to use their economic power collectively to fight their disempowerment. This led to a greater use of Islamic symbols (taxis, phone ring, dress, mosque attendance, veils). It was not Islam that had failed Muslims, but Muslims who had failed Islam by relying on the West for guidance and development.

The turn to Islam has been motivated by the spiritual emptiness of secularism as much as by the poverty imposed through neocolonialism. This revival of religion is not unique to Islam. In recent decades, there is growing influence of religion in politics involving all major religions—Christianity, Judaism, and Hinduism have all experienced movements of revival, and developed a politicized version, all claiming to promote the authentic, original form of their religions. Hinduism and Judaism have been politicized in opposition to Islam in the twentieth century—due to the partition of India, in the case of the former, and the creation of Israel and subsequent wars, in the latter—and are associated with their ethnic roots. Christian revivalism across the dozens of Christian sects has become captive to Zionism and is thoroughly embedded in modern day imperialism, having long ago acquiesced to the 'separation of church and state' and accepted the role of willing handmaiden to the imperial project.[3]

In the current 'great game' (what I call Great Game III in *Postmodern Imperialism*), where the communists of Great Game II are defeated and the global market is now unrivalled, the planet's 1.5+ billion Muslims get on with their daily lives in the midst of a wide range of political realities, so far mostly still reluctantly under the imperial thumb. Some live in secular nations like **Turkey**, governed by a devout president who does a delicate dance with Ataturk's ghost and his NATO 'partners'. Others suffer in states under direct threat of invasion by the West, like **Palestine**, **Iran** and now **Syria**, because of their resistance to empire. Then there is pro-US authoritarian 'Islamic' **Saudi Arabia**. Some live under secular dictatorships like **Uzbekistan** and **Algeria** where Islamist parties are the ever-ready, ever-suppressed, *de facto* opposition. In democratic **Pakistan**, Islamic parties collude with a more or less pro-US corrupt secular regime. Still others live in war-zones like **Iraq, Afghanistan** and **Somalia** where the presence of foreign troops has exacerbated sectarianism and civil strife and where 'Islamist' militias mete out vigilante 'justice'. Far from the birthplace of Islam, in **Malaysia** and more recently **Indonesia**, democratic and Islamic institutions are functioning well. A growing umma lives in the heart of the empire, in majority Christian countries where Zionism and Islamophobia are ever-present like the **US**, **Britain** and **France,** obsessed with *la laicité.*

Beginning in the 1970s, governments in Turkey and Egypt used Islamists to weaken leftist opposition. In Pakistan, too, Zia's dictatorship tried to use Islam against Bhutto's socialism. In Afghanistan, the cynical use of Islamists by the imperialists and a Pakistani government intent on self-aggrandizement took the logic of using Islamists to stave off socialism to its absurd conclusion—'destroying the state to save it', and in actuality creating a terrorist[4] haven dominated by premodern tribes. Islamic forces were still following the imperial 'map' of the world. Even Iran's Islamic revolution, like the 'jihad' in Afghanistan, decimated its socialists, who might have been accommodated within a society based on social justice, but who were killed or fled into exile, the secular-religious divide proving too deep to bridge.[5]

The US-blessed chaos in Afghanistan backfired on Pakistan, spilling back across its amorphous borders, creating a weak state riven by tribal succession movements. The same thing happened in Iraq, which like Afghanistan suffered the ignominy of full-scale US invasion. Meanwhile, Saudi Arabia's monarchy continues to use Islamic rhetoric to divert increasing frustration with the corrupt, accommodationist monarchy, making it a center of simmering unrest and an ongoing source of funding and recruiting for violent premodern Islamists across the umma.

The catchwords of twentieth century Islamism have been 'sharia' and 'Islamic state'. The concept of an Islamic state is a problematic one, the direct offspring of the western political order, dating from the Treaty of Westphalia (1648). Sharia is clearly at the heart of the Islamic project, and the assault on sharia in western media as a medieval relic has more to do with the West's desire that the legal structures built up during colonialism—to the imperialists' advantage—remain in place.

Both concepts have come to mean very different things to different people. Are they still the litmus tests for genuine reform which can withstand the pressures of empire and produce robust Islamic governance? Following the Arab Spring, the Egyptian and Tunisian MBs have been careful to dismiss the intention of declaring an Islamic state, and downplayed their intention of broadening the use of sharia, even as the MB triumphed in elections. "Today you are the source of this power. You give this power to whoever you want and you withhold it from whoever you want, with God's blessings," Mohamed Morsi told the crowds in Tahrir Square, Cairo, during his informal swearing in as president 30 June 2012, *prior* to his official swearing in before the Supreme Constitutional Court. This was to demonstrate that the MB is taking its authority from the umma rather than the previous political order, dominated by a secular justice system and the army.

Official Islamic governments/ states/ republics include Saudi Arabia (1932),[6] Pakistan (1956), Mauritania (1958), Iran (1979), Afghanistan (1992) and Sudan (1993), but they have little in common, and all have shortcomings in terms of economic development and political life, to say nothing of the actual practice of Islam. In the face of unremitting hostility from the West, it is hardly surprising that Islamists have failed so far to show that claims to be following Islamic politics and economics or sharia law automatically guarantee citizens a better life. Sardar and others reject the notion of an Islamic state, seeing the concept as a reaction to the nation state of imperialism and the vacuum created by the abolition of the Caliphate in 1924. They argue that Islam is a universalist movement, not bound by geographical borders.[7]

Turkey (75 million, 73% Sunni/ 25% Alevi[8]) has evolved from radical secularism towards a renewed Islamic neo-Ottoman role in the Middle East, hinting at the possibility (in combination with the BRICS[9] or with a future configuration of Islamic or Muslim-majority states) of a new rival to US world hegemony, though economically neither Turkey nor the BRICS have yet to venture far from the western neoliberal model.

Its transformation since the 1970s is remarkable. The 1971 coup in Turkey followed the rise of Erbakan's Islamist National Order Party, and was repeated in 1980 when Erbakan's successor National Salvation Party was poised to form a government (it had already briefly served in a coalition in 1974 during the Cyprus crisis).

The corruption of the secularist government was dragging down the statist economy, socialism was not acceptable as an alternative, and the army was forced to acknowledge the Islamists as a necessary 'evil'. After the 1980 coup, intended to suppress *both* militant leftists and Islamists, it nonetheless became government policy to allow religious instruction in schools. At the same time, neoliberal reforms were undertaken under the military-approved Prime Minister Turgut Ozal (1983–1989), a former World Bank official, loosening state control and stimulating industry, in line with the WB and IMF demands for privatization with a focus on export-led growth.

The Kemalist state-led reforms and economic development had created a small middle class dependent on state patronage. As the liberal project soured and Turkey turned to neoliberalism under IMF pressure in the 1980s, this middle class was weakened, and turned to the now more public Islamists. At the same time, a new entrepreneurial middle class from the Anatolian heartland was developing, the natural constituency of the Islamists.

In the 1990s, Erbakan's successor Just Order movement used civil society associations and elections to emulate MB grassroots success in Egypt. A devastating earthquake in 1992 exposed the inadequacy of the secularists—both the complicity of corrupt officials in shoddy construction and the government's inability to respond quickly and compassionately. Islamist groups reacted quickly and made a major contribution to the relief effort. Erbakan finally became prime minister in 1996 as head of the Welfare Party[10] but in yet another 'soft' coup was pressured by the military to step down the next year, and, like his earlier parties, Welfare was banned. The members immediately regrouped as the Virtue Party, which in turn was banned in 2001, prompting the creation of two parties—the Justice and Development Party (AKP) and Felicity, the former more accommodating, led by the up-and-coming Erdogan, the latter by Erbakan.

Erdogan was first elected to parliament in 1991 as a member of the Welfare Party but barred from taking his seat. In 1994, he was elected mayor of Istanbul, and proved to be pragmatic in office, successfully tackling such chronic problems as water shortage, pollution and traffic chaos. He was again banned from office and sentenced to a prison term for reciting a popular poem during a public address in 1997 including the words, "The mosques are our barracks, believers are our soldiers and the minarets are our arms." After six months in prison, Erdogan went on to found the AKP, which won nearly two-thirds of the parliamentary seats in 2002.

Since coming to power, the AKP has achieved three consecutive majority governments, a first in Turkey, continuing the neoliberal policy of privatization, promoting globalization and deepening Turkey's economic ties to Europe. In contrast to Erbakan, Erdogan favors joining the EU, and more or less conforms to NATO policy in Afghanistan, Libya and Syria, though he refused use of Turkey's NATO base for the invasion of Iraq in 2003. Clearly Erdogan's faction of Islamists decided to compromise with the secular order ruled by US diktat. In a 2010 interview with the *Times*, President Abdullah Gul rejected any notion that Ankara had turned its back on the West. Turkey "was now a big economic power that had embraced democracy, human rights, and the free market." It had become a "source of inspiration" in the region. "The U.S. and Europe should welcome its growing engagement in the Middle East because it [is] promoting western values in a region largely governed by authoritarian regimes."[11]

In Afghanistan, Turkey positioned itself as a low-key but vital ally in the "war against terrorism", providing 1,800 troops in strictly noncombat roles, such as providing security around Kabul and training troops, "not with paternalism or the imperial arrogance of an occupying power," according to Aydemir Erman, Turkey's coordinator for Afghanistan from 1991–2003.[12] According to Turkish MP Burhan Kayaturk, Turkey, which has the goodwill of the Afghani people, "can help win the hearts and minds of the Afghani people, who like the Turkish soldiers", and can "steer them away from militancy by strengthening the infrastructure in education, health and industry." Claims Erman,

> As a historically trusted friend of the Afghan people, Turkey, alone among members of the NATO alliance, has a 'soft power' ingredient in its arsenal that is key to winning the hearts and minds of the population. No Afghan was ever killed by a Turkish bullet [and] no Afghan trained by Turks has ever betrayed his country.[13]

In keeping with the policies of Erbakan, the AKP has pursued a "zero problems" policy with its neighbors, upgrading its relations with Armenia, Iraq (including Kurdish Iraq where it funds a Turkish university) and Iran. Visa-free travel was initiated with Albania, Jordan, Lebanon, Libya and Syria in 2009 and in 2010 with Egypt. Referring to Turkey's "strategic depth" in former Ottoman lands, Foreign Minister Davutoglu said in Sarajevo in 2009: "We will reintegrate the Balkan region, Middle East and Caucasus ... together with Turkey as the center of world politics in the future."[14]

However, this policy has run into problems as the Turks pursue their own hegemonic interests in the region and at the same time try to keep in American good books. The decision to drop the alliance with Assad and support the largely Sunni Islamist insurgents in Syria reflects the AKP's decision to comply with Saudi/ Gulf Islamist sympathies, combined with the US desire to overthrow Assad for his hostility to Israel and alignment with Iran.

Turkey's Kurds (14 million) and Alevis (15 million), which together make up 40% of Turks'[15] are directly affected—the former in sympathy with Syrian Kurdish rebels, the latter in sympathy with Syrian Alawi supporters of Assad. Erdogan's decision to back the insurgents aligned Turkey directly with US-Israeli interests. Clearly Erdogan saw Syria as another Libya, and as there, switched to what he expected to be the winning side.

The failure to oust Assad has left Turkey in a precarious situation, with Kurds now supporting their rebellious brothers in both Iraq, Syria and Iran, and Alevis supporting Assad's regime. Abandoning Assad worsened Turkey's relations with Russia, Iran and China—the source of much of its trade, especially oil and gas, leaving it relying on vague US/ Saudi/ Gulf support. But the latter cynically support a dubious array of neo-Wahhabi insurgents, and are not very keen on yet another MB-dominated government, whom they view as potential rivals to their autocratic monarchies.

Turkey finds itself in a very similar role to the one played
by Pakistan during the 1979-89 Soviet-Afghan war. Some
of the groups Pakistan nurtured during those years have
now turned on their patrons. Will Turkey become the next
Pakistan? One Syrian insurgent said that many of the rebels
were stockpiling ammunition for "after the revolution".[16]

The flip side of Turkey's "zero problems" foreign policy was to
distance itself from the regional troublemaker—Israel. In 2004 Turkey
denounced the Israeli assassination of Palestinian Sheikh Ahmed Yassin
as a "terrorist act" and Israeli policy in the Gaza Strip as "state-sponsored
terrorism". In 2009, Erdogan famously refused to share the platform with
Israeli President Shimon Peres at the World Economic Forum after the Israeli
invasion of Gaza. When Israeli commandos killed nine Turkish citizens aboard
a relief convoy to Gaza a few months later, Turkey withdrew its ambassador,
insisting on an apology and reparations, which Israel grudgingly complied with
under US pressure in 2013, though relations remain strained. Even NATO is
no longer a pillar of Turkish foreign policy. Whereas in 2004, 67 per cent in
Turkey saw NATO membership as essential for national security, only 41 per
cent did so in 2011.[17] The decision to participate in NATO's missile defense
'shield', clearly meant to protect Israel from any retaliation for a western
invasion of Iran, further alienated the AKP's Muslim base.

Its foreign relations have thus frayed after its early successes.
Straddling the geopolitical divide is not conducive to "zero problems". Turkey's
support for US-European intervention in Libya and Syria, its perception in the
Arab world as having its own national agenda, Kurdish unrest, and domestic
friction with its large secular community and still-powerful military have
weakened the Islamists. What was meant to be the crowning touch to the new
Turkish role—Erdogan's co-founding of the Alliance of Civilizations with
Spanish Prime Minister Zapatero at the UN General Assembly in 2005—is
rather threadbare, with Turkey not the center of a peaceful new Islamic order,
but the center of inter-ethnic fighting and international intrigue. The Turkish
Islamists' 'map' is clearly flawed.

The AKP's chief claim to fame is Turkey's economic performance
(see Chapter 5), a hopeful sign that Islamists can beat the capitalist West at its
own game—a powerful symbol to the Muslim world that it is both possible
and desirable to have avowedly Islamic politicians in control, even if their
policies are influenced by their own geostrategic interests. Despite the current
political turmoil, Turkey's new Islamic image also marks the beginning of a
major shift in political power in the Middle East against the US and Israel.

While **Egypt** (90 million, 85% Sunni, 15% Christian) distanced itself
from the imperialists under Nasser, it failed to provide a credible alternative

secular socialist model for the Arab/ Muslim world, allowing Sadat to reverse Nasser's gains, make 'peace' with Israel, impose a US-approved secular capitalist model, and assist the US in its use of Islamists to destroy the Soviet Union in the 1970s. Starting in the 1970s, thanks to Sadat's appeal to Islamists as allies in his neoliberal *infitah* (opening), the MB were able to quickly renew their network of cells by absorbing the new student Islamic Society (founders including Abul Futuh and Erian),[18] which immediately dominated student councils in eight of the 12 universities including Cairo, Minya and Alexandria, with the support of Sheikh Qaradawi. The more militant elements refused to join what they saw as a movement that had had its day, and formed Islamic Jihad.

Sadat approved a 1971 constitutional amendment declaring sharia "a principal source of legislation", welcomed home MB exiles returning mostly from Europe and Saudi Arabia, as he flirted with Islamization.[19] His neoliberal policies led to the 1977 bread riots and an end to any pretense of democracy. Adding insult to injury, he shocked everyone (including his closest advisers) by traveling to Jerusalem, announcing peace with Israel, and signing the Camp David Accords in 1978. In 1979, even the docile Arab League expelled Egypt and moved its headquarters from Cairo to Tunis.[20] In 1981 Sadat was assassinated by Islamic Jihad member Lieutenant Khalid Islambouli.

At the same time as he was making peace with Israel, Sadat approved secret operations to recruit and train mujahideen for the CIA for deployment in Afghanistan against Soviet troops and Afghans who supported the socialist regime there, even as he arrested 1,320 moderate Islamists who disapproved of his peace with Israel and his *infitah*. On US urging, Sadat sponsored local Islamic fundamentalist groups Tabligh Islami (spreading Islam) and Nahda (renaissance), setting up a base in Upper Egypt for training and an airport for transporting them to Afghanistan. Fundamentalists were recruited from Tunisia, Algeria, Morocco, Lebanon, Syria, Jordan and of course Saudi Arabia. They killed tens of thousands of Soviet soldiers and Afghan socialists, themselves died in the thousands, resulting in the deaths of hundreds of thousands of civilians, paid for by the US and Saudi princes living off US petrodollars. And when the mujahideen 'went home' in the early 1990s, they picked up in Egypt (and elsewhere around the world) where they had left off in 1979.

Upon coming to power in 1981, just as had Sadat before him, Hosni Mubarak initially released most of the Islamist political prisoners who Sadat had hurriedly arrested just prior to his assassination, and as a sop to them, changed Sadat's 1971 sharia clause in the constitution from "a" to "the" in 1980.[21] But the corruption and mass poverty precipitated by the *infitah,* and the new neocolonial turn in Egypt's regional policies meant that leftists and Islamists were now united (as had happened under the Shah in Iran in the 1970s). Mubarak's attempt to portray himself as more democratic, less pro-US and more devout than his erratic predecessor convinced no one. The reality even left most Egyptians pining for the 'less bad' days of Sadat.

The MB made good use of its window of opportunity and set up the Socialist Labor Party (1978), headed by Marxist-turned-Islamist Adel Husayn. The MB was able to strike an alliance in 1984 with New Wafd and gained 8 seats in the parliament. In 1987 it allied with Amal (labor) and Ahrar (liberal) parties and gained 36 seats, coining the slogan "Islam is the Solution", to become the largest opposition group. It again allied with Wafd in 1995. In 2000, it captured all the seats which Mubarak allowed the opposition (17).

The small, educated middle class of the Nasser period was swamped during Sadat's hurried privatization campaign, as a new middle layer of speculators used the *infitah* for self-enrichment without contributing to economic development.[22] The dismantling of Nasser's stern but just welfare state created a "soft state"[23] where most activity, be it economic or political, is controlled not by the state but by a tiny elite in consultation with western advisers. Protecting this weakened mafia-state required a huge increase in police and security forces. The elite was by definition non-MB, and as people became more desperate, they turned to the most respectable and uncorrupt opposition around—the Islamists.

During the 1990s, MB activity was inspired not by Qutb, but by Banna, offering both education and social services as the soft state shed its responsibilities (health insurance, maternity benefits, social funds, pensions, housing assistance, holidays, loans). It captured control of the larger unions of the middle class engineers, lawyers and doctors, who are more religious and socially conservative than the *infitah*'s nouveau riche. MB members came to dominate professional associations from the mid-1980s on, including doctors (Abdul Futuh, Erian), engineers (Osman Ahmed Osman, Abu al-Ela Mady), scientists, pharmacists, agronomists and others. By the early 1990s, al-tayyar al-islami (Islamist current) controlled the important lawyers and journalists associations, replacing the leftists/ Nasserists in these key positions. Eventually, 21 professional associations with 2 million members, Egypt's educated middle class, came under the sway of the MB.

Osman, the engineering syndicate chairman from 1979–1990, built private hospitals, established a social welfare fund, and arranged for members (eking a meager living on government salaries) to buy apartments and discount goods. He also arranged for MB members to work abroad before Mubarak could have them (or him) arrested. It was only a matter of time until the discredited government shut down 5,000 MB offices and arrested leaders of the doctors' union (Erian) and the lawyers' union (Khalid Badawi) in 1995. Erian and Abdul Futuh were among hundreds of MBers unjustly imprisoned from 1995–2000. The professional associations helped "map out a new Egyptian identity, no longer subservient to the demands of 'westernization' that have little to offer the common man. This shattered the corrosive myth that the Islamists were bent on recreating a medieval Arabian 'paradise' by violence if necessary."[24]

As in Turkey in 1992, there was a major earthquake in Cairo the same year which killed over 500, and the MB-led medical and engineers unions were immediately mobilized to provide relief.[25] The official response was lackadaisical, much of the aid embezzled, and the embarrassed government reacted by ripping down MB tents in the holy Sayeda Zeinab Square and forcing donations to go to the state-run Red Crescent Society, confirming the government's incompetence and venality.

Mubarak was forced to support the US-led invasion of Kuwait/ Iraq in 1991, which was uniformly unpopular among Egyptians, tens of thousands of whom had worked (and were still working) in Iraq, remitting precious earnings to their poverty-stricken families in Egyptian villages.[26] The engineers' union dared to protest the war, and again, in 1993, the Oslo peace accord, prompting a new crackdown on MB leaders. In response, the government passed the Associations Law to take control of the syndicates, but the MB mobilized its grassroots and continued to win elections. Then the government resorted to the *hirasa* law (literally, sequester, issued in 1952 to confiscate aristocrats' property) to seize engineers and lawyers syndicates' property and provincial syndicates.

The regime was caught in its own web of lies, using the state apparatus to suppress autonomous Islamic opposition groups while at the same time permitting the "creeping Islamization" of the state as a cover for its intentions.[27] It preserved itself but in the process conceded terrain to the most intolerant elements of the Islamic establishment, repressing moderate MBers along with leftists and suspected terrorists, encouraging terrorism, further discrediting itself and building admiration for the MB.

The culmination of the MB's gradualist strategy was that by the 1980s the 'infrastructure' of an Islamic society was being put into place in Egypt. The "Islamic passive revolution represents a managed Islamic restoration" where the state maintained official control.[28] The state had tried to use Islamists to weaken its socialist critics, allowing them to head up professional unions and to become providers of welfare, education, even investment in the era of the 'soft state', but the Islamists had turned the tables. Erian argues that the Egyptian state was in a sense already Islamic, reflecting the hegemony of Islamism which had imposed its framework and language on the state. The oppression of devout Muslims only further legitimized them among the umma and increased religiosity, as evidenced by an opinion poll that found that 98% of Egyptians considered themselves religious vs 82% of Iranians/ Americans, and 24% of Japanese.[29] The soft state had lost its legitimacy in public discourse.

The MB was now the elephant in the room, illegal, officially invisible, but altruistically flexing its muscle in the open, making Egypt's threadbare modernity ever more Islamic. Each move Mubarak made merely further discredited his soft state. The popular Sheikh Omar Abd al-Kafi was banned from preaching in mosques and on TV in 1994, but recordings of his *khutbas* (sermons) circulated and were played in microbuses and at mosques.

In 1993 the MB's reformist current held a forum in the Ramses Hilton with other oppositionists ranging from communists and Nasserites to jihadists, and signed the National Pact, a kind of common front among the opposition.[30] In 1996 the Islamist Wasat Party (moderation) was founded by Abu el-Ela Mady and attempted to register as an official party independent of the MB, supported by Qaradawi and, initially, by MB Murshid Akef. Mubarak's Parties Committee rejected its application and arrested Mady and the MB leaders.[31] Karama (dignity), a Nasserist party, was also founded though not officially recognized.

The year 2000 marked a new stage in Egyptian politics. The Palestinian Intifada protesting the PLO sellout in the Oslo Accords resulted in a spontaneous mass mobilization around Palestine, further invigorating the MB. The Egyptian Popular Committee for Solidarity with the Palestinian Intifada, the Egyptian Anti-Globalization Group, the National Campaign Against War on Iraq and the Committee for Defense of Workers' Rights were all popular NGOs with MB involvement. There was an explosion of satellite TV, the establishment in 2004 of new parties Kifaya (enough) and Ghad (tomorrow)—the latter, a liberal, secular party even recognized by the 'soft state'—and the dissident *al-Misr al-Yowm* (*Egypt Daily* private newspaper), showing the inability of the Mubarak regime to control the growing movement for change. Mubarak increasingly came under pressure from Washington with its 'democratize the Middle East' campaign, which it began with the invasion of Iraq in 2003.[32]

The nouveau riche continued to make fortunes by bribing underpaid government officials responsible for privatization, speculation, the lucrative import-export sector, and financial services. They found ways to spirit their illicit gains abroad, especially once the Egyptian pound was made 'convertible' in 2003 under IMF pressure. This starkly emphasized to the population the widening gap between the official 'soft state' and the incorruptible social and economic institutions being forged by the MB, accelerating the move towards revolution.

In anticipation of the 2005 elections, the MB joined with socialists and the liberal Wafd and Ghad parties to create the National Alliance for Reform and Change, and MB Supreme Guide Mahdi Akef stated publicly, "No matter how much we are hit, how many of us are thrown in prison, we will not be hostile to anybody."[33] Under pressure from the US to institute a democratic electoral facade, Mubarak loosened the reins, permitting MB candidates to run as independents and win 88 seats (20% of the total, the legal opposition winning only 14 seats), despite ballot rigging and the arrest of hundreds of its supporters. The Brotherhood became "in effect, the first opposition party of Egypt's modern era",[34] outshining the historic Wafd and the threadbare Nasserists.

Accounts differ over the Brotherhood's record in parliament.

> While many secular critics fear that the Brotherhood harbors
> a hidden Islamist agenda, so far the organization has posed a
> democratic political challenge to the regime, not a theological
> one. The Brothers formed a 'parliamentary kitchen' with
> committees on various subjects; the committees, in turn,
> organized seminars to which outside experts were regularly
> invited.[35]

The MB was praised for an "unmatched record of attendance", forming a coalition to fight the extension of Egypt's emergency law, and generally attempting to transform "the Egyptian parliament into a real legislative body, as well as an institution that represents citizens and a mechanism that keeps government accountable".[36] The MB's efforts in parliament to combat what one member called the "current US-led war against Islamic culture and identity" led the very liberal Minister of Culture Farouk Hosny to ban the publication of three novels on the ground they promoted blasphemy and unacceptable sexual practices.

The MB remains fundamentally conservative on social and economic issues. The 2004 "Muslim Brotherhood Initiative: On the general principles of reform in Egypt" calls for transforming the society by reforming the individual who is the victim of "negligence and selfishness" and "immediate desires and materialistic values", who must be purified on "a base of faith, straightforwardness and good manners".[37] Its 2007 draft platform called for regular parliamentary and presidential elections, along with appointment of a council of clerics to advise the government on legislation and executive policy in matters of sharia. It rejected a woman or Copt (Christian) as president then and again in 2011.[38] The 2010 election of Mohamed Badie as the new Murshid (supreme guide) and the subsequent expulsion of the moderate Abdul Futuh from the Guidance Office and the MB represented a victory for the old guard.

The *eminence grise* of the MB is Khairat el-Shater, deputy supreme guide, a former socialist and presently (very rich) businessman, engineer by training, who served 12 years in prison, and was the MB's preferred candidate in the 2012 presidential elections. He was banned from running on a technicality (his conviction had been overturned after the 2011 revolution). Nay-sayers, pointing to the Shaters, are quick to dismiss Islamists in power, arguing that the

> rhetorical appeal of political Islam as representing 'freedom,
> under God, from the dominion of man over man'—the
> source of its capacity to mobilize people against tyrannical
> regimes—[is] producing Machiavellian-style pragmatism

that can prove to be no less corrupt or authoritarian than the system it replaces ... The shift in emphasis from economics to morality may be to the advantage of free enterprise while appealing to the values of recently urbanized rural immigrants and the religiously observant middle class of small businessmen.[39]

Even if they are correct, one of the main benefits of the Turkish AKP has been the dramatic improvement in the (neoliberal) economy due to a sharp reduction in corruption and the prosperity of these new small businessmen, who are the main and acknowledged source of jobs in capitalism—everywhere.

Neither the AKP nor the MB's political arm, the Freedom and Justice Party (FJP), particularly court the working class, relying on the presumed religiosity of workers and promises to act paternalistically in their interests. The MB has never initiated revolutionary moves, its strategy throughout its history being an evolutionary one. The 25 January 2011 revolution was sparked by liberals and leftists, largely secular internet-savvy youth, but also by MB youth, who were soon joined by the leadership (and more belatedly by the Salafis) when it became clear that the uprising would remain largely peaceful. This cautious *realpolitik* is both understandable and pragmatic, as unlike a liberal-led revolt, with the West attentive and supportive, an MB-initiated uprising would have been ruthlessly dealt with, with little protest from Mubarak's western sponsors. Power was handed to the US-backed thoroughly secular army leadership, who spent the next year trying to make sure the Islamists didn't come to power, and failed.

Complaints by the liberals that the revolution was stolen by the Islamists are empty words. Without the decades of institution building by the MB and their persecution over the previous decades, the young secular revolutionaries would not have had the inspiration or courage to take on the security state.[40] The Islamic social movements mobilized and newly legalized to defend the revolution today are built on the hard work of the MB as it Islamized Egyptian society from the ground up during a time when an increasingly remote 'soft state' was no longer in touch with much of civil society (unlike the earlier 'strong state' of Nasser, which regulated people's lives to a great extent—for better or for worse).

Following the 2011 revolution, the MB was officially recognized—for the first time in its 84-year history. The Brotherhood supported the constitutional referendum in March which was also supported by the Egyptian army, and opposed by Egyptian liberals, who feared early elections would give the Islamists a majority and allow them to write the new constitution. The MB's FJP won almost half the seats in the Egyptian parliamentary elections for both the lower house (people's assembly) and upper house (shura or consultative council) and the presidential election of June 2012, though on the eve of the presidential election, the Supreme Constitutional Court, under army pressure, declared the lower house elections unconstitutional and disbanded it.

The MB have some experience in political power, but they are faced with highly experienced US-western forces, pressuring them to continue the neoliberal policies of Mubarak, on the one hand. On the other hand, they are faced with Saudi pressure, both political and economic, not to join Egypt's natural ally politically—Iran—now that it has 'caught up' with Iran's 1979 revolution, which would leave the premodern Saudi and Gulf absolute monarchies isolated.[41]

Iran and Egypt might finally be in sync, but there are questions:

- Has the MB lost its compass and become accommodationist in the meantime?
- Do Sunnis have the same revolutionary spirit as Shia?
- Is the revolution too late? Turkey too had its 'revolution' delayed by the heavy hand of Kemalism and the secular army, which prevented the Islamists coming to power until 2002, providing the secularists with an extra four decades.

The MB supported the overthrow of Gaddafi in Libya and is now supporting the overthrow of Assad in Syria—both high priority *western* objectives, but from the MB perspective sadly understandable, given the persecution of many devout Muslims, in particular the MB, by both regimes. That Egyptian President Mohamed Morsi met with the Gaza Hamas leader Ismail Haniyeh within weeks of his election, opened the Rafah crossing to Gaza, prevented another Israeli invasion of Gaza, and has increased economic and political cooperation with Iran are all encouraging signs. This was a very difficult period for the MB, with both the Egyptian army and the liberal opposition conspiring with the old regime remnants and the West, as the 3 July coup confirmed, to make its honest efforts to improve Egyptians' lives fail.

While the MB triumph in elections following the Arab Spring was more or less expected, the surprise was the strong showing of the Salafi, especially in Egypt. Their main party in the parliamentary elections, al-Nur (light), in coalition with al-Asala (originality) Party and the Islamic Society's Construction and Development Party, garnered 28% of the vote, second only to the MB's 38%. Until the revolution in 2011, they were concerned solely with *dawa* and helping the poor,[42] and they initially refused to participate in the uprising.[43] As politicians, they are concerned with strengthening Islamic appearances and institutions such as *awqaf*, and observing Islamic principles in economic and cultural policy. Effectively, they are acting as an Islamic watchdog over the MB, who are suspected as likely to compromise with the West.[44] They call for sharia-based law and are generally supportive of Saudi Arabia. Part of their popularity is attributed to their victimization by the largely secular media: "The liberal media is focused on us. They smear us, and then people see what we do on the ground, the people understand that there is something wrong with the media ... not with us," al-Nur spokesperson Muhammad Nour says.[45] Their satellite channels in Egypt are popular, and have introduced their leaders to a wider audience. Their initial hesitation to participate in the uprising is gone now, as *niqab*-wearing women are frequently seen with children at demonstrations, and their work among the poor will no doubt increase with the new freedom.

They are reportedly well funded by Saudis, but at the same time function as the 'communists' of the Egyptian revolution, being closest to the project of social justice, and intent on ridding society of western decadence, which should translate into a willingness to replace western capitalism by a more just system, even if it means a rejection of growth and western economic integration. However, their lack of political savvy and experience and innate conservatism may on the contrary translate into merely using Saudi money to provide charity to mitigate the effects of capitalism, without confronting the pro-imperialist subtext behind their lavish Saudi petrodollar funding.

There is talk of the Salafization of the Muslim Brotherhood. Hossam Tamam argues that traditional MB religious and social thought has increasingly given way to the influence of Salafi ideas within the organization, due to the oil boom of the 1970s and 1980s, which saw millions of Egyptians, including many MB supporters, migrate to the Gulf to work. A large proportion went to Saudi Arabia, and returned home infused with Wahhabi attitudes, a process assisted by the collapse of Nasserism.[46] Ex-members of the formerly terrorist Islamic Jihad and the Islamic Society[47] have joined the MB's ranks, further deepening Salafi influence.

Nonetheless, terrorist threats remain in Islamic Egypt. By 2012, al-Qaeda's post-Bin Laden leader, the Egyptian Zawahiri, was focusing his efforts on the disintegration of the Assad regime in Syria *and* the MB government in Egypt.[48] European jihadists come to Cairo to study Islam or Arabic in Nasr City, but then head for al-Qaeda training camps in Egypt, the Sinai or Libya. Unlike Bin Laden, who targeted western powers, Zawahiri has always been focused on combating local regimes and Arab rulers.[49]

The current unrest in **Syria** (21 million, 74% Sunni, 13% Shia, 10% Christian, 3% Druze[50]) has its roots in failed MB uprisings in Aleppo in 1979, inspired by the Iranian revolution (Islamists killed 83 Alawi cadets), and in Hama in 1982, inspired by the assassination of Sadat (intended as a prelude to an Iranian-style general uprising, which ended in the killing of up to 10,000 Islamists by Assad senior). There was no clear plan to seize power, the (Sunni) ulama was not supportive, the Baathists were socialist and had support among the poor. 'Independent' Syrian politics is rife with ethnic sectarianism, with the Baathists dominated by the Shia Alawis who were traditionally looked down upon by Sunnis. At the same time, the MB-linked Palestinian Hamas had its offices in Damascus with full Syrian government support, evidence that Syrian state solidarity with the Palestinians trumped solidarity and coordination between the different MBs.

Assad senior became convinced in 1982 that "he was wrestling not just with internal dissent, but with a large scale conspiracy to unseat him, abetted by Iraq, Jordan, Lebanon, Israel and the United States,"[51] and repression of all dissent doubled. The Assad dictatorship was passed from father Hafez to son Bashar in 2000, with the latter trying to heal the wound at the heart of Syrian society with a 'Damascus spring'. But the paranoid mindset inherited from his father remained, and he was unable to budge the army, which was entrenched as the leading political force.

The current attempt to force Assad's resignation continues at a terrible cost in human lives, abetted by the West and Israel, intent on another regime change and possible partition as achieved in Libya,[52] and as a stepping stone to an actual military encounter with Iran. Israeli support for the overthrow of Assad is in line with its own 'divide and conquer' strategy for the region, despite the risk of instability next door. The MBs in the region and the Gulf monarchies are also eager to bring Assad down, each with their own interests in mind. The specter of both Iraq and Libya hangs over Syria, and indeed they are intimately connected in US strategy. US 'Ambassador' to Libya Chris Stevens, at the time he was assassinated by al-Qaeda on 11 September 2012 in Benghazi, was facilitating the transfer of *Libyan* arms to *Syrian* rebels (many of whom are Iraqi al-Qaeda jihadis). The US compound in Benghazi was in fact a CIA post. *Iraqi* forces subsequently arrested 250 Saudi (read: US)-backed fighters who were on their way to Syria.

While both Qatar and Saudi Arabia were quick to finance and arm the Syrian rebels, their interests soon diverged when it became clear that Assad was not going to be toppled so easily. Qatar backs the Muslim Brotherhood and soon began backing a brokered deal to end the insurrection, betting that the MB could win control of the post-Assad government, while Saudi Arabia was determined to destroy Syria, both Assad and the MB, its interests directly paralleling those of both the US and Israel. Their intent is to remove Iran's main ally in anticipation of a US-Israeli invasion of Iran, and to undermine the Shia government in Iraq. Once again Wahhabi and neo-Wahhabi (really just Saudi tribal) interests coincide with US-Israel interests.

Lebanon (4.3 million, 27% Sunni, 27% Shia, 5% Druze, 39% Christian), suffered a decade and a half of civil war from 1975–1990 stoked by Israel, causing 120,000 deaths and resulting in a million refugees. Israel invaded in 1982, briefly occupied Beirut, driving the PLO into exile, and abetted a Maronite militia-led massacre of 1,000–3,500 Palestinian refugees and Lebanese, Iranian, Syrian, Pakistani and Algerian civilians at the Sabra and

Shatila camps. Following the civil war, Israeli occupation of southern Lebanon continued until 2000, when Israeli Prime Minister Ehud Barak ordered a full withdrawal. Syrian troops left Lebanon in 2005.

Hizbullah (1982, Party of God) is the Shia organization which emerged in response to the Israeli invasion of Lebanon, inspired by the Iranian Revolution and the Palestinian resistance, and which in turn inspired Palestinian Hamas. It helps the poor and resists Israel through militant MB-type grassroots organizations. Its popularity, deriving especially from the defense of the country against the Israeli 2006 aggression, has meant participation in coalition governments since 2005. Its current leader is Sheikh Hassan Nasrallah (b. 1960), a follower of the Iraqi Mohammad Baqir al-Sadr.

In **Jordan** (6.2 million, 92% Sunni) the Muslim Brotherhood was allowed to participate in the 1989 elections, and formed the Islamic Action Front (IAF) in 1992. Jordan's demographics are complex, with a large Palestinian refugee community, and a substantial (unsympathetic and not especially religious) Bedouin element which supports the monarchy. King Hussein (r. 1952–1999) supported Saddam Hussein during the 1991 US invasion under popular pressure, but then went on to sign a peace treaty with Israel in 1994 under US pressure. The IAF is the largest party in the parliament,[53] which has virtually no power, the prime minister being appointed by the king. The weakness of the parliament has disillusioned most voters, many of whom vote along tribal lines merely to get a few handouts from their local clans. Following the Arab Spring, Jordan was invited to join the Gulf Cooperation Council (GCC) (as was Morocco), even though it's not in the Persian Gulf,[54] making clear that the real purpose of the GCC is to unite reactionary autocratic Sunni regimes. Given Qatar's plans for 'pipelinestan' (see below), it will probably work now to turn Jordan into a more constitutional monarchy, giving the MB a modicum of power.

After the 1967 war, resulting in Israeli occupation of all of **Palestine** (Israel 7 million, 20% Sunni; Occupied Territories 11 million, 75% Sunni, 8% Christian, 17% Jewish), Israel borrowed a leaf from secular regimes in Turkey, Egypt and even Pakistan, and began to support political Islam as a counterweight to the secular PLO. Between 1967 and 1987, the year Hamas was founded, the number of mosques in Gaza tripled from 200 to 600. During that time, the Brotherhood established associations, used zakat for aid to poor Palestinians, promoted schools, provided students with loans, used *awqaf* to lease property and provide employment. Because the MB refused to engage in active resistance to Israel, its activist followers moved to Hamas when the latter was founded in 1987 in Gaza as a wing of the Brotherhood.

During the first Intifada (1987–1993), Hamas militarized and became the strongest Palestinian militant group. Gaza's stronger militancy is due to the fact that it consists mostly of refugees from the wars of 1948 (when it was under Egyptian occupation) and 1967 (under Israeli occupation). Hamas rejected the Oslo Accords in 1993 and sponsored suicide attacks against Israeli targets starting in 1994, resulting in hundreds of Palestinian/ Israeli deaths. It was also the mainstay of the second Intifada (2000–2005), and won elections in 2006. The Hamas takeover of the Gaza Strip in 2007 was the first time since the Sudanese coup of 1989 that an MB-linked group ruled. In power, it has had little room for maneuver, faced with the hostility of both the West/ Israel, who ignored the Hamas victory, and the secular PLO, which refused to relinquish power. It has mostly tried to keep Gazans alive without compromising Palestinian resistance, and as such has become a powerful symbol that has mobilized millions of supporters around the world, giving Islam further claim as the main global ideological force countering imperialism. Fatah in the West Bank, the main party in the PLO, cancelled the 2010 elections when it was clear it would lose again. In municipal elections in 2012, which Hamas boycotted, Fatah lost five of 11 main towns to PLO rebels and leftists.

But more radical groups than Hamas were also founded. Palestinian Islamic Jihad (PIJ) was formed in Egypt and the Gaza Strip in the 1970s and is noted for its military wing, the al-Quds Brigades. Unlike the MB and Hamas, the PIJ was committed to armed struggle. It takes its inspiration from both the MB and the Iranian revolution and has links with Hizbullah. There are also groups in Palestine affiliated with al-Qaeda[55] which have attacked both Israel and now Egypt's Sinai. In the wake of the August 2012 attack on Egyptian border troops, Hamas was pressured by Egyptian officials to crack down on these groups, but Hamas is hardly in a position to do so. In October 2012, an Israeli drone killed Tawhid and Jihad leader Abu Walid al-Maqdisi (see Chapter 3), suspected in the attack on Egyptian border troops. Maqdisi had been released by Hamas just two days before the August attack.

In **Libya** (6.5 million, 90% Sunni, 7% Ibadi[56]) in the 1980s, Reagan began a campaign to undermine Gaddafi, his sin as suspected Soviet proxy compounded by his defiant support as a Sunni for Shia Iran in the 1980–1988 war with Iraq. Gaddafi continued to provide financial support and even token weapons support to the PLO, the Irish Republican Army and other groups he deemed anti-imperialist, and remained the most outspoken Arab critic of the US empire and Israel, a lightning rod for western anti-Arab sentiment, but an eccentric, ineffectual leader for Arab nationalists, and a ruthless persecutor of genuine Muslims. He most notoriously 'disappeared' Syrian Shia Sheikh Musa al-Sadr in 1978 supposedly at the request of Syrian President Hafez al-Assad. The suppression of a riot at the Abu Salim prison in Tripoli in 1996 claimed over 1,000 deaths according to Human Rights Watch.[57]

The West took advantage of the February 2011 uprising in Benghazi to launch an invasion to oust Gaddafi, mobilizing disaffected Libyans, both liberal and MB/ Salafi/ al-Qaeda. This gross return to Great Game I was supported around the world by most leftists and Muslims, so isolated had Gaddafi become. Chaos reigns in the post-Gaddafi vacuum, now flooded by arms, with rebel holdouts and al-Qaeda active as evidenced in the assassination of US Ambassador Chris Stevens in September 2012. Current Prime Minister Ali Zidan (b. 1950) is a liberal who defected from Gaddafi's government in 1980, set himself up as a 'human rights lawyer' in Switzerland and formed the National Front for the Salvation of Libya.

Abdelhakim Belhadj (b. 1966), leader of the Salafi al-Watan Party, is a veteran of the Afghan jihad, ex-emir of the Libyan Islamic Fighting Group (which carried out three assassination attempts on Gaddafi in the 1990s), and ex-Taliban member, 'rendered' to Libyan jail by the US in 2004. He was freed in 2010 under a "de-radicalization" drive championed by Saif al-Islam Gaddafi, and a few months later became a military leader of the insurgency against Gaddafi.

There has been an underground branch of the Muslim Brotherhood since 1949 but members ended up in prison or were executed.[58] From the outset of the 2011 uprising and western-backed overthrow of Gaddafi, the Brotherhood was supportive of the National Transitional Council. The Libyan MB modeled its new Justice and Construction Party (JCP) after Egypt's Freedom and Justice Party and came a distant second with 10% to the liberal National Forces Alliance (48%) in the July 2012 elections. Al-Watan did not win any seats in the July 2012 elections.

The US, NATO and France—and the neo-Wahhabis—were the winners in the overthrow of Gaddafi. The former were celebrated as the liberators from the Gaddafi dictatorship, giving the pro-West secularists the edge in elections, though neo-Wahhabis such as Belhaj have been given a non-electoral boost, now operating freely, funneling Libyan arms and jihadis to Syrian rebels with US approval.[59] The MB emerged as the major Islamist force and is gaining strength; however, the collapse of Gaddafi's Libya allowed western businessmen and EU state-builders to flood the country and give it a make-over *a la* Kosovo. This will shape Libyan society for many years to come, with western 'security' firms, NATO training missions and EU administrators and educators weaving close ties to the new Libyan elite.

In an irony of imperialism witnessed throughout the region, Islamists in **Tunisia** (11 million, 98% Sunni) were repressed far more after 'independence' in 1956, than before under the French. Bourguiba was pushed aside in a coup in 1988, and his secular (and far more corrupt) successor Zine al-Abidine Ben Ali, was president for 23 years. Just as both Sadat and Mubarak initially courted the Islamists only to turn against them, members of Tunisia's MB-linked group al-Nahda (1981, renaissance) were allowed to participate in the 1989 elections as independents and, despite blatant repression and vote rigging during the elections, garnered 17% of the vote. This show of electoral democracy by the dictator Ben Ali was cynically used two years later, when Ben Ali had 25,000 of these publicly-declared supporters of Nahda imprisoned.

The self-immolation of Mohamed Bouazizi in December 2010, a fruit vendor in Tunisia, was the spark that set off the 2011 Arab uprising. Nahda won 89 of the 217 seats in the elections of October 2011 to lead a left-Islamic coalition government. Prime Minister Nahda Hamadi Jebali, leader of Nahda, and President Moncef Marzouki, a former dissident exiled in France, headed the new government, in a power-sharing deal between Nahda and its smaller secularist leftist coalition partners Takkatol and Marzouki's Congress for the Republic. Marzouki, author of *Dictators on Watch: A Democratic Path for the Arab World*, argued during the election campaign that progressive forces should unite with moderate Islamists in recognition of the importance of Islam in the Arab world. During the election campaign, he criticised the "old left, secular and Francophone, and totally disconnected from the real problems of Tunisian society".

Algeria's (36 million, 99% Sunni) pre-independence ulama was repressed both before and after the revolution in 1962, creating a vacuum in Islamist leadership that militants came to fill during the jihad against the Soviet Union in the 1980s. The traumatic history of Algeria under imperialism had created a culture of bitterness, xenophobia and violence. The brutal French occupation left it with no experience in pluralism, and the post-independence secular socialist government left no room for an MB-style Islamic revival.

Boumedienne died in 1978, just as the Iranian Islamic revolution was erupting, and Colonel Chadli Bendjedid (r. 1978–1990), a moderate, took his place, intending to institute pluralism. However, the 1980s fall in oil prices by two-thirds caused severe economic hardship, and after riots in 1988 and with a new constitution allowing political parties other than the ruling FLN, the hastily-formed Islamic Salvation Front (FIS) won more than 50% in municipal elections in June 1990 and was poised to take power national elections in December 1991. The elections were cancelled and Algeria's *second* civil war began.

Algeria's dynamic is yet another gruesome example of *realpolitik*'s 'divide and conquer' tactic, used with such effect in Afghanistan against socialist Afghans backed by the Soviet Union in the 1970s–1980s, and in Egypt and Syria in the 1980s–1990s, where Muslims also killed Muslims in the name of Islam. The Algerian civil war was merely an extreme version of Egypt's Sadat/ Mubarak nightmare, with France and the US supporting the secular military government (in Afghanistan and Syria they *opposed* the secular governments because their 'enemy', the Soviet Union, was supporting them). Between 1992–2002, an estimated 200,000 people died.

Some of the most notorious Islamic Armed Groups (IAGs) were in fact creations of the Algerian secret services, as even the French backers of the military were forced to admit.[60] "On the domestic front, their purpose was to commit atrocities in the name of Islam that would discredit the FIS. On the international front, the aim was to convince the West that Islamism needed to be "eradicated". [61] IAG *takfiri* (excommunication) ideology, like the fatwas of Zawahiri and Salim, targeted civilian populations.

Abdelaziz Bouteflika,[62] current president of Algeria, played the harsh but forgiving schoolmaster, amnestying thousands of members of the FIS based on a "Civil Concord" approved in a referendum in September 2000, but there are still occasional bombings in the name of al-Qaeda in the Islamic Maghreb (AQIM). The Islamist Green Algeria alliance, which includes the MB's Movement for a Peaceful Society (MSP),[63] won a paltry 59 of the 462 seats in the People's National Assembly in May 2012, one less than in 2007 'elections', with a turnout of 42%. The successors to the FIS refuse to participate in elections, accusing the government of rigging them. The Islamists are being held in check, but Algeria's trauma is far from over. The Washington-Paris scenario for the Muslim world is gruesomely unfolding as planned in its Algerian laboratory.

Morocco (35 million, 99% Sunni), became the most westernized Arab state after 'independence' in more than just name.[64] It continues to be a tourist playground for Europe, and exporter of fruit, vegetable and phosphorus, primarily to Europe, but lacks oil. It was granted "major non-NATO ally" status by the US in 2004 and has signed free trade agreements with the US and EU.

In defiance of the UN and the African Union (AU) Morocco annexed the Western Sahara when Spain relinquished it in 1975. Algeria broke off relations as a result and the borders between the two countries have been closed for most of the subsequent period. Morocco withdrew from the AU in 1984 when the AU supported the independence of the Sahrawi Arab Democratic Republic in the Western Sahara. Morocco also has territorial claims against Mauritania.

A glance at history reveals that this is an attempt to return to the pre-imperial order. The *French* expanded Algeria at the expense of Morocco in the nineteenth century because of Morocco's support for Algeria's anti-colonialist leader, Amir Abd al-Qadir, who proclaimed his allegiance to the Moroccan Sultan Moulay Abderrahmane. The Sahrawis, who fought *Spanish* occupation in what is now called the Western Sahara, also traditionally proclaimed allegiance to the Moroccan sultan. So it is no wonder when Morocco got its independence in 1956, it refused to accept the so-called Cairo Declaration in 1964, binding nations to accept the borders they inherited from colonial regimes, which would have meant *relinquishing* the struggle for independence. Not surprisingly, it was Algeria's current President Bouteflika, then foreign minister, who piously defended the Cairo Declaration.

Morocco existed as a sovereign state for centuries. Most of its dynasties originated in the Sahara—the Almoravids, who founded Marrakesh as the capital of their empire, were from Mauritania. Most natives north of Senegal and the 'Algerian' Sahara paid allegiance to the Moroccan sultan and conducted Friday prayers in his name. "These were the markers of sovereignty in pre-colonial Muslim societies, not the precise territorial boundaries that European states had to establish to sort out their own feuds."[65] Moroccan monarchists argue that they are not trying to conjure up 'greater Morocco' (which once extended into Libya and Spain) but merely to reunite people who had expressed their attachment to Moroccan sultans in the immediate pre-colonial period. It is part of the modern process of decolonization—no more, no less. As if confirming this, Polisario Secretary General Mohammed Abdelaziz (b. 1947) is a native of Marrakesh. Moroccans see the push for independence of Western Sahara as western 'divide and conquer' in collusion with Algeria. Of course, it is impossible to return to the pre-colonial status quo, and Morocco's repression of activists advocating independence for the Western Sahara faces condemnation, especially from Europe.[66]

By the 1990s, King Hassan II finally ended his executions of Islamists, releasing hundreds of political prisoners in 1991, and allowing the opposition Alternance to assumed power, for the first time in the Arab world. However, as in Jordan and the other monarchies, all authority in the constitution was in the king's hands, and, as in Jordan, the opposition was merely discredited for being powerless.

The MB's Popular Democratic and Constitutional Movement existed in Morocco from the 1960s but was persecuted along with all the other opposition. It was finally able to register its Justice and Development Party (JDP) in 1998. Large and persistent public protests organised by the 20 February youth movement in 2011 suddenly made genuine elections an important weapon in King Mohammed VI's (r. 1999) arsenal, and he immediately announced a process of constitutional reform and promised to relinquish some of his administrative powers.[67] There is still widespread cynicism; only about 25% of Moroccan adult citizens actually voted. Nonetheless, the JDP won a plurality of seats and, in alliance with center-leftists, its head, Abdelilah Benkirane, was appointed prime minister.

As in Tunisia and Egypt, the new government is committed to economic growth, improved education and greater Arab and Muslim unity, but has no chance of making any major changes in economic direction. Morocco was invited in 2012 to join the Gulf Cooperation Council along with Jordan, clearly an attempt by the absolute monarchies to help put the brakes on Morocco's Islamists, who reject monarchy and have embraced electoral democracy. The movement for a republic remains strong. [68] Corruption is rampant, headed by Mohammed VI, whose fortune is estimated by *Forbes* to be worth $2.5 billion. One-third of Moroccans are unemployed, 20% live in poverty and illiteracy is 40%.

The political situation post-Arab Spring is fluid. Islamists such as Mohamed al-Marouani, founder of the moderate Islamic movement al-Oumma in 1998, sentenced to twenty-five years in prison for "conspiring against state security", were released in the wake of Morocco's 20 February Movement. Al-Oumma finally was registered as a political party. The voices of Morocco's Sufi orders and Salafis have also joined the more open debate about Morocco's future.

The 1972 truce between north **Sudan** (35 million, 97% Sunni) and south Sudan (8.2 million, 18% Sunni) was undermined by Nimeiri's insistence that Islamization include the application of sharia in the south in 1983. Northerners argued, not without reason, that Christianity was mostly a legacy of imperialism, and tried to turn the clock back to make Islam the unifying principle for a truly independent 'Islamic state'. This did not convince the animist-Christians,[69] who looked back on colonial days with nostalgia, as they were the privileged ones then.

Turabi, Nimeiri's attorney general from 1979–1985, presided over the implementation of sharia in both north and south, culminating in the execution of Mahmoud Mohammed Taha for apostasy in 1985, soon followed by a renewed outbreak of civil war and Nimeiri's overthrow. At the same time Turabi supported women's right to vote—his MB[70] ran women candidates—and he proposed a broad understanding of the ulama to include professionals in every science and discipline, who must be inculcated with an Islamic responsibility for *ijtihad*. He argued that "*hudud* were applicable only in an ideal Islamic society from which want had been completely banished."[71]

Lieutenant-General Omar al-Bashir's coup in 1989 put an end to a series of weak coalition governments and declared Sudan an Islamic state. Nimeiri and Bashir tried to use Islam to prop up their shaky quasi-socialist military dictatorships, in the dysfunctional nation state bequeathed to them by the British, but this only made matters worse. The civil war raged until a Comprehensive Peace Agreement was signed in 2005, leading to a referendum and independence for the south in 2011, though there is no end to the simmering civil war across artificial, porous borders where the many tribes share traditional pasture rights and where oil wealth and unused, potentially irrigable land make Sudan a pawn in imperial games. Though hardly much worse than other third world dictators, Bashir became a target for the West,[72] as he harbored Bin Laden from 1992–1996 and because of the suffering of Christians in the civil war. Sudan is seething with unrest and could suffer further dismemberment in the 2010s.

Mali (16 million, 90% Sunni) has been in crisis since a coup in March 2012. While mainstream media framed the 2012 crisis as a result of radical Islam, it is rather a direct consequence of the West's intervention in Libya (and of course the 'nation state' bequeathed by imperialism). Mali's colonial era borders were fashioned by the French, lumping the desert north (sparsely populated by light-skinned nomadic Arab-Berber and Tuareg), and the more fecund south populated by dozens of darker, sub-Saharan tribes.

The Tuaregs[73] have staged unsuccessful revolts four times since Mali won its independence from France in 1960. Gaddafi had long supported the Tuaregs in their war for independence, and many Tuaregs served in the Libya armed forces. The invasion of Libya 'liberated' thousands of Tuareg, along with huge caches of arms. The 'Malians' among them went to northern Mali,[74] soon joined by battle-hardened al-Qaeda elements. They used their new weapons (courtesy of the West) against the largely ineffective (neocolonial) Malian army. Al-Qaeda-types[75] only moved in after the Tuareg Movement for the National Liberation of Azawad (MNLA) had expelled the Malian army from the north and declared a separate 'nation'. It is these neo-Wahhabi groups, not the Tuaregs, that enforced a rigid sharia law, stoned and beheaded, tore down Sufi shrines, and destroyed ancient artefacts. The Tuaregs were pushed aside, and many of them returned to the desert, abandoning cities like Timbuktu, Gao, and Kidal to the well-armed and ruthless neo-Wahhabis.

The idea of the old colonial power, France, invading in January 2013 was to 'defeat the terrorists' in the north and push Mali back into its pre-2011 shaky electoral democracy. There is no chance of success for the western plan to impose its one-size-fits-all electoral democracy, given the pressing social problems and the impossible ethnic stand-off which led to the collapse of the previous government. The French military intervention to prop up the brittle neocolonial regime is also intended to prop up similarly dysfunctional pseudo-democracies in Mali's neighbors Mauritania, Burkina Faso and Niger.

But Mali merely highlights the dilemma of modern imperialism: al-Qaeda-type groups endeavor to *entice* western intervention, in order to transform nationalist conflicts into confrontations with the West. Ultimately, if western powers are truly interested in political stability, they must avoid falling into this "intervention trap"[76] and encourage negotiated resolutions to local demands. Attempts by the Tuareg's MNLA to reach out to the occupiers, calling for joint efforts to expel the al-Qaeda elements, establish autonomy and provide uncorrupt economic development assistance, were ignored. Instead, the crisis was used by power-hungry chauvinist politicians from southern Mali to call for ruthless suppression of the MNLA as a 'Trojan Horse for terrorists'. And while the West bemoans the few dozen cases of cutting off of limbs of criminals and the loss of manuscripts and shrines in Timbuktu, they say nothing of the killing and forced exodus of thousands of Tuareg as a result of the invasion.

But US plans for the region long predate the sudden concern for electoral democracy, or the unfortunate victims of AQIM's *hudud* punishments which began in 2012. In 2011, the US declared the Sahara desert a breeding ground for terrorism and inaugurated the Trans-Sahal Counter Terrorism Initiative (2002).[77] The US African Command (AFRICOM, 2008) took over the 'Initiative' and began working directly with countries in the region, including Mali, and is now burrowing into Niger.[78]

> The US military is training the armed forces of dozens of African nations. A Malian army captain [Amadou Sanogo] used that aid and training to pull off a coup that now threatens to turn into a regional war. Will Morocco use US aid to fight terrorism or tighten its grip over the mineral rich Western Sahara and re-ignite its war with the Polisario Front? Will Niger fight "terrorists" or crush Tuareg resistance to French uranium mining in the Sahara? Will Algeria go after the AQIM or its own outlawed Islamist organizations? Will aid to fight terrorism in Nigeria be diverted to smash resistance by local people to oil production in the Niger Delta? Bayonets won't defeat the source of terrorism and instability in Africa. Indeed, military solutions tend to act as recruiting sergeants for groups like AQIM.[79]

The regional grouping ECOWAS (see Chapter 2) was mobilized by the French under a UN mandate to act as a cover for the blatant reoccupation of the region by the empire. ECOWAS and the West African Monetary Union,[80] 'postmodern'[81] attempts to break down the artificial borders forced on these largely Muslim states and recreate some of the peaceful cross-border trade that characterized the region before the arrival of the imperialists, are now the Trojan Horse for blatant US-French reconquest of the resource-rich Sahel hinterland. Christians in the region, the result of the French occupation, have a privileged position, identifying with the West (and Israel), and are a useful trump card justifying interference and intervention on 'humanitarian' grounds, the so-called R2P (responsibility to protect).

As in Libya and Syria, Russia and Iran exposed the hypocrisy of this: "Those whom the French and Africans are fighting now in Mali are the [same] people who ... our western partners armed so that they would overthrow the Gaddafi regime," Russian Foreign Minister Sergey Lavrov told a news conference angrily in January 2013.

The Algerian role is not so clear; there is no love lost between it and its former colonial master, but the secular government is still fearful of its own Islamists and AQIM terrorists, as underlined by the hostage crisis in In Amenas in January 2013 where 67 died. Egypt's President Morsi condemned the French invasion. The US and France continue to manipulate the political unrest in pursuit of the region's raw materials (especially gold, uranium and of course oil), oblivious to the devastation wrought on the local population or the long term consequences of what can only be seen as a return to the outright imperialism of Great Game I.

Nigeria (163 million, 51% Sunni, 48% Christian), instituted sharia law in the predominantly Muslim north in 1999, but the country is still plagued by an al-Qaeda-type local group Boko Haram (2002, "Western education is forbidden") intent on establishing a northern Muslim state along the lines of the Uthmanid caliphate dismantled by the British in 1903. The secretive sect is blamed for nearly 1,400 killings since 2009, involving a campaign of terror that has seen bomb and gun attacks on government buildings, police stations, communication facilities, churches and even mosques.

Nigeria is Africa's top oil producer with vast reserves of natural gas, its petrochemical wealth concentrated in the Christian south. During the insurgency in the Niger Delta by the Ogoni tribe in the 1990s, Shell reportedly colluded with death squads to quash that insurrection. It is widely suspected that Boko Haram, which only adopted violent tactics in 2009, is manipulated by western oil interests intent on encouraging the south to secede. This terrorism gives the US an excuse to extend its reach through AFRICOM, and as in Algeria and Mali, it kills mostly Muslims.

Despite oil export earnings of $45 billion a year and more than five decades as a major producer, Nigeria remains one of the poorest (and most corrupt) countries on earth. The curse of oil is likely to spread across West Africa as it becomes a major new oil-producing region, with recent discoveries in Ghana and Niger and offshore fields in the Gulf of Guinea.[82]

By 2006, **Somalia**'s (10 million, 100% Sunni) broadly-backed Islamic Courts Union (ICU) had almost united the country riven by civil war, subduing warlords for the first time since 1991, but it was not recognized by the West, which accused it of being in league with al-Qaeda. The West patched together a Transitional Federal Government from émigré Somalis, and encouraged Ethiopia to invade in 2007. The ICU splintered into a more radical faction, Shabab (youth), which defiantly pursued insurgency, this time in league with al-Qaeda. The Ethiopian invasion rallied Somalians against the occupiers, and the Shabab succeeded in uniting a large section of the population against the occupation, despite its association with al-Qaeda. Thus, a small, extremist group that was marginal in the UIC became the backbone of the resistance thanks to western meddling. "The end result of the US-backed invasion was driving Somalia into the al-Qaeda fold," says Somalia's former foreign minister Ismail Mahmoud Hurre.[83] The MB Reform Movement (1978) is a member of the transitional parliament, but its following is limited as it operates mostly in Mogadishu.

Djibouti (900,000, 97% Sunni), formerly French Somaliland, is a port carved out by the French and given 'independence' in 1977. Some 1,500 US

Marines are deployed at Lemonier, a French Foreign Legion base in Djibouti, and drones take off hourly to Somalia and Yemen. The US also has facilities in Kenya, Uganda, the Central African Republic, Ethiopia, Mauritania, Burkina Faso and the Seychelles islands, and is establishing bases in Niger and possibly South Sudan.

Ethiopia's (85 million, 34% Sunni) former communist regime (1977–1991) failed, weakened by civil war with **Eritrea** (6.1 million, 48% Sunni) which finally gained independence in 1991. In 1998, a border dispute with Eritrea led to the Eritrean–Ethiopian War, which ended in a stalemate. Eritrea is accused of aiding the Shabab in Somalia (presumably to weaken Ethiopia), and is subject to UN/AU sanctions. Eritrea recognizes Israel, and is treated as its "strategic ally" because of Eritrea's Red Sea port. It has had border disputes and clashes with all its neighbors—Sudan, Ethiopia, Djibouti, even Yemen over islands. Overall, religious strife is less than elsewhere, given the strength of nationalism, where Muslims represent a minority.

The **Saudi Kingdom** (28 million, 85% Sunni, 15% Shia), now headed by King Abdullah under the spiritual guidance of the Wahhabis, was consolidated under the watchful eye of the British in the 1920s and bequeathed to the Americans in the 1930s. With the subsequent discovery of vast oil fields, this meant that there were two Arab worlds by the 1970s, when oil wealth in the Gulf and high prices for oil provided a happy coincidence for the once-poor Bedouin tribes there. One world—most of the umma in Africa and Asia—is poor, populous and (until recently) secular, the other—a handful of sheikhdoms allied to the imperialists (including Bahrain, Oman, Qatar and the UAE)— fabulously wealthy, their security tied to the empire. This catapulted these premodern Islamic tribes into the heart of twentieth century empire strategy, making them second in importance only to their protagonist Israel, forcing an awareness and tolerance of Islam (however distorted the understanding may be by the empire), mortgaging the empire's well-being to these oil-producing sheikhdoms. (What happens if they fall, like the Shah's Iran?)

Throughout the post-'independence' period from the 1920s, Saudi Arabia took no initiative not approved by the US—except once. In 1973, King Faisal initiated an oil boycott of countries supporting Israel, in support of his new friend, Egyptian President Sadat, who had ended Egypt's experiment with secular socialism, allowed exiled MB members to return from Saudi Arabia and pushed Israel back in the October war that year.. The US government was not happy, and the oil embargo was lifted after only six months—despite the refusal of Israel to withdraw from Sinai and the Occupied Territories— and Faisal was assassinated in 1975, [84] and replaced by the more compliant King Fahd, who went as far as to accept a permanent US military presence on Saudi territory,

It is speculated that the boycott was actually orchestrated by oil companies not so much to threaten Israel, but to jack up the price of oil—

delivering a huge bonanza to the sheikhs, western oil companies and banks. 1979 oil revenues were 30 times those of 1970, and, after a brief fall in the late 1980s, have continued to climb ever since, creating starvation in many third world countries (including many Muslim ones), causing a huge transfer of wealth from them to the sheikhs, oil barons and international bankers.

To deal with this massive disruption to the international financial order, the United States-Saudi Arabian Joint Economic Commission was set up, which funneled billions of petrodollars back to the US, "entrenching the US deeply in the Kingdom, fortifying the concept of mutual interdependence" at the same time as the US turned a blind eye to Saudi financing—both official and private—of Islamists, outside of American purview.[85]

The US plan for 'jihad' in Afghanistan against the Soviet Union, which was put into full gear by 1979, was a Saudi dream-come-true. The Saudis were now flush with petrodollars and eager to see a Saudi-groomed Sunni Islamic state beside Pakistan as a counterweight to newly militant Shia Iran. The Saudis guaranteed to match the US dollar-for-dollar for arms and logistics (in fact the Saudis provided most of the funding). It was coordinated by Saudi intelligence, headed by Prince Turki al-Faisal, in close liaison with the CIA. Drug smuggling was an additional major source of funding.[86]

The sudden windfall allowed the Saudi and Gulf 'states' (really tribal principalities) to undertake ambitious modernization programs. The Saudis gave western corporations blank checks to build state-of-the-art infrastructure, and the kingdom guaranteed its people free health care and education, its men jobs—a kind of medieval Islamic socialism—even as it imported tens of thousands of experts, laborers and domestic help from abroad. The Wahhabi doctrine to keep women covered and chaperoned or out of sight, and the encouragement of polygamy, continued to the *faux* disapproval of the West. Fabulously rich (and backward) Arab sheikhs are a Hollywood staple, or at least were until 911.

However, all was not well, as evidenced in the 1979 seizure of the Grand Mosque in Mecca during the hajj by disgruntled Saudi youth (one of whom claimed to be the Mahdi), denouncing the moral laxity of the royal family and demanding the expulsion of foreign military and civilian specialists, the unspoken motivation being the Iranian revolution.[87] Though quelled, the uprising shook the government, which gave the ulama more powers in regulating education and controlling the media. Retail establishments were forced to close for daily prayers, and princes were told to better hide their decadent ways. State and private funding of *dawa*, mosques, and schools abroad (Indonesia, east Africa, Pakistan, Europe) increased—there was a seemingly bottomless pit of petrodollars. It was at this time that *hadd* penalties were enforced with increasing frequency.

There was still no parliament (let alone universal suffrage)[88] or an independent judiciary, but only the feudal-style process of negotiations among king, tribal leaders and ulama. There is virtually no culture—music, creative literature and art are essentially banned.[89] The Saudis are "as indifferent and even opposed to traditional Islamic art as are the partisans of modernism". They are the worst per capita polluters in the world. In effect, they are in the same position with respect to re-emergent Islamic civilization as liberal assimilationists (viz., their common wholesale adoption of western technology), with the difference that they get their western science and life style paid for by oil, in the process, fueling imperialism's war machine against Islam. "At best, God is remembered as Truth, at least on a certain level, but He is forgotten as Presence. Beauty becomes incidental, and the Islamic character of architecture and city planning is of total inconsequence."[90]

A growing middle class, many of whom were educated in sciences and management in the US, were and are dissatisfied with the economic and political privileges of the ruling family and the cultural desert of Arabia, and understandably want changes that the Saudi monarchy is incapable of providing. Shia, living in the oil-rich east, suffer extreme discrimination, benefiting not at all from their oil wealth, with the Saudis' western sponsors oblivious.

However, there is almost no articulate Saudi dissident movement, either liberal or traditionalist, in reflection of the negative influence of Wahhabism on all forms of thought, and the influence of the tribal political structure on the ordinary people, 25% of whom live in poverty, despite the oil wealth. The most prominent individuals include Saad Rashed Mohammad al-Faqih (b. 1957), a professor of surgery at King Saud University who fled to London in 1994 and set up the Committee for the Defense of Legitimate Rights[91] along with fellow exile Mohammad al-Massari. They are both effectively Wahhabi but anti-royalist and are disapproved of by the US since they seek the overthrow of the Saudi monarchy by force. The main Saudi opposition is the Shia minority. Since 1979, dozens of Qatif protesters have been killed (the US uses the nearby Dhahran Air Base). There were large demonstrations in Qatif from February 2011 on, demanding the release of political prisoners (there are thousands in Saudi Arabia, mostly Shia). There are also semi-clandestine groups of MB supporters, including the Brotherhood of the Hejaz, part of a broader social movement Sahwa (awakening) which began in the 1970s, and which Bin Laden joined.

As such, the Wahhab-inspired Saudis and Gulf monarchies have provided little in the way of a meaningful intellectual contribution to the debate about how Islam can accommodate modernity, or how modernity can accommodate Islam (other than to fence off Muslims 'lucky' enough to have lots of oil money). Despite their control of the holy cities and the hajj, and their extensive funding of mosques and Wahhabi-inspired Islamic education around the world, Saudi efforts have resulted in only a faint echo of Wahhabism being followed elsewhere. And just as the neo-Wahhabis destroy shrines in Timbuktu, Wahhabi control over the holy cities has proved to be disaster for Islam's heritage, resulting in the destruction of 95% of the 1,000-year-old buildings in the two cities in the past 20 years. [92] Their claims that such sites are not important looks suspect when the targets are sites particularly revered by Shia as well as reminders of the (anti-Wahhab) Ottoman past.

Their main influence on the Muslim word has been indirect, with the rise of Wahhabi-inspired terrorism, and the negative role model that these politically isolated, tribal states have played as allies to the US empire after WWII. The message of premodern accommodationism to the empire is: 'If you leave us alone, and protect us discretely, we'll use your imperialist map of the world, and you can do what you like in the Middle East and anywhere else for that matter. Islam is 'above politics'. You can even station your troops here if necessary. If this happens to contradict Islam, so be it.'

The Saudis were furious when, after supporting the US invasion of **Kuwait** (3.6 million, 64% Sunni, 21% Shia) in 1991, the reinstalled Kuwaiti Sheikh Jaber al-Sabah (r. 1977–2006) was pushed to institute a more meaningful elected consultative assembly, curb the religious police and give more freedom to women. His US patrons, after all, had to justify the costly invasion with a pretense of bringing democracy. Women were finally given the vote in 2006 and in 2009 four women were elected. There are no parties in Kuwait, only parliamentary blocs (Salafi, Popular (Bedouin, Shia), Liberal), and elections are marred by vote buying and tribalism. The Salafis have dominated the elections and began impeaching ministers in 2010. Emir Sheikh Sabah has dissolved the unruly parliament four times, but the opposition are demanding a constitutional democracy, much as the MBs are in Morocco, Jordan and Bahrain. The era of absolute monarchies is almost over. The new parliament elected in 2012 is just as Salafi-angry as the previous one (they demand that all western cultural symbols be removed) and October 2012 saw 100,000 demonstrators turn out to the biggest protest in Kuwaiti history.

The other Muslim world—those without oil—resent that this wealth is under the control of such a tiny minority of Muslims. Even though millions of penurious Muslims have traveled to the Gulf sheikhdoms to serve their rich cousins and earn US dollars to remit to their relatives at home in, say, Egypt or Pakistan (enduring terrible working conditions, earning low wages with few benefits, unable to form trade unions), most Muslims fervently hope for radical change in these feudal fiefdoms, so that they share the wealth more generously among the world umma.[93]

These premodern accommodationists have financed or at least condoned all the US wars against their fellow Muslims—against Iran (1979+), against Iraq (1991), against Afghanistan (2001+), against Iraq (2003), against Yemen, Bahrain, Libya and Syria (2011+), and no doubt elsewhere at US behest. Together Saudi Arabia and the Gulf states use their oil revenues to contain and shape the politics of the Sunni Arab states, undermining the socialist experiments (Egypt, Libya, Syria, Iraq), and offering aid to poor Muslim countries in exchange for a political shift to the right. They were staunch supports of the Cold War throughout the twentieth century, and were instrumental in destroying the Soviet Union and any hope of a secular alternative to capitalism.

Just as they feed the imperial war machine and support its policies, Saudi Arabia and now Qatar in particular, have acted as a catalyst in promotion of western interests in the Middle East, including terrorism, which has primarily victimized the world's Muslims, thereby gravely weakening the world umma, and stifling innovative reforms within Islam to meet the demands of the modern world. Their aim is a proliferation of Wahhabi-style Islamic states, and their version of sharia throughout the Muslim world. Their official strategy is promotion of premodern accommodation, while the unofficial tactic of many millionaire princes in and out of power (Osama Bin Laden is the tip of the iceberg) is terrorism.

To give the Saudi monarchy credit as Muslims, they have made at least a partially positive contribution to the process of Islamization in the Muslim world, publishing and mailing free Qurans and hadiths to all comers around the world. Faisal was the best of the Saudi monarchs—intelligent, competent, uncorrupt, sincerely promoting his conception of Islam (and was conveniently assassinated—see endnote 84). He founded the (anti-communist) Muslim World League (1962), the Organization for Islamic Cooperation (1969), the International Islamic News Agency (1972) and the Islamic Development Bank (1975) (disparaged as "American Islam" by Khomeini). Since the 1960s, the Saudis have funded Islamic education (achieving close to universal literacy at home), though the intent was more to undermine secular Arab regimes which were carrying out mass literacy programs.[94]

The **United Arab Emirates** (8.2 million, 76% Muslim) is a federation of seven emirates[95] with capital Abu Dhabi, whose rulers retain absolute power but acknowledge a figurehead UAE president. Only 17% of the population are natives (85% Sunni, 15% Shia), 23% other Arabs, and 62% other guest workers. The Abu Dhabi Fund for Development (1971) has provided $6.5 billion in soft loans and grants mostly to Palestine and African nations for emergency relief—a modest fraction of its oil revenues following the hike in oil prices from 1973 on. It maintains close ties with Saudi Arabia and the US, and advertises itself as a duty-free shopper's paradise for westerners, but beware—prison terms, lashings, even death are experienced by foreigners for what in the West would be considered acceptable behavior.[96]

Oman (2.8 million, 75% Ibadi, 24% Sunni) was a British protectorate until 'independence' in 1972, when the British felt it was safe to officially leave, having facilitated a coup against the isolationist Sultan Said bin Taimur, who was faced with a secessionist movement in Dhofar funded by Saudi Arabia. Pro-British Sultan Qaboos bin Said (r. 1970) instituted social reforms and modernization, and by 2010 Oman was awarded the UNDP's prize for the country "most-improved in the past 40 years". A lesser oil state, like the other GCC members it is run as an absolute monarchy, though there are elections (no political parties). The eccentric Qaboos is PM, chairman of the central bank, and minister of defense, finance, foreign affairs, what-have-you. An aficionado of western classical music, he funds a 120-piece orchestra composed of Omani youth and regularly imports entire European orchestras for concerts. His accession day and birthday are national holidays.

In addition to Qaboos, the odd-men out in the Gulf are **Bahrain** (1.3 million, 70% Shia) and Qatar. The Sunni Sultanate of Bahrain, 'independent' since 1971, remains a defiant hotbed of unrest. The Saudi-backed crackdown against the Shia uprising in 2011 drove protesters from Pearl Square in the capital Manama into the villages where smaller groups of demonstrators clash with security forces almost daily. As in all the absolute monarchies, there are elections to a toothless parliament, though here they must be doctored to prevent an embarrassing manifestation of the Shia majority. The large US naval base in Bahrain means that no 'democracy' rules apply.

Qatar (1.9 million, 75% Sunni) is headed by the ambitious Prince Sheikh Hamad bin Khalifa al-Thani, who overthrew his laid-back father in 1995, set up Al-Jazeera TV a year later, and has used his power as absolute monarch sitting on one of the world's largest supplies of natural gas to guide the Arab secular dictatorships towards some kind of Islamic democracy.[97] He gave Salafi/MB exiles such as Egypt's Qaradawi the chance to reach a worldwide satellite audience on the understanding that "they could speak to the world and arouse the fury in Egypt or Libya, but they would have to leave their revolution outside of Qatar."[98] The international Muslim Brotherhood dissolved itself in Qatar in 1999, as "the kingdom was in compliance with Islamic law", according to Jasim Sultan, an ex-member who now heads the Qatar state-funded Awaken Project, publisher of moderate political and philosophical literature. Sheikh Hamad finances Doha thinktanks and conferences where western liberals debate the future of the Arab world with likeminded Arabs.

Qatar has traditionally had a testy relationship with Saudi Arabia since its independence in 1971, which worsened when Sheikh Hamad pushed aside his father in 1995 and started stirring up trouble, unwilling to leave regional affairs in Saudi hands. Saudi Arabia uses geography to try to bring Qatar to heel. Qatar is the world's largest LNG (liquefied natural gas) producer, and was frustrated by the Saudis in 2009 when they blocked a pipeline from Qatar to Europe through Saudi Arabia and Turkey. The discovery of a new gas field near Israel, Lebanon, Cyprus, and Syria opened new possibilities to bypass the Saudis and further expand. Only Assad in Syria is in the way.

The rival sheikhs are at present scheming together to overthrow Assad, each with his own agenda, not to mention the agendas of the US and Turkey. They are united in their aversion to Iran and its $10 billion Iran-Iraq-Syria gas pipeline project. If they 'succeed' in overthrowing Assad, the Saudis will presumably be forced to allow Qatar's pipeline (same South Pars gas field as Iran) whether or not it goes through Saudi Arabia. The Turks and Qataris appear to have the edge in the scheming, both wanting to install the Syrian chapter of the Muslim Brotherhood to block Saudi Arabia's efforts to install a more fanatical Wahhabi regime.[99] Where concern for the umma is in all this cynical scheming is hard to see.

Similarly, in Libya, Qatar joined NATO in overthrowing Gaddafi, looking to a future MB-dominated government to work with it in preference to Saudi Arabia. The bankruptcy of Wahhabism is starkly revealed in tiny Qatar's ability to outfox the natural regional hegemon, though this involves a marriage of convenience between the autocratic Sheikh and the MBs in the region, which have had to gain power without money, relying on genuine religious and popular support, and the alignment could change:

> Qatar's influence could be crowded out by a rising Egypt or even Iraq in the future. Furthermore, if the Arab Awakening spreads from Bahrain into other Gulf emirates, Doha may need to reign in its international ambitions and address its democratic deficit at home. Indeed, when it comes to democracy in the Gulf, the two [Saudi and Qatari] kingdoms are rivals no more.[100]

With the collapse of the Soviet Union, the (socialist) People's Democratic Republic of **Yemen** was forced in 1990 to join north Yemen, run by secular autocrat Ali Abdullah Saleh (r. 1978–2012) in the Republic of Yemen (25 million, 53% Sunni, 45% Shia). The Muslim Brotherhood is Islah (1990, reform), the largest opposition party. After a grueling year of demonstrations and virtual civil war in 2011, culminating in the resignation of Saleh and the 'election' of his vice president, Abd Rabbah Mansur al-Hadi, Islah became part of the interim government. Al-Qaeda is strong in this failed state, and US drones regularly kill supposed terrorists and innocent civilians. Most likely

Yemen will continue to disintegrate, the south and the Shia al-Houthi rebels establishing their own *de facto* governing structures.

In **Iraq** (33 million, 63% Shia, 33% Sunni), the Iraqi MB-affiliated Islamic Party was formed in 1960 but banned in 1961, re-emerging after the fall of the Saddam Hussein regime in 2003 as one of the main advocates for the country's Sunni community. In the north of Iraq there are several Islamic movements inspired by the MB. The Kurdistan Islamic Union (KIU) holds seats in the Kurdish parliament, and is the main political force apart from the two main secularist parties, the PUK and KDP.

But Iraq is a Shia-dominated state—the only Arab state where Shia are the majority. Current Prime Minister Nour al-Maliki (b. 1950) fled Iraq for Iran in 1979 under a death sentence as an official of the Islamic Dawa Party (1957), which aims at establishing an Islamic state where the authority is from the umma rather than the ulama (Mohammad Baqir al-Sadr was a founding member).

Dawa gained strength in the 1970s recruiting from among the Shia ulama and youth, and waged an armed insurgency against the government of Saddam Hussein, opposed to the secular Baathist ideology and inspired by the Iranian revolution. In 1979, Dawa moved its headquarters to Tehran. In 1980, Saddam Hussein had Mohammad Baqir al-Sadr assassinated. During the Iran–Iraq War, Iran backed the Dawa insurgency against Saddam Hussein. The Dawa Party was thought to have been behind the 1983 bombing of the US embassy in Kuwait as punishment for Kuwaiti, American and French military and financial assistance to Iraq in its war against Iran. One of those convicted in the bombing was Dawa member Jamal Jafaar Mohammed, now a member of Iraq's parliament.

The inspiration for Saddam Hussein's socialist secular nationalism, Egypt's Nasser, died in 1970, and the Iraqi and Syrian Baathists had fallen out even earlier. Saddam Hussein was on his own by the time he invaded Iran in 1980 and then Kuwait in 1990—both implicitly approved of by the US,[101] which counted on him to create sufficient havoc to lead to his overthrow or, in the worst case scenario, justify a US invasion, which finally happened in 2003.

The US and Saudis prepared for the overthrow of Saddam Hussein by funding the Iraqi National Accord (1991) and the Iraq National Congress (1992), bringing together secular and religious opposition forces. Up to that point, Dawa was viewed as a terrorist organization because of its support for Iran during the Iran-Iraq war, and was accused of assassination attempts in Iraq against Hussein's foreign minister, Tariq Aziz, in 1980 and Saddam Hussein himself in 1982 and 1987.[102] After the end of the Iraq-Iran war and with the Iraqi invasion of Kuwait, the interests of Dawa and the US converged, and it joined the US-backed Iraqi National Congress, which promised "human rights and rule of law within a constitutional, democratic, and pluralistic Iraq".

The main alternative Shia organization is the Supreme Council for the Islamic Revolution in Iraq (SCIRI), founded in 1980 in Iran and composed of Iraqi exiles. It approved of Khomeini's theocratic government, although SCIRI has distanced itself from its Iranian sponsors since then. After the 2003 US invasion of Iraq—which Dawa opposed—both Dawa and SCIRI returned to Iraq. Dawa and SCIRI are the two main parties in the Shia United Iraqi Alliance, which won a plurality of seats in the 2005 elections. Dawa Prime Minister Maliki lived in exile in Iran until the US invasion in 2003, and became prime minister in 2006 after fellow Dawa member, Ibrahim al-Jaafari (now head of National Reform Trend).

SCIRI (renamed Islamic Supreme Council of Iraq (SIIC)) is associated with Ayatollah Sistani, and its militant Badr Brigade competes for popularity with Muqtada al-Sadr's Mahdi Army. The Badr Brigade was trained by Iran's Revolutionary Guards, and fought alongside Iranian troops during the Iraq-Iran war and in the 1991 uprising of Iraqi Shia following the US-led invasion of Iraq. It is the *de facto* government in Basra.

Shia have joined the new Iraqi security forces in large numbers, eager to cement their control of the new state, and the continued bombings of primarily Shia are clearly the work of Sunni insurgents (backed by the Saudis and possibly the US). The anti-occupation Iraqi resistance has been Sunni-dominated from the start, determined to end both the occupation (now 'occupation lite') and Shia control. The resistance demands Shia join them, despite the obvious sectarian divide now,[103] which prevents a united resistance to the US-imposed order and ongoing US military presence. The (Wahhabi) Saudis are using these bombings targeting Shia both to provoke a Shia backlash leading to outright civil war, and to show the US that violence will continue unless the US abandons its Shia 'partners'. This is also the strategy of (neo-Wahhabi) al-Qaeda, which formed in Iraq after the US occupation and was led by the Jordanian Abu Musab al-Zarqawi (1966–2006), once again showing how Saudi/ al-Qaeda interests converge (their only difference being over the sanctity of the Saudi royal family).

Iran's (75 million, 93% Shia, 5% Sunni) Islamic revolution and ongoing anti-imperialist resistance gives it a towering role in the re-emerging Islamic civilization, despite it being relatively isolated as a militant Shia state in a world where Shia represent only 12% of the world's Muslims. Unlike the Turkish generals after 1980 or Egypt's Sadat after 1973, the Shah was in no position to encourage the Islamists in order to neutralize the leftist challenge to his liberal nationalism. Ayatollah Khomeini became the symbol of resistance to the Shah by 1963, and the special role that the *Usuli* ulama play in Shiism[104] put the issue of theocracy on the agenda of the revolution. The 'divine right' of monarchs was replaced by the 'divine right' of those with a legitimate claim on knowledge of the Divine Will. The message of social justice was co-opted by

Khomeini, the liberals and leftists were crushed after a coup attempt in 1981, hounded into prisons or exile, but the heady dreams of quickly achieving an Islamic utopia gave way to the reality of war with Iraq, boycott and subversion by the West, cynicism and weariness.

The Khomeini version of Islamic democracy put into place after 1979 consists of:

- the Council of Guardians of the Constitution, a 12-member body half appointed by the Supreme Leader and half elected by parliament from jurists nominated by the head of the judiciary (who is appointed by the supreme leader). It supervises elections of the Assembly of Experts, the presidency and parliament, (regularly disqualifying liberals and leftists from running in elections), approves/ vetoes laws passed by parliament.
- the Assembly of Experts, a body of 86 *mujtahids* elected from a list of candidates by direct public vote to eight-year terms. It elects and can remove the Supreme Leader, and supervises his activities.
- the Supreme Leader, the highest ranking political and religious authority, elected by the Assembly of Experts, and who appoints half the Council of Guardians, the head of the judiciary, and other senior civilian and military officials, and can dismiss the president.

This system was devised by Ayatollah Khomeini in 1970 and engraved in the constitution at the height of the revolution in 1980. In addition,

- the Expediency Council was set up by Ayatollah Khomeini in 1988 (out of his frustration with the ulama who disapproved of land reforms), a kind of upper house,[105] to be appointed by the Supreme Leader to resolve conflicts between parliament and the Council of Guardians and advise the Supreme Leader.

The effect of this complex electoral system has been to leave most power in the hands of the ulama, and to discourage reformists and women from running for parliament, although given the extreme pressure that Iran is under from outside, this conservatism is hardly surprising.

While Iranian scholars, the broad public and western critics debate the validity of political rule by the ulama and just how far popular democracy should extend, the day-to-day reality of life in Iran has been one of economic hardship and political fractiousness. The turning point came with the end of the Iraq war in 1988, when Khomeini tried to enact land reforms but was stopped by the Council of Guardians. Khomeini had been able to balance left and right forces, and his death in 1989 "removed the charismatic and unifying figure who had made the revolution possible."[106]

The more conservative Ayatollah Ali Khameni had served as president (1981–1988), balanced by his more left-wing Prime Minister Mir-Hussein Mousavi. Khameni replaced Khomeini as Supreme Leader in 1989, ending the leftist pretensions of the government. The post of prime minister was abolished and Mousavi disappeared from political life. Postwar reconstruction and the beginnings of neoliberal reform took place under President Ali Akbar Rafsanjani (r. 1989–1997), a pillar of the revolution, but anxious to return Iran to capitalism and its position among western nations. He redefined property rights to legitimize private capital accumulation, and at the same time changed labor laws to help the poor. He proceeded with modest land reforms, confiscating 2.1 million acres which were distributed to 220,000 farmers, but also privatized hundreds of companies, and coaxed exiled businessmen to return and take back their businesses.

His success in these changes, coupled with the collapse of living standards for the urban middle class following the revolution[107] and the often violent clamp-down on the press and critics, gave rise to a strong liberal movement, which, headed by Muhammad Khatami, swept into power in 1997. But the conservative ulama prevailed, undermining the weak president and chipping away at the liberals in subsequent elections. The brain drain (3 million educated Iranians emigrated) and capital flight continued, and by 2002, liberalization was dead. The populist Tehran mayor Mahmoud Ahmedinejad was elected president in 2005, identified as a 'conservative', though this is misleading, as in economic terms, he was more socialist (though his supporters would simply call him more Islamic), refusing to implement the neoliberal agenda of privatization, using oil revenues to subsidize food and fuel. He appealed to both nationalists and Islamists, pursuing Iran's legitimate right to nuclear power, strongly supporting the Palestinians and attempting to dispense with dollars in the oil trade.[108] Like Khomeini, he has been battling the ulama establishment, though whether their differences are over fundamentals or more due to political intrigue is difficult to determine.

Iran's post-revolutionary experience in many ways recapitulates that of other revolutions, for example Cuba, where unremitting US hostility and the inevitable post-revolutionary disarray resulted in 'revolutionary justice'[109] and a mass exodus of the (mostly western-trained) elite, and a largely negative image in the western media, which claims violation of human rights of those who would undo the revolution.

Charges in the western media that the 2009 presidential elections were fraudulent had little basis in reality. To imagine that the iPod uprising by westernized urban youth could have toppled the regime and ushered in a 'post-Islamic' era of assimilation is to fly in the face of reality. Recall the defiant words of Ayatollah Ali Khamenei, now Iran's supreme leader, during the hostage crisis in 1979: "We are not liberals like Allende and Mossadeq, whom the CIA can snuff out." Even western opinion polls put Ahmedinejad well ahead of former Prime Minister Mousavi. Though a socialist before the revolution, Mousavi was by 2009 the real conservative, calling for greater privatization as well as more freedom of expression and less corruption, a program that appealed to the urban elite. The state's heavy hand against Tehran's rioting protesters, who were trying to orchestrate another color revolution (it was deceptively dubbed "Green" for Islam even as the movement itself sought to move away from the Islamist government and towards the West), was hardly surprising, given Iran's recent past and the pressures Iran's government ·faces. On the contrary, there is a lively open domestic debate across the country about political issues.[110]

Despite its uniformly bad press in the West, Iran, with its principled position of upholding its Non-Proliferation Treaty (NPT) right to nuclear power in defiance of the US, and its support for the Palestinians in the face of intense western opposition, continues to impress the rest of the Muslim and anti-imperialist worlds to say nothing of the growing Palestinian support movement around the world. Iranian leaders from Ayatollah Khomeini to presidents Khameni, Rafsanjani, Khatami and on to Ahmedinejad have all pursued peace initiatives with the West, without bowing to western arrogance. 2001 was declared the UN "Year of Dialogue among Civilizations" as a result of a resolution of Khatami. It was followed immediately after 911 by Iranian overtures to help resolve the tragedy of Afghanistan, which were greeted by a deafening silence in Washington.

The revolution in Shia Iran, the rise of Shia power in Lebanon as a result of the 1975–1990 civil war, the formation of a Shia-friendly government in Afghanistan and a predominantly Shia government in Iraq have created a new constellation of forces in the Muslim world, the so-called Shia crescent. This has caused great worry in Washington, Tel Aviv and among Saudi/ Gulf accommodationists, supposedly over the possibility of increased terrorism, even though the impulse for terrorism in the Muslim world comes not from Shia, but from Wahhabi and neo-Wahhabi Sunnis, to say nothing of US-Israeli instigated false flag operations fingering/ targeting Muslims. The real reason is that they are afraid of what Davutoglu calls "the restoring of the natural flow of history" in the Middle East.[111]

Though Iran was not an immediate factor in the Arab Spring, the revolutions in the Arab world have vindicated Iran and contributed to an improvement in relations with Egypt. Add to this Turkey's rapprochement with Iran under its AKP Islamists, along with that of Iraq under the Shia post-occupation coalition, Afghanistan under the US-installed Karzai regime, and Pakistan's enduring good relations with Iran, and it is clear that Iran is now the most powerful regional power, despite its economic problems. Only the Saudis and Gulf Arabs are unhappy, pressuring their poor Arab cousins with monetary bribes and encouraging US-Israeli plans to invade their Shia nemesis, further discrediting them in the eyes of the Arabs.

Iran has a murky reputation among western progressives, as did the Soviet Union in its day, ironically, largely for the same reasons (human rights, censorship, ideological rule). Iran can be described as a socialism-averse socialist state, where the 'reformers' are hell-bent on jettisoning the remnants of socialism and obediently following the dictates of the IMF. If Iran goes the IMF route and makes peace with Washington, it is clear whose 'human rights' will flourish: the current Iranian economic elite's. Many are naively pro-western, just like many Soviets were (to their eternal chagrin now that they've joined the Brave New West). As in the Soviet Union, along with the naive and the few genuine and brave human rights dissidents, the budding capitalists crave the commercial freedom of the West and are eager to join the American empire as junior partners. They will be the first to send their profits offshore, scoop up state industries, and repress workers and students when the last remnants of morality are swept from the economy.

Afghanistan (31 million, 85% Sunni, 15% Shia), following the communist coup in 1978, became the only Muslim socialist state apart from south Yemen. This led to ten nightmarish years of foreign-sponsored civil war,[112] ending in a brief truce from 1989–1992 under President Najibullah,[113] followed by three more years of civil war as an "Islamic state", and six austere but relatively peaceful years under the Taliban as an emirate, where Osama bin Laden was given safe haven after he was forced to leave Sudan in 1996. Whatever Bin Laden's sins (the US never indicted him for involvement in 911), he was the Taliban's friend from the days of their joint 'jihad' against the Soviet Union. Whatever the real story is behind the CIA, Bin Laden and 911, there is no question that Islamic jihad in Afghanistan was a CIA initiative, initially launched in 1979 during the Carter administration (see Chapter 2 endnote 77 and text). The CIA-sponsored guerrilla training was even integrated with the teachings of Islam.[114] But once the US was done with 'jihad', and given the Taliban were not willing to acquiesce to US plans for the region, they had to go.

In the West, the Taliban are best known now, not for disarming a population awash in arms and eradicating opium production, but for their massacre of 8,000 Shia Hazara in 1998,[115] blowing up the Buddha statues in Bamiyan in March 2001,[116] and, of course, providing a home to Bin Laden. Recognized only by the Saudis, the UAE and Pakistan, the original Taliban out-did the Saudis in their attempt to emulate a seventh century Islamic lifestyle as they conceived it (thanks to their Saudi-financed education in Pakistani madrassas in the 1980s), including a ban on all music and modern media except for recitations from the Quran and lectures on Islam. A decade of occupation and civil war made Afghanistan an extreme version of what imperialism can lead to—a genuinely premodern society, but one stripped of its rich premodern culture, brutally occupied, fragmented, starving, with no prospect for extricating itself except by yet further armed struggle. Any notion of Islamic reform has been obliterated by the machinations of imperialism.

Oh yes, desperate for legitimacy, Karzai announced in 2004 that Afghanistan was now an "Islamic republic"—under the watchful eye of his US patrons.

The 'independence' of the **five 'stans'**—Kazakhstan, Uzbekistan, Turkmenistan, Kyrgyzstan and Tajikistan (57 million, 95% Sunni)—and **Azerbaijan** (9.2 million, 83% Shia, 13% Sunni) in 1991 proved even more disappointing than previous 'liberations' of Muslim lands. Standards of living dropped drastically from Soviet days, *faux* nationalisms and tight border controls have made the 'independent' republics prisons policed by corrupt security forces, where—apart from tiny, impoverished Kyrgyzstan[117]—torture is rampant, Islamists repressed, and elections rigged. Tajikistan's Islamists rose up and in the sparsely-populated remote 'nation' waged a hopeless civil war in the 1990s against the corrupt dictator Emomali Rahmon (r. 1994) demanding a return to Islam as the principle guiding society. They were suppressed with Russian help but the unrest remains.

The **Caucasus** Muslims (3.5 million, 90% Sunni) and **Crimea**n Tatars (350,000, 90% Sunni) were accused of collaboration with the Germans, and were deported at the end of WWII. The Caucasus nationalities are the source of continued Islamist unrest today, financed by a cynical array of forces, from Israel and the US to Saudi Arabia. (Chechen Tamerlan Tsarnaev, accused in the 2013 Boston Marathon bombing, was apparently working with the FBI.) The brutal wars in **Chechnya** (1994–1996, 1999–2009) stoked Islamophobia in Russia's heartland and killed tens of thousands. Sporadic killings and terrorism continue, both there, in Dagestan and in the Russian heartland. Similarly China's **Xinjiang** is the scene of a Muslim and national revival of the Uighurs (8 million, Sunni), occasionally erupting in violence, protesting Chinese immigrants who are diluting the Muslim character of the remote region. China also has a Han ethnic group of Muslims, Hui (10 million, Sunni), who live and prosper throughout China.

The Indian subcontinent, where the largest Muslim umma lives,[118] is still suffering from the repercussions of the 1947 partition. One of the chief problems left behind was Kashmir, which is predominantly Muslim, but whose prince was pressured by the British to remain in India (recall that the vast majority of Muslims in the Indian subcontinent wanted to remain in a united India).[119] Pakistan's state of war with India continues today over Kashmir, a senseless and massive drain on both the Indian and Pakistani budgets.[120]

Pakistan (178 million, 80% Sunni, 15% Shia, 5% Ahmadis, Hindus, Christians) is "struggling to free itself from the clutches of a cynical military dictatorship that promises Kemalism even while nurturing fundamentalism".[121] As elsewhere in the Muslim world, the rise in Islamic influence in politics unfolded from the late 1970s. Maududi supported the newly 'Islamist' General Zia ul-Haq's 1977 coup against Prime Minister Zulfikar Bhutto and his own cosmetic Islamization. In December 1984, sharia law was established in

Pakistan, even as Zia was feted by Reagan and showered with money and arms for the 'jihad' in Afghanistan. The threads of the concerted campaign against the Soviet Union were already being pulled together, coordinated by the Safari Club, a secret network of western intelligence agencies set up in 1976, and Bhutto was not a reliable enough quisling. Zia boasted he would Islamize Pakistani society *a la* Iran, even as he became America's trust ally in the region against India, Afghanistan, but above all, the Soviet Union. Given the growth of Islamism in the 1970s, the imperial strategists had to adjust to mollify the Arab world, and a patina of Islamism was tolerated, as long as it was directed at the Soviet Union, rather than Israel, now zealously colonizing the occupied territories.

The main effect of Islamization under Zia was to increase the number of traditional madrassas from 900 to 33,000. They were nominally Deobandi, but uncontrolled as to content and quality. Funded largely by Saudi Arabia, they became indoctrination centers for Wahhabi-style extremism.[122] Zia imposed superficial, authoritarian policies—a ban on political parties and alcohol (leading to bootlegging), introduction of sharia law and *hadd* penalties (there were a few floggings but no doctors would amputate limbs), and encouragement of interest-free banking. The main result was a sharp increase in sectarian tensions between Sunni and Shia and among Sunni groups, as the basis for the national implementation of sharia was the Sunni Hanafi school, alienating the remaining 20% of the population. "Politics was dominated by ethnic tension, rivalries and corruption scandals."[123] There was little to cheer about from a reform perspective. Islamization did not affect politics, the economy remained integrated in the western imperial order, and 'Islamic' Pakistan became ever more a tool of the US, a chaotic, unstable state plagued by tribal separatist movements and now hosting millions of Afghan refugees.

After Zia died in a mysterious plane crash in 1988, there was a backlash against his unconvincing US-sponsored 'Islamic' dictatorship, and Bhutto's daughter, Benazir, and her Pakistani People's Party were elected. Pakistan's politics remained mired in corruption (the Pakistani Muslim League under Nawaz Sharif was equally corrupt and differed little in terms of policies). There was another military coup by Kemalist General Pervez Musharraf, who brought the corrupt, chaotic democracy to an end in 1999, leading to yet another unholy alliance with the US, now *against* the very forces Zia had promoted, the Wahhabi-inspired Taliban, allowing the US to pursue its own invasion of Afghanistan. This meant an end to US sanctions on Pakistan[124] and a massive inflow of US military aid, providing a temporary boost to the economy, but with the inevitable result of an increase in terrorism and a further weakening of the state.

Terrorism has plagued Pakistan's 'soft state' since the Afghan war in 1979, and can only be described as 'reaping what you sow'. Pakistan saw its own geopolitical interests served by supporting the US in its war against the Soviet Union, even infiltrating Soviet Central Asian states, a plan the CIA only agreed to reluctantly in October 1984, and then supporting the Taliban. Pakistani leaders continued this support even after the Taliban were declared America's enemy and after the US installed its own government in Kabul "due to a perceived need to counter India's influence"[125] and to exert some kind of hegemony of its own over Afghanistan. When the US forces leave, Pakistan's politicians/ generals will still be controlling the shots, so the thinking goes. In the meantime, suicide bombings have created urban havoc, US drone attacks have killed thousands, and Pakistan's tribal regions are in constant revolt, reflected notably by the 2007 Red Mosque siege and the temporary takeover of Swat District in 2009 by the Pakistani Taliban.

Like Egypt (and to a lesser extent now, Turkey), Pakistan is still run in the background by the all-powerful military, and in the countryside, it is still feudal, making a mockery of electoral politics. The main militant group, Lashkar-e Tayiba (1990, army of the good), was encouraged by the Pakistani state to create havoc in Kashmir, borrowing the neo-Wahhabi promotion of terrorism against civilians there as a legitimate 'individual duty' even without state sanction or consensus of religious scholars. It was banned in 2002 but continued to thrive, and was held responsible for the 2008 Mumbai bombing. Now the state is powerless to suppress it (Musharraf tried, but survived six assassination attempts in the process), as it provides much needed social welfare support, *a la* MB, through its humanitarian wing, Jamaat-ud-Dawa (society for invitation).[126]

Britain and then the US wanted to have their cake and to eat it—to have a Muslim, anti-socialist ally, but like Saudi Arabia, a nonthreatening one. However, Pakistan is not a desert ruled by a tiny tribe with lots of oil, but rather a large, desperately poor hodge-podge of Muslim sects and ethnic groups which quickly descended into sectarian tensions after independence and remains mired in them, and where US-abetted extremists continue to embrace violent jihad against other Muslims in the absence of a genuine, charismatic Muslim political leader *a la* Khomeini who dares to throw off the US yoke. Pakistan started as a US pawn against the Soviet Union, which made it a hub of terrorism, and then was forced to become a key ally in the 'war *against* terrorism'. [127]

Things have only gone from bad to worse since then. Relations with the US deteriorated rapidly in 2011 with the continuation of drone attacks (more than 3,000 civilian deaths since 2004) and US covert activities, including the assassination of Osama bin Laden and the killing of 24 Pakistani soldiers while they slept in their barracks, in a US air strike in 2011. The government was forced by popular pressure to cut off the NATO supply route to Afghanistan and to try to reduce US military activity. At the same time, it increased its military cooperation with China and Iran. US policy is pushing its once subservient ally into the hands of its 'enemies'.

India's Muslims are 14% (85% Sunni, 15% Shia) of India's 1.2 billion people, the third largest community in the world (after Indonesia and virtually tied with Pakistan). Despite a state of war with Pakistan over Kashmir, relations between Hindus and Muslims were relatively peaceful after the partition until recently. Two Muslims have served as president of India, the first female Supreme Court judge was Muslim, Muslim women have been governors of several states, movie stars and leading scientists have been Muslims. But with increased terrorist violence, attributed to Pakistan and militant Muslim groups supported by it, Hindu nationalism has increased. Officially, discrimination is outlawed, but most Indian Muslims remain at the bottom of India's economic ladder, not much better off than the dalit (untouchables). The Aga Khan Ismailis have prospered in India, though they are *non grata* in Pakistan, considered along with the Bahai and Ahmedi sects to be apostates. India's support for the current Karzai government in Afghanistan and its considerable involvement in reconstruction is resented by Pakistan, seriously complicating US withdrawal strategy.

Bangladesh (150 million, 90% Sunni, 10% Shia) became 'independent' twice—most recently from Pakistan in 1972, becoming the world's fourth largest Muslim nation after Indonesia, Pakistan and India. It has stayed out of the western headlines since then, apart from hosting the world's second largest annual Islamic gathering (after the hajj) north of the Dhaka, where the Biswa Ijtema (World Muslim Congregation) is held every January.[128]

In the 1973 elections, the first after declaring independence from Pakistan, the mainstream center-left secular Awami League gained an absolute majority. After two years of famine, Mujibur Rahman initiated a one-party socialist rule but was assassinated by mid-level military officers. Bangladesh has been plagued by intermittent army coups since then, notably in 1977 when Lieutenant General Ziaur Rahman took over the presidency. Ziaur reinstated multi-party politics, introduced free market reforms, and founded the Bangladesh Nationalist Party (BNP). His rule ended when he was assassinated by elements of the military in 1981. Ziaur's widow, Khaleda Zia, led the Bangladesh Nationalist Party to victory in 1991. The Awami League, headed by Mujib's daughter Sheikh Hasina, won the next election in 1996. In 2007, a soft military coup was followed in 2008 by the reelection of the Awami League, but the military continues to keep watch over a 'soft state', as in Pakistan and Egypt.

Indonesia, the world's largest Muslim nation (203 million, 87% Sunni, 9% Christian, 3% Hindu), emerged from General Suharto's pro-US secular dictatorship in 1998, when the dictator of 33 years was forced to resign by widespread rioting. Abdurrahman Wahid (1940–2009) was elected by parliament as the first post-Suharto president in 1999 (with Sukarno's daughter, Megawati Sukarnoputri, his vice president) as head of the National Awakening Party (PKB). Wahid was head of the powerful Islamist Nahdlatul Ulama, which was founded by his grandfather, Hasyim Asyari.

Instead of a boring 'modern' coup, where the military brings in the tanks and disposes of the previous dictator, the Islamist was allowed to take power, but in the new unstable, bankrupt environment, without the necessary political skills or powers, Wahid's amateurish attempts to weaken the army's hold on the country and to expose corruption were easily resisted. As rioting and instability in Aceh and Maluku continued, he turned to his up-and-coming General Susilo Bambang Yudhoyono[129] in desperation. It was too late. An array of political forces in the parliament impeached him on dubious corruption charges, with the implicit backing of power-hungry secularist Megawati (whose father was ironically the victim of the army coup by Suharto). As vice president, she was able to rehabilitate her father (much like the other famous secularist Muslim father-daughter Zulfikar and Benazir Bhutto in Pakistan) and became president (r. 1999–2004) till the next scheduled elections, which she lost to the army candidate Yudhoyono not least because of her own poor political skills. The 'postmodern' coup was perfected in Indonesia, putting the (US-trained) army back in control, with a popular mandate willingly given by simple people who just want stability and a tolerable level of corruption at the top.

Wahid, though head of the nominally conservative Islamists, was never persecuted for his faith, and largely supported Suharto during the 33 years of dictatorship, during which he became a great fan of Israel, visiting it six times, and calling for establishing diplomatic relations. "They believe in God," was his rationale. The maverick leader also stated that "Nahdlatul Ulama is like Shiism minus Imama". The political scene in Indonesia today reveals a lively but fragmented Islam-inspired array of parties, which combined could probably form a government.[130]

There is some neo-Wahhabi militancy, "reflecting the close historical contact between that area and Arabia",[131] especially Laskar Jihad (jihad army) since 2000 in the Maluku islands. Aceh demanded and was granted more autonomy and implementation of sharia law in 2001. There are many movements representing a wide range of Islamic thought, including the Islam Liberal Network and Hizb ut-Tahrir Indonesia, which, like its affiliates elsewhere, strives to implement a caliphate in the Muslim world. The post-Suharto order is well integrated with the US War on Terror, which remains a constant inspiration for further terrorist acts and subsequent persecution of Islamists.

In **Malaysia** (30 million, 61% Sunni, 20% Buddhism, 9% Christianity, 6% Hinduism), Mahathir bin Mohamad (b. 1925) became prime minister (r.

1981–2003), and pursued various Islamic initiatives, including founding the International Islamic University Malaysia and an Islamic bank (1983).

Since the late 1990s, Malaysian politics has been embroiled by the scandal involving Anwar Ibrahim (b. 1947). Anwar was founder of the Muslim Youth Movement of Malaysia (1971), which criticizes westernization and calls for an Islamic state. However, in 1982, Anwar the Islamic radical shocked his supporters by joining the governing UMNO, and moving quickly up the political ladder to become Mahathir's chosen successor as prime minister. Anwar boasted in public of his 'son-father' relationship with Mahathir. In 1997, Mahathir appointed Anwar acting prime minister while he took a two-month holiday. The relationship with Mahathir deteriorated shortly afterwards, when during the 1997 Asian financial crisis, as finance minister, Anwar supported the IMF recovery plan, which would have introduced an austerity package to cut government spending by 18% and defer major projects. Although many Malaysian companies faced bankruptcy, Anwar declared: "There is no question of any bailout. The banks will be allowed to protect themselves and the government will not interfere." Anwar advocated a free-market approach to the crisis, including foreign investment and trade liberalization. He also attacked what he described as the widespread culture of nepotism and cronyism.

Mahathir blamed currency speculators like George Soros, and instituted currency controls and tighter regulation of foreign investment, saving Malaysia from the financial meltdown that engulfed the other so-called tiger cub economies (Thailand, Philippines and Indonesia). Not surprisingly, this was not appreciated in the West, and it was Anwar that *Newsweek* named "Asian of the Year" in 1998. Mahathir saw a conspiracy and dismissed Anwar, and in 1999, Anwar was sentenced to six years in prison for corruption, and in 2000, to another nine years for sodomy. After release from prison in 2008, he taught at Johns Hopkins University's School of Advanced International Studies in Washington DC, at Georgetown University, and is honorary president of the London-based Institute of Social and Ethical AccountAbility and chair of the Washington-based Foundation For the Future. Despite these rewards for his suffering in the cause of neoliberalism, scandal clings to him.[132] A 'man with a mission', he won re-election in a by-election in 2008 and returned to parliament as leader of the Malaysian opposition. Meanwhile, Mahathir's Malaysia is considered a post-colonial success story. The Islamic Party of Malaysia (PAS), part of the opposition alliance, which calls for sharia and an Islamic state, has formed several state governments in the north since 1999.

Indonesia and Malaysia (the division is artificial) became Muslim under the influence of traders and Sufis, and with their large minorities of Chinese, Hindus and others, their version of Islam includes Sufism and in Malaysia, Hindu practices and social structures. There is a thriving art scene and openness to different cultures. There is still a sense of the pre-imperial

Islamic civilization, which in southeast Asia was a Golden Age of modest prosperity and peace, and one which is not so distant historically. Thus, Islam thrives and the idea of a renewed world umma is a popular one here. Mahathir in retirement is a widely respected world statesman and advocates that Muslim countries work more closely together, that rich Gulf states invest their wealth in the poorer Muslim countries to reduce the income gap, and that the Muslim world establish a gold dinar. Not to be outdone, Anwar compares Malaysia to Moorish Spain with its ideology of *convivencia* (coexistence) where all three groups—Muslims, Christians and Jews—lived peacefully together. Neither Indonesia nor Malaysia recognizes Israel, despite Wahid's urgings.

Muslims constitute only 10% of the **Philippines** (95 million), and have suffered much like their African counterparts, from continual attempts at their conversion to Christianity and assimilation to a secular, now US-dominated order. The Moro National Liberation Front (MNLF) held large protests in 1968 and inconclusive talks in 1976 in Tripoli, Libya. In 1984 the movement split, with the Moro Islamic Liberation Front (MILF) being formed, divided along ethnic lines, which morphed into the violent Abu Sayyaf Group, an al-Qaeda spin-off, in 1991. A truce was signed between MILF and the government in 2009 and a Framework Agreement signed in 2012 which continues the current Autonomous Region in Muslim Mindanao (opposed by Christian communities). Now, after 40 years of struggle that has claimed 120,000 lives and displaced more than 2 million people, MILF has broken with Abu Sayyaf and the Jemaah Islamiyah (blamed for the Bali nightclub and Jakarta bombings), and in February 2013, inspired by the agreement in Northern Ireland, signed an agreement with President Benigno Aquino. Bangsamoro (land of the Moors) will become autonomous in 2016, and the Philippines applied to join the Organization of Islamic Cooperation as an observer. MILF's 12,000 fighters will be integrated into a civilian police force, taking over responsibility for security from the army. Oxfam's Mindanao program has developed partnerships with local organizations to improve access to basic education and boost awareness of the peace process and the rights of the non-Muslim Lumad indigenous people, though Christian settlers are unhappy, having been lured there in the past much like Christian settlers in North America, on the understanding that the natives would be pushed aside.

Indonesia, Malaysia and the Philippines were all founding members of the US-sponsored Association of Southeast Asian Nations (ASEAN) in 1967.[133]

Today, 13–17 million Muslims live in western **Europe**: 6 million in France, 4 million in Germany, 3.3 million in Britain. Europe's Muslim population has grown throughout the twentieth century, firstly due to its vestigial colonial connections. Britain's Muslims are primarily from the Indian subcontinent, (concentrated in northern industrial cities and London's east end). The attempt to secularize Algeria in the 19th–20th centuries led to a large emigration of Algerians to France from the 1930s on as low-paid laborers. France's control of Morocco until 1956 and its colonization of West Africa, which formally ended in 1960, resulted in significant Muslim immigrant communities, mostly in the south and in urban ghettos. As Europe's population aged after WWII, millions of north Africans and Turks came—legally and illegally—to fill low-paid jobs throughout Europe. Despite immigration restrictions, higher birth rates, reuniting of families and Europe's need for cheap labor means that its Muslim population will continue to increase. Over the next 20 years, Europe's Muslim population is projected to grow to nearly 30 million—8% of all Europeans.[134] As is the case with refugees from US-British wars in Iraq, Afghanistan, etc. in North America and the UK, immigrants from former French colonies, in particular Algeria and now Mali, are viewed with suspicion as France reasserts its colonial prerogative in pursuit of 'humanitarian intervention', so-called R2P (right to protect).

This has led to increasing civil conflict due not only to paranoia over possible blowback, but to abiding European racism. In contrast to more immigrant-friendly North America, "Britain has historically received newcomers with a combination of curiosity, hostility, and indifference", fostering a "self-absorption in immigrant communities".[135] This goes for all of Europe and accounts for the greater militancy of European Muslims.

After WWII, US-style 'separation of church and state' was transplanted to Europe and, buttressed by French *laïcité,* led to a sharp decline in religiosity and the rise of a super-secularism, a culture that produced legalized prostitution, and where the blasphemous Muhammad cartoons published in Denmark in 2005 were acceptable.[136] The state now enforces secular-inspired norms such as gay marriage, divorce, etc., and imposes other laws which in many cases directly target the Muslim community (banning of head scarves, minarets). "In Britain, race-based equality laws protected Sikhs and Jews as minorities, but not Hindus and Muslims."[137] This radical secularism is aided by Europe's post-WWII state socialism, providing a secular safety net absent in the US, where traditional church charity still plays an important role as welfare provider. Issues such as AIDS are more easily stripped of their moral (religious) aspect in Europe and dealt with in purely functional terms ('safe sex') where the (secular) state is responsible for health care.

Euro-Islamophobes have an even more fertile ground than the US, as Europe's main geopolitical and spiritual rival until the rise of imperialism was the Islamic world. They portray Europe today as in danger of a new Muslim conquest, a recap of 711AD, with politicians and mass media egging on the likes of Norway's mass murderer, Anders Breivik, who called for the ethnic cleansing of all Muslims from Europe, much like Christian conquerors expelled Muslims and Jews following the reconquest of Spain in the fifteenth century.

Soeren Kern points out that "the UAE, together with Libya [sic] and Morocco" paid for the construction of the Great Mosque of Granada. Says Abdel Haqq Salaberria, a spokesman for the mosque: "It will act as a focal point for the Islamic revival in Europe. It is a symbol of a return to Islam among the Spanish people and among indigenous Europeans."[138] Worse yet for Islamophobes, Muslims in Cordoba are demanding that the Spanish government allow them to worship in the main cathedral, which was originally the Great Mosque of Andalus and is now a World Heritage Site.

The rise of Islamophobia prompted the founding of the Alliance of Civilizations, sponsored by Spanish Prime Minister José Luis Rodríguez Zapatero and Turkish Prime Minister Recep Tayyip Erdogan in 2005, as a way to "bridge the divide" between the West and Islam, through projects in youth, education, media, and migration. Forums have been held in Madrid (2008), Istanbul (2009) and Rio de Janiero (2010). Spain is now rediscovering its Islamic Golden Age before the Christian reconquest of Spain. While Andalus lasted eight centuries, the post-Islamic period of Spain has lasted only six centuries, and has been characterized by religious intolerance in comparison to the Islamic Golden Age that preceded it.

Given the current tyranny of money that characterizes western civilization, it is not surprising that the Zapatero/ Erdogan attempt at bringing peace and understanding among the founding faiths of Spain and the Middle East is greeted with sneers and resentment by Israel and its supporters in the West. Israel-firsters such as Kern twist the positive moves to bring East and West together as a cover for "Muslim countries in the Persian Gulf and North Africa funneling large sums of money to radical Islamic groups in towns and cities across Spain".

But there is a more enduring dialectic at work in Europe. The wave of revulsion against Israeli apartheid continues to grow throughout Europe, but especially in Spain. Ilan Pappe describes how all Israeli ambassadors to Europe are more than glad to end their terms, complaining about their inability to speak at universities. The Israeli ambassador to Spain, Raphael Schutz, finished his term in Madrid in 2011, and in "Why the Spanish hate us" in *Haaretz*'s Hebrew edition (not in its English edition)[139] he charged that he was the victim of local and ancient anti-Semitism, comparing the situation to the Inquisition of five centuries ago. He ignores the fact that Muslims were also victims of the Inquisition, that Jews fought and suffered side by side with their Muslim allies as the Christian armies invaded, and that subsequently, many Jews found refuge in Muslim-ruled lands.

At the same time, Islamophobes such as Marine Le Pen, leader of France's National Front, are not without cause when they criticize their governments for allying with the premodern Saudis and Gulf monarchs. Campaigning for the 2012 presidential elections, Le Pen said Qatar was "playing a double game" by presenting itself as an "enlightened" country to western democracies while at the same time supporting Islamist groups in the Middle East and north Africa. Qatar is also building a "mega-mosque" on Sicily, "a reference point for the 1.5 million Muslims in Italy."[140] At a conference "Muslims and European Values" in Barcelona in 2011, Moroccan imam Noureddine Ziani argued that the construction of big mosques would be "a useful formula" to fight Islamic fundamentalism in Spain. "It is easier to disseminate fundamentalist ideas in small mosques set up in garages, than in large mosques that are open to everyone." Islam must be incorporated into the national fabric; if Islam remains outside, a fringe belief, "unregulated 'underground Islam'" can inculcate terrorism.[141]

Ziani asserted that Islamic values are compatible with European values and that so-called western Judeo-Christian civilization is really an "Islamo-Christian" one. The cultural construct "Judeo-Christian heritage" entered the English language only in the 1940s as a reaction to Nazism, and is used by the imperial elite in its 'clash of civilizations' targeting Islam. It's a concept which has been useful to a largely Christian empire where Jewish elites play a powerful role, but is rejected by serious scholars, both Christian and Jewish. Talmudic scholar Jacob Neusner calls it a "secular myth favored by people who are not really believers themselves". Not only Ziani but American scholars such as Richard Bulliet argue for the use of "Islamo-Christian" to characterize western civilization.

Spain suffered several terrorist bombings in the wake of 911, notably the 2004 bombings in Madrid, but no evidence was ever presented to suggest al-Qaeda was behind it.[142] The reality of Spain today is not the existence of any external threat from Islam, but on the contrary, domestic unrest due to the economic crisis and political paralysis. This gloomy situation prompted concerned young people to boycott Spain's elections in May 2011 and emulate their largely Muslim Arab Spring heroes by constructing tent cities in protest at the lack of meaningful democracy. Just as Egyptian revolutionaries borrowed nonviolent techniques from their western counterparts in an effort to throw off their taskmasters, so Spaniards are emulating them in turn—a true 'alliance of civilizations'.

Britain's riots in the summer of 2011 prove that Muslims are a boon to European society, being inherently peaceful and law-abiding. Muslims from the East London Mosque and the Islamic Forum Europe played an important role in helping to fight the looting and preserve public safety. Three Muslims died in Birmingham defending shops from looters, though in the media they were merely called Asians. "When accused of terrorism we are Muslims, when killed by looters, we become Asian," a Muslim student told Al-Jazeera bitterly.

Islamophobia in Europe came to a climax in the summer of 2011, incited by Islamophobes such as Oslo-based American Bruce Bawer, author of *While Europe Slept: How Radical Islam Is Destroying the West from Within* (2010), who argues that Europeans are yielding up their freedoms to Muslim invaders, and that Muslims are reproducing "beyond the point of no return", which will soon mean "subservience or civil war" in Europe. Fellow Osloite Anders Breivik made 22 references to Bawer's writing in his online justification of the murder of more than 70 Norwegians in July 2011.[143]

The rise of right-wing, anti-immigrant parties has led several European countries to impose poorly thought-out policies, insofar as

> restrictions on Islamic dress, mosque-building and reunification of families through immigration law are counterproductive. Paradoxically, people for whom religion is otherwise not all that important become more attached to their faith's clothing, symbols and traditions when they feel they are being singled out and denied basic rights.[144]

The accommodation of Islamic religious practices, from clothing to language to education, does not mean capitulation to fundamentalism. On the contrary, only by strengthening the democratic rights of Muslim citizens to form associations, join political parties and engage in other aspects of civic life can Europe integrate immigrants and give full meaning to the abstract promise of religious liberty. As Davutoglu argues, "A city with different cultural artifacts in its silhouette produces more and more pluralistic citizens."

The French Council for the Muslim Faith, the German Islam Conference, the Committee for Italian Islam and the Mosques, and Imams National Advisory Board in Britain are all state-sanctioned Islamic organizations set up in the past decade. Whoever is responsible for 911, the resulting clash of civilizations has also produced the will for greater understanding and a resolve to greet re-emerging Islamic civilization positively.

The great tragedy for Muslims in Europe in the twentieth century occurred during the civil war in Yugoslavia, precipitated by western powers intent on dismembering the most viable socialist country. Serbia tried to prevent the secession of its immediate neighbor Bosnia-Herzegovina, a complex mix of Bosniak Muslims (45%) and Serbian/ Croatian Christians (55%), who had previously lived peacefully in the federation, intermarrying and working side by side. The civil war continued from 1992–1996, resulting in over 100,000 deaths, mostly Muslims, abetted by both the West and thousands of al-Qaeda fighters, fresh from Afghanistan.[145] As a result of western intervention, Bosnia-Herzegovina became an independent, sectarian federated state, and Kosovo was separated from Serbia and emerged as Europe's only nominally Muslim state, dysfunctional, a center of illegal drugs, arms and human smuggling, the site of the largest US European base (Camp Bondsteel).

The lack of militancy of Soviet and Bosniak Muslims prior to the 'independence' of their countries can be explained by the fact that while professedly atheistic or at least radically secular, the socialist countries largely observed the Quranic economic values of social justice through extensive social welfare and tight control over banking and speculation. The weakness of communism as conceived by Marx and the Jewish-Christian-atheist revolutionaries of the nineteenth century, was its belittling of the spiritual realm. It was only with the collapse of the socialist bloc that Islamists gained any following, as the lack of any kind of social justice in the post-socialist reality now pushed Muslims to look for it in their own traditions..

The Muslim community in **North America** has grown rapidly during the last half of the twentieth century, largely through regular immigration channels (especially via university studies), though Canada's colonial tradition means most immigrants there are from the Indian subcontinent, as is the case in Britain. The lifting of immigration restrictions in the late 1960s has allowed a steady immigration of Muslims from around the world to both the US and Canada.

The US is built on a culture of mass immigration and rapid assimilation, and despite the Islamophobia of especially the post-911 era, Muslims have adapted well to life in America and have prospered. There are more Muslims than Jews in the US now—approximately 5 million. They are the most diverse of all American believers, one-third Afro-American, many of whose ancestors were African Muslims, the rest—immigrants fleeing the legacy of imperialism in their homelands, mostly from southeast Asia, Africa, Iran, Syria, Lebanon and Jordan, who generally have founded mosques along ethnic lines. Traditionally they have voted Republican, but have shifted to Democrat and Green parties in recent years.

In the US, the absence of an anti-clerical tradition and the cultural presence of Protestantism as a 'civil religion' have combined to make Christianity—the religion of 86% of the population—a more enduring element in public life, despite its disestablishment.[146] However, at the same time as Christian fundamentalists demand a more moral politics (defined in their terms), they campaign against encroachment of the state on what they see as their domain—the cultural life of America, where, as in Europe, the state increasingly enforces its secular norms (sexuality, education), albeit legislating against discrimination. This provides a degree of protection of Muslims against Zionist and fundamentalist Christian bigotry.

The US is probably home to the most scholar-reformers of Islam, with dozens of centers of Islamic studies, many of which date from the early post-WWII period,[147] when the US tried to discretely promote conservative Islam as an antidote to the more dangerous (so it seemed at the time) Arab nationalist and socialist movements. These centers are staffed by non-Muslims more than

Muslims (the latter mostly secular émigrés), and are focused on supporting or advising the US government on policy towards the Middle East. As such they are at best liberal-assimilationist in advocacy.[148] Independent Muslim scholars and writers are few and face victimization, though their numbers are increasing despite attempts by the Israel Lobby in the US to police campuses and restrict academic freedoms.[149]

Until the 1960s, Hollywood created a romanticized fantasy of Arab life in the American imagination, at the same time disdaining the Arabs' supposedly primitive and exotic ways. Orientalism, really a British project, entailed serious academic study of languages, anthropology, etc., albeit at the service of empire; in America it was different, less academic, and metamorphosed into Islamophobia, especially after 911. It never dawned on Americans interested in the Middle East that the Islamists were qualitatively different from the comprador Christian clerical establishment they were used to in the West. The remarkable growth in the Palestinian solidarity movement at US universities and the post-911 anti-war movement have sparked greater interest in Islam and contributed to a lively process of experimenting with new forms of worship and political involvement.[150] Popular student pressure has meant that these centers and universities are becoming more open to an appreciation of Islam, as opposed to merely serving as a weapon in imperialism's arsenal in the war against it.

The Holy Land Foundation (HLF) was the largest Islamic charity in the US. In 2007, it was shut down, charged with funding the Palestinian Hamas and other "Islamic terrorist organizations". The 2008 trial of the charity leaders was dubbed the largest terrorism financing prosecution in American history, and its founders, including an official of the Council on American-Islamic Relations (1994, CAIR), America's largest Muslim lobby and civil liberties organization, were given life sentences for providing $12 million to Hamas, funds which were intended to support refugees in Jordan, Lebanon, and the Palestinian territories. The HLF also provided support to victims after disasters and wars in Bosnia, Kosovo, Turkey, and the United States (after Iowa floods, Texas tornadoes, and the Oklahoma City bombing). CAIR, headquartered on Capitol Hill, grew out of the Palestinian support movement, and has regional offices in 50 cities. CAIR's mission statement is "to enhance understanding of Islam, encourage dialogue, protect civil liberties, empower American Muslims, and build coalitions that promote justice and mutual understanding". It fights discrimination, profiling and harassment. Though an outspoken critic of terrorism, its prominence and support for Palestinians has made it the target of Zionists, and in 2009, the FBI broke off formal outreach contacts with CAIR, following the HLF trial.

Sharia has slipped into western legal systems. The US federal arbitration law, passed by Congress in 1925, allows religious tribunals, and their judgments are given force of law by state and federal courts. Recent attempts to outlaw sharia (notably a referendum in Oklahoma) failed on First Amendment appeals. After all, US Jews have had their *beth din* religious courts for more than a century, and there are now Christian conciliators for those Christians who prefer canon law to the secular law of the land. US courts "have been positively encouraging [its] use since the 1980s" for inheritance, business, and matrimonial disputes, "sorted out by Islamic scholars according to the sharia. The precepts of Islamic law, like those of other religious codes, therefore have judicial force in the US already."[151] Christian fundamentalists would find that Muslims are their best allies on cultural issues such as gay marriage, prostitution and cultural restrictions to limit denigration of religion in popular culture.

The Muslim community in the US is slowly gaining confidence in the face of concerted Islamophobia. The American Israel Public Affairs Committee (AIPAC) prompted Muslims in the Democratic Party Asian-American Caucus to organize the American Muslim Political Action Committee (AMPAC) in 2012, and plan a "Million Muslim March" on the White House in September 2013, demanding the establishment of a real 911 Commission and protection against rampant Islamophobia,[152] citing the following American victims:

- Imam Luqman Ameen Abdullah of Detroit, Michigan, was murdered by the FBI in 2009
- Neurophysicist Dr. Aafia Siddiqui was kidnapped and tortured by US authorities, and sentenced to life imprisonment in 2010
- Anwar al-Awlaki, his son and grandson were killed by US drone strikes in Yemen in 2012
- Federal agents and Anti-Defamation League[153] types infiltrate and provoke Muslim groups in FBI-concocted terror plots
- As of 2006, the US had already kidnapped and tortured more than 80,000 Muslims worldwide since 2001, including many Americans.[154]

***

APPENDIX
Al-Azhar University in the 1980s–2010s

Al-Azhar University was founded in 970 as a madrassa (center of Islamic learning). It played a very different role in relation to the Islamic establishment in Egypt in the build-up to the 2011 revolution than did the Iranian religious establishment in Iran's revolution. Azhar's contribution to the resistance to the secular dictatorship and the 25 January revolution was mixed.

The leading Sunni authority is Azhar's Grand Imam. Gad al-Haq Ali Gad al-Haq (r. 1982–1996) was appointed Grand Imam by Mubarak to be a pliable supporter of his regime, but 'betrayed' him, instead, becoming the most powerful thorn in Mubarak's westernizing agenda. He called for large families at the UN Population Conference 1994, refused to outlaw polygamy or female circumcision, or to agree to quotas for women in parliament, and barred visits to holy sites in East Jerusalem under Israeli occupation. Mubarak was more careful next time, and appointed the pliant Mohammed Sayyed Tantawi (r. 1996–2010), who overturned the Jerusalem visit ban, agreed to quotas, met with Israeli chief rabbi Yisrael Meir Lau 1997 at Azhar, and even attended a Lions Club meeting. The current Grand Imam is Mohamed Ahmed el-Tayeb, whose position on the MB and the political situation is not clear.

Mubarak appointed as Grand Mufti (the second most important Sunni figure) Ali Gomaa in 2003, who supported Mubarak against the MB, and was denounced by the MB as "civil servant ulama".[155] On Gomaa's obligatory retirement at age 60, Shawki Ibrahim Abdel-Karim Allam was elected Grand Mufti in February 2013, the first elected Mufti since the 1952 revolution, and not the MB's preferred candidate, belying the incessant worries that the MB was now calling all the shots.[156]

Sadat and Mubarak's strategy of using Azhar to promote their westernizing agenda was just a cynical replay of Nasser's nationalizing of religion in the name of promoting socialism, which from the Islamist point of view created a "generation of rejectionists", strengthening the MB and street sheikhs by bringing these outsiders and the non-elite ulama together to find common cause against the government and its sycophants within the religious establishment, and contributing to undermining government legitimacy in the 1990s.[157]

ENDNOTES

1   "Surely never will Allah change the condition of a people until they change it themselves (with their own souls)." (13:11)

2   Vernon Egger, *A History of the Muslim World since 1260: The Making of a Global Community*, New Jersey: Pearson, 2008, 459, 462.

3   Catholic US Defense Secretary Leon Panetta had an audience with Pope Benedict XVI, who told him, "Thank you for helping to protect the world." Panetta: "Pray for me." *New York Times*, 17 January 2013.

4   Terrorist here refers to willful targeting of civilians, Muslim and non-Muslim, who are not directly complicit in *hiraba*, murder and *fitna* (see Chapter 1).

5   Is an accommodation between secularist and Islamists possible given the hostility of the West to any form of genuine Islamic government? Iran still suffers from the secularist MEK, which was recently absolved of its official US terrorist status despite its continued subversive activities, and in Egypt the secularists are openly collaborating with old regime supporters to undermine the popularly elected Islamic government. This recapitulates the standard practice of western subversion of any genuine anti-imperialist alternative using proxies.

6   Saudi Arabia is an absolute monarchy which claims to be governed by Islam.

7   This recapitulates the Trotskyist argument about the impossibility of 'revolution in

one country'.

8   Turkish Alevis are not directly associated with Syrian Alawis, though both venerate Ali. They are specific to Turkey and are seen as more secular and syncretic, combining Sufism and a Turkified version of Islam where men and women can pray together.

9   Brazil, Russia, India, China, South Africa, accounting for 40% of the world's population and 25% of global GDP.

10   Erbakan was banned from politics by a constitutional amendment suspending members of banned parties, which narrowly passed in a 1987 referendum.

11   Svante Cornell, "What Drives Turkish Foreign Policy?" *Middle East Quarterly*, Vol. XIX: No. 1, Winter 2012.

12   Aydemir Erman, "How Turkey can help NATO in Afghanistan", *Christian Science Monitor,* 10 February 2010.

13   bid.

14   See Cornell, "What drives Turkish foreign policy?"

15   There are no official statistics on Kurds, who are considered to be Turks. Alevis are members of a religious sect closer to Shiism that includes some Kurds.

16   Conn Hallinan, "Turkey haunted by hubris", *Foreign Policy in Focus*, 3 November 2012.

17   Eric Walberg, "Turkey vs the US: A kinder Middle East hegemon", *Al-Ahram Weekly*, 21 July 2011.

18   Both now prominent post-Mubarak political figures.

19   Sadat was a member of the MB in the 1940s. A popular anecdote of the time was: "Instead of Nasser's 'Socialize Islam!', we have Sadat's 'Islamize socialism!', i.e., privatize the economy.

20   In 1989 the League re-admitted Egypt and returned its headquarters to Cairo.

21   Geneive Abdo, *No God But God: Egypt and the Triumph of Islam*, Oxford: Oxford University Press, 2000, 165.

22   A popular joke is: If you weren't imprisoned under Nasser, you never will be; if you didn't become rich under Sadat, you never will; if you haven't begged under Mubarak, you'll never be a beggar.

23   Gunnar Myrdal coined the term to refer to a state that "passes laws but does not enforce them. Elites can afford to ignore the law and pay bribes, everything is for sale" (including building permits, licenses to import illicit goods, tax rebates), and corruption is generalized, further weakening the state. See Galal Amin, *Egypt in the Era of Hosni Mubarak 1981-2011*, New York: AUC Press, 2011.

24   Abdo, *No God But God,* 105.

25   This same dynamic was witnessed in Iran under the Shah and in Pakistan. Islamists in southeast Asia—indeed, in the US and everywhere where Muslims have organized— have long been vital in providing this kind of relief.

26   A popular Egyptian film "Storm" (2000) directed by Khaled Youssef centers on the tragedy of two brothers, one conscripted by Iraq to fight the invaders, the other confronting him as a reluctant conscript in the invading Egyptian army.

27   Carrie Wickham, *Mobilizing Islam: Religion, Activism and Political Change in Egypt*, USA: Columbia University Press, 2003, 212.

28   Asef Bayat, *Making Islam Democratic: Social Movements and the Post-Islamist Turn,* Stanford University Press, 2007 12.

29   In "World Values Survey", ibid., 147.

30   The old-guard MB leadership refused to sign.

31   The Wasat founders resigned from the MB and the MB leadership went as far as to call on the government to reject Wasat's appeal. Wasat was legalized after the revolution, ahead of the legalization of the MB and the registration of the MB's Freedom and Development Party.

32   In his 2005 Inaugural Address, President Bush traced out the logic of a new post-911 American foreign policy: "It is the policy of the United States to seek and support the growth of democratic movements and institutions in every nation and culture, with the ultimate goal of ending tyranny in our world."

33   "Egypt's Brotherhood rejects violence", *Gulf Times*, Qatar, 30 March 2005.

34   James Traub, "Islamic Democrats?", *New York Times,* 29 April 2007.

35   Ibid.

36   Joshua Stacher and Samer Shehata, "The Brotherhood Goes to Parliament", *Middle East Report*, 2007.

37   Alison Pargeter, *Muslim Brotherhood, 2010: The burden of tradition*, London: Saqi, 2010, 55.

38   But President Morsi said, "I will not prevent a woman from being nominated as a candidate for the presidential campaign. This is not in the Constitution. This is not in the law. But if you want to ask me if I will vote for her or not, that is something else, that is different." *New York Times*, 22 September 2012.

39   Malise Ruthven, *Fundamentalism: The Search for Meaning*, UK: Oxford University Press, 2003, 147.

40   The broad respect that Egyptians hold for the MB was brought home to me at the 2007 Anti-imperialist Conference in Cairo, grudgingly allowed by the government, where dozens of MB youth pleaded with journalists to publicize the illegal arrests and persecution of their parents and friends. Official leftists present (Tagammu members, Nasserists and others) appeared to be doing little of any value in fighting imperialism, including its local manifestations in Egypt.

41   Fearing the MB as a model for renewing Islamic civilization, Saudi Arabia's intelligence head Prince Bandar and Abu Dhabi Prince Mohammad Ben Zayed reportedly financed the Mubarak candidate Shafiq in Egypt's presidential election of 2012, and continue to fund the secular opposition in order to destabilize Egypt. See Esam al-Amin, "Showdown in Egypt", *Counterpunch*, 30 November 2012.

42   The roots of the organization go back to 1977, when the MB dominated the Islamic Society at Alexandria University. In reaction, students with Salafi convictions, mainly in the faculty of medicine, formed the Salafi School, arguing against the Muslim Brotherhood's domination of Islamist activism. By mid-1985, the Salafi School had contacts throughout Egypt, though the movement's leaders were prevented from leaving Alexandria without travel permits. It had its own educational institution, the al-Furqan Institute, a magazine, *Voice of the Call*, and a social service network.

43   "They would have bombed us from the air if they saw our beards in Tahrir!" said one of the Salafi leaders afterwards.

44   Salafi critics of the MB call them the *ikhwan muflisin* (failed brothers).

45   Omar Ashour, "Egypt's Salafi challenge", *Project Syndicate*, 3 January 2012.

46   Mohammad Khawly, "Egypt: Muslim Brotherhood and al-Azhar follow Salafi lead", *al-akhbar.com*, 23 March 2012.

47   See above and Chapter 4 "Jihad vs Terrorism".

48   Jabhat al-Nusra (support front) is aligned with Zawahiri in Syria. Islamic Jihad members Jamal al-Kashef and Sheik Adel Shehato were arrested in October 2013, charged with planning attacks in Egypt.

49   Thomas Joscelyn, "Report: Al-Qaeda emir's hand in Egypt and Syria", *longwarjournal. org*, based on "Has Syria become Al-Qaeda's new base for terror strikes on Europe?", *Die Welt*, December 2012.

50   An ethnically defined Shia sect.

51   Patrick Seale, *Asad of Syria: The Struggle for the Middle East*, USA: University of California Press, 1988, 335.

52   One possible partition scenario would be the formation of separate and 'independent' Sunni, Alawi-Shia, Kurdish and Druze states. Mohammad Rasho, "Syria and the Partition Scenario", *kurdishtribune.com*, 6 February 2013.

53   In the 2003 elections, the IAF got 25% of the vote.

54   The term Persian Gulf has been disputed since the 1960s with the rise of Arab nationalism. The UAE actually forbids the use of the term. Despite US usage of Persian Gulf since 1917, and UN usage since 1945, the US military since 2009 has started to use Arabian Gulf.

55   Ansar Bayt al-Masqdis, Tawhid and Jihad, Ansar al-Sunnah, Mujahideen Shura Council.

56   Ibadism is a branch of Kharijism, with beliefs in between Sunni and Shia, like the Shia, denying the legitimacy of the Caliphs after Ali, and believing the Quran was created by God at a certain point in time. See Chapter 1.

57   There is only one source for the estimate of deaths (by a kitchen worker at the prison). The government admitted that many were killed, including 200 guards, though an investigation after Gaddafi's fall has not yielded anything definitive. A claim by the National Transitional Council in September 2011 that a mass grave of 1,200 bodies had been discovered was disproved by CNN.

58   The MB were called "wayward dogs", and were executed, imprisoned or fled into exile under Gaddafi. "Gaddafi left the Salafis alone because they were not interested in politics. The Muslim Brotherhood were educated and willing to engage in politics so he tried to damage our image." Mary Fitzgerald, "Introducing the Libyan Muslim Brotherhood", *foreignpolicy.com*, 2 November 2012.

59   Tony Cartalucci, "The geopolitical reordering of Africa: US covert support to Al Qaeda in Northern Mali, France 'comes to the rescue'", *Global Research*, 15 January 2013.

60   In 1996 seven French monks were kidnapped in the Medea region south of Algiers. The French secret services attempted to contact the Islamist kidnappers directly and discovered that the kidnapper Jamal Zitouni was an agent of the Algerian government. The monks were then murdered by the Algerian junta as punishment for the French going over their heads.

61   Fouzi Slisli, "The Algerian Civil War: Washington's Model for 'The New Middle-East'", Association of Concerned Africa Scholars, August 2007.

62   Bouteflika was foreign minister under Ben Bella, convicted in 1983 of embezzling state funds, and amnestied by Bendjedid.

63   The Algerian Muslim Brotherhood formed the Movement of Society for Peace, and did not join the FIS. After the 1992 coup canceling the elections, and throughout the civil war of the 1990s, the MB remained a legal political organization and enjoyed parliamentary and government representation. In 1995, MB Sheikh Nahnah ran for president of Algeria finishing second with 25% of the popular vote. During the 2000s, the party was a member of a three-party coalition backing President Abdelaziz Bouteflika (r. 1999).

64   The Arabic name for Morocco, Maghreb, means west.

65   Said Temsamani, "Historical facts about the 'Moroccaness' of the Sahara", *eurasiareview.com*, 6 November 2012.

66   In February 2013, 24 Sahrawi human rights activists from the Moroccan Occupied Territory were given sentences from two to 30 years for constructing a 'peace camp' Gdeim Izik in 2010, attracting condemnation internationally.

67   Following a referendum in July 2011 with 70% turnout and 98% approval, the new constitution was ratified and parliamentary elections then held. In the new constitution, the king gave up his power to appoint the prime minister, agreeing to appoint the leader of the largest party as PM and allow him to appoint senior civil servants, cabinet members, and to dissolve parliament—in consultation with the king's ministerial council.

68   Morocco's more radical (illegal) MB-affiliated Justice and Charity Group was established in 1987 and is headed by the Sufi Sheikh Abdul Salam Yassine, who spent many years in prison. The group rejects the king's authority, strives to establish an Islamic republic and boycotts the party system, which it considers window-dressing for the king.

69   Estimates of the prevalence of animism vs Christianity vary widely, and both the Anglican and Catholic churches insist that they are the majority. Christianity's ability to absorb earlier religious beliefs (which accounts for its weakness in the face of the secular onslaught) and impoverished locals looking for foreign support contribute to this confusion. See Chapter 1.

70   Renamed the National Islamic Front in 1989 when Bashir staged his coup. Turabi served as speaker of the National Assembly in the 1990s.

71   John Esposito and John Voll, *Makers of Contemporary Islam*, UK: Oxford University

Press, 2001, 132.

72   Bashir was the first sitting head of state indicted by the ICC, a decision opposed by the African Union, Arab League, Non-Aligned Movement, and the governments of Russia and China.

73   The Muslim Tuareg are the indigenous population of the central Sahara and the Sahel, numbering up to 3 million. Over 800,000 live in Mali, followed by Niger, Algeria, Burkina Faso and Libya. In addition to the rebellions in Mali, there have been three in Niger, and ongoing unrest in Algeria.

74   The Tuareg tribes have controlled the Sahara trade routes for millennia, united under their legendary queen Tin Hinan in the fifth century, and Timbuktu was long a kind of capital for these nomadic tribes.

75   al-Qaeda in the Maghreb (AQIM), Ansar al-Din (Helpers of the Way), al-Tawhid wa al-Jihad (Movement for Oneness and Jihad in West Africa (MOJWA)).

76   Olivier Roy, "The Intervention Trap", *New Statesman*, 7 February 2013.

77   It includes Algeria, Burkina Faso, Libya, Morocco, Tunisia, Chad, Mali, Mauritania, Niger, Nigeria, and Senegal.

78   The crisis of 2012–2013 proved to be a boon for AFRICOM, which Niger tentatively agreed to host, giving permission for US drones to be stationed on its territory.

79   Conn Hallinan, "The War in Mali", *Counterpunch*, 28 August 2012.

80   UEMOA (1994) includes Benin, Burkina Faso, Cote d'Ivoire, Mali, Niger, Senegal, and Togo.

81   'Modern' nations still have their own foreign policy, while 'postmodern' nations are weak nations which take their lead on policy from the US. See Walberg, *Postmodern Imperialism.*

82   Finian Cunningham, "West using Terror to plunder Nigeria's oil resources", *Press TV*, 8 October 2012.

83   Jeremy Scahill, "Blowback in Somalia", *The Nation*, 7 September 2011.

84   By his half-brother's son, Faisal bin Musaid, recently back from 'studies' in the US.

85   John Perkins, *Confessions of an Economic Hit Man*, USA: Berrett-Koehler, 2004, 130.

86   See Walberg, *Postmodern Imperialism*, 57–59.

87   At least 255 died, including 127 military. In 1987 Iranian hajjis rioted, provoked by Saudi police, and 402 were killed.

88   After the 'liberation' of Kuwait, the Saudis felt compelled to hold municipal elections in 2005 and again in 2011 (for half the seats), though women still cannot vote.

89   In Saudia Arabia and the Gulf states, there are western-style universities and media with highly-paid western staff, with ulama providing a patina of Islamic-correctness to studies, lots of western-built museums and discrete night life for the elite and their western friends. The UAE and Qatar have imported western cultural symbols, such as the Dubai Desert Rock Festival and the Doha Film Festival. The Bahrain Formula One race was cancelled in 2011 and calls continue to boycott it. Presumably, these borrowings from (and pay-offs to) westerners are intended to show how 'enlightened' these absolute monarchies are, despite lack of meaningful elections, rigid control of media, and financing of neo-Wahhabis.

90   Ibid., 237.

91   In 2009, Mohammad Fahd al-Qahtani and Abdullah Hamad founded a similar (also banned) group in Saudi Arabia, the Saudi Civil and Political Rights Association that documents human rights abuses, calls for a constitutional monarchy and elections. They were sentenced to 10 years prison in 2013.

92   According to the Washington-based Gulf Institute. Saudi authorities maintain they have the sole right to decide what should happen to the historic sites in Medina and Mecca. In 1925, they leveled the cemeteries in Medina (where the Prophet's grand-sons Hasan and Husayn and Imam Jafar al-Sadiq are buried), and Mecca (where the Prophet's mother, wife Khadija, grandfather and other ancestors are buried). They built the 600m tall Abraj al-Bait (Royal Hotel Clock Tower, second tallest building in the world after the Dubai Khalifa tower) beside the holy mosque of Mecca. It houses luxury hotels and apartments on a five-storey shopping mall, where the Ottoman

Ajyad fortress (1781) once stood, built to defend Mecca from Bedouin bandits like the Saudis. Currently, as part of their plans to turn the Masjid al-Nabawi in Medina into the world's largest building (capacity 1.6 million), they are threatening to destroy the thirteenth century green dome which holds the tombs of the Prophet, Abu Bakr and Umar, mosques dedicated to Abu Bakr and Umar, and the Masjid Ghamama, built to mark the spot where the Prophet gave his first prayers for the Eid festival. The Saudis have announced no plans to preserve or move the three mosques, which have existed since the seventh century and are covered by Ottoman-era structures. A pamphlet published in 2007 by the Ministry of Islamic Affairs, and endorsed by Grand Mufti of Saudi Arabia Abdulaziz al-Sheikh, called for the dome to be demolished and the graves of Muhammad, Abu Bakr and Umar to be flattened.

93   The Quran calls for Muslims to share their wealth: "Let the man of means spend according to his means: and the man whose resources are restricted, let him spend according to what Allah has given him." (65:7) Saudi Arabia donates 4.2% of its GNP to aid (almost exclusively to Muslim majority countries) vs 0.35% by developed nations, but the overwhelming share of oil revenues ends up back in western coffers.

94   Faisal also founded the Islamic University of Medina in 1961 with Maududi a trustee, and King Abdul Aziz University in 1967. Maududi, the Brotherhood and Wahhabis had convinced the king that Azhar in Cairo was too close to Nasser, so the Islamic University was lavishly funded in competition to promote Wahhabi-style apolitical Islam. 85% of students were foreign, expanding from 3,265 students in 1965 to more than 113,000 in 1986, so the Wahhabis could spread their quietist ideology everywhere, now with the assistance of the CIA.

95   Members Abu Dhabi, Ajman, Dubai, Fujairah, Ras al-Khaimah, Sharjah, and Umm al-Quwain, formed from Britain's Trucial States in 1971.

96   "Dubai Kissing Couple: Jail Sentence Upheld For UK Couple Arrested For Kissing", *huffingtonpost.com*, 4 May 2010; "Briton 'beaten to death' in a Dubai police cell after being arrested for swearing", *dailymail.co.uk*, 14 April 2011; "British woman 'arrested in Dubai after being raped'", *telegraph.co.uk*, 1 July 2012.

97   Qatar's Al-Jazeera TV and press was a vital tool of revolutionaries in the Arab world in 2011. Qatar unashamedly uses western petrodollars and technology to help overthrow secular Arab regimes, while funding the Islamic opposition.

98   Felix Imonti, "Qatar - Rich and Dangerous", *Oilprice*, 17 September 2012.

99   Pepe Escobar, "Why Qatar wants to invade Syria", *Asia Times*, 27 September 2012.

100   Giorgio Cafiero, "Saudi Arabia and Qatar: Dueling Monarchies", *Foreign Policy in Focus*, 27 September 2012.

101   In 1990, as Iraqi military preparations to occupy Kuwait were under way, Saddam Hussein was told by US ambassador April Glaspie that Washington, "inspired by friendship and not by confrontation, does not have an opinion ... on the Arab-Arab conflicts." See "Twenty years on, shockwaves of Kuwait invasion are still felt in Middle East" *www.dw-world.de*, 2 August 2010.

102   Saddam Hussein was hanged for the Dujail massacre, the judicial murders and torture carried out following a Dawa assassination attempt on him in 1982.

103   Stoked both intentionally by the US, worried about the 'Shia crescent' which it inadvertently helped create by invading Shia-majority Iraq. Hence, the likelihood that not only the Saudis but the US is behind the ongoing terrorism against Shia, despite Saudi frustration with the US for allowing the Iraqi Shia to form a government.

104   See Chapter 3 endnote 72.

105   There are 39 members in the current council. See Ervand Abrahamian, *A History of Modern Iran*, UK: Cambridge University Press, 2008, 183.

106   Egger, *A History of the Muslim World since 1260,* 503.

107   Per capita real income by 1989 was half the pre-revolutionary level.

108   US sanctions targeting Iran have ironically further undermined the dollar, as China, Japan, India, Russia and Turkey now are forced to trade with Iran using their own currencies, Iranian rials and/or gold. South Korea uses barter. Vietnam, Indonesia, Sri Lanka and others are eager to join this non-dollar trade club.

109   From 1979–1981 Iran's revolutionary courts executed 500 political opponents. The first post-revolutionary president, Abulhassan Bani-Sadr, and Mujahideen-e-Khalq tried to overthrow the government in June 1981 at the height of the war with Iraq, resulting in assassinations and leading to a new purge. From 1981–1985 8,000 oppositionists were executed. In 1988 a final mass execution of 2,800 was ordered by Khomeini after the war with Iraq ended in a UN-mediated ceasefire, which Khomeini compared to "drinking from a poisoned chalice". Shortly before he died in 1989, Khomeini issued the fatwa against Salman Rushdie as an apostate. These final acts can only be explained as necessary "to leave behind disciples baptized in a common bloodbath." See Abrahamian, *A History of Modern Iran*, 182. Ayatollah Hussein Montazeri, who had been groomed to be the next Supreme Leader, resigned in protest and went into retirement in Qom.

110   Kadri (*Heaven on Earth*) was impressed by the articulate criticism he heard at conferences in Iran. The current victimization of Iran in the western media is a replay of the Cold War propaganda against the socialist bloc and has little to do with reality.

111   Eric Walberg, "Turkey and the Middle East: Carpe Diem", *Al-Ahram Weekly*, 24 March 2011.

112   Gulbuddin Hekmatyar, founder of Hizb e-Islami (Islamic Party), was particularly notorious for his cruelty and murders, yet Charles Wilson, a Texas Republican who was the leading congressional advocate for the Afghan jihad, approvingly noted that Zia was "totally committed to Hekmatyar, because Zia saw the world as a conflict between Muslims and Hindus, and he thought he could count on Hekmatyar to work for a pan-Islamic entity that could stand up to India."

113   Najibullah's rule is now remembered fondly by Afghanis of all stripes despite his communist beliefs..

114   Michel Chossudovsky, "Al-Qaeda in the Islamic Maghreb: Who's Who? Who is behind the terrorists?" *Global Research*, 21 January 2013.

•115   The Hazara had sided with the western-backed Tajik opposition who eventually replaced the Taliban as the government after the US invaded in 2001.

116   According to the *New York Times* (18 March 2001), as well as Taliban ambassador-at-large Sayed Hashemi, the Taliban were furious that foreign aid groups were more interested in restoring the statues than helping starving Afghans, and faced pressure from radical clerics who had been campaigning for years to destroy the statues as idols. Bin Laden is said to have convinced Afghan leader Omar, who was originally opposed, to allow their destruction.

117   Kyrgyzstan demonstrates the meaninglessness of elections in societies dominated by tribal/ ethnic allegiances, where the minority Uzbeks have suffered severe discrimination at the hands of the majority Kyrgyz, despite the most honest (western-style) electoral system in the former Soviet Union.

118   The combined Muslim population of Pakistan, India and Bangladesh is 480 million vs Indonesia's 203 million. See "Mapping the Global Muslim Population: A Report on the Size and Distribution of the World's Muslim Population," 7 October 2009.

119   Kashmir was "created rather off-handedly by the British after the first defeat of the Sikhs in 1846, as a reward to a former official who had sided with the British". Kashmir's Maharaja Hari Singh was Sikh, but its population was 77% Muslim and it shared a boundary with Pakistan. When Singh hesitated to join Pakistan, "Pakistan launched a guerrilla onslaught meant to frighten its ruler into submission," but Singh appealed to Governor General Mountbatten for assistance, and the governor-general agreed on the condition that the ruler accede to India. The UN was invited to mediate but no plebiscite has been held to allow the population to decide and Pakistan and India have fought two more wars over it (1965, 1999). India has control of about half the area of the former princely state of Jammu and Kashmir, while Pakistan controls a third of the region. Quotes from Burton Stein, *A History of India*, Oxford University Press, 2010, 358.

120   An astute political leadership in Pakistan would admit the situation is a stand-off, as the far more powerful India will never cede territory unilaterally. The only solution is

complete peace and open borders between the two countries (*a la* Bangladesh-India) which will allow families to unite in Kashmir, with a 'special economic zone' status, allowing it to flourish, borders no longer relevant—an 'Islamic' solution.

121   Vali Nasr, *The Shia Revival: How Conflicts within Islam Will Shape the Future*, New York: Norton, 2006, 226.

122   Egger, *A History of the Muslim World since 1260*, 472.

123   Karen Armstrong, *Islam: A Short History*, USA: Modern Library, 2000, 163.

124   Imposed for Pakistan's testing of a nuclear bomb in 1998.

125   Vali Nasr, *The Shia Revival*, 209.

126   It was first on the scene with relief in Kashmir in 2005. Hizbullah in southern Lebanon similarly cannot be touched by a weak government as it has protected the country from Israeli attacks and provided support to the poor. In contrast, the avowedly non-violent MB in Egypt was persecuted by the Egyptian state when it provided relief after the 1992 earthquake.

127   In his memoirs, Musharraf says that US Deputy Secretary of State Richard Armitage told ISI head Mahmoud Ahmed that the US would "bomb Pakistan back to the Stone Age" if it didn't co-operate in the US invasion of Afghanistan. Pervez Musharraf, *In the Line of Fire: A Memoir*, Free Press, 2006.

128   Begun in 1964, in 2013, more than a million Muslims came, including 30,000 foreigners from more than 100 countries, according to Tabligh Jamaat.

129   Yudhoyono used a newly formed 'Democratic' Party as his personal vehicle. He had been close to Suharto and supposedly tried to coax him to return stolen public wealth but was unsuccessful. After the October 2002 Bali bombing, he oversaw the arrest of those responsible, and negotiated with the Free Aceh Movement, gaining a reputation both in Indonesia and abroad as the Indonesian politician to talk to about the War on Terrorism. Wahid discussed his suspicions regarding the involvement of the Indonesian government and Indonesia's armed forces in the terrorist bombings on Bali, in "Inside Indonesia's War on Terrorism", 12 October 2005.

130   Prosperous Justice Party (PKS), loosely associated with the MB, in fourth place with 8%. In 2004, it tied President Yudhoyono's secular Democrat Party, but Yudhoyono adopted the PKS call for clean and effective government and won the 2009 elections handily; National Mandate Party (founded by reformists, including Muhammadiyah chairman Amien Rais) in fifth place with 6%; United Development Party, crafted by Suharto to unite the Muslim parties in 1971, continuing its close relationship with the ruling military as it did under Suharto, with several ministers in the current government, in sixth place (5%); Wahid's National Awakening Party (PKB) 5%.

131   Vali Nasr, *The Shia Revival*, 320.

132   Upon his appointment to the Foundation for the Future, he immediately requested the transfer of Paul Wolfowitz's lover, Shaha Riza, to the Foundation in 2006, after the scandal at the World Bank surrounding the pair erupted, and Riza needed to get out of the spotlight. Wolfowitz resigned as president of the World Bank the next year. In May 2010, Bnai Brith International condemned Anwar in a letter to the United States Senate Committee on Foreign Relations, claiming that he was a "purveyor of anti-Jewish hatred". The current Malaysian Prime Minister Najib went so far as to say Anwar "would make a good prime minister for Israel".

133   Along with Singapore, Thailand, and later Brunei, Myanmar, Cambodia, Laos, and Vietnam.

134   Jonathan Laurence, "How to integrate Europe's Muslims", *New York Times*, 24 January 2012.

135   Sadakt Kadri, *Heaven on Earth: A Journey Through Sharia Law from the Deserts of Ancient Arabia to the Streets of the Modern Muslim World*, USA: Farrar, Straus and Giroux, 2012, 273.

136   The Louvre's new Islamic art section shows (rare) depictions of Muhammad from earlier periods and places where they were not so strictly proscribed, a more subtle state-sponsored provocation of Muslim sensitivities.

137   Laurence, "How to integrate Europe's Muslims".

138   Soeren Kern, "Muslim countries financing Jihad in Spain", *gatestoneinstitute.org*, 4

August 2011.
139   Available at <www.haaretz.co.il/hasite/spages/1235352.html>.
140   Soeren Kern, "Qatar financing Wahhabi Islam in France, Italy, Ireland and Spain", *stonegateinstitute.org*, 9 February 2012.
141   Laurence, "How to integrate Europe's Muslims".
142   Moroccan Jamal Zougam and Spaniard Emilio Trashorras were eventually convicted. Many observers point to Basque and other independence movements as complicit, or even the Spanish police themselves as part of a false-flag operation.
143   Eric Walberg, "Islam and Europe: An equal and opposite reaction", *Al-Ahram Weekly*, 18 August 2011.
144   Laurence, "How to integrate Europe's Muslims".
145   Bin Laden and other al-Qaeda members were issued passports by the rebel Bosnian government in 1993.
146   Ruthven, *Fundamentalism*, 52.
147   In 1947 Princeton University set up the first Near East Center in the US.
148   For instance, Pakistani Fazlur Rahman (d. 1988), who was appointed head of Pakistani government's Central Institute of Islamic Research in 1961 but was attacked by the Pakistani ulama and moved to the University of Chicago in 1969. Akbar Ahmed is another liberal academic from Pakistan, a professor at American University. Khaled Abou al-Fadl (b. 1963, Kuwait) is a professor of Islamic law at the UCLA School of Law, formerly on the Board of Directors for Human Rights Watch, currently on the Advisory Board of Middle East Watch, appointed by President George W. Bush as a commissioner on the US Commission on International Religious Freedom.
149   Joseph Massad at Columbia University, Palestinian Nadia Abu El-Haj at Bernard College, M Shahid Alam at Northeastern University.
150   US citizen Amina Wadud drew on tenth-century scholarship to lead a mixed congregation in worship in New York in March 2005. We "mustn't use consensus or *ijtihad* to override explicit textual provision set down by the Quran or a sound hadith ... Verses justifying manumission point the way to behavior more in accordance with God's long-term aims. And what is true of slavery might also be true of other aspects of the divine law." Kadri, *Heaven on Earth*, 284.
151   Muftis near Birmingham UK set up the "Muslim Arbitration Tribunal to offer consenting parties the right to have their commercial and family disputes resolved according to Islamic law, for a small fee." Kadri, *Heaven on Earth*, 279.
152   Kevin Barrett, "Muslims to march on White House next September 11th", *PressTV*, 8 February 2013.
153   The ADL (1913) is the most militant legal Zionist organization worldwide.
154   Duncan Campbell and Richard Taylor-Norton, "US accused of holding terror suspects on prison ships", *Guardian*, 2 June 2008.
155   Ibid., 139.
156   One of the first legislative victories approved under the military-controlled interim Egyptian governments of 2011–2012 was to provide greater independence for Azhar to elect its leadership independent of government interference.
157   The outstanding example of this is the Islamic Society's work in the 1990s in what came to be known as the "Islamic Republic of Imbaba", a poor neighborhood of Cairo where, in the absence of any meaningful state support for the poor and unemployed, Salafi Islamists created an unofficial locally-governed community, largely manned by self-appointed street sheikhs, to maintain order and provide some relief for the poorest by creating "alternative codes of conduct". It was suppressed in the 1992 siege on the pretext of fighting terrorism. See Bayat, *Making Islam Democratic*, 139.

CHAPTER FIVE

CONTEMPORARY ISSUES IN ISLAM

Nationalism and the Sunni-Shia Divide

In the postmodern imperial era, that is, since the collapse of the Soviet Union in 1991 and the attempt to forge a New World Order (NWO) under US hegemony, nationalisms everywhere—except for the US-Israeli variants—have lost their drawing power. The French and British are grey Europeans, lost in a complex web of multiculturalism, with immigration the order of the day. Afghani refugees in New York pledge allegiance to the stars and stripes, Egyptians in Toronto brush shoulders with Jamaicans and Chinese, and claim allegiance to Queen Elizabeth, despite what these symbols represent to these peoples historically. The reality of imperialism is secured by faceless international institutions like the IMF and NATO before which everyone is 'equal', their rights or obligations guaranteed by a global financial and military order. In this NWO, even countries like Italy or Germany without a significant history of imperial occupation, but with economies already capitalist and with a developed financial sector, have the necessary clout to number among the dominant nations and the "deciders" in the various "Gs"—G7, G8, G20 ...

Nationalism in the Muslim world of the 1950s–1960s was based on military dictatorships, artificial borders, and supported especially by Shia minorities (as a defense against Sunni chauvinism). Traditional monarchies (Morocco, Jordan) have indulged the nationalism of nostalgia and survive. As guardians of the holy cities, the Saudis have sought to nationalize Islam. Pakistan tried 'Muslim nationalism', but Pakistan barely worked from the start as a nation, as it was comprised of a polyglot hodgepodge of tribes forged in civil war. Republican Yemen too has not progressed much beyond the tribal level.

Pan-Arabism has also had little resonance. Nasserism disintegrated after 1967. The Arab League of 22 states has advanced not one step on the road of political and economic integration, was helpless during the Yemen civil war in the 1960s, the Jordan-Palestine crisis in 1970, the Lebanese civil war 1975+, the Iraq-Iran war in the 1980s. It was split 12/21 on the 1991 'liberation' of Kuwait, and has been unable to cooperate with Iran against the US/Israel to stop the blatant colonization of the Occupied Territories. Sadly, the BBC Arabic service and Qatar's Al-Jazeera are more 'uniting' than the Arab League.

The only effective coalitions have been the pro-western UAE and GCC cliques (the latter formed hastily in 1981 in response to the Iranian revolution), and the French West African UEMOA. Europe entices the region through its Mediterranean Dialogue. The increasingly powerful institutions of the New World Order such as the World Trade Organization, and bilateralism with the US, EU, China, and other large economic forces, weaken any attempts at regional Arab solidarity. False-flag operations turn Muslim against Muslim. The Muslim world continues to be under the dominion of others.

The Shia-Sunni divide has been particularly problematic for the success of the nationalist project. The Sunni are seen to be the pragmatists, accepting rulers not because they are the best Muslims but because they performed leadership functions well, provided order, with the proof of their worth their ability to grab and hold on to power. They believe that the fact that Shia imams, beginning with Ali, were not able to win power made them *ipso facto* unworthy of having it, "a fact that has not been lost on modern-day Arab dictators."[1]

As a minority in the Muslim world,[2] Shia have traditionally supported nationalist and leftist movements which downplay religious sectarianism. Shiism's implicit identification is with the poor and dispossessed, and Shia activists seek to focus politics on ideology that distracts attention from religious identity. The Iraqi Communist Party (which Saddam ruthlessly repressed despite its support for him) was largely Shia. Pakistan's founder Jinnah and the Pakistan People's Party leaders Zulfikar and Benazir Bhutto were Shia. This prominence leads to resentment by fundamentalist, quietist Sunnis.

Arab nationalism was Sunni at heart, and at the same time had the potential to be a bridge to overcome the Sunni-Shia-Christian divide. Arab Shia and Christians such as Aflaq intuitively recognized this and supported Arab nationalism. Sunnism inherits the mantle of the Umayyad and Abbasid Caliphates and Ayyubid and Mamluk monarchies—the historical expressions of Muslim and Arab power. Egypt, Syria and Iraq had been the traditional seats of Sunni power. To promote his own role as Arab nationalist, Alawi Hafez al-Assad had Imam Musa al-Sadr and Ayatollah Khomeini issue fatwas in 1973 declaring Alawis Shia and hence acceptable allies to Sunnis in their common Arab cause.[3]

The whole nineteenth century reform thrust was made to look Sunni, though Afghani was himself Shia and Abduh was nonsectarian, campaigning for an end to the Sunni-Shia animosity.[4] After the Caliphate was abolished in 1924 and replaced by colonialism, Shia and Sunnis cooperated (the Khilafat Movement). Iraqi Shia ulama supported the Sunni rebellion against the British, and Iranian ulama went to the Caliphate Conference in Jerusalem in 1931 to try to restore the Caliphate.

Anti-Shia polemics come from the Salafis and to a lesser extent the Muslim Brotherhood. Sunni extremists identify Shia as American agents supporting the US in Iraq and Afghanistan. Shia parties opposed these invasions but then accepted the occupations as *faits accomplis*, but really had no alternative, and naturally attempted to improve their lot under the circumstances. The Sunni resistance movement in Iraq expects Shia to join them, even as they persecute Shia. The charge of being agents of imperialism is belied by the fact that Iran is the only outspoken Islamic critic of imperialism and is the subject of unrelenting subversion for its trouble.

Both liberals and socialists used nationalism to buttress their regimes, but they were bound to fail, faced with the western agenda. When regimes collapsed during the Arab Spring, Islam understandably filled the vacuum.

Traditional monarchies in Morocco and Jordan have so far survived primarily because they rely on a softer form of nationalism embedded in their past. Both dynasties claim they are related to the Prophet's family, satisfying Shia and Sunni citizens alike, however accommodationist these monarchies are. Similarly the Saudis and Gulf tribal leaders, and the Pahlavis in Iran promote(d) their rule as monarchs, appealing (however tenuously) to a pre-imperialist Islamic tradition.

Where Shia are a large minority (Syria, Saudi Arabia, Pakistan, Yemen) or a majority under Sunni rule (pre-invasion Iraq, Bahrain), they have become hostage to political power struggles. Saddam Hussein, in hiding after the 2003 invasion, proclaimed: "Just as [the Mongol] Holagu entered Baghdad, so did the criminal Bush, with the help of Alqami."[5] After elections in Iraq which allowed the formation of the first majority Shia government, random bombings of Shia shrines and police stations, where Shia youth came to apply for jobs, became rampant. Even after US troops departed, the bombings—presumably by the Sunni resistance—continue unabated. The long-suffering Iraqi Shia meanwhile continue their MB-style provision of social services for the poor, and consolidation of control of the rump Iraq state, leaving the Sunni (both pro- and anti-US) behind.

Ethnic-based nationalism 'works' where the Sunni majority have the Shia minority on board (pre-1980 Iraq and Pakistan, Lebanon, and to a lesser extent, Syria[6]), promising a level playing field for Shia. Shia Aga Khan supported Pakistani independence. Jinnah was Ismaili by birth and a Twelver Shia by confession, and Pakistan has had three Shia prime ministers, and Shia governor-generals, military leaders and many intellectuals.

But modern authoritarian leaders such as Saddam Hussein or Zia ul-Haq undermined their policy of promoting nationalism as the social force of cohesion by using the Sunni-Shia divide to shore up their own personal authority. Shia Zulfikar Bhutto was hanged by Sunni Muhammad Zia ul-Haq after the Supreme Court recommended commutation. The 1977 coup used (Sunni-based) Islamization to buttress the Zia military dictatorship and ended Pakistan's experiment with inclusive 'Muslim nationalism', done in by political manipulation of the sectarian divide. Pakistani Shia have been persecuted ever since.

Then there is the role of the imperialists, who jump at the chance of exacerbating Sunni-Shia tensions as part of their 'divide and rule'. The British did this in India, the French in Syria. Much of the violence in post-invasion Iraq has been attributed to US strategy to cow the Iraqis into accepting the occupation, a variation on the so-called Salvador Option. US Special Forces and Pentagon-hired mercenaries like Dyncorp helped form the sectarian militias that were used to terrorize and kill Iraqis and to provoke civil war.[7]

Nationalism flopped in Iran as the father-son Shahs were using it to distract Iranians from the injustice of their rule and to undermine the ulama. When he declared himself Shah in 1925, Reza Shah 'Pahlavi'[8] tried to cultivate Persian nationalism, but with a Shia flavor. The eighth Imam was Reza; hence, Reza Khan became Reza Shah, though he was a secularist, and had no royal blood, seizing power in a coup. His successor Mohammad Reza Shah Pahlavi took nationalism to its absurd extreme with his celebration of 2,500 years of 'Persian royalty' in 1971.

The Iranian revolution in 1400EH took on millenarian overtones, celebrating recent Shia martyrs Musa al-Sadr (reputedly killed by Gaddafi/Assad) and Mohammad Baqir al-Sadr (killed by Saddam Hussein). Iraqi Muqtada al-Sadr calls his militia the Mahdi Army in the cause of twelfth imam. Since the 1979 revolution and the leading role of Shia in defense of the Palestinians, Shia have been at the forefront of the re-emerging Islamic civilization, calling the Arab Spring an Islamic re-awakening.

Khomeini, as the champion of Islamic revival and revolution, downplayed Sunni-Shia differences, eager to unite the Muslim world and all anti-imperial forces. He admired Banna and Maududi and was himself an inspiration not only for Sunni militants concerning revolutionary strategy, but for secular leftists in Indonesia, Turkey and Lebanon to look at Islam with renewed interest. The Iranian revolution also pushed secular Sunni dictators to enact superficial Islamic symbols in Egypt, Iraq and Indonesia to shore up their regimes. This spillover was a direct result of the common anti-imperialist cause, and was only possible in the absence of a strong sense of nationalism. Warnings by leading Sunni clerics like Qaradawi and former Azhar Grand Mufti Ali Gomaa to Iran to stop trying to convert Sunnis in Egypt[9] reflect the respect that Iranian defiance of imperialism and Israel have engendered among the Sunni masses, though the idea that Sunnis will convert to Shiism is far-fetched. It is more a case of the Sunni ulama diverting attention from their own weakness and trying to assert a territorial imperative.

There is a tradition within Sunnism too of downplaying the Sunni-Shia divide, exemplified by Azhar Grand Muftis Abduh (r. 1899–1905) and Shaltut (1958–1963).[10] Saudis have no interest in Sunni-Shia reconciliation, unless it means Shia being strictly subservient and out of sight, despite King Abdullah Aziz's promise to Iranian President Ahmedinejad at the 2012 OIC summit in Mecca of a center for promoting peace "between Islamic sects". On the contrary, he continues the policy of King Faisal who 'stopped Arab dominoes from falling' to what the Saudi sheikhs saw as Shia-inspired Arab nationalism/ socialism.

The Saudis see the US as complicit in the current Shia revival, which indeed undermines the House of Saud, not only in the region, but at home, where the monarchy's chief opposition comes from its large, persecuted Shia minority. With a Shia government in Baghdad, Riyadh can't claim to be sustaining Sunni dominance in the region. Its Wahhabi version of Islam is in peril. However, the Saudi monarchy must ultimately bear the responsibility for its own low standing in the Muslim world. And the US certainly did not intend to create a 'Shia arc'. Whatever it intended, its policies are part of a broader imperial strategy (which is not necessarily in Saudi interests, and in any case appears to be out of control). Even as the 2003 invasion of Iraq empowered extremist Shia death squads via the new Ministry of the Interior, the CIA continued to support Salafi Sunni militias throughout the region.

In 2008, Zawahiri lambasted Iran and Shiism and said he would like to see both destroyed at American hands: "The possibility of the US striking Iran is real. We hope that war saps both Washington and Tehran."[11] The white elephant in the room is the premodern Wahhabis, who are responsible for *Sunni* terrorism, and who "pose the greatest threat to US interests. Religious and political ideology among Sunnis in the Middle East, unlike among Shia, is moving in the wrong direction, toward militancy and violence."[12] Arab nationalism has warped into anti-Shia Arab Sunnism, serving the imperial agenda. In keeping with Ben Johnson's 'Patriotism is the last refuge of a scoundrel', it should not be long before the Saudis reverse themselves and try to *revive* Arab nationalism in a desperate attempt to save their regime.

Democracy in the Arab and Muslim worlds will bring to power more Shia majorities (Bahrain, Azerbaijan) and give greater voice to Shia minorities (Saudi Arabia, Pakistan, Afghanistan). There is no reason for Sunnis like the MBs to fear this development, as Sunnis and Shia have every reason to work together against their common enemies, as they have done at key historical junctures in the past.

Jihad vs Terrorism

Inner jihad, defensive jihad, expand-the-caliphate-to-give-opportunity-to-accept-Islam jihad eventually morphed via Ibn Taymiya and Wahhab into jihad against-pseudo-Muslim-rulers, and via al-Qaeda even against civilians supporting them or merely caught in the crossfire, a permanent damn-the-consequences revolution. This perversion of the original intent was not inherent in Islam, but rather motivated by frustration and humiliation under occupation by imperial powers.

There is nothing peculiarly Islamic about armed resistance against invaders and martyrdom in the cause of religion,[13] which is common to all peoples, including Christians and Jews. One can only admire Aceh's resistance to the Portuguese in the sixteenth century. Even the nineteenth century Saudi resistance to the already decadent and weakened Ottoman court deserves respect, though the Saudi Bedouin were notorious for their cruelty and killing of captives, in violation of sharia.

The PLO hijackings of the late 1960s–early 1970s (recall Leila Khaled) were classic jihad: individual duty (*fard ayn*) in defense of one's home and religion, heroic and justified given Israeli aggression and unwillingness to negotiate the return of Palestinian lands. Similarly, Hamas and Hizbullah resistance today has nothing to do with neo-Wahhabism. Unlike the neo-Wahhabis' nineteenth century European anarchist models (who genuinely wanted to overthrow the monarchies and/or imperialism), the neo-Wahhabis are actually just serving the same tribal interests—Saudi—which their hated Wahhabi-inspired princes represent, as revealed time and again when they establish austere little 'emirates' in Yemen or Mali, lording over the local Muslims and alienating them in their zeal to emulate Wahhab.

The involvement of mujahideen in imperialist Cold War strategies (in fact a private army funded by the US and Saudis: see Chapter 2) was a perversion of the intent of jihad, though it indeed destroyed the Godless Soviet Union and has pushed the US empire to its limit, as Bin Laden intended. However, it did this at a horrendous cost to all, especially Muslims, and the name of Islam has been seriously harmed. If anyone deserves the *hadd* punishment for *fitna*, it is those who kill innocent civilians in the name of Islam.

Throughout the age of empire, the British and US had coddled and allied with conservative, nonpolitical Islam. When the Soviet Union was destroyed and the Arab nationalists weakened, it was time for the imperialists to abandon their Islamist allies and put them in their place, to 'reform' Islam and incorporate it *a la* Christianity into the West's secular, democratic order. It was also necessary to extend the empire's reach along the Silk Road—the Eurasian region of the Caucasus through to Afghanistan and China—newly opened for business, and populated by Muslim countries.

But what looked relatively simple in the early 1990s, over the next decade became much more complex, spinning out of control. The Islamists had not lost any of their fervor. Algeria's Islamic Salvation Front, denied the fruits of their electoral victory, began using terrorist tactics perfected in Afghanistan to fight for power at home, and the Algerian junta declared a "counter-Jihad". Denied the ability to gain power at the polls, some Islamists resorted to similar terrorist operations in other countries, now—horror of horrors—targeting their former allies, the US and its compliant Middle East regimes, even as Iran's Islamic regime remained vigorously anti-imperialist, the only one in the region.

Apart from hijacking airplanes, the most sensational 'terrorist' act now associated with the Muslim world is suicide bombing. The first Muslim suicide bombing (the Tamils 'popularized' the technique) was during the Lebanese civil war, the Shia bombing in Beirut that killed 299 US marines and French forces in 1983, motivated by the US-French support for Israel's invasion of Lebanon, prompting the US to evacuate, but by no means ending the civil war or Israeli occupation. Palestinian suicide bombings in Israel in the 1990s–2000s shocked the world, bringing the reality of the occupation into western homes, though again their actions did not end the occupation. Afghan martyrs kill occupation troops almost daily, not ending the occupation, but forcing the occupiers to abandon their long term plans to subdue the country. These tragic acts are justified by *maqasid* or the right of self-defense against attacks on Islam and threats to life, as confirmed by Islamic scholars such as Qaradawi, though he condones them only within the Occupied Territories.[14]

Suicide bombings should not be confused with politically-motivated hostage-taking where the intent is to force officials to comply with justifiable demands, though at considerable risk to the lives of innocent civilians as well as the lives and cause of the perpetrators. Like suicide bombings, hostage-taking must be considered in context. There have been very few after the spate of airplanes successfully hijacked by Palestinians up to the early 1970s. Consider the hostage-taking by Palestinians at the 1972 Munich Olympics, by the Chechens at a Moscow theater in 2002, the Shalit affair in Gaza in 2006, and the Algerian In Amenas gas plant incident in 2013. Only the Shalit affair entailed a successful negotiation (due to the overriding Israeli concern for the safety of Shalit) resulting in the freeing of at least 450 Palestinian political prisoners. The others ended in by 'rescuers' massacring both perpetrators and hostages, and, sensationalized in the media, did great harm to the cause of the hostage-takers. Hostage-taking is in fact a common occurrence around the world for purely monetary motives by run-of-the-mill criminals, so the few high-profile instances perpetrated by 'terrorists' must be judged in context and according to the likelihood of their 'success'.

The untargeted violence perpetrated by the al-Qaeda types is something else: a direct result of Enlightenment thinking, imported along with the weapons to carry it out (see Chapter 3). The Saudi 'map' came to include the western mapmaker over time. Whether or not 19 al-Qaeda members (15 Saudis) carried out 911, the wannabe Bin Ladens, studying their business administration courses and enjoying their petrodollars, were shaped by their western sponsors in ways that had nothing to do with Islam, and have continued to carry out other acts (not nearly so spectacular and sophisticated, but equally un-Islamic), following the western-influenced map.

The 1980s–1990s in Egypt, that witnessed the most al-Qaeda-type terrorism in the Muslim world at that time, entered history as a shameful and humiliating period, with a government more pro-imperialist and corrupt than at any time in its history, one which turned its back on its natural allies. As in Algeria, Saudi Arabia, etc., the young radicals, many of them battle-hardened heroes of the Afghan 'jihad', saw the same old quisling government kowtowing in the same old way to the US, and understandably turned against it and its western sponsors, armed with their new skills, experience, and fatwas by Ibn Taymiya, Wahhab, Bin Laden and modern self-appointed *mujtahideen* (authorized issuer of legal rulings), promising them martyrdom.

The dean of the terrorists, Bin Laden, had returned to his homeland in 1990, hailed in the Saudi media as a hero of jihad, who along with his Arab legion, "had brought down the mighty superpower" of the Soviet Union. The dying gasps of Arab nationalism—the Iraqi invasion of Kuwait in 1990 and Saddam Hussein's pan-Arab republicanism—suddenly put the Saudi monarchy at risk, and Bin Laden offered King Fahd his mujahideen fighters to protect the kingdom, warning him not to depend on non-Muslim troops. Bin Laden believed the presence of foreign troops in the 'land of the two mosques'[15] profaned sacred soil, and when King Fahd welcomed a half million primarily US troops and allowed the US to launch its invasion of Iraq from Saudi soil, Bin Laden turned against the monarchy. He fled into exile in Sudan in 1992, now determined, like his newly energized, battle-hardened comrades across the world, to overthrow all the pseudo-Muslim rulers who were playing along with the imperialists.

This Enlightenment jihad, once lauded (and funded) by Reagan as a 'fight for freedom', reached the shores of America with the World Trade Center bombing of 1993, for which the Egyptian Islamic Society 'Blind Sheikh' Omar Abdel-Rahman was sentenced to life imprisonment. Neither the Islamic Society nor Islamic Jihad was a 'spin-off' of the Egyptian MB, as claimed by western analysts. On the contrary, when Sadat allowed Islamists to function openly again in the early 1970s, the Islamic Society had split, with most members joining the reconstituted MB, and the extremists, seeing the MB as passé, staying put. They were rather a spin-off of Sadat's peace accord with Israel and the US-sponsored 'jihad' in Afghanistan (see Chapter 3).

By 1997 the entire Islamist movement had become paralyzed. Tarred with the terrorist brush, 20,000 Islamists (only a handful of whom were involved in any way with violence) were in custody in Egypt and thousands more had been cut down by the security forces. In July of that year, a deal was brokered between the Islamic Society and the Egyptian government, called the Nonviolence Initiative, whereby the movement formally renounced violence. The next year the government released 2,000 members. Leading the opposition to this attempt to stop the terror campaign was Bin Laden's lieutenant, Egyptian Islamic Jihad leader Zawahiri, who termed it "surrender" and proceeded to carry out the Luxor massacre in November 1997, turning Egyptians overwhelmingly against terror. This was the last gasp for this strategy of targeting innocent people in Egypt, confirming the real opposition to Mubarak to be the MB.

The project to forcibly reform the Muslim world to meet the needs of imperialism received a most unexpected Godsend in 911. It was as if Bin Laden, the supposed perpetrator of the collapse of the World Trade Center, was in cahoots with the US political establishment, and had provided the pretext on demand. While the many contradictions and inconsistencies surrounding the official 911 story make his actually having committed the act unlikely, it did, however, instill in Muslims a burning and urgent purpose: to affirm their belief, and to let the world know what Islam and jihad stand for—which has nothing to do with blowing up innocent people.

While Bin Laden had been in common cause with the CIA in Afghanistan, his continued existence over the years—now as enemy—provided an excuse to invade Afghanistan, Iraq and elsewhere. And where genuine terrorist acts were lacking, there was always the possibility of false-flag terrorist acts, which have been a staple of imperialist policy from time immemorial.[16] As with the Taliban, so too the "al-Qaeda" brand serves as a label of convenience, for the West and militants alike.

911 is the terrorist black box, a one-off miracle too far-fetched to accredit to a man in a cave, in comparison with the incompetent litter of genuine terrorist acts by frustrated fundamentalists both before and after. And rather than inspiring greater and greater acts of destruction, the WTC towers' collapsed coincided with terrorism's swan song in Egypt. The Islamic Society renounced bloodshed in 2003, and in September 2003 Egypt freed 1,000 members, citing what Interior Minister Habib el-Adli called the group's stated "commitment to rejecting violence". In 2006 the Egyptian government released another 1,200 members. Following the Egyptian Revolution of 2011, the Society formed a political party, the Building and Development Party, which gained 13 seats in the 2011–2012 elections (12 in Upper Egypt and one in Suez) to the lower house of the Egyptian Parliament as part of the Islamic Alliance led by the Salafi Nur Party.

The Saudi-Yemeni Bin Laden was officially killed in 2011 and succeeded by the Egyptian Zawahiri as al-Qaeda's chief, but al-Qaeda had been a ghost for years,[17] quite possibly kept alive by the very US that helped create it and now claims to be its mortal enemy, needing it to justify US terrorism in defense of empire. Now its 'affiliates' are even openly courted by the US, as seen in recent events in Libya and Syria. They include:

- Al-Qaeda in the Arab Peninsula (AQAP), led by Nasser al-Wuhayshi, a Saudi who served as Bin Laden's personal secretary in the 1990s in Yemen. It supposedly masterminded (and bungled) three incidents since 2009 intended to blow up commercial airliners bound for the US. A fourth attempt in May 2012 was reportedly thwarted when the suicide bomber turned out to be simultaneously working for the Saudi, British and American intelligence agencies.[18]
- Militants with ties to 'al-Qaeda in Iraq', formed as a result of the US invasion of Iraq, who have now moved into neighboring Syria, where they are called the Jabhat al-Nusra and are supported by the western-Saudi-Gulf states.[19]
- Al-Qaeda in the Islamic Maghreb (AQIM), which has pulled off a few kidnappings for ransom, and received a boost when the West overthrew Gaddafi and opened Libya to western briefcases, AQIM and other local jihadis. To the extent that AQIM is now flush with arms and former political prisoners, it is again thanks to western intrigue.

The terrorist incidents since 911 most trumpeted in the West are:

- The 2002 Bali bombings (202 killed)
- The 2004 Madrid train bombings (191 killed)
- The 2005 London metro bombings (52 killed)
- The 2005 bombings in Jordan (60 killed)

Like 911 they are all attributed to al-Qaeda, though none proved to be directly carried out by al-Qaeda. The Bali bombings were carried out by the Indonesian Islamic Society, the Madrid and London bombings were not connected to al-Qaeda at all, and the Jordan bombings were carried out by Iraqis. The main scene of post-911 random violence against civilians has been in post-US-invasion Iraq. And the overwhelming majority of deaths are of Muslims, there and in Afghanistan. According to the FBI, extremist Muslims commit only 6% of the few terrorist attacks that do happen in the West.[20]

The logical implication of US promotion of 'Islamic terrorism' in Afghanistan in the 1970s–1980s—as clear as day to anyone with half a brain—was that the Afghans would be free to institute an Islamic state, and that the mujahideen would return to their own countries and foment Islamic revolutions there. The inevitable result would be the triumph of Islamists throughout the Middle East when those 'jihads' were successful, which would end the need for such jihads.

Of course, this is not what was intended by the strategists in Washington; in fact, very much to the contrary. Instead the US continued to support secular dictatorships throughout the region in the 1990s–2000s, and tried to stuff the Islamic genie back into the bottle, beginning in Algeria,[21] and after 911in Afghanistan and Iraq, provoking further 'Islamic terrorism'. Considering that false-flag terrorist provocations have been a part of imperial policy from at least the 1960s, the *lack* of provable al-Qaeda-type terrorist operations, especially in the West, and especially in the last seven years, looks suspicious.

The question arises: Is the lack of terrorist events in the West after 2005 due to the 'War on Terror', the massive increase in surveillance and illegal operations by western secret services, or because there is no further need for such false-flag operations, as these NWO-type 'security' agencies already have their *carte blanche* in terms of funding and powers to spy, render and torture?

Even if the US is innocent of false-flag terrorism, the US-instigated scenario of wholesale retaliation was guaranteed to let al-Qaeda and similar groups spread rapidly, creating an unwinnable cycle of violence everywhere, the "intervention trap" (see Chapter 4 endnote 76). The momentum from the US-sponsored jihad in Afghanistan continues today. After US and NATO intervention in Libya, the threat has percolated to the Sahel, destabilizing Mali, Chad, Niger, Mauritania and even Nigeria, putting pressure on secular governments to allow AFRICOM to 'help' them maintain stability.

Egyptian terrorism burned itself out after the Luxor bombings, though following the revolution in Egypt, it flared up in the security vacuum in Sinai on the border with Israel,[22] and such violence continues in Iraq, Afghanistan, and now Libya, Syria, Nigeria and Mali, fueled by imperialist intrigues.

The logical outcome of the US-sponsored terrorism in Afghanistan— that Islamists would come to power in the Middle East—is coming to pass, not as happened in Afghanistan, but through the return of Islam to the lives of the people, undoing the humiliation of imperialism and 'independence' wrought on Muslims.

Muhammad finally achieved victory over his enemies by negotiations, and entered Mecca peacefully leading to an upsurge of faith that his *dawa* inspired. The Quran opposes force and coercion in religious matters. Violent jihad is wrong when peaceful *dawa* and reconciliation are possible, affirming the strictures of the Quran to "Fight in the cause of God those who fight you, but do not commit aggression." (2:195)

Hadd Laws

The blind application of *fiqh* has led in some cases to the very opposite of Quranic principles being realized. The seventh century harsh penalties were first revived in the 1920s in Saudi Arabia, as a result of the fall of the Ottoman Caliphate. Starting in the 1980s, based on certain hadiths, some countries reinstituted stoning for adultery (nowhere mentioned in the Quran), and made *hudud* (extreme) punishments the norm,[23] whereas the Quran would avoid almost all capital punishment. "If any one slew a person—unless it be for murder or for spreading mischief in the land—it would be as if He slew the whole people." (5:32) Life is precious.

In Iran, this began with a spontaneous self-righteous binge after the 1979 revolution. Perhaps the most notorious case there was in Kerman in 1980, when zealots convicted four Iranians of sexual misconduct *(zina)*—two prostitutes, one homosexual and one rapist—and decided they should be buried up to their necks and stoned to death. Meanwhile, clerically supervised mass hangings and shooting of "supposed drug dealers, perverts and leftists" were proceeding apace.[24] Pakistan, Mauritania, Sudan and the UAE formally adopted traditional *hadd* penalties in the 1980s, and Somalia, Yemen, Afghanistan and northern Nigeria in the 1990s. Even secular Iraq issued a 1994 decree that robbers and car thieves should lose their hands.

Despite all the publicity surrounding Islamic punishments (for which there are no reliable statistics), it should be pointed out that, apart from a rash of 50 amputations in Sudan from 1983–1985 (which led to the overthrow of President Nimeiri),[25] almost no stonings or amputations were carried out except in Saudi Arabia.[26] In the entire 1980s, even as the US and Saudis were conducting an orgy of blood-letting in Afghanistan, where torture and gruesome deaths by western-backed forces were celebrated as heroic, honorable acts, four stonings were carried out and 45 amputations by the Saudis. In Nigeria there were two amputations,[27] in Libya one, in Iraq and Pakistan none (doctors refused to supervise and/or conduct the operation), and in Iran none from 2002 on.[28] *Hadd* penalties always had a symbolic value far in excess of their practical importance. Authorized application has now virtually ceased, apart from the administration of lashes, beheadings and rare amputations in Saudi Arabia[29] and the Gulf. It should be remembered that the guillotine was the standard method of capital punishment in France until the death penalty was abolished in 1981.

As concerns apostasy, it is not punishable by death except in Saudi Arabia and Pakistan; the sentence is rarely carried out in the former[30] and never in the latter. Iran did not put a law against apostasy in the 1991 penal code and has not executed a Muslim-born citizen for abandoning the faith since the late 1980s.[31] Amendments to the Iranian criminal code in 2012 expand national security crimes liable to capital punishment to include activities of political dissidents who engage in armed opposition or are affiliated with terrorist organizations. The new definition also includes activities such as "publishing lies", "operating or managing centers of corruption or prostitution", "damaging the economy", or "seriously disturbing the public order and security of the nation", consistent with the punishment for *hiraba*. Under the current penal code, authorities have executed at least 30 people since January 2010 on the charge of "enmity against God" or "sowing corruption on earth" for their alleged ties to armed or terrorist groups, making it clear that these are what in the West would be labelled political crimes, but here are being expressed in religious terms.

Egyptian scholar Nasr Abu Zayd was convicted of apostasy in 1995, on a private citizen's charge, for questioning the divinity of Quranic texts.[32] Zayd fled to Europe. Muhammad Taha in Sudan in 1985, who claimed Mecca suras were more authentic, denying abrogation,[33] was not so lucky and was executed—the first and last execution for apostasy in recent times, apart from al-Qaeda-type unofficial 'justice' and the Saudi political prisoner Malallah (see endnote 30). On the contrary, a hadith states, "The difference of opinions of my Companions is a mercy for my Ummah."[34]

For Iranian Bahais[35] and others who 'stray', there is an Iranian "don't ask, don't tell" policy, in line with the hadith "If you sin, hide it."[36] This tradition of discretion in the public interest in Islam, of course, is especially relevant to sexual orientation issues. It led Foucault to defend the Iranian revolution despite its persecution of those discovered committing homosexual acts.[37] Yet, Shia Iran has dealt with sexual issues more openly than any other Muslim country. There are seven times as many gender change operations in Iran as in the EU. No Sunni jurist of note is publicly in favor of sex changes (though the operation is allowed in Egypt).

The reason for the condemnation of Islam by western critics today has more to do with guilt over Christianity's past sins[38] than it does with Islamic practice, just as recent calls by some Muslims for criminalizing apostasy has more to do with the relentless subversion of Islam by the West. Considering how seriously Muslims take their religion, their calls to criminalize hate speech directed against them is hardly surprising. The West itself has laws against hate speech, but they prosecute only people accused of anti-Semitism or 'holocaust denial'. The heightened Islamophobia spread over the internet, the scurrilous Danish cartoons of Muhammad widely published in 2005, and the quasi-pornographic film "Innocence of Muslims" in 2012, which caused riots in the Muslim world, are clearly part of a concerted campaign to provoke simple Muslims, who riot, die and kill—to be captured on western media, thereby impugning Islam and Muslims in general as part of the West's Islamophobic campaign.

A significant reason for the West's condemnation of sharia is the worry that sharia-compliance will affect state policy in their former colonies, interfering with western hegemony in the Middle East. For instance, according to sharia the Sadat-Mubarak peace treaty with Israel violates the spirit of Islamic law, which requires that Muslims help each other under attack. The billions of dollars Egypt accepts from the US is seen as a bribe to Egyptian leaders to protect Israel's hegemony and to promote the oppression of Muslims, putting

Egyptian "national interest" above sharia. The whole argument for a 'secular state' is to let this injustice continue, to let the *government* avoid following sharia. Similarly, with regulation of the economy (see below).

Women in Islam and Converts

The greatest single weapon in the anti-Islamic arsenal after accusations of terrorism and hand-chopping is Islam's supposed bias against women. On the contrary, for the first time in history, Islam gave clear support to women's rights. Popular figures in Islamic history include Mary mother of Jesus, the Prophet's wife Khadija, his daughter Fatima and his last wife Aisha, all strong, intelligent women. There are women scholars as well; in the first place, the Sufi 'saint' Rabia al-Adawiya, who "is credited with introducing the concept of unconditional love of God into Sufism, thus transforming 'somber asceticism into genuine love mysticism'." In Islam, the feminine is valued, even sacred ("Be at your mother's feet and there is paradise"[39]), unlike in the West today, where "ideals and concepts pertaining to womanhood and the family are no longer regarded as sacred, but on the contrary, as stigmatizing and stereotyping."[40]

In western modernity, the emphasis is on the human ego, while Islam "focuses attention on Divinity, the centrifugal force that unites all life. ... In relation to the Divine Unity, all multiplicity is a veil ... This [male/female] differentiation is a reflection of a complementarity within the Divine Attributes and is a most profound feature of what constitutes human nature."[41] Western laws, such as the decision to allow women to take part in combat, which treat men and women as undifferentiated, are based on a "least common denominator between the two sexes", but

> Islam bases itself on the norm and not on departure from the norm without denying that some departures also exist, for example, in the case of homosexuality, which has always existed in certain sectors of Islamic society as it has existed in other societies. To destroy the norm, however, means ultimately to sacrifice and compromise the eternal life of man and woman for an apparent earthly justice based on a uniformity that fails, ultimately even on the purely earthly level, since it does not take into consideration the reality of that which constitutes on the deepest level the human state in both its male and female forms.[42]

Based on his studies of the evolution of modern, secular society, where more invasive forms of social control, disguised as legal 'rights', replaced religion and tradition, Foucault came to a similar conclusion that the clinical, legalistic framework of premodern social relations were less totalitarian than modern bourgeois social relations, including marriage, with their normalizing subtext.[43]

Western-style women's emancipation, which directly continues the 'liberatory' trajectory of modernity by abandoning the strictures of bourgeois marriage altogether, and embracing legalized promiscuity and androgyny, is for a woman "actually a disguised form of exploitation of her body, deprivation of her honor, and degradation of her soul," as evidenced in legalized prostitution and the far higher incidence of rape in the West vs the Muslim world.[44] This is the subtext to the October 2007 Egyptian MB political platform, which asserts "equality between men and women in terms of their human dignity," but warns against "burdening women with duties against their nature or role in the family."[45]

The right of women to a dowry and to inherit property fulfilled the goal (*maqsid*) to guard against need. These social principles account for the different shares in inheritance which so obsess western critics, with men (sole breadwinners at the time) getting more than women. By implication, in a society where both men and women work, sharing financial burdens equally, a son and daughter would get equal shares in any inheritance. Today, even Saudis give the deceased's pension to his widow for family support. There is nothing in sharia which prevents 'innovation' (*bid'a*) to adjust legal relations between the sexes.

The problem of 'absent fathers' is a serious one even for the western norm of monogamous marriages. Fully half of the children in North America are now born to single mothers,[46] and this in turn has ushered in a new social reality, the "feminization of poverty". Islam refused to abandon the traditional marriage contract in favor of single mothers, 'two mummies' or 'two daddies', as it inevitably affects a child's character formation negatively. That monogamy is the preferred norm in Islam is suggested by the fact that Muhammad only married multiple wives after his first wife died (unusual for the times) and his children were well on their way to maturity.[47] The verse condoning polygamy in fact puts the stress on monogamy: "If you fear that you shall not be able to deal justly (with them), then only one." (4:3, also 4:129) Of all the world's major religious groups, Muslims are the least likely to have sex outside of marriage. And as a country's Muslim population grows, the rate of premarital sex declines for all residents, even non-Muslims.[48]

The confrontation between Islam and western modernity poses both problems and opportunities for traditionalists. The un-Islamic features of relations between men and women observed in many Muslim societies are compared to the often more equitable relations which women have achieved in the West. In Morocco, a new family law was introduced in 2003 adopting some western features:

- the marriage age for women was raised from 15 to 18
- women have the right to marry without the legal approval of a guardian, the right to divorce and full inheritance rights
- men can take additional wives only with the full consent of the first wife and the approval of a judge.

Similar reforms are being made in Egypt, Malaysia, Indonesia and Turkey, clearly under pressure from the West, which finances NGOs and provides funds to shape official attitudes to women's issues in the Muslim world, sometimes with good cause. (Ironically, the West's *bête noire* Iran encourages women to specify her attitude concerning a second marriage in a prenuptial contract.) The long road towards secularism and capitalism finally gave women in the West a "least common denominator" equality with men, while in Muslim societies, pre-Islamic patriarchal relations remained and need adjusting.

That said, the current alliance of western feminism with secularists in Egypt and other Muslim countries struggling to extricate themselves from imperialism's grip is a problem. At the 57th session of the UN Commission on the Status of Women in March 2013, Pakinam el-Sharkawy, President Morsi's political adviser and the Egyptian government's representative, faced western criticism for the formulation of some clauses. Asked about what was called an attempt to shield marital rape from legal prosecution, Sharkawy turned the tables on her western critic: "Marital rape? Is this a big problem that we have?" She dismissed this concern as a western imposition and pointed to sexual harassment in the streets as a far greater concern in Egypt.

> Should we import their concerns and problems and adopt them as ours? We're talking about things that aren't widely agreed upon, like abortion. We can't give women the freedom to have abortions whenever they want. Do not pick issues not pressing in Egypt, and then tell me that I'm in a conflict with the international community.[49]

The most well-known Muslim feminist is the Moroccan Fatima Mernissi (b. 1940), author of *Beyond the Veil* (1975), a study of the wives of Muhammad, *The Veil and the Male Elite: A Feminist Interpretation of Islam* (1987), and *Dreams of Trespass: Tales of a Harem Girlhood* (1994). As professor at Mohammed V University in Rabat, she has written on the development of Islamic thought, casting doubt on the validity of some of the hadith dealing with women.

Even as the Muslim world adopts certain secular standards which help women, the sterility of the secular agenda in human relations is pushing westerners—both men and women—to re-evaluate Islamic traditions, and even to adopt them. Western converts to Islam have increased since the 1960s, and accelerated following 911, and two-thirds of them are women.[50]

There are problems. First generation Muslim immigrants tend to live in like-minded émigré communities, and their practice of Islam is steeped in ethnic customs. When westerners intermarry and convert to Islam, they are pressured to adopt the entire 'package', which, given secular civil codes, has given rise to "Islamic feminism" and, among second and third generation western Muslims, a nascent gay movement. This development is not surprising—cultural traditions include not only language, ethnicity and cuisine, but local, sometimes tribal interpersonal relations, which are confronted with secular androgyny and commodification—an explosive cocktail, as the incidence of honor killings in the West confirms.[51]

In an echo of the Mutazilite claim that the Quran is only the historical (human, and hence temporally expressed) manifestation of God's eternal truth, Inji Icli, a convert and feminist argues that "there are traces of patriarchal culture within the Quran because it was sent to a patriarchal culture. It was sent to them in their language, their conception, their worldview. I know that it constituted progress for women back then but this progress is incomplete. We need to look at the text ourselves and reinterpret it."[52] Thus the call for a

> Swedish Islam—Islam interpreted through Swedish/ European experiences. Our way is the creation of new culture. Swedish Islam tries to find alternative methods and ways to educate and promote *dawa*, incorporating Swedish values.[53]

It stands to reason that over time, as the immigrant communities assimilate, and with new (Euro-American) converts, new geo-specific variants of Islam incorporating local cultural features will "creolize".[54] For instance, Islamic kindergartens in Sweden use the Montessori system, deemed by local Muslims to be in accordance with Islamic pedagogics. The goal is an Islam "which raises up the classical Islamic culture as a beautiful heritage to pass on in the Swedish language, which represents a deep spirituality rooted in the Islamic orthodoxy as well as in the mystical path of Sufism".[55]

The attraction of Islam to western women is a direct response to the rise of feminism, its "collateral damage".[56] Most women converts

> find the price of freedom promised by American feminism to be too steep and dehumanizing. Feminists, they believe, are complicit in freeing men from a sense of responsibility toward women and the family and have revolutionized society to the end that it has brought about the breakdown of family values ... 'Feminism has not liberated women; rather, it has liberated men from responsibility. In the process it has enslaved women. They have become imitators of men, not

free to be themselves, always in the process of measuring up to the men.'[57]

The essential equality, or better—equity[58]—between men and women in Islam is stated plainly in many verses (2:178–180). 'Equality' that forces women to measure up to male norms is seen by the convert quoted above as a continuation of patriarchy as much as it is providing women with other (hopefully, more appropriate) behavior models. The Islamic rejection of this ironically recalls the original cutting-edge version of feminism, called radical lesbian separatism, which argued that women needed special separate institutions from men in order to flourish in all aspects, since men by nature tend to dominate (at least in certain key areas). So this would entail separate schools, colleges, etc. much like what many Islamists advocate.

The importance of the family, the careful regulation of male-female relations, the sacralization of all aspects of life, and Islam's strong rational side "makes it the most convincing religion as compared to the other monotheistic options" for many women.[59]

In Britain, the number of Muslim converts in the past decade doubled to 100,000, according to a survey conducted by an inter-faith group called Faith Matters, again—two-thirds of them women, 70% white and the average age at conversion 27. In France, an estimated 70,000 French citizens have converted to Islam in recent years according to France 3 public television. In Italy, Ambassador Alfredo Maiolese, an Italian MP, recently became a Muslim and now dedicates his time trying to improving the image of Islam in the West. In Germany, at least 20,000 people have converted to Islam in recent years, according to RTL television. In the US, there have been an estimated 10,000 'white' converts in recent years.[60]

Arnoud Van Doorn, a member of the Dutch parliament and The Hague city council for Geert Wilders' far-right PVV party, announced his conversion to Islam in March 2013 on Al-Jazeera, driven by his party's anti-Islam discourse to study the religion more objectively. In Switzerland, Daniel Streich, a former member of the Swiss People's Party, who rose to fame for his campaign against the construction of minarets for mosques, converted to Islam. He now says Switzerland needs more mosques.[61] Ex-head of the Swiss Migration Office Alard du Bois-Reymond described the Central Islamic Council of Switzerland, which was founded and is run by Swiss converts to Islam, as "the most radical group in Switzerland".

There is a gut anti-imperialism to those who refer to themselves as

'symbolic migrants' [who have] moved away from central Dutch values, but do not feel they are outsiders. Islam offers them an alternative system from which they criticize Dutch views on morality and such western values as individualism and materialism. Islam provides them a way of distancing themselves from their western background.[62]

The strangeness of Islam—its roots in desert Arabia—is even an advantage for those who find themselves drowning in an ocean of consumerism. The western obsession with competition and privilege, be it race, place, status, sex, dissolves. "The only way a person can be better than another is if they are better Muslims."[63]

The personal reasons for conversion by both men and women, white, black and Hispanic, include

- aversion to alcohol and drunkenness
- the "lack of morality and sexual permissiveness" and "unrestrained consumerism" of western culture
- insecurity concerning sexual relations and gender roles
- issues of self-esteem
- transcending the white/ other divide
- where one's work is menial or meaningless, Islam becomes an "alternative career".[64]

Converts invariably cite what they see as weaknesses in Christianity: the Trinity vs the unity of God, Jesus as the son of God vs Jesus as a prophet, the Bible as being written and modified over time by humans vs the unchanged perfection of the Quran, original sin vs no original sin, and the incompatibility of the Bible with modern science.

Many converts are attracted by Sufism.[65] For others, conversion is political, and can be either right or left. "Islam, the religion of praxis that does not on principle distinguish between the 'city of men' and the 'city of God', just prefers to overlay them, and seems to be an ideal way of 'spiritualizing' a militant commitment that previously was only social or political,"[66] Foucault's "political spirituality".

Skeptics look at Islamic norms with nostalgia as if they were quaint shibboleths—like Christian America of the 1800s: head scarves, strictures against promiscuity and homosexuality, parental consent in marriage, honesty and frugality; in short, a mix of Puritanism and Catholicism. "I know very well the reasons for the uneasiness I feel in front of Islam: I find in it the universe I come from: Islam is the West of the East."[67] This is superficial at best, as you would have to go back five centuries to find a reasonably close parallel in East-West mores, and even then, the differences were significant. The grain of truth here is: this was before the total secularization of society and the complete penetration of capitalism into social life as well as the economic order. These 'quaint shibboleths' provide a moral and ethical norm to structure your life, a sense of decorum and restraint which minimizes social tensions.

Black converts are in many cases returning to their roots, as 10–25% of slaves were Muslims. Christian missionary Edward Blyden, known as the father of pan-Africanism, reconsidered his proselytizing, and, in his *Christianity,*

Islam and the Negro Race (1887), began promoting Islam as an alternative for blacks to Christianity, devoid of racism, which would "globalize their religious-political discourse".

Elijah Muhammad (1897–1975), came to Islam through the spiritual guidance of Wallace Fard Muhammad, founder of the Nation of Islam in the 1930s in Detroit, then perhaps the largest and now still a significant self-supported African American organization, advocating black separation if blacks could not find just treatment by whites in America. He inspired such 1960s revolutionaries as Malcolm X (1925–1965), who referred to himself as an "ex-smoker, ex-drinker, ex-Christian, ex-slave", and who, as a Muslim, advocated pan-Africanism (as opposed to black nationalism), harking back to pre-colonial Africa, where Islam was the most powerful single religion.[68] World boxing champion Cassius Clay (Muhammad Ali) is the most famous member. Warid Deen Muhammad (son of Elijah) founded the American Muslim

Mission as a continuation of the Nation of Islam but in strict conformity to Sunni Islam.[69]

Louis Farrakhan (b. 1933) the effective successor to Elijah Muhammad, now heads the Nation of Islam, but has adjusted the organization's beliefs in conformity with mainstream Islam. Farrakhan's 1995 Million Man March in Washington, DC may be the most significant and sizeable African American public demonstration ever, followed by a second march of almost the same size. The themes of the 1995 march were Affirmation/ Responsibility and Atonement/ Reconciliation, to the dismay of some who hoped for slogans more manifestly political.

The well-heeled western 'defectors' from Christianity and Judaism, who include journalists such as Yvonne Ridley and Lauren Booth (Tony Blair's sister-in-law), as well as other members of the West's elite (see Chapter 3), prompted Cold War author Philip Knightley to brand their ilk as "the new Philbys". They were running from privilege, he suggested, driven as much by a sense of guilt at what they had as wonder at the mysteries of Islam. The fact that Kim Philby's father happened to have converted to Islam was taken to support the accusation. But take Joe Ahmed-Dobson, the son of the former British Health Secretary—a child of New Labour and the opposite of a rebel. He works on inner city regeneration, finds spiritual satisfaction in Islam's "constant impetus to do the right thing", and credits his first-class degree to the structure his faith has brought to his life.

Islam's true 'danger' for the West lies not in isolated terrorists incensed by (a product of, and sometimes abetted by) the imperialists and the gross injustices of colonialism, but in the scholar-activist converts like Pickthall and Asad and the tens of thousands of ordinary westerners, disgusted by Zionized Christianity, Judaism and secularism, who are drawn by the Quran's argument that the earlier People of the Book have yet again been corrupted in their interpretation of God's message, leaving the clear message of Islam as the only true guide in a disintegrating world.

The significance of conversion is not just Islam's sheer scale and its capacity to penetrate various cultures, but the fact that a person who converts steps through the 'doors of perception' into Islamic culture, which immediately opens up a new understanding of events in the world, particularly as they impact the Muslim world, and necessarily is weaned from the US/Israeli orientation which is at the heart of the postmodern imperial order.

Islamic Economics

The ever-increasing power of economics to shape our private lives and dictate our politics and our way of life (and threaten to destroy it) has put the moral and ethical issues raised by Islam back at the center of the world's attention. The Islamic call for social justice, including the prohibition of usury/ interest, is the bedrock of Islamic economics (see Chapter 1).

Since the 1970s, reflecting the re-emerging Islamic civilization (not to mention the enormous wealth of the Gulf states), there has been a surge in "sharia-compliant" financial 'products', i.e., without overt recourse to interest charges or risk. This movement to avoid interest has led to the following 'innovations' in Islam:[70]

- *murabaha*—an item (a car) is purchased for the client by the bank, which sells it to him for a mark-up (the majority of 'Islamic' transactions),
- *mudaraba*—a loan to finance business where the bank gets collateral in the form of a share in the business venture during the loan period, but no interest, and at the end of the loan period gets a percentage of net profits for a designated period,
- *ijar*—for mortgages, the investor/bank buys the house and gets 'rent' payments from the occupant who is part of a consortium,
- *sukuk*—bonds which use asset returns to pay investors a premium, i.e., sharing risk in the economic growth which the bond presumably finances.

The development of this Islamic financing has taken place in three stages:

- 1975+ double *mudaraba* (on the liabilities side of the balance sheet, borrower = financier, bank = entrepreneur; on the asset side, depositor/ borrower = entrepreneur, bank = financier), replacing one-sided interest with profit-sharing,
- 1991–2001 deregulation (created more room for Islamic financial products), Arab-Malaysian convergence,
- 911+ rapid expansion of Islamic financing.

The concept of sharia-compliancy was first considered in the 1950s–1970s. Sharia recognizes the "time value of money but not as a predetermined quantity calculable at a predetermined rate",[71] which became the accepted practice of banking as developed in fourteenth century Europe. The Islamic banking principle of sharing risk is an "incentive to be sure the borrower is doing something sensible with the money [and] make the free market system more open, you might say more democratic."[72] Needless to say, it also encourages the lender to make sure the loan is going to be productive. It is shared risk that keeps out "moral hazard".

Ahmad el-Naggar founded a savings bank based on profit-sharing in the Egyptian town of Mit Ghamr in 1963, which led to eight other similar local banks being founded by 1967 and provided a model later adopted by the Gulf countries and Malaysia. In response to the deluge of petrodollars in the Gulf,

- In 1973, the Bank of Credit and Commerce International was founded, purportedly an Islamic bank, though in fact it was nothing of the sort (see endnote 80).
- In 1975, the inter-governmental Islamic Development Bank,[73] which funds infrastructure projects and offers private sector financing, was set up in Jeddah, and the first modern commercial Islamic bank opened in Dubai (Dubai Islamic Bank).
- In 1976, the first International Conference on Islamic Economics was

held in Mecca and the Islamic Economics Institute was set up at King Adullaziz University in Jeddah.

- In 1984, the International Association of Islamic Economics was organized.
- The Accounting and Auditing Organization for Islamic Financial Institutions (AAOIFI) was established in Bahrain in 1991, and has 200 institutional members from 45 countries, including central banks and Islamic financial institutions.
- In 2005, the International Center for Research in Islamic Economics was established in Malaysia with Saudi funding.
- In 2009, the first Arab Economic and Social Development Summit was held in Kuwait, followed by one in Sharm el-Sheikh in 2011, and one in Riyadh in 2013, promoting regional "investment flows".

The above institutions, of course, all rely on western financial specialists and all operate within the bounds of the current world economic order. Nonetheless, Islamic finance is the fastest-growing segment of the global financial system. Assets increased six time between 2000–2010 and there are now more than 300 banks with total assets $1.6 trillion in 103 countries, including the UK and the US,[74] as well as an additional 250 mutual funds that comply with Islamic principles, representing approximately 1% of total world assets. Iran, Saudi Arabia and Malaysia have the most sharia-compliant assets. Iran holds 40% of the world's Islamic financial assets valued at $235.3 billion, far more than Saudi Arabia.

In a fatwa in the 1900s, Abduh rejected Postal Savings Fund interest payments and proposed *mudaraba* contracts, rejecting any overt interest payment. This view held in most Arab countries until the 1960s, though banking has always been condoned in practice, which is justified by their avoiding "excessive interest", this being the more liberal view of the prohibition of riba as "excess".[75]

The broader definition defines *riba* to include any monopolistic profit, speculation or hoarding, rejecting arguments about 'excessive interest', and the use of *mudaraba* contracts etc. as legal tricks allowing pro forma 'sharia compliancy'.

The experience of banking without any interest varies across the umma: Pakistan, Egypt, Malaysia and Saudi Arabia gradually adopted dual banking systems but only Malaysia has a significant amount of assets (12%) that are sharia-compliant. Saudi Arabia piously insists it has always been Islamic in its practices, despite all the evidence to the contrary.[76] Ayatollah Vaezzadeh Khorasani argues that since all Iran's banks are state-owned, and the state is Islamic,

an Islamic state can pay and charge interest, and the Islamic state bank can receive interest from loans granted to private or government sectors. 'Within-the-family' state loans transfer money from the public to the representatives of Muslims, i.e., the Islamic state. [77]

'Profit rates' on 'profit-and-loss-sharing accounts' are even used by the nationalized banking system as an instrument of monetary policy. Modern *mudaraba* includes cash distribution of profits, or employee stock ownership plans and worker representation in management.

Critics of Iran's experience argue that the attempt to replace interest by calling it 'profit' changed nothing. There was no genuine move towards 'risk sharing'. The only effect was higher fees, more fraud, redistribution using lotteries and gifts. Where inflation is high, outlawing interest on savings accounts even transfers wealth from lower-middle class savers to big borrowers (corporations, government), and discourages savings. Iran's chronic inflation discourages long term financial activity and risky operations. *Mudaraba* contracts for productive investment have been rare.[78]

Nonetheless, non-Muslims too are increasingly using Islamic banks, notably in South Africa and Kyrgyzstan,[79] attracted by the concept of shared risk, and concerned that the funds are not used to promote gambling, pornography, alcohol or tobacco. At the same time, western Muslims have decided that a very restricted use of interest—for mortgages on private homes—is acceptable, "a need which ... becomes a constraining necessity", according to a fatwa issued by the European Council for Research and Fatwas (ECRF) and the League of Scholars of Sharia in the US, using Hanafi *fiqh*. Interest is allowed, but only for Muslims living in non-Muslim societies in dealings with non-Muslims to protect the property of Muslims.

Islamic banks weathered the financial crisis of 2008 better than western banks, primarily because they do not trade in government debt, or allow derivative transactions, sub-prime loans (sale of debt without clear asset backing), credit default swaps (*gharar*), and short-selling. While secondary effects from the 2008 meltdown on asset prices and the real economy have hurt Islamic banks, western casino capitalism is actually conducive to the introduction of Islamic monetary products, allowing them entry to the market. They are now seen as a safe alternative to western banking, where interest charges are in any case less important, given deregulation, than fees and profits earned from speculation, and where 'anything goes'.

Whatever its advantages over western-style banking, Islamic banking is of no benefit to the 90% of those in the Muslim world who don't have bank accounts, or the 60% living below the poverty line. Furthermore, many financial institutions currently offering Islamic banking services are majority-owned and staffed by non-Muslims, making their actual 'sharia-compliance' doubtful. One

Malaysian Islamic-based investment fund was found to have the majority of these funds invested in the gambling.

Even without the scandals, this 'compliancy' is merely reacting superficially to the glaring sins in the western economic order, and implicitly endorses the capitalism/ imperialist economic model in which the Muslim world is immersed. A Rothschilds is adviser to Qatari Sheikh Hamad, the supposedly Islamic Bank of Commerce and Credit International outdid by far any kafir bank in murder, theft, drug laundering and arms dealing for terrorists,[80] all thanks to Saudi/ Gulf petrodollars (i.e., directly complying with and buttressing imperialism economically).

Turkish-American Timur Kuran argues that not only the ban on interest, but the very concept of Islamic economics is simplistic and largely irrelevant to present economic challenges, that its practical applications have had no discernible effects on efficiency, growth, or poverty reduction. Islamization is a gimmick "to demonstrate the distinctness, continuing social relevance, and priority of Islam", useful to lower the aspirations of the lower-middle classes, and reconcile them to a puritanical lifestyle, "like the fox who decided the grapes he couldn't reach must be sour."[81]

He and other liberals such as Fazlur Rahman and Nasr Abu Zayd criticize *riba* (recall its literal meaning of "excess"), as opposed to interest, as 'bad' only when it is excessive, pushing defaulters into enslavement, creating political instability—the 'excessive' interest argument above.[82] The interest that a modern bank charges on a loan, or that it offers to a depositor, they assert, involves no such danger.[83]

Interest, Kuran insists, is indispensable to economic life as it allocates capital and risk efficiently.[84] Efforts to eliminate interest from financial transactions are futile, and sharia-compliance is a ruse to make interest appear as a return to risk. Fazlur Rahman couches much the same argument in more Islam-friendly language: we must adapt Islam to modernity, "the market should determine the rate of return to modern loans via interest just like any other price, determined by demand and supply for loans." He incongruously concludes that, "Islamic economic policy must be based on the establishment of the spirit of cooperation and solidarity demanded by the Quran."[85]

Critics of Islamic banking from the perspective of Islamic orthodoxy such as the Sufi Murabitun movement, like liberals such as Kuran, also dismiss Islamic banking as a gimmick, but for very different reasons: *murabaha* involves "two transactions in one" which "disguise a loan with interest under the pretence of a sale". It is hard to disagree with Vadillo that

> When it comes to the Islamization of bonds and derivatives, the original [*fiqh*] sources are completely forgotten. What is used as the basis of reasoning is the "judgement" of

the previous generation of Islamic Bankers. The result is absurdity upon absurdity. The 'Islamization' of the futures market is the latest, yet not the final move, of this unrestrained development of deception called the 'Islamization of the economy'.[86]

Vadillo criticizes the modernists who reject the use of precedents (*taqlid*) and go directly to the Quran and hadith, 'deriving' the goal (*maqsid*) of 'no interest' and then, using a slight-of-hand, applying their halal charge to anything from bonds to derivatives, including options, swaps, shares, and also credit cards, loans and debt trading. The principle public benefit (*maslaha*) is interpreted as including just about anything.[87]

While there is no inherent need for Islamic banking to reject paper scrip,[88] it *is* necessary to reject *riba*. Kuran, Fazlur and apologists for capitalism justify interest: 1/ as compensation for the lender's risk, 2/ as deferred enjoyment, so-called opportunity cost, 3/ as the true price of capital as determined by the market.

But, in the first case, what about the borrower's risk? Why not share all the risks? In any case, there is risk even in holding capital without lending it. In the second case, when you say people should prefer 'now' over 'later' then you say that the interests of the current generation of humanity outweigh the interests of later generations of humanity. This is a moral and ethical judgment which is inherent in the economic problem and must be made explicit. In the third case, this confusion of the interest rate with some kind of 'price' of money/ capital is carrying the belief in the magical 'money making money' formula to its (il)logical extreme. Rather than trying to circumvent the Quran, it is better to deal with these issues openly.

One of the great metaphors of the Quran concerns making a loan, not to another person, but to God: "Loan to Allah a Beautiful Loan" (73:20), for Allah "will increase it manifold to his credit." (57:11). This embodies Wright's theory about cultural evolution involving positive-sum interactions. This truth has even become a popular liberal meme of "paying forward" a good deed rather than paying it back. Refusal to make such 'loans', which put one's assets into circulation, is hoarding, which is condemned:

> The Holy Prophet said: Your own property is only that which you have sent forward (for the good of your Hereafter), and whatever you held back indeed belongs to the heir.[89]

To address the endemic instability, inequality and risk-prone nature of the global market economy—casino capitalism—which results from banker hegemony, US economist James Tobin proposed a tax on international speculation,[90] which finally resulted in the implementation of a Financial Transaction Tax by eleven EU countries in 2013, intended to reduce speculative transactions by imposing a 0.1% tax on *all* financial transactions to dissuade speculation and tax evasion. This is a 'rediscovery of the Islamic wheel', since sharia is in effect an international legal system intent on penalizing speculation and redistributing wealth more equitably.

A sensible position on the goals of Islamic banking is set out in the Ethica Institute of Islamic Finance *Handbook of Islamic Finance,* which calls for an end to fractional debt-reserve banking, the promotion of equity-based structures like *mudaraba,* a reduction of expedient structures like *murabaha,* and the establishment of a globally recognized gold-based currency.[91]

There are weaknesses in the economic practices in Islamic history:

1. The accumulated problem over time of wealthy people's *awqaf* and state endowments to the ulama (as in Iran in the eighteenth century), which removed large tracts of land from production, contributing to long term economic stagnation. Laws were revised in Egypt (1946), Lebanon (1947), Syria (1949) to keep productive land in use despite private wills, serving the public interest, in the teeth of conservative ulama opposition.[92]

   Opposition to agrarian reform even played a role in Islamist uprisings (Iran 1963, Afghanistan 1978), despite the fact that those who were intended as beneficiaries in the land distribution were landless farmers. The Egyptian MB supported Mubarak's law to force poor peasants off the land they were renting cheaply as a result of Nasser's reforms, and return it to its pre-1952 owners. Maududi condoned the vast holdings of land by the 'aristocracy' as their private property.[93] Olivier Roy believes this is primarily because it would "imply a reexamination of the concept of ownership", and in particular "throw into question the *waqf* endowments whose revenue ensures the functioning of religious institutions."[94] In Iran, *waqf* holdings are very large (in Khorasan Province, 50% of the cultivated lands belong to the religious foundation Astan-i Quds). Khomeini's attempt at land reform in 1988 was stymied by the entrenched interests of the powerful ulama, much as they protested the Shah's 1963 reforms that made Khomeini the symbol of anti-Shah resistance. The Shah's assets were given to Islamic foundations which were uncontrolled, unaccounted for, and led to charges of corruption and waste (see below).

2. The strict individualism of Islamic economic law and its lack of a

concept of corporation, has hindered organizational development, and contributed to keeping civil society weak. There was little need for the concept of an unlimited-in-size corporation in the seventh century, when production and trade were by individuals. Suitable forms of organization are needed to accommodate large-scale production. Socialism proposes state control. Islam has yet to develop a better alternative, and state control was Iran's only option in 1979, despite aversion to socialism as a system.

3. The Quran has few specifics on economics, and the differences between the seventh century and today make it vital for Muslims to develop new mechanisms to regulate economic affairs. Taxation was traditionally via private and/ or state charity (zakat).[95] In today's economy, dominated by services and industry, with most 'wealth' in the form of salaries, zakat should be based on not only wealth/ assets but on both wealth *and* income. Furthermore, all wealth (including *awqaf*) can be used productively, if only as collateral.

Current attempts to try to replace taxation with zakat in Sudan, Pakistan and Malaysia have yielded only 3–5% of government revenues. The *maqsid* for zakat in the Quran is just redistribution of wealth, but currently, this 'redistribution' via traditional zakat is mostly "only amongst the poor and the very poor"[96] Most devout Muslims and most poor (and very poor) Muslims are in the traditional sectors (agriculture, retail trade, crafts), and it is impressive that the Quranic intent is at work especially among the poor helping their starving brothers, while the superrich are oblivious. The issue is: "How can an institution such as zakat be integrated ... [making it] a duty for everyone to make a contribution to the satisfaction of others?"[97]

Until Egypt's parliament was annulled in 2012, there was a bill aimed at Islamizing taxation, proposed by Nur MP Mohamed Talaat, which provided for the establishment of a *bait al-mal* (treasury-house) to collect money paid annually by Egyptian Muslims as zakat and ushur (religiously-decreed charitable donations and tithes). Talaat declared that the establishment of this institution would signal "the beginning of the dream of the restoration of the Islamic Caliphate". Azhar's Office of the Mufti had itself put forward a similar idea in 1997, but it was blocked at the time by parliament and the Cabinet—then headed by Prime Minister Ganzouri.[98] (Ganzouri was the military-appointed interim PM in 2012 when the parliament, including Talaat, was dismissed.)

4. It is clear in the Quran that the state should guarantee that the umma can earn or at least have a minimum standard of living. The issue of trade unions is not one the Quran addresses, as there was no large-scale industry in the seventh century, most labor being family members or slaves. Medieval Islamic civilization was dominated by guilds, governed by religious principles, where working conditions and payment were established and unchanging. In the context of capitalism/imperialism, the MB's pre-1952 demand for a "moral economy"[99] was essentially the demand for a welfare state, and was the inspiration for Nasserism. This is why the 1950s–1960s are remembered by Egypt's working class as a Golden Age. People could earn their living honestly and disparities were minimal (at least compared to before and after). It was and is not so much a question of capitalism vs socialism for Egyptians, but of a moral economy.

Apart from Nasser's Egypt, the best times for Muslim workers were in King Faisal's Saudi Arabia, Zulfikar Bhutto's Pakistan, and Iran from 1977–1983, when the Shah's grip was weakening, and in the early days of the revolution. After executing Bhutto, Zia ul-Haq used Islamization to promote a pro-business agenda, undermining what unions there were. In Iran, after 1983, Iran Islamized its labor councils, which are now composed of management, selected workers representatives and government appointees, returning superficially to the Shah's policies.[100] Egypt's MB has not put much energy into labor activism. It made an alliance with the Socialist Labor Party (SLP) in 1981, but the socialists were angered that Islamist union officials did not initiate mass struggle around labor issues or support others' protests. The MB condemned the 1989 occupation by workers of Helwan Iron and Steel plant, which was brutally suppressed by the government. The MB-socialist alliance collapsed in the late 1990s when the government cracked down on both the MB and SLP and passed a "flexibilized" labor law in 2003 (similar to Morocco and Tunisia).[101]

The **Turkish** AKP's experience with wresting control of the economy from the military and reducing corruption is encouraging. The economic success of the AKP over the past decade is notable on several counts:

- There has been a sharp reduction in corruption.
- GDP, exports and foreign investment inflows have all surged.
- Inflation was brought under control.
- The IMF debt of $23.5 billion was reduced to $6.1 billion by 2010, and is projected to be paid off in 2013.

- Economic relations with Russia improved dramatically, including with the Turkic Central Asian republics.
- Turkey is poised after the Arab Spring to become a major economic actor in the Middle East after almost a century of orientation towards Europe and the US.
- Its relations with Saudi Arabia and the Gulf monarchies have also improved. President of the Union of Chambers Commodities and Exchanges Rifat Hisarciklioglu told Gulf sheikhs at a conference in 2012: "Let's make investments together. You have the money, but we have the courage." Trade between Turkey and the Gulf states increased from $1.5 billion in 2002 to $11.9 billion in 2011.[102]

The **Muslim Brotherhoods** in the region have come to power following the Arab Spring, with promises of economic improvement for the masses. They head governments in Morocco, Tunisia and Egypt, and are strong in Libya and Jordan. They are faced with common problems: high rates of poverty and unemployment, declining productivity and competitiveness, low levels of integration with the global economy, acute disparities between classes and regions, corruption, high domestic and foreign debt, and more. The MB plans are not yet clear, but so far there is no major change in direction. The Moroccan and Jordanian monarchies have been forced to give cosmetic power to their MBs, but continue to hold the reins of power and are unlikely to allow any changes that will significantly affect their very considerable personal wealth. All vow to end corruption, promote small-scale business, replace price subsidies on basics with targeted help for the poor, and introduce progressive income taxes.

Tunisia's MB leader Ghannouchi said: "I believe that we must adopt the form of social democracy practiced in Sweden and the other Scandinavian states. Economics must be dominated by social values, and not simply the aggressive forces of the free market." Corruption—financial, judicial, administrative, or media related—is responsible "for draining half of Tunisia's wealth".[103] According to the party's guiding document, work is both a right and an obligation, and economic life must be based upon humane foundations and a just distribution of the country's wealth. Ghannouchi actually repeated the communist slogan: "To every man what he has earned; to every man what he needs."

Egypt has revoked some corrupt sales of enterprises under the previous regime and/or demanded additional compensation. It appears that its free trade zone with Israel, requiring a minimum Israeli content in order to get access to the US market, will expire. Sales of gas to Israel were halted, and Gaza saw an easing of its isolation. Already in Egypt, a reduced ceiling and increased floor were imposed on state salaries by the interim administration. The MB's Freedom and Justice Party platform emphasizes more equitable growth with a minimum level of corruption, strengthening public supervisory bodies, reforming privatization to allow more purchase of shares by workers and the public, and monitoring enterprises after they are privatized, tying employees' salaries to performance instead of education or years of experience, improving health care, education, and other public services, and increasing public spending on vocational training programs to meet the needs of the labor market.

MB leaders include wealthy businessmen, who now see a new prospect for honest economic activity:

> When I was in prison and [Mubarak's son] Gamal Mubarak was taking over, I was thinking of not working anymore and leaving the business to my children and doing charity work. But now I feel it is a responsibility to bring investors and build factories. The idea is not to amass money or build wealth as much as it is to develop the country.[104]

"We will accept the [IMF] loan. But we told them that we have to take into account the social dimension. They can't impose on us conditions that are not good for Egypt. Our society should become self-reliant from now on," says Hassan Malek, chairman of the Malek Group which runs the Egyptian branches of a Turkish furniture company, Istikbal, and a clothing brand called Sarar. Malek and MB heavyweight Khairat el-Shater are business partners who spent more than four years in jail together until their release after the revolution. MB businessmen have launched the Egyptian Business Development Association.

Critics are disdainful of such effusions of piety:

> The Muslim Brotherhood is a reformist power, not revolutionary. They have never taken a radical position against authority because they believe they should change gradually. The working people and farmers will suffer because of this new class of businessmen. One of the big problems with the Muslim Brotherhood now—they have it in common with Mubarak's old political party—is the marriage of power and capital. The big difference is which private sector you are talking about.[105]

The Mubarak regime focused on mobilizing investment, but the beneficiaries were those who were already well-connected. Today, a Muslim Brotherhood-led economy could open up opportunities to those who never had them, perhaps giving rise to an entirely new business class. "If they succeed in doing this, I think that will be the best model for the so-called private-led growth. We can't just tax and subsidize—it's not sustainable," says Magda

Kandil, executive director of the Egyptian Center for Economic Studies. The big unknown for Egypt is the extent of its military-industrial complex and whether the MB is able to make it respond to its plans for economic development.

The **oil states**—with the notable exceptions of Iraq and Libya— continue to live in a fool's paradise, as if neocolonialism is the Divine Order and will never end. These economic exceptions prove the rule: if you are wealthy or strategic, you had better accept the neocolonial order. Their experience, supposedly pursuing an economic model based on Islamic principles, falls far short of providing an alternative paradigm. Saudi Arabia and the Gulf have merely skimmed off enough profits from the international oil companies to buy off their citizens with social welfare, fully adopting the premises of western economics with minor tweaks to avoid violating the letter of the Quran with respect to interest and zakat. Oil-rich Kazakhstan's secular dictatorship does a better job, more inspired by a crude sense of social justice based on Soviet socialism than Islam. Malaysia was fortunate to have principled leaders who adjusted a skewed post-independence economic order to provide a fairer distribution for the umma, without the massive corruption and harsh dictatorships of its neighbors Philippines and Indonesia, though corruption is the bane of all the above.

Iran's economic difficulties following the revolution and the immediate imposition of sanctions, war, unrelenting subversion, and a major drop in oil revenues after 1985, resulted in endemic inflation and a mediocre standard of living. However, Islamic principles of welfare have been incorporated into state planning—there is universal education, modest guarantees for adequate housing, medical and legal aid. Mohammad Baqir al-Sadr's theories promoting small-scale capitalism as an ideal were pursued after the revolution, rather than Shariati's advocacy of socialism (see Chapter 3). There were spontaneous workers' councils and wholesale nationalization initially, but early utopian visions faded with the general economic collapse, as many rich capitalists and landowners fled with their wealth, and the secularists that stayed resisted Islamization.

During the early days of the revolution, it was declared that the rule of *mustazafin* (the oppressed) will be established. Land would be distributed; the poor were promised housing, free electricity, no-interest loans, and even dowries for their daughters and free pilgrimages to the holy cities. Rafsanjani, then the speaker of the Majlis, gave Friday *khutbas* on social justice, summarizing Sadr's views about social balance.

But soon the mood shifted, and as the economy suffered during the post-revolutionary period, Khomeini too dropped his socialist rhetoric,[106] and the *modarresin* (teacher-scholars) working with traditional western-trained economists published *An Introduction to Islamic Economics* (1984)—a conservative manifesto rejecting the utopian interpretations of Islamic economics swirling around at the time. The economic problem was once again "scarcity" (for war-torn embargoed Iran, all too true), and social welfare is optimized by competition, requiring firm property rights. Economic growth should take precedence over equity, and the activity of those with more means should not be limited just to maintain "social balance". There was no connection or even reference in this treatise to the works of other conservative Islamic economists, particularly Maududi and the so-called King Abdul Aziz school of Islamic economics (western economic theories modified to exclude interest and to include zakat).

The *modarresin* argued there should be no limitation on accumulation of capital and wealth from legitimate economic enterprises. Like Maududi, they called loudly for a return to the moral values of the 'Golden Age' while supporting the status quo in the social relations of production. They most likely were looking longingly at the Saudi Arabia and Gulf sheikhdoms. The failure of Iranian populism to breach the Shia-Sunni gap, spark Sunni revolutions, and to substantially improve the lot of most Iranians economically meant a retreat to "cultural and symbolic dimensions of Islamization":[107] segregation of work/ study, interest-free banking in name, institutionalized zakat taxation, but not much improvement for the urban masses.

By 1988, GNP per capita had declined to one half of what it was in 1977. The state tried to prevent a corresponding decline in the level of consumption and standard of living by relying on subsidies for basics and extensive control over the economy. The result was a sharp decline in investment, development of black markets throughout the economy, including a network of rent-seeking activities (to allow for interest), and formation of monopolies. The apparent failure of 'Islamic economics' opened the door to the liberal reformers of the 1990s, in parallel with the Russian neoliberal reformers of the times, mesmerized by promises of economic miracles by introducing privatization and unregulated competition, which supposedly would allocate scarce resources.

Those behind the reforms were in fact more interested in the promise of a mass transfer of wealth from the poor to the rich, as state enterprises could be sold cheaply to cronies and subsidies on staples lifted. This would of course drastically lower real income for the poor, but would scarcely be noticed by the rich. Just how much investment would increase as a result, allowing for a trickle-down effect to the poor and unemployed was—and remains—a risk the rich and the reformers were willing to take. The same process in secular Egypt in the 1990s was a spectacular failure, merely creating a class of superrich, who famously spirited their windfall gains abroad to western banks to 'earn' interest, unwilling to risk them in domestic industrial development (as theorized by the IMF, the promoter of this neoliberalism).

By 1994, public opposition to the liberalization policy forced President Rafsanjani to retreat, though the yearning by the elite for neoliberal economic reform continued as Muhammad Khatami became the president in 1997 in a landslide victory won on his campaign for cultural and political liberalization. The high price of oil was a boon for him, but the conservative political hierarchy above him scuttled all attempts to cement a new liberal cultural and political order along with a neoliberal economic order, and in the 2005 presidential elections, the culturally conservative, populist mayor of Tehran, Mahmoud Ahmedinejad, came from nowhere to win the highest elected office. *Iqtisad al-islami* (meaning both Islamic economics and economy) "once a revolutionary shibboleth, is now absent in all official documents and the media. It disappeared from Iranian political discourse [in 1990]."[108]

An important part of the Iranian economy is played by *bonyads*, founded as charitable organizations to promote the Shah's rule, in line with *awqaf*, though they had little to do with charity; instead, used for tax-free property development, such as the Kish Island resort, and retail sales oriented to the middle and upper classes. After the revolution, they were nationalized with the declared intention of redistributing income to the poor and families of martyrs in the Iran-Iraq war. The assets of dissidents were also confiscated and given to the *bonyads*. Today, there are over 100 *bonyads*, controlling as much as 20% of the economy[109] and they are criticized for many of the same reasons as their predecessors. They form tax-exempt, government subsidized consortiums receiving religious donations and answerable only to the Supreme Leader. The *bonyads* are involved in everything from soybean and cotton to hotels, soft drinks, car manufacturing and shipping lines. In addition to the very large national ones, almost every Iranian town has its own, affiliated with local mullahs. Estimates of how many people they employ ranges from 400,000 to as many as 5 million.[110] They compete with Iran's private sector, with the advantage of political connections providing government permits and subsidies. As charity organizations they are supposed to provide social services to the poor and the needy; but lack of proper oversight and control has hampered the government's efforts in creating a comprehensive, central and unified social security system in the country.

Nonetheless, there is much to admire in post-revolutionary Iran. Despite the war with Iraq and the constant subversion and boycotting by the West:

- Peasants got land and created thousands of cooperatives.
- Agricultural prices were raised and the country became self-sufficient in cereal production.
- The literacy campaign meant all Iranians can now read and write.
- Roads, electricity, clean water, and health clinics came to villages.
- The poorest peasants now have some access to modern consumer goods.
- Life expectancy went from less than 56 in the 1970s to 70 in 2000.

- Infant mortality went from 104 per 1,000 to 25 per 1,000.
- The UN praised Iran's birth control program which began in the 1990s.
- For workers, basic goods are subsidized, there are labor laws regulating the work week and providing job security, and May Day rallies are celebrated with Tudeh-type slogans.[111]

Bangladesh has produced modest economic success, mainly by avoiding war and extreme corruption; per-capita income having doubled from 1975 levels. It produced a reformer who has achieved a hopeful economic breakthrough for poor farmers. Muhammad Yunus (b. 1940) started a movement of "microfinancing" of small businesses to alleviate rural poverty. The movement expanded quickly around the world and earned him a Nobel Prize in 2006 (the first economics prize for a Muslim). Over the years, his Grameen Bank, now operating in more than 100 countries, has loaned nearly $7 billion in small sums to more than 7 million borrowers—97% of them women, and 98% of the loans repaid. One of the more reputable spin-offs, Kiva, a charity to raise funds to be distributed as microloans, has been criticized for allowing local moneylenders to charge usurious rates of 25%. Such loans are no solution to long term poverty, and the project have been increasingly plagued by negligence, corruption and extortion.[112] This initiative is supposedly in line with Islam's obligation to help the poor, but the insidiousness of banking logic (and the enduring validity of the Quranic injunction against usury) shows yet again how difficult it is to accommodate the current economic order without abandoning ethical principles.

***

APPENDIX
The United Nations *Arab Human Development Reports*

All Muslim countries are below the world average in per capita income except the oil-rich Saudi Arabia, GCC and Kazakhstan (just barely), as well as Malaysia, also resource-rich and where the economy is largely in hands of non-Muslim Chinese.[113] There are many reasons for this sorry state of affairs, tied to the distortions resulting from imperialist occupation, and the subsequent disruption when the occupiers were finally kicked out. The colonial administrations pointedly did not encourage mass education, as they had no intention of leaving or promoting local development beyond that necessary for wealth extraction. The denigration of Islam, despised by the occupiers, continued after independence, as the poorly-trained new elite attempted to ape its western partners.

The United Nations Development Program (UNDP) has been working intensively in the Arab region since 2002 to analyze development challenges facing the countries there, producing five volumes of *Arab Human Development Reports* (AHDR, 50 reports), which

> highlight the root causes and the deep drivers of development challenges in the region, and outline a vision for the fulfillment of human development through increased access to education and knowledge, full enjoyment of freedom as the cornerstone of good governance, empowerment of women, and the guarantee of human security for all. [114]

Not surprisingly, coming from the UNDP, the reports are rigorously secular in nature, based on western definitions of the economic and political terms "freedom" and "democracy", emphasizing rights of independent actors rather than responsibilities to the community. The problem in the UNDP view is that "political forces, in power and in opposition, have selectively appropriated Islam to support and perpetuate their oppressive rule," especially via the "trap of the one-off election", a ploy used by Arab regimes apprehensive about the accession to power of Islamist groups, to rig elections in their own favor. "[Fear of Islamic dictatorship] is also cited to justify foreign interference to prop up authoritarian Arab regimes."[115] This assumes that the basic western economic model is sound, and everything would be just fine if only the local Islamists and the potential foreign interferers would lay off. That the interferers are in fact the *authors* of the AHDR's western economic model, and are interfering more in order to pre-empt their use of bombs and troops, to make sure all nations comply with it, is not mentioned.

According to the 2009 AHDR "Challenges to Human Security in the Arab Countries", about 30% of Arab youth are unemployed. Considering that more than 50% of the people in Arab countries are under the age of 24, 51 million new jobs are needed by 2020 just to avoid an increase in the unemployment rate. The 2012 AHDR "Empowerment: The Will of the People" calls for

> a transition to more accountable and effective governing systems, a revitalization of development progress which benefits all, not only the few, and efforts to promote social cohesion at a time when pluralism and consensus have never been as needed.

Coded language for: western-style secularism, multi-party electoral democracy, with aid tied to the dominant neoliberal agenda to support industry, implemented by specialists from or trained in the West. But whether western-style electoral politics allows for a "transition to more accountable and effective governing systems" which don't have the pitfalls of the current international economic order, or at least without a powerful infusion of ethics, available only via committed Islamists, is doubtful. "Bold thinking holds the key to realizing grand visions for the future," reads one edition of the report. Precisely.

The very words "progress" and "development" are restricted to the material realm (at best, including education). But as Nasr points out, "the goal of development as indefinite material growth" does not accord with Islam [116] any more than it accords with the resource/ pollution capacity of the planet.

The only acknowledgment of Islamic economic principles is the adjustment by western banks to allow for "sharia-compliant" financial 'products', i.e., without overt recourse to interest charges or risk.

ENDNOTES

1   Vali Naser, *The Shia Revival: How Conflicts within Islam Will Shape the Future*, New York: Norton, 2006, 96.
2   Primarily Saudi Arabia, Yemen, Lebanon, and Pakistan. Arab Shia are a majority only in Iraq. Persian Iran, Bahrain and Azerbaijan, and Arab Iraq are the only majority Shia states.
3   The Syrian Sunni opposition to the Assad regime is in part due to the resentment by the majority Sunni of rule by the Alawis, a resentment which is fed by both western and Saudi/Gulf support for the rebels today. Rifaat al-Assad, Hafez's younger brother, head of Syrian security (later in exile), told the Iranian ambassador in 1978 that (Sunni) Gaddafi was responsible for the murder of (Shia) Sadr, who was Iranian by birth.
4   In 1959 Azhar began teaching Jafari jurisprudence, and the rector, Mahmoud Shaltut, recognized Shia law as the fifth school of *fiqh*.
5   Ibn al-Alqami was the last caliph's Shia vizier. Ibn Taymiya (d. 1328) denounced Shia as the enemy within, facilitating the fall of caliphate during Mongol invasion, pointing to Alqami.
6   The popular, nonsectarian Baath rule became a dictatorship under (Shia) Alawi Hafez al-Assad, causing sectarian tensions to increase over time.
7   See Walberg, *Postmodern Imperialism*, 137.
8   The Shah insisted people take surnames as part of his westernization drive. 'Pahlavi' refers to the Persian language at the time of the Sassanids, the last pre-Islamic empire.
9   The 10th–12th century Fatimid Caliphate in Egypt was Shia (an Ismaili 'Sevener' sect), and even founded Azhar. The Fatimid heir, the Aga Khan, has provided funds in recent years to restore historic Cairo.
10 Azhar teaches Shia *fiqh* as a legitimate school.
11 Vali Nasr, *The Shia Revival*, 65.
12 Ibid., 250.
13 "Those who are slain in the Way of Allah—He will never let their deeds be lost. Soon will He ... admit them to the Garden which He has announced for them." (47:4–6)
14 Magdi Abdelhadi, "Profile of Sheikh Yusuf Qaradawi", *BBC News*, 7 July 2004.
15 Al-Masjid al-Haram (Mecca) and al-Masjid al-Nabawi (Medina).
16 Operation Northwoods. See Walberg, *Postmodern Imperialism*, 75–76.
17 CIA director Leon Panetta told ABC's "This Week": "There are at most 50–100, maybe less. There's no question that the main location of al-Qaeda is in the tribal areas of Pakistan." *ABC News*, 27 June 2010.
18 Ewen MacAskill, "Underwear bomb plot: British and US intelligence rattled over leaks", *Guardian*, 11 May 2012.

19   Eric Schmitt, "As Al-Qaeda loses a leader, its power shifts from Pakistan", *New York Times*, 7 June 2012.

20   Sabrina Park, "Only 6 percent of terrorists are Muslim", *dailytitan.com*, 13 September 2010.

21   "The US has much to learn from Algeria on ways to fight terrorism," said assistant secretary of state for Near East Affairs William Burns approvingly during a visit to Algiers in 2002.

22   The August 2012 murder of 16 Egyptian border guards, supposedly by Yemeni militants.

23   Based on hadiths, married adulterers should get capital punishment, while not-married adulterers should be flogged 100 times.

24   Sadakat Kadri, *Heaven on Earth: A Journey Through Sharia Law from the Deserts of Ancient Arabia to the Streets of the Modern Muslim World*, NY: Farrar, Straus and Giroux, 2012, 217.

25   Peter Woodward, *Sudan After Nimeiri*, USA: Routledge, 1991, 157.

26   There are no statistics for these punishments during Taliban rule in Afghanistan. The public stonings (or walls collapsing on offenders) that took place were sensationalized in the West. Given the cruelty that became daily fare from 1979 on, it is hardly surprising that these primitive forms of punishment were not seen as anything special. The Disney "The Kite Runner" (2007), in a complete perversion of the actual situation, depicts the Taliban as sadistic, homosexual pedophiles, regularly stoning women to death (and Soviet soldiers as thieving rapists).

27   The Nigerians were fed up with colonial-based law which served only the rich and victimized the poor. Sharia has the aura of simplicity and universality, but the old ulama, poorly trained and experienced only in domestic affairs, were unable to deal with the complex, class-ridden economic problems that were the real issue, and ended up outraging all by falling back on what they knew, prescribing stoning for adultery, though no stonings were actually carried out. This highlights the pressing need for much better education in the Muslim world, or else "Islamic reform can be stillborn." (Ziauddin Sardar, Introduction to *The Britannica Guide to the Islamic World*, London: Robinson, 2009, xxvii.)

28   As of September 2010, stoning is included in the laws in Saudi Arabia, Pakistan, Sudan, Yemen, the UAE, and some states in Nigeria and in Aceh (Indonesia). In Iraq after the US invasion, in Somalia and in northern Mali, there have been a handful of stonings by al-Qaeda militants. In June 2013 Iran's Guardian Council amended proposed changes to the criminal code to again allow stoning for adultery, though this looks more like a show of defiance against the West.

29   There were 69 beheadings in Saudi Arabia in 2012, says Human Rights Watch. Rape, murder, armed robbery and drug trafficking are all punishable by death.

30   The only documented case in recent times was the 1992 execution of the Shia Saudi citizen Sadiq Abdul-Karim Malallah, who was arrested in 1988 for throwing stones at a police patrol, was tortured and pressured to convert to Sunni Islam and refused. Malallah was most likely just a political prisoner.

31   Given the revolutionary situation this charge was no doubt conflated with treason/ sedition.

32   There is no law against apostasy in Egypt. Zayd's *Criticism of Religious Discourse* (1992) states: "The text, from the moment it descended over the Prophet, has been transformed from being a divine text to a human understanding because it changed from revelation to utterance. The Prophet's understanding of the text represents the first stages of transformation to an interaction of the text with a human mind." The case against Zayd was pursued by Azhar's Islamic Research Academy. At the same time, Azhar Grand Imam Shaltut, Grand Mufti Gomaa and others argue that apostasy is not punishable by death.

33   The principle that subsequent revelations take precedence over earlier ones. The Meccan suras preceded the Medinan suras. The scandal surrounding Taha's case led to Sudanese President Nimeiri being deposed two months

after Taha's execution.

34   This militates against rigidity and conformity, and teaches tolerance, which the Quran exemplifies in many passages. Whether or not Muhammad said it, its enduring popularity reflects the intent of the Quran. Hadith scholars such as al-Suyuti consider its actual attributability to Muhammad as weak.

35   Their leader declared himself successor to Muhammad in the 1860s. During and after the 1979 revolution, they openly sided with the West, permanently damaging their reputation as loyal citizens.

36   "Whosoever covers (the sins of) a Muslim, Allah covers (his sins) on the Day of Judgment." Hadith reported by al-Bukhari. "As far as our own sins are concerned, we should always try to hide them and not make them public." See "Exposing the sins of your fellow Muslims", *turntoislam.com*, 1 May 2008.

37   Foucault argued that premodern sexual relations were freer in the sense that they were not so tightly categorized and control as happened with the rise of modernity. He critiqued the gay/ straight categories as reinforcing division between heterosexual (normal) and homosexual (pathological). Gay identity meant acknowledging one's pathology, for "to betray the law of normality means continuing to recognize its existence." Janet Afary and Kevin Anderson, *Foucault and the Iranian Revolution: Gender and the Seductions of Islamism*, USA: University of Chicago Press, 2005, 29. This persecution is a direct consequence of the attempt to foist western legal norms on the Muslim world (see endnote 45).

38   See Chapter 1 endnote 129.

39   Hadith reported by Ibn Marjah (*Sunan*: 2771).

40   Haifaa Jawad, "Female Conversion to Islam", in Karen van Nieuwkerk (ed.), *Women Embracing Islam: Gender and Conversion in the West*, USA: University of Texas, 2006, 163–164.

41   Seyyed Hossein Nasr, *Islam in the Modern World: Challenged by the West, Threatened by fundamentalism, Keeping faith with Tradition*, USA: Harper One, 2010, 34, 65.

42   Ibid., 72.

43   *The History of Sexuality*, vol. 1, 1974, in Afary, *Foucault and the Iranian Revolution*, 25.

44   Abdur Rahman Doi, *Women in Shariah*, London: Ta-Ha Publishers, 2nd ed., 1989, 10. "A woman is beaten *every nine seconds* in [the US]. It's the number-one cause of injury to American women." <http://readersupportednews.org/opinion2/273-40/15693-focus-a-rape-a-minute-a-thousand-corpses-a-year>.

45   Similarly, the hostility of Islamists towards homosexuality is another instance of serious misunderstanding and misrepresentation. Persecution of msm (men having sex with men) was non-existent in Muslim societies until recently, and, like the Leninist revolutionary strategy of radical Islamists, was a direct result of western invasion, this time cultural invasion, as the neocolonial center tries to impose its secular, genderized ideology of artificial equality. Traditionally, homosexual acts have been tolerated if kept discrete (the rule of four witnesses ensures that prosecution is virtually impossible), and even if discovered, punishment could be waved if the guilty parties repent, which is the intent of the only mention of consensual msm in the Quran (4:16). The story of Lot focused on public orgy and rape.

46   Jason DeParle and Sabrina Tavernise, "For women under 30, most births occur outside marriage", *New York Times*, 17 February, 2012.

47   Muhammad's subsequent marriages were more about diplomacy, helping out widows and orphans, and spreading Islam.

48   See the *American Sociological Review*, October 2012. In Megan Gannon, "Muslims least likely to have sex outside of marriage", *livescience.com*, 21 October 2012.

49   David Kirkpatrick and Mayy el-Sheikh, "Muslim Brotherhood's Statement on

Women stirs liberals' fears", *New York Times*, 14 March 2013.

50   The lack of formal organizational structure in Islam means there are no pre-cise records for conversion, nor do national censuses include a conversion category, but that Islam is the fastest growing religion is suggested in various studies. See Nieuwkerk, *Women Embracing Islam,* especially Wolhrab-Sahr, "Symbolizing Distance", 78–79, Haifaa Jawad, "Female Conversion to Islam", 154, Gwendolyn Zoharah Simmons, "African American Islam as an Expression of Converts' Religious Faith and Nationalist Dreams and Ambitions", 174.

51   See Eric Walberg, "Where is the sense of honour?" *Al-Ahram Weekly*, 2 February 2012.

52   Nieuwkerk, *Women Embracing Islam*, 212.

53   Ibid., Anne Sofie Roald, "The Shaping of a Scandinavian 'Islam'", quoting Swedish convert Alba, 57–58.

54   Ibid., 65. This ability of Islam to thrive in radically different cultures is its strength, and accounts for its rapid spread around the world.

55   Nieuwkerk, *Women Embracing Islam*, 67.

56   Ibid., Yvonne Haddad, "The Quest for Peace in Submission", 34.

57   Ibid., 34.

58   See Jamal Badawi, *Gender Equity in Islam: Basic Principles,* USA: Amer Trust Pbns, 1995. Also Chapter 1 endnote 106.

59   Nieuwkerk, *Women Embracing Islam*, 107.

60   Nieuwkerk, *Women Embracing Islam*, 79.

61   Soeren Kern, "Europeans increasingly converting to Islam", *stonegateinstitute. org*, 27 January 2012.

62   Ibid., also Nieuwkerk, *Women Embracing Islam*, "Gender, Conversion, and Islam", 106.

63   Ibid., an interviewee, 107.

64   Nieuwkerk, *Women Embracing Islam*, Monika Wohlrab-Sahr, "Symbolizing Distance", 80.

65   Unfortunately, Sufism has attracted many westerners for the wrong reasons—because it's more aesthetic, more esoteric and secretive, hence, more elitist, and not as simple and democratic as Islam truly is.

66   Ibid., Stefano Allievi, "The Shifting Significance of the Halal/Haram Frontier", 123.

67   Claude Levi-Strauss (1955), quoted in Nieuwkerk, *Women Embracing Islam*, 146.

68   See Y.N. Kly, *The Black Book: The True Political Philosophy of Malcolm X*, USA: Clarity Press, 1986.

69   Dropping the belief that Fard was Allah and Elijah Muhammad the last prophet.

70   *Fiq al-muamalat* (jurisprudence concerning social affairs) is open to evolution and change according to *maqasid maslaha, darura, urf* (public interest, need, custom). "*Maslaha* and *darura*—the need to achieve economic welfare and meet the requirements of the global economy—usually trump theological or legal concerns." Ibrahim Warde, *Finance in the Global Economy*, 2nd ed., UK: Edinburgh University Press, 2010, 12.

71   Ibid., 21.

72   "A Survey of Islam", *Economist*, 1994:10, in Sohrab Behdad and Farhad Nomani (eds), *Islam and the Everyday World: Public Policy Dilemmas*, New York: Routledge, 2006, 161.

73   Founded by Saudi Arabia with co-founders Libya, Iran, Nigeria, Qatar, Egypt, Turkey, UAE and Kuwait and 56 members, all members of the Organization of Islamic Cooperation. The IDB has since set up the Islamic Research and Training Institute, the Islamic Corporation for Development of the Private Sector, the Islamic Corporation for Insurance of Investment and Export Credit, and the International Islamic Trade Finance Corporation.

74   Warde, *Islamic Finance in the Global Economy*. In the US, the Michigan-based

University Bank.

75   The Egyptian Abd al-Razzaq Sanhuri drafted the 1948 Civil Code of Egypt and also in Syria, Libya, Iraq, Kuwait, forbidding compound interest. Azhar Grand Imam Tantawi issued a fatwa allowing simple interest in 1989.

76   The Saudi economy was developed from the 1930s based on investments by Standard Oil and Texaco, which formed Aramco with the Saudi rulers, and financial affairs have been managed through western banks. It was only the huge increase in oil revenues in 1974 and the challenge of the Iranian revolution that spurred the Saudis to give their economic affairs a degree of Islamic window-dressing.

77   Sohrab Behdad, *Islam and the Everyday World*, 215.

78   Ibid., 116.

79   Shamil Murtazaliev's EcoIslamicBank was launched in 1997 to "break the monopoly" of the western-style banking system in Kyrgyzstan. Murtazaliev became the representative for the IDB.

80   BCCI was founded in 1973 by Pakistan *muhajir* (uprooted aristocrat from India forced to settle in Pakistan in 1947) Agha Hasan Abedi who claimed the bank had a divine destiny. Abedi was able to ingratiate himself with the Gulf Sheikh Zayed bin Sultan al-Nahayan of Abu Dabi and gain access to the elites of Kuwait, Bahrain and Saudi Arabia in the 1960s–1970s, seducing them with hunting trips, and then shopping and dancing girls in London. Zulfikar Bhutto nationalized Abedi's prototype United Bank in 1972 and put him under house arrest, but Abedi bounced back, setting up BCCI the next year, in time for the petrodollar bonanza, even befriending the unwitting Bhutto. The bank grew spectacularly, a conduit for CIA illicit funds and Mossad, until its collapse in 1991. "BCCI was friends with everybody." BCCI chief financial officer Masihur Rahman's sister famously quipped: "I looked into his eyes and saw God and the Devil sitting in perfect harmony." From Jonathan Beaty and S.C. Gwynne, *The Outlaw Bank: A wild ride into the secret heart of BCCI*, USA: Random House, 1993, 80, 135.

81   Mehran Kamrava, *The New Voices of Islam: Rethinking Politics and Modernity, A Reader*, USA: University of California Press, 2006, 43. See Timur Kuran, *Islam and Mammon: The Economic Predicaments of Islamism*, Princeton: Princeton University Press, 2004.

82   Nasr Abu Zayd, "The Nexus of Theory and Practice", in Kamrava, *The New Voices of Islam.*

83   Though the cost of a house is tripled, credit cards effectively charge usurious rates of 28%, student loans leave many people in hock for the better part of their future.

84   The Quran does not prohibit interest as an abstract concept to help determine the rational allocation limited capital resources, as one factor in deciding between investment opportunities, but it clearly forbids the one-sided *payment* of interest to the lender.

85   The only neutral 'interest rate' for society which does not distort income distribution would be one reflecting the increase in technological change (to the extent that it can be measured), but in keeping with Islam's prohibition of having idols, any increase in production which results should itself be neutrally distributed or used to strengthen society and the faith that holds it together, and not accrue to an economic elite, let alone an abstract corporation.

86   Umar Ibrahim Vadillo, "Fatwa on Banking and the Use of Interest Received on Bank Deposits", October 2006.

87   Vadillo calls for the use of gold-based e-Dinars (*www.e-dinar.com*).

88   The first paper money in general use was only in eleventh century China, so it is not surprising there is nothing about it in the Quran. True, European paper money, unlike that in China, was issued not by the government but by a private group of businessmen (goldsmiths) who began to issue credit based on *frac-*

tional deposits. They seized the power that Kubla Khan (i.e., the state) had to issue money and adapted the ancient practice of usury as their revolutionary tool. This is what is haram: creating money out of nothing. Money based on community exchange systems and barter based on LETS (Local Employment and Trading System) are compatible with the Quran, being based on the community's resources, contrary to claims by such as Vadillo who insist on only seventh century gold dinars and silver dirhams.

89 Hadith of al-Bukhari, al-Nasai, and *Musnad* Abu Yala. In western usage, 'You can't take it with you.'

90 The Tobin tax on currency transactions was first proposed in 1972.

91 But this insistence on a gold standard needs qualification (see endnote 88).

92 See Dale Eickelman and James Piscatori, *Muslim Politics*, USA: Princeton University Press, 1996.

93 Maududi also called for the use of *awqaf* along with medieval partnerships to promote capital investment without exploitative interest. See Marshall Hodgson, *Rethinking World History: Essays on Europe, Islam and World History*, Cambridge University Press, 1993, 238.

94 Olivier Roy, *Failure of Political Islam*, USA: Harvard University Press, 1994, 136–138.

95 2.5% on gold, 5% on agricultural produce from irrigated land, 10% from rainfed land, on animals, buried treasures (but not on 'unproductive' wealth such as art), as well as land-, poll-, *jizya-*, import-taxes.

96 Behdad, *Islam and the Everyday World,* 160.

97 Johan Galtung quoted in Hans Kung, *Islam: Past, Present and Future*, USA: Oneworld 2004, 577.

98 Bisan Kassab and Mohammad Khawly, "Egypt: Muslim Brotherhood and al-Azhar follow Salafi lead", *al-akhbar.com*, 23 March 2012.

99 Behdad, *Islam and the Everyday World,* 116.

100 In theory, there is no reason that such 'state unions' can't function to meet workers' demands in the context of social stability, given the Quran as inspiration. The Soviet Union's unions were based on the principle of social harmony where the workers were in control, but the system lacked the moral foundation to make this work.

101 Ibid., 133.

102 "Turkey offers Gulf perfect match up", *hurriyetdailynews.com*, 25 August 2012. Deputy Prime Minister Ali Babacan proposed building a railway line "to link the Gulf with Europe and Central Asia". This was a reference to the historic Hejaz railroad built in early twentieth century by Germany with the Ottomans, which ran between Damascus and Medina.

103 Ibrahim Saif and Muhammad Abu Rumman, "The Economic Agenda of the Islamist Parties", Carnegie Paper, May 2012.

104 Interviewee quoted in Suzy Hansen, "The economic vision of Egypt's Muslim Brotherhood millionaires", *Business Week,* 19 April 2012.

105 Sameh Elbarqy, a former member of the Brotherhood who parted ways with the group after he disagreed with its refusal to register as an official nongovernmental organization, which would have forced "transparency", quoted in Hansen, "The economic vision of Egypt's Muslim Brotherhood millionaires". However, the MB is much more than a run-of-the-mill NGO, and registration as such is hardly an option, given the MB's experience in the past.

106 Murtaza Mutahhari (d. 1979), a disciple of Khomeini who defended Islamic orthodoxy against Shariati's socialism, moved in the opposite direction, conjecturing in a posthumous MS published in 1983 and immediately banned that, "The new capitalism is a separate, independent and unprecedented phenomenon and requires separate and independent jurisprudential considerations." In Behdad, *Islam and the Everyday World,* 27. No individual can claim for himself the 'surplus' that modern mass production technology produces.

107   Ibid., 31.
108   Sohrab Behdad, "Revolutionary surge and quiet demise of Islamic Economics in Iran", USA: Denison University, 2005.
109   Afshin Molavi, *Soul of Iran*, USA: Norton, 2006, 176.
110   Kenneth Katzman, "Iran's Bonyads: Economic strengths and weaknesses", 6 August 2006, quoted from <http://en.wikipedia.org/wiki/Bonyad>.
111   See Abrahamian, *A History of Modern Iran*. Tudeh is the (outlawed) Communist Party.
112   See Hugh Sinclair, *Confessions of a Microfinance Heretic,* USA: Berrett-Koehler, 2012.
113   Monaco is at the top of the Word Bank per-capita-per-year list at $173,000 and Somalia at the bottom at $139—200 times less per capita than a Monacan, 100 times less than a Norwegian. See *en.wikipedia.org*.
114   The *Arab Human Development Reports* are at *arab-hdr.org*.
115   Ibid., "Towards Freedom in the Arab World", 2004, 12.
116   Nasr, *Islam in the Modern World,* 120–121.

CHAPTER SIX

POSTSECULARISM
MUHAMMAD AND MARX

The Dialectic between Revelation and Reason in Islam/ the West

The events in the Middle East over the past two centuries described here have been following the imperial 'map'. But that map is not the only one. Events can be interpreted in many ways, leading us along different paths, in keeping with our postmodern era.

Though most philosophers, historians and social scientists are secular these days, there is still a sense in the West that the path chosen by western civilization was 'divinely' appointed. The 'chosen people' meme infuses both Jewish and Christian thinking (see Noble's *Promised Land: Myth and Movement*). The once genuinely divine linear trajectory of history began with the Axial Age and was supposed to culminate in apocalypse, but in the process there arose an 'enlightened' secular trajectory for history,[1] which culminated instead in capitalism and imperialism (with Islam still resisting), where 'God is dead'. On the revised map, the old apocalypse was replaced by two scenarios: Marx's alternative, still apocalyptic— the destruction of the exploitative capitalist system, and Fukuyama's non-apocalyptic 'end of history' (Margaret Thatcher's TINA—There Is No Alternative), reflecting capitalism's final entrenchment. Both rejected society as spiritually-centered in favor of an obsession with material production and consumption.

The current system—and its map—like its apocalyptic precursor, is grounded in the belief that man is basically sinful (now, merely greedy), and that through a process of social evolution (formerly called social Darwinism) the strongest (craftiest, greediest) would come to control the system, whipping the less endowed into line with appropriate material incentives, producing a cornucopia of goods, bringing history to an end, be it peaceful or apocalyptic. The Invisible Hand of the market (or the worker-friendly plan) and an appropriate legal system would regulate society.

The actual history of this system belies both Marx and Fukuyama. Western civilization from the Enlightenment on has been an apocalyptic one of violence, war and environmental destruction, every bit as apocalyptic as the New Testament Revelation and Marx's *Kapital*, and continues to be so today, though replacing the market has proved harder than Marx thought. Marx's critique of capitalism zeroed in on the problem: exploitation of man by man, which in its highest form is interest—a belief in a miracle, that money can produce more money. Ultimately such a system must collapse, as it is contrary to nature, including man's nature—whatever it may be.[2]

Marx brought the theory of history to a higher level. Competition and class struggle propel changes in both the productive forces and economic relations, giving history its continuity and dynamism. Men make their own history but "not exactly as they choose". The material legacy of history defines and limits their possibilities. He saw the outlines of the way to transcend capitalism: individual rights must include social rights such as good working conditions, an adequate standard of living and relatively equal distribution of the wealth produced by society. Contrary to the musings of Thatcher, there *is* a society,[3] and there *is* an alternative, though the vague one Marx proposed requires considerable fleshing out.

Marx left no room in his formulation for the evolution of man's spiritual life, but his point that, "The aim of philosophers is not just to understand and comply with the world but to change it" is not value-neutral in this respect, and could be a hadith. Replace 'philosophers' with 'Muslims', and recall the ayat, "Surely never will Allah change the condition of a people until they change it themselves (with their own souls)." (13:11)

Islam presented the closest rival to Marxism in its revolutionary ideological potential as it relates to the pursuit of social justice. Like Marxism, Islam believes in the unity of theory and practice. Unlike Marxism, however, it provides a belief in the spirit and afterlife that gives meaning to the human conditions of death, suffering, and evil. Islam, like Marxism and unlike Buddhism, takes history seriously. Unlike Christianity, Islam recognizes no demarcation between the spiritual and temporal realms. The unity of temporal and spiritual authorities in early Islam (and at many other times and places) is the ideal state which inspires Muslims today.

Secular capitalism rejects revelation, as does the Marxian reaction to it, leaving them both without a clear moral and ethical grounding. Yes, capitalism is wrong because workers were exploited; it is unstable and will ultimately collapse. The workers must understand all this and overthrow it to establish a more just system, which they can construct based on rational principles. But this vision relies solely on reason and the vagaries of history to bring about its demise, and fell into the same apocalyptic trap as that of the millenarial Christians and Jews, who were eager to accelerate God's plan and take a shortcut to their respective 'end times'.

The brutalized, mostly illiterate incipient working class was an unlikely savior of history—an inexperienced and ill-prepared mass 'movement' based more on shared hardship than genuine solidarity. The dispossessed worker, a radically new individual, like the slave of the Roman Empire, with nothing to lose but his chains, thus became the hope for overthrowing the entire system in a destructive revolution. Like the Roman slave, this individual was not even a 'cog in the machine' as he was replaceable by any other individual, and hence dispensable.

The history of the working class struggle from the nineteenth century on is certainly heroic and tragic, but given the brutality of the system of capitalism and imperialism, produced its own demons. Faced by an implacable enemy, the twentieth century revolts against capitalism resulted in horrendous wars and insurgencies which resulted in tens of millions of senseless deaths, far surpassing the brutality of even Genghis Khan, and all in the name of Enlightenment ideals of liberty, equality and brotherhood. In WWI&II, both sides alike slaughtered millions of innocents, "only following orders", culminating in the dropping of atomic bombs on Hiroshima and Nagasaki by the US.

The most tragic episode for those opposed to capitalism was surely the cruelty of Stalin's regime in revolutionary Russia, which decimated communists in the first place, and the many failures of 'real existing socialism', especially with regard to forced collectivization and the imbalance between individual and collective life, all in the name of the workers (and, by implication, all mankind). This to a large extent discredited the very idea of communism and socialism as the answer to the unjust order of capitalism. At the same time, in the West, working class leaders were suppressed or co-opted. Some became the most militant standard bearers of the capitalists. The workers' 'reason' and the vagaries of the economy were not enough to overthrow the system, contrary to Marx's fervent belief.

The truly satanic disregard of morality witnessed in the twentieth century is condemned in the Quran where, says Satan: "I had no authority over you except to call you, but you listened to me: then reproach not me, but reproach your own souls." (14:22)

European Romanticism of the nineteenth century attempted to formulate a different map opposed to modernism, yearning to recapture the more 'unified' consciousness of premodernity by elevating art, the senses, emotions.[4] It erred by rejecting both revelation *and* reason, striving instead for the immediate and unmediated, instinct, passion, innocence, the sublime, over the alienated, guilt-ridden, future-oriented quest laid out in the Old Testament, the dry, soulless calculations of the modernists. Harking back to Gilgamesh, its touchstone was Nature, and its notion of time was cyclical, eternal. It came to be embodied in Nazi Germany, which embraced the romantic, organic view of society, was still captive to the chosen people myth (despite its disdain for the Abrahamic monotheisms), and, without a universal moral grounding, led to results that were all too tragic. It survives in the ecology movement and New Age cults of today, but it could not triumph in the face of capitalism either.

While the twentieth century western drama played itself out, the forces of Islam were left on the sidelines, forced to concentrate on survival in the face of the powerful secular devil. The relatively peaceful Muslim lands were subjected to invasion and occupation, and the Muslim 'empires'—the Indian Moghul and

Persian Qajar dynasties, and the Ottoman Caliphate—were now controlled by the imperialists. The collapse of the Caliphate was a devastating blow to the world umma, comparable to the effect of the collapse of the Soviet Union and socialist bloc in 1991 on the world socialist movement. Both these monumental events were brought about by the capitalist/ imperialist steamroller that has been creating a new—flat—playing field for its 'great games'.

But those opposed to the steamroller have been resisting its inexorable drive. Marx provided an immanent critique of capitalism, confirming dialectically the revelations about usury and distributive justice in the Quran. He separated and analyzed production, circulation and distribution under capitalism so they could be rationally determined. But value, as with interest, is an abstraction, a variable in a mathematical equation, without any reality until assigned one by human actors. *Kapital*'s weakness—the labor theory of value—is a materialist *reductio ad absurdum,* denying the 'value' of 'unproductive' labor (the elements brought to bear by the capitalists related to securing markets, research, innovation, factors management), like positivism, setting art and morals aside (in Marx's 'superstructure'). Going beyond Marx, the catalytic role of 'nonproductive labor' must be recognized in organizing society, as well the role of morality and ethics, as confirmed by Foucault's radical support for the Iranian revolution, based on his seminal critique of modernity.[5]

How to distribute this wealth among workers, capitalists, bankers, scientists, engineers, etc., is also a value judgment, a social decision. Some people are very talented organizers, very far-sighted, able to solve complex social problems. Others are brilliant thinkers, able to solve abstract mathematical problems which practical engineers can translate into inventions, which hardworking 'productive' workers in turn can use to produce material goods. The capitalist, financier, scientist and engineer all 'work' (organize/ finance/ invent)—though their labor is 'unproductive' in Marx's narrow definition of embodied physical labor—and they need to be rewarded 'appropriately', according to society's values. That said, Marx's clarification of the class structure of society is necessary before it can be overcome. Roles in production are identified, the productive/ nonproductive (in material terms) aspects spelled out, so that producers/ consumers can rationally solve their material needs in a way that satisfies their spiritual ones.

But neither capitalists nor workers can participate in any material production for the good of the society unless they have a moral and ethical framework—principles—to structure their efforts. We *have* to assign values when drawing our maps, indicating what signposts are of importance to us. For Marx, 'progress' meant class struggle and worker ownership of means of production. Islam believes in the unity of the umma, where belief transcends class, spiritual values transcend material values (a 'successful' person is one who best follows the deen), by asserting, not man's but God's ownership of everything and role in creating/ facilitating all that is good. People are equal as God's creatures, whose relative merits pale to insignificance before the majesty of their Creator, who is the source of these merits, and to whom alone all praise is due. We cannot be sure of being able to do what we intend (hence the pervasive *insha' allah*) or what the next day will hold. Each day, we remind ourselves that we are 'at the mercy' of God. As all wealth is God's bounty, there is a duty for the rich to share with the poor. The early Christian vision was much like this, reflecting the teachings of Jesus.

This is where Marx meets Muhammad. For instance, 'Work efficiently using technology!' Yes, but all activity should be imbued with spiritual striving, and material pursuits should be conducted both in moderation (they are a mundane concern rather than a spiritual enterprise),[6] and in a way to employ everyone. Not, 'Work/ spend till you drop!', and the specter of mass unemployment.

Marx's quip that religion is the "opium of the people" can be understood now in historical context. Foucault argues that it is correct for a particular period in history—the rise of capitalism in Europe, when the state and churches colluded to induce workers to 'accept their fate'. But not "as a general statement on all eras of Christianity, or on all religions."[7] The full quote published in 1844 in the *Deutsch Franzosische Jahrbuche* reads very differently: "Religion is the sigh of the oppressed creature, the heart of a heartless world, and the soul of soulless conditions. Religion is the opium of the people." The flip side of this is that Marx's analysis is also historically determined. Foucault saw the potential globally of the forces that the Iranian revolution unleashed, and recognized it as his desired "rejection of [the] European form of modernity", and that its global impact would surpass Marxism "which was not as deeply rooted in society", that the result of an Islamic revolution would be "much stronger than the effect of giving [revolution] a Marxist, Leninist, or Maoist character".[8] The Marxian conscious working class becomes the umma mobilized to realize their spiritual journey here on earth, centered on the Quran and hadiths, their focal point the mosque, which serves as catalyst for this purpose.

Islam, in contrast to Judaism/ Christianity and/or Marxism, does not look to an apocalypse and/or revolution to put human evolution back on the 'straight path'. Nor is it enough to rely on reason to achieve the good life. Revelation, belief, faith *must* be acknowledged (after all, what is 'money creates more money' but a belief, and a most absurd one at that?). And Islam just happens to have the most credible version of this revelation. Revelation and reason are the two poles of the dialect underlying history. Hegel's being and nothing, Marx's value and use value, Hanafi's value and fact.[9]

In light of this, the Rothschild-Clausewitz 'laws' underlying modern capitalism (see Chapter 1) and Islam's rejection of them lead us to certain conclusions. First, if the past 2,000 years of western history, where Jews were both despised and the moneylenders of last resort, is proof of anything, it is that there seems to be a role for chrematistics (money-making) in social affairs, only it must be very strictly circumscribed, as it is a dangerous, even 'sin'ful *practice*. Rational management of economic resources requires rational tools. But they are tools in the hands of humans, not magic wands which, like the sorcerer's apprentice found out, can take on a will of their own and create havoc. They must be informed by spirituality and social values, and incorporate human activity within the context of the larger natural world.

Secondly, and similarly, all empires become malignant when unchecked, choking the energy of the people, inciting them to harmful, even 'sin'ful actions. The American spirit of entrepreneurship, self-reliance, and local self-government is something to be proud of. Likewise, if harnessed, the incredible cultural and scientific richness of Israel's Jewish heritage could transform the Middle East in a benign way. But the American and Israeli empires—lacking a sense of morality and ethics grounded in a universal spirituality—have become malignant. The Russian revolution led to the death and exile of millions in the drive to demolish the old order, producing uniformity and environmental decay just as deadly in its own way as its militarist-consumerist antagonist. Unchecked, the Nazis unleashed their own version of apocalypse.

The US and the EU are multicultural, open to immigrants, and at least officially tolerant to Muslims; at the same time, they function according to these laws, making them both intolerant and warlike, i.e., *dar al-harb*, despite their pious claims to be protecting the world's human rights. Their legacy of imperialism lives on and must be confronted.

A new modernity must incorporate both revelation and reason, morality and materialism, Muhammad and Marx. We must use *ijtihad* in our jihad against US-NATO imperialism. This *ijtihad*-jihad process is in a sense just a more comprehensive version of Marxian praxis, emphasizing:

- social unity rather than class struggle
- the family and spiritual life rather than material production
- evolution rather than revolution.

Left secularists such as Azmeh, Bayat and Dabashi dismiss Islam as having 'run its course'—they ignore Foucault's startling and prescient embrace of the Iranian revolution and his call for a "political spirituality", finding the inherent conservatism of Islam distasteful. But their secular, radical discourse does not in*spir*e the masses. Dabashi's analysis in any case ultimately rests on an inner revolutionary personal transformation (what is this but revelation?) and a coming-together of secular leftists and Muslims in an anti-imperialist alliance: Occupy Wall Street and Aung San Suu Kyi meet Tahrir Square.[10] It's hard to argue with that, but without an adequate map to follow, these protest movements are easily absorbed.

Social Evolution and Islam

Overcoming the contradictions of science vs religion, the individual vs society, means vs ends, salvation vs liberation requires grappling with the revelation-reason dialectic. Finding a balance between revelation and reason continues to bedevil humanity. As argued by Schumacher, Foucault, Habermas and other critics of modernism, after the Enlightenment, the "Big Three" cultural values of art, science, morality were separated into distinct disciplines, and science—restricted to what can be measured and proved—crowded out the other two, which were relegated to second place, a matter of taste or opinion.

The religious experience, which still concerns itself with all three, has been relegated to the periphery of the modern world, the true meaning today of the 'separation of church and state'.[11] Hegel and Kant wrestled with modernity's desacralization of the world, postmodernists formalized it by arguing there are only interpretations, contextual-dependent constructions, some of them nihilistically arguing that any interpretation is equally valid. Only hardnosed positivist science held out in the face of this relativism.

Social evolution now is all about reintegrating the Big Three, bringing morality and art back into the way we organize our daily lives. Hamza Yusuf's lecture on *taqwa* (see Chapter 3) is all about achieving a higher nature, transforming and transcending our anger and desire for vengeance, striving for a higher level of personal consciousness and behavior. Similarly, for a Sufi, life is all about trying to achieve a glimpse of God-consciousness[12] through right living, meditation, and good deeds, moving to a higher level both consciously, unconsciously, individually *and* socially.

Western civilization's love affair with quantity produced predictable results—degradation of humanity and Nature—as production of material goods skyrocketed. Global commercial culture, where Nature is desacrilized, is really the material 'it' colonizing the spiritual 'I/We'[13] in both center and periphery. All interior dimensions of 'I' and 'We' are reduced to exterior surfaces of objective 'its'. Thomas Friedman's flat-earth globalization[14] is a postmodern moral flatland.

A critique of (post)modernity that relies on a material base is inadequate. But it is not enough to return to premodern magical or crude mythical worldviews. Both the disasters of the West, but also its great advances have been due to the differentiation of the Big Three (art, science, morality). Empirical facts can refute patently false beliefs (though empirical thinking errs in dismissing *all* beliefs or at least relegates them to second place). Of course, individuals should have constitutional rights (as well as roles/ responsibilities in society). But for that matter, Nature has 'rights' too, as Ecuadorans now assert in their constitution.

All along, there was a civilization that hadn't lost sight of the Big Three, where the I and We were not colonized by the it, where quality and value were held in higher esteem than mere quantity, where both revelation and reason were respected. From the sixteenth century, when the positivist shift in the worldview in the West really got underway, threatening the foundations of Islamic deen, the ulama took a defensive stance towards western science—a powerful weapon in the hands of the oppressors—rather than engaging with it. Finally, under pressure from the imperialist onslaught, various efforts were made to 'catch up' by adopting western science, as the very existence of Islamic civilization came into question.

All along, Islamic thought never lost sight of the revelation side of the revelation-reason dialectic.

> The Islamic perspective is based upon the intellect as a
> supernaturally natural faculty within human beings that is a
> sacrament and that, if used correctly, leads to the same truths
> as those revealed through prophecy. The doctrine of unity
> (tawhid) dominates the whole message of Islam.[15]

God is "spirit-in-action", as Hegel conceived him, and God's realm is to be realized on earth by building and nurturing the umma following the path laid out by God in the Quran. The means and ends are one; spirit's goal is the path itself (the Sufis call their practice the *tariqa* (path)). The mapmaker includes himself on his map.

Sufis share with Islamists the desire to reform a corrupt and materialistic society. In the post-'independence' Muslim world, "in a sense they wish to complete the process of decolonization that took place half a century ago politically, but not culturally and socially."[16] It's the chicken-egg controversy, Koestler's commissar, Ahmed's Deoband, concerned with the outer transformation of society (dedication to action, providing the material freedom for inner transformation) vs the Yogi or Sufi, concerned in the first place with that inner-world transformation (achieved through prayer and meditation). But unlike Koestler, Muslims see these opposites as complementary facets of Islam: the deen is a path *(tariqa)* for inner transformation where renewed Muslims will build a road for political renewal inspired by the *tariqa*, incarnating it. Sufis become Islamists and vice versa (Ghazali, Banna, Tariq Ramadan[17]). As Islamists captured the headlines from the 1970s on, Sufis continued to celebrate festivals of Muslim saints. In 2003 even the Saudis allowed discrete Sufi festivals. At the same time, following the Arab Spring, Sufi shrines were destroyed by holier-than-thou Salafis as smacking of idol worship. All three of Ahmed's facets are embodied in a well-rounded Muslim: Deoband (orthodox, traditionalist), Aligarh (liberal) and Ajmer (Sufi).

Any reform attempt is stuck with the scientific and industrial revolution spawned by the West and capitalism over the past two centuries. Traditionally, there is no lack of inventiveness in the Muslim world. In the past, Muslim scientist-philosophers conjured up mechanical devices though more for amusement that profit, preserved technologies inherited from past civilizations which were useful in agriculture and crafts, but never developed the West's passion to use reason merely to 'make money', including 'things' which would harm the umma. The rapid advance in killing machines and firearms (the rifle, machine gun, grenade, bombs, drones, poison gas, WMDs) developed since the Middle Ages all came from the West. The results of technopoly's indiscriminate pursuit of profit include production forces and products which are useful, but also many which are harmful—and worse yet, a consumer lifestyle and tolerance for war and aggression that arguably outweighs the 'good' in our goods.

Pursuing their 'reason-based' projects, the Muslim (liberal) political nationalists in the 1920s–1950s and the (primarily socialist) economic nationalists in the 1950s–1980s failed to create vibrant independent, secular states, both capitulating to neoliberal capitalism and/or invasion by the 1990s. There was no place at the center's table for the Muslim johnny-come-latelies. The lack of a vigorous traditionalist Islamic response—except by the Muslim Brotherhood and in Iran—shows how misguided is the patience of academic Islamists, who, like the Sufis, stress the need "to revive ethics by reforming Islamic society from within"[18] and reject political activism.

Meaningful engagement in the political process opposing the continual encroachment of imperialism, whether by traditional Islamists, Sufis, socialists/ Marxists, or even liberals, is essential. This inner-outer dialectic of social development is a variation on the revelation-reason dialectic; it is not enough to wait for people's inner transformation through *dawa* and education—but no transformation will take place if the umma lacks spirituality and is illiterate.

That is, of course, unless we take the Saudi/Gulf road, which gambles that one can have one's cake and eat it—use the imperial map, live high off the capitalist hog and somehow preserve the faith on the side by distributing Qurans to help individuals transform, in the pious hope that they will stumble upon the 'straight path' in the end. The ecological record of the Saudis and Gulf monarchies, along with their key role in propping up imperialism over the past half century, and the neo-Wahhabi reaction—'Islamic terrorism', undermine the credibility of this option. The Wahhabis, like the liberals, ended up supporting the imperialists, and neo-Wahhabis use revolutionary Enlightenment tactics to try to defeat imperialism through violent revolution, which they suppose will result from their terrorist acts. Both fall into the traps laid by their nemesis.

The communists got half the answer: mobilize politically to get rid of interest and distribute profit rationally, harness technology to social welfare, introduce systemic elements to buttress the pillar of morality. But in their rush to embrace secular truth, they too suppressed spirituality, undermining their system in the end. 'Man shall not live by bread alone.'[19]

Each century brings its reformer/ renewer (*mujadid*), according to a hadith of Abu Daud, referring to such figures as Shafii, Hanbal, Ghazali and Ibn Taymiya. The year 1400HE (1979) marked the beginning of the end for the Soviet anti-capitalist experiment, and the triumph of Islam in Iran under Khomeini, starting the era not of end-of-history capitalism, but of the Islamic-led revolt against secularism.

Can the Arab Springers move beyond the western economic straightjacket by repositioning traditional Islam into the center of life in all its aspects? Iran's theocratic answer to western secularism will not be duplicated in the Arab world even in Shia-majority Iraq, but theocentric Islamic traditionalists are in power in some fashion—or soon could be—almost everywhere in the umma. Unlike the neo-Wahhabis, they will not be going away soon, and will increasingly work together, unless the imperialists once again succeed in *their* 'traditionalist' policies of 'divide and conquer'. Number one on the agenda of all reformers and even the Wahhabis is Wali-Allah's greater literacy, which is essential to meaningful reform, and will contribute to Islam's long term renewal.

The ultimate stumbling block for skeptics is religion's belief in 'the afterlife'. What of the Quran's visions of the afterlife, the fires of Hell and the gardens and flowing streams of Heaven? This work cannot pretend to provide answers to such theological questions, other than to hint that the realm of the spirit is beyond our conception, that it is anybody's guess what 'soul' and 'spirit' or consciousness really mean, or even whether 'there is an afterlife'. Humans are not just motivated by physical needs but by a shared perception of reality within which a community exists, requiring a set of symbols. And what more appropriate symbols for inner peace for the first Muslims—surrounded by the harsh desert—than gardens and rivers?

There is no need for a concrete heaven/ hell, as Islamic philosophers from Farabi, Ibn Sina and Ibn Rushd to Iqbal, Asad and Sardar have argued. And not only Muslims and People of the Book, but most non-Muslims can be assured of eventual salvation[20] by belief in the oneness of God, as Ghazali argues in *The Decisive Criterion for Distinguishing Belief from Unbelief*. Ibn Sina's "return is to the same place whence one came",[21] or Iqbal's argument that heaven and hell are representations of inner character and states of mind rather than locations, suggest that the Quranic visions of the afterlife can be understood as inspiring metaphors rather than physical realities.

The essence of belief in the Hereafter, our continuation beyond this life, is a kind of answer to:
- 'Why do bad things happen to good people?'

The answer:
- 'Because while humans cannot always understand God's greater plan

or fathom beyond the immediate or apparent effect of events, it will all be resolved with justice in the Hereafter, where each soul will be rewarded according to the merits of his deeds and belief.'

'The Hereafter' (whatever it is) is "exactly the reason to persevere in doing as much good as one is able, despite the bad things that happen".[22] A balance of hope and fear is what characterizes a Muslim's attitude towards one's eternal state, serving as a deterrent against wrongdoing and assurance of divine mercy. In the Sufi Sardar's view, paradise is not a place of arrival but a way of traveling, a kind of continual becoming, a way of thinking and questioning, which requires constant attention and questioning to ensure the right path is being taken as the landscape and surroundings continually change. The metaphors of the Quran are "guides to shape these journeys",[23] codewords for the fact that we can never understand the higher dimensions of the world beyond our current level of consciousness.

As for soul and spirit, the existence of higher levels of consciousness has been 'proved' by science at least indirectly, by registering sensory-motor effects of EEG brain patterns during meditation, though a "deep science of the spirit" requires the experimenter himself to meditate to experience the inner realm of spirit. EEG is merely external evidence, but the 'value' (vs 'fact') of the experience requires that the individual enter the experience, not merely record its physical manifestations.[24]

If indeed we have the potential within for spirituality (inner voices from the right hemisphere), why do we even need a prophet like Muhammad? Why not just 'listen to the inner voice'? The answer: Very few people are able to understand the inner voice that speaks in them. Most of us are trammeled by our personal interests and desires. To follow 'one's own heart' would lead to moral chaos.

Going beyond the simple question of 'Is there a God', Robert Wright[25] posits that the advent of man and the first civilizations heralded a new process of evolution—cultural evolution—allowing large scale social organization and extreme division of labor (viz., a self-aware anthill). This corresponds to the Axial Age theory, when monotheism arose. Negative- and zero-sum games are over time replaced by positive-sum games. This is clear in Islam, which strives to replace the negative-sum game of war[26] and the basic 'Invisible Hand' positive-sum game of trade, with higher order ones based on a moral bottom line (the law of equity in sharia). What is the "beautiful loan" which reaps a manifold reward (57:11) but a positive-sum transaction, brought about by following the Quran?

For a Muslim, God is immanent in the patterns of daily life, physical and mental work. Religion is the living embodiment of the moral truth, which helps people align themselves with the moral axis of the universe. By thanking God, asking God to help them stay righteous, seeking forgiveness from God for lapses, people can strive to live a moral life. This is possible without religion, but requires a highly developed moral sense.

In Wright's terms, the 'designer' is both a meta-natural-selection process (as witnessed in life and nature around you) *and* something inside you, an incarnation of nonzero-sum logic. The moral imagination was 'designed'/ evolved by what secularists would call "natural selection" to help us cooperate (i.e., exploit positive-sum opportunities). *This* is 'enlightened self-interest', not the Invisible Hand, which reduces positive-sum trade to a zero-sum game for the (selfish) individual trader, and which ignores the vital (moral/ ethical) question of how the increased wealth is distributed.

However, after a certain point, accumulation of physical wealth and population growth is counterproductive for both individual, society and Nature. The culturally-evolved 'instinct' for cooperation then passes on via knowledge/ learning rather than physically via genetics. This suggests that man's higher purpose is not just the mundane transmission of genes on earth, but rather to transcend the material realm, to 'return to God' (Hegel, Ibn Sina), creating and ensuring the continuity of *God's* realm here and now, where worship, self-reflecting, and suffering is understood as *soul*-building.

This social 'instinct', the converse of zero-sum logic, is the very essence of morality, the essence of Abrahamic logic—social salvation through individual moral behavior. Where this cultural innovation came from is a seeming miracle.[28] Wright calls it the "evolution of God". It is now embodied for eternity in the 'word of God', most clearly in the Quran. To benefit from it, one must be open to others' worldviews to facilitate nonzero-sum interactions, "beautiful loans", which require tolerance and universalism. The greatness of the Abrahamic scriptures is to reveal "the coherence of the relationship between social order and moral truth".[29] This is nothing but James's "alignment with the moral axis of the universe",[30] the Stoics' belief that happiness is attuning one's life and character to the Logos or universal reason which orders all things, and the Cynics' belief that virtue is its own reward. To be free is to live in conformity with God's will. The Sufi's 'God is love', in cultural evolutionary terms, proceeded from family and race (Judaism), to fellow believers (Christianity) and then to all (Islam).

The Caliphate is the Islamic Version of Globalization

Those who approve of, or at least are resigned to our postmodern moral flatland see the collapse of the Caliphate and the Soviet Union as proof of Thatcher's TINA—there is no room for a multi-ethnic world order which is not based on profit and interest.

But critics of the post-imperial world, if it is to survive at all, realize that, on the contrary, we must move towards a political and economic map with morality at the center, moving beyond the material concerns of existence, returning humanity to the natural order. Capitalism, based on exploitation, is the root cause of the current world financial crisis, characterized by massive currency speculation (90% of all financial transactions),[31] weak, unstable governments blackmailed by the interests of empire, leading to environmental devastation and outright war and piracy. As more and more states are undermined and 'conquered' by the American empire and chained to the international financial system, and the threat of war continues, we are slowly being brought to the brink of the Armageddon preached by the Axial Age religions.

Soon after Islam was founded, it spread quickly around the world. Islam continued to thrive and expand its reach over the centuries, despite invasion and setbacks. The past three centuries have witnessed the attempt to destroy Islam through invasion and/or the import of western secularism just as today attempts to discredit Islam are made through linking it to terrorism. The goal of the New World Order is to make the entire world capitalist, functioning according to the dictates of a globalized, coordinated system of central banks and based on the Almighty Dollar as global currency. The resilience of Islam in the face of this onslaught has been remarkable. Animist civilizations, from the natives of North America to Borneo, continue to disappear along with their languages and priceless understanding of Nature and social organization. Only Islamic civilization has survived relatively intact in the face of imperialism.

Interestingly, the fuel driving the imperial system physically—oil—is found predominantly in Muslim countries, where imperialism's vital principle of 'money making money' (interest) is condemned. No doubt Marx would sigh if he were to be told that "Yes, world capitalism is doomed to collapse, but so is socialism, and it is ancient Islam that will survive to rebuild economic relations built on stewardship of Nature, social justice, the gold standard and prayer."

Muslims base their identity first and foremost on Islam. Islam being a universal religion, they will overcome nationalism and work together to realize the Quran's ideal state. The very concept of nationalism is a western one and became the predominant political force surprisingly late, only with the triumph of capitalism and the ascendancy of secularism in the nineteenth century. It reached its most criminal form in Nazi Germany and today in the US and Israel. It must be abandoned in favor of the unity of all Muslims, rejecting the ineffectual, postmodern nationalist regimes sponsored by imperialism—first British and now American—that keep Muslims divided.

The collapse of the Caliphate did not end Islam as a unifying anti-imperialist force, just as the collapse of the Soviet Union did not end the appeal of socialism as the secular anti-imperialist counterpart to Islam. The impact of the Arab Spring—the Islamic reawakening—will continue to be felt in the Muslim world as a clarion call for Muslims to unite around their beliefs to find a way out of the current global nightmare.

There are more than 60 million Central Asians,[32] with rich resources and ethnically close peoples. When combined with Turkey's 75 million, Iran's 75 million, the Indian subcontinent's 480 million, the Middle East's 230 million and southeast Asia's 220 million, it is easy to envision a superpower in the making second only to China and more diverse, based on a unifying belief system grounded in social justice, not ethnicity, greed and violence.

The time for reconstituting the Caliphate, uniting Muslims throughout the Middle East and Central Asia and on to Indonesia and Malaysia, is coming. The dominant influence that British and US imperialism (the Soviet Union/ Russia, too) have enjoyed, training and propping up secular political leaders (fluent in English or Russian and trained in the London, Washington or Moscow), will soon be over. The Soviet Union pushed too far in trying to incorporate Afghanistan into the socialist fold, and the US even farther with its invasions of Afghanistan and Iraq. Just as imperialism destroyed its secular nemesis, the Soviet Union, in the region, it has been hard at work ever since undermining any Islamic alternative there.

Now, with mass literacy—only a prospect by the 1970s in the Muslim world—and instantaneous worldwide communications via the post-1990 rise of the internet, there is the possibility of more widespread debate and *ijtihad,* and the possibility of creating many and then one government inspired by Islam as a "crystallization of political idealism based on religious community and concord".[33]

The project for a renewed caliphate will seek to take the place of the imperialist project, which left a painful trail of tribal and linguistic divisions, disrupted trade routes, declining local economies, and quisling local leaders tied to the center, caught in a vicious circle of war and exploitation. What better argument for the logic of a renewed caliphate today: dissolve the artificial borders (already effectively removed by global neoliberalism), provide a common, truly just legal code, and protect minority communities of belief, as under the original caliphate more than a millennium ago?

Postmodernism is the new imperial western culture that pretends to give marginalized cultures a voice, but actually undermines their worldviews as they join the marketplace of globalized cultures. Here, all are equal and increasingly the same—though some cultures (western pop culture) are decidedly 'more equal than others' not because they are inherently better but because they are the postmodern versions of the missionaries of yore, arriving in the wake of the western guns and briefcases. A similar situation holds for religion in general, as all religions are okay now, as is the lack of religion, or the defamation of religion (especially Islam).

An alternative, "transmodernism", a synthesis between tradition that is open to change, and "a new form of modernity that respects the values and lifestyles of traditional cultures",[34] recalling Davutoglu's vision of Turkey as a "litmus test of globalization", is beginning to take shape in the Middle East, where a new Turkey-Iran-Egypt axis is becoming a reality. How and when Africa, the Levant, Central Asia, the Indian subcontinent, Iran and southeast Asia will join in is not so clear. With cyber grassroots activism picking up steam in the West and with the continued renewal of Islam around the world, this will eventually lead to a coalition of forces determined to bring morality and ethics back into the world. The major stumbling blocks are the unholy pact of the Saudi/Gulf monarchies with imperialism, and the continued colonial enterprise of Israel. Overcoming these will depend on when the US dollar loses its hegemony and how the US will adapt to the collapse of its empire.

So far, the US and Israel have dominated the Middle East as a non-Muslim pretender to the caliph's throne. When they are dethroned, the main contender as neocaliph is **Turkey**. The revival of Islam in Turkey can put it in a position to both bring Islam to Europe as a moral force, and at the same time, embrace the Muslim world to the south and east. The only solution to the ethnic conflicts in Central Asia, for the Kurds, and the externally exacerbated Sunni-Shia divide is to base society on its one common denominator: Islam.

Turkey's recent renewal of ties with both Iran and the Arab world under the AKP has been dubbed neo-Ottoman. A less pejorative description is Davutoglu's vision, similar to Ramadan's, where the imperial periphery reasserts its authority and unity, and begins its 'soft invasion' of the imperial center through immigration, bringing with it Islam. The EU will be transformed through this multiculturalism, including a renewal of Christianity in dialogue with Islam, where Islam acts as an "inoculation" against moral disease, and Turkey acts as a catalyst for world civilizational change.

At the Leaders of Change summit (2011) in Istanbul, Davutloglu said, "Islam and democracy are side by side" now, and Turkish entry into the European Union will show that "Europe can have a Muslim country." At the sixth Al-Jazeera Forum "The Arab world in transition: Has the future arrived?" in Doha, Qatar a few days earlier, he condemned the colonial divide-and-conquer policies of the 1930s–1950s, carving up the Middle East and cutting the organic relations of Arab countries, and the subsequent Cold War, which distorted and weakened the region and turned nations like Turkey and Syria, which had lived together for centuries, into enemies. We are not witnesses of the end of history, but, on the contrary, the return of the Middle East to "the normal course of history" after a century of distortion, when ancient civilizations were torn apart by the invaders. Davutoglu advised:

> We need to reconstruct and restore the political systems in our region, just as we would rebuild our houses after a tsunami. We must become subjects of change, like the people in Tahrir Square. Turkey understands the region better than others precisely because it is part of the region,

but the people of each country must lead the way. Davutoglu endorsed Erdogan's call to eliminate visas, envisioning a day

> when people can pass from a free Palestine through Istanbul to London. That's our vision. Not building walls around Turkey, but opening up to share with our neighbors. In Cairo,

> we are the Middle East, in Europe we are Europeans. We
> must shape history with all the nations around us.

Erdogan added that this applies to the West too, that following the international financial crisis of the past three years, "we need to develop an economic order based on justice, and a social order based on respect and dignity." Middle East developments today hold out the promise of showing the way towards a "global, political, economic and cultural new order".[35]

When the Soviet Union collapsed, Russia quickly became Turkey's largest trading partner, and Turkey lost its *faux* strategic importance as a NATO outpost. But this was in fact a plus, as it was now able to forge its own rational relations with its neighbors and the world at large, "the renewal of the natural flow of history".

Turkey envisions the equivalent of the European Union or the North America Free Trade Agreement for a reconstructed caliphate, but not based solely on economic relations. Istanbul/ Constantinople as the last seat of the Caliphate has been the natural center and capital of the Middle East since the fourth century, with its long history of ties to the Middle East, the Balkans, North Africa, and as a crossroads of Christianity, Islam and Judaism. Its visa-free regime with Albania, Jordan, Lebanon, Libya and Syria in 2009 and in 2010 with Egypt was a first step.

But its path to regional hegemony is proving to be perilous (see Chapter 4). Its high stakes geopolitical intrigues may derail its neo-Ottoman pretensions, and even turn Turkey into another Pakistan, plagued by neo-Wahhabi insurgents and independence-seeking minorities, next-door to a failed Syrian state. Whatever happens in Syria now, Turkey will have a difficult time incorporating it into a Turkish-led neo-Caliphate, much as Germany has faced severe indigestion after swallowing up the remains of civil-war victim Yugoslavia (not to mention Greece) in the EU.

Turks are not the only claimants. There are the **Saudis** and their sort-of ally, **Qatar**. They both have plenty of money, and the latter has a powerful media tool, Al-Jazeera. They, rather than Turkey, are the main beneficiaries of the NATO attack on Libya, and they have invested a lot of resources in the destabilization of Syria, though events there make it look more and more like a negative-sum game for all sides. So far these premodern accommodationists are working together with both the US and Turkey, and even Egypt's MB.

When the non-Muslims (even Islamophobes) now directly and indirectly ruling the US-Israeli regional 'caliphate' are dethroned, the Saudis will demand the title, as 'guardian of the holy places'—indeed, they think they are the regional hegemon even now—though this will likely not happen. Their close alliance with the US, their absolutist monarchical rule, their Wahhabi brand of Islam cannot unite the various Islams around the world, and their neo-Wahhabi offspring will not be easily placated. The Qatari Sheikh knows this and promotes the more traditionalist, democratic Muslim Brothers everywhere as the logical heirs of the Caliphate to counter the serious Turkish bid. Qatar's shifting alliances at present put it more in league with Turkey than Saudi Arabia, even as Saudi Arabia tries to bring Morocco and Jordan into the GCC fold and cement Arab monarchy as the preferred political path. Just how Qatar's absolute monarch will square his commitment to republicanism is hard to understand.

While **Egypt's** revolution was very much about domestic matters—bread and butter, corruption, repression—it has had wide repercussions regionally and abroad. It's been a long time since Egypt loomed so large in the region, to both friend and foe. Apart from bellwether Tunisia, 12 of the 22 Arab League countries are now affected by the Arab Spring: Algeria, Bahrain, Djibouti, Iraq, Jordan, Libya, Mauritania, Morocco, Sudan, Syria, Yemen and yes, Saudi Arabia. Unrest continues in them all, inspired by Egypt, now the most democratic and open Arab state, led by the MB. But just as powerful has been the resonance in Israel. It has no precedent for an assertive, democratic neighbor—except for Islamist Turkey. Egypt's MB President Morsi made some changes in relations with Israel and Iran, and condemned France's invasion of Mali, but Egypt has far to go in recouping its leadership in the Arab world after 30 years in the wilderness.

Given Turkey and Saudi Arabia's inability to extricate themselves from the US embrace, Egypt holds the key to forcing Israel to finally negotiate a reasonable peace with Palestine, giving backbone to other Arab governments to push Israel to the table. Just as in the days of Nasser, when Egypt led the Arab world against imperialism, today, all Arabs and Muslims have gained a new sense of pride as Egypt's Islamists take control of the reins of power and begin to transform Egypt domestically and regionally.

A Nasserist variant on the Caliphate was proposed by Hamdeen Sobahi in Egypt's 2012 presidential election. He envisions the restructuring of ties between Nasser's three main circles: the Arab circle in which Egypt is a key player; the African circle of the Nile Valley; and the Islamic circle (see Chapter 2) involving the Arabs, the Turks, and the Iranians. "We have all been engaged in proxy wars that benefited America and Israel, not the Arabs and definitely not the Egyptians." He is inspired by policies undertaken by Brazil, Turkey, Indonesia, India, and South Africa. "The revival project we prepared is based on the experience of these five countries. I am particularly impressed with what Lula da Silva did in Brazil, for within eight years he turned the Brazilian economy around. I find the Turkish experience to be quite relevant. And I think that we should take the Iranian economic experiences seriously, especially regarding subsidies."[37] But Sobahi has joined the increasingly militant opposition in Egypt, which appears intent on 'destroying the village to save it' from the Islamists. Egypt's disarray could knock it out of the equation for the foreseeable future.

Probably Turkey is the more realistic claimant than either Egypt or Saudi Arabia: it is a big, prosperous, modern country; its orthodox Islam has a strong touch of Sufism. "Historically, the holy cities of Mecca and Medina were unable to keep the seat of Caliph to themselves; probably they will fail this time, too, unless they are willing to moderate their goals and play second fiddle to Turkey."[38] However, if an Egyptian-Turkish-Iranian alliance can be secured, and decides to take on Israel, the current blockade of Gaza will look like child's play. Egypt controls the Suez Canal, Turkey—the eastern Mediterranean, and Iran—the Persian Gulf. One can only marvel that it has taken over 60 years for Israel's powerful neighbors—with more than 30 times the population of Israel—to realize their collective power and ability to impose a just regional order without any kowtowing to Washington.[39] At the same time, they can easily be sabotaged by a ruthless US-Israeli "empire-and-a-half"[40] which can orchestrate a currency collapse, false-flag terrorism and boycotts through its overwhelming global military and economic power.

How **Pakistan** will fit into this fluid political scenario is difficult to predict. Its status from 'independence' on, as a dysfunctional state, and its long history of subservience to the imperial agendas of both Britain and the US, is a hard legacy to shake. China has been its closest non-US ally since the 1970s, but this also has been strictly an alliance of convenience. The imperial map in AfPak[41] is presumably to be shredded when the US troops pack up, and leave AfPak a series of sectarian, feuding 'nations', whose elites will continue to reach out to the empire (so goes the logic) in the face of holdouts Iran, Russia and China.

But the holdouts—Russia and China, the heirs to the communist foe of yesteryear, Iran the Muslim heir to the anti-communists of yesteryear—are now key players in the current 'great game', the only ones who play to beat the reigning imperialists, not just to hold them to a draw or stalemate. As the prospect of the US losing the game in Iraq and Afghanistan looms, Iran gains greater regional importance, without having to do much except survive the intense efforts by the empire to subvert it. From a distance, China similarly must only be patient, continuing to expand its economic might. Both these countries, unlike AfPak, Libya, Iraq and Syria, are united around a strong sense of historic destiny and national self-awareness—in the end, impossible for the empire to successfully subvert.

America's increasingly unwilling Pakistani ally is increasingly turning to them. In the wake of the recent collapse of US-Pakistani relations (over drones, other 'friendly fire' and a complete disregard for Pakistani sovereignty), Pakistan confirmed its gas pipeline project with Iran would be online by 2013, flouting US pressures to nix the deal and wait for the trans-Afghanistan pipe dream (excuse me, pipeline). Iran need not drop bombs or invade its neighbors (it ended any imperial pretensions in the seventeenth century), but like China, may well seduce them economically. The pipeline will also export gas to Turkey, Armenia and even Iraq. Iran has excellent relations with nearby India, Russia and China. But of course, Pakistan's main lifeline is still the US.

Whether the western intervention in Libya and Syria will turn those 'nations' into willing (if conservative Islamic) allies of imperialism *a la* Saudi

Arabia, Morocco and Pakistan or simply failed states, is yet to be seen. But this is the game plan of the empire.[42] Only by wresting itself from the US embrace, dropping the unrealistic demand that India give up Kashmir unilaterally, and by working with the regional players to stabilize Afghanistan, can Pakistan acquire a worthy role, say, the caliph's vizier, in the process facilitating the transformation of the whole region following US withdrawal in 2014.

Though it can never pretend to the role of caliph, on many fronts, **Iran** holds the key to readjusting the playing field and establishing rules of a new geopolitical game that can lead away from the deadly game being played by the US and Israel, the empire-and-a-half, including in Afghanistan, Iraq, and with implications for nuclear disarmament, EU-US relations, but above all, for the continued role of the dollar as world reserve currency.

Iran's key energy partner is China (12% of its oil comes from Iran). Soon there will be pipelines uniting all of Eurasia, with Iran as the hub. India and Iran are jointly constructing power plants and plan to exchange electricity via Pakistan. Tehran is already exporting electricity to Turkey, Armenia and Afghanistan. As Iran gains experience in nuclear power, it is poised to become the energy powerhouse in Central Asia.[43]

Islamic economics requires a monetary system which is just, not one imposed on an unwilling world by an imperial hegemon. As a step in this direction, Iran has been trying since 2008 to trade all its oil in any currency but dollars, notably the euro, yuan and ruble. This lonely call for free choice of trading currency became a chorus by 2010, most notably from other oil exporters such as Russia, Venezuela, Norway, Beijing—even the Emirates. This is a primary reason (second only to US domestic Zionist pressure) behind the US drive to overthrow the Iranian regime. The end of the petrodollar means the end of the dollar as the world's reserve currency.[44]

Once the imperial playing field is remade—remapped—the chief existing joint structures—the Arab League and the Organization of Islamic Conference—can begin to act more forcefully on behalf of the umma.

Tariq Ramadan criticizes the caliphate project, which he identifies narrowly with Hizb ut-Tahrir. He also criticizes the MB's ground-up mobilizing to achieve the caliphate, claiming both are stuck in the early or mid-twentieth century, subject to "a binary thought process". Turkey and Iran are caught up in *realpolitik*. "Strictly political power is highly relative, subject to impositions, pressures, and influences that reduce, undermine, or altogether prevent its actual exercise." In the age of globalization, "the autonomy of politics" has shrunk, economics is international, the third world is not an independent political power.[45] The global market system was 'created' by imperialism, and has never been 'independent' anyway, and its 'soft states' are still in thrall to the imperial agenda.

Islam today has the makings of a new-old world civilization which, in alliance with socialist efforts in the non-Muslim world, can provide an antidote to the New World Order. For instance, the BRICS are gaining a reputation for working towards a non-imperial world order, having established a development bank in 2013 aimed at breaking the monopoly held by western-backed financial institutions. It will provide a collective foreign exchange reserve for bilateral and multilateral trade deals, and a fund for financing development projects in poor economies, using the BRICS own currencies. China and Brazil have agreed to conduct nearly half their trade without resorting to US dollars.

So far, all of the Arab Spring revolutions are continuing along their neoliberal path by inertia, rather than pursuing a radically different social set-up. This is not surprising, as the elites are all western-trained and the economies are part of the neoliberal global system. Politicians like Ghannouchi will make minor adjustments but can't venture far on their own. They will have to team up with the other anti-imperialist force in the world—the heirs of the communists.

Hugo Chavez of Venezuela and Mahmoud Ahmedinejad of Iran

Both the Islamic and socialist alternatives depend on grassroots organizing ("Think global, act local") to provide a truly democratic alternative to the nation state, long compromised by its ties with global capitalism (and now in the process of being undone by it). This would enable a return to a loosely-knit political organization of the umma (read here: all people concerned with reviving the spiritual side of human life, and with social justice). This is not so radical, as the general consensus in the West among reformers is towards decentralization and reducing the importance of borders, reminiscent of the original intent of the caliphate.

Ramadan rightly bemoans the dumbing down inherent in western-style electoral politics, since the timing of social reforms does not correspond to electoral political schedules[46] but this merely confirms the necessity of supplementing electoral politics with something like the MB's long-term grassroots strategy.

There is much to learn from the West. Egypt will only achieve some return of its stolen wealth if it takes a page from Ecuador's experience. President Rafael Correa fought off the IMF and cut Ecuador's debt in half legally, identifying loans which were knowingly provided to corrupt officials and wasted, and renegotiating Ecuador's foreign debt using the "odious debt" procedure.[47] The rise of "postmaterialism" in the West since the 1970s represents a new morality reacting against consumerism.[48] The new generation in America and Europe lacks the Cold War paranoia about socialism: Americans under 30 are "essentially evenly divided" as to whether they prefer capitalism" or "socialism".[49]

Egyptians support US workers[50]

There is also much for the West to learn from the Islamic experience. The Islamic resurgence has inspired mass political actions such as Boycott Divest and Sanctions (BDS), and the 99% movement and Wisconsin public service worker protests which sprang up shortly after the Arab Spring began in 2011, bringing Arab activists in direct touch with their western counterparts.

The positioning of the Wahhabis at the heart of the empire may not have resulted in many conversions to Islam, but it did allow them to spread copies of the

Quran and build mosques freely around the world and to support the new Muslim immigrant communities in Europe and the US. More in spite of the Wahhabis, there has been a growing appreciation of Islam among disaffected western critics of capitalism, as the modest but steady process of conversion demonstrates.

Muslims, both in the West and in the traditional Muslim world, must ally with western critics of capitalism and imperialism, as "the principles held by Muslims are essentially opposed to the economic logic of today's world."[51] They must not treat the West simply as *dar al-harb*, or in the case of Muslims living in the West, retreat into a ghetto to avoid contamination by western culture. The paradigm is not "A good Muslim is an invisible Muslim" in the West. 'Integrate' does not mean abandoning traditions and beliefs, but 'integrating' them into the local society one lives in. Muslim activist philosophers like Tariq Ramadan insist they don't want special treatment as a "religious minority", but a fair application of secular laws: "real equality for all (Jews, atheists, Muslims)", recognizing that "power and people reading the law in a specific way" can be discriminatory.[52] Western Muslims must discard their "minority" self-perception and integrate,

> find a selective approach to [music, photography, and television]. Not everything produced in the West ... is of very high quality or very moral, but it is erroneous ... to allow it to be thought that everything is perverted and useless. [It is necessary to apply] in a positive way the Islamic principle of integrating all that does not contradict the prohibitions and making it our own...[53]

exactly as did Afghani and Abduh, as the reform movement got underway more than a century ago.

Twenty-first Century *Ijtihad*: Interpreting Sharia in Today's World

Looking back today on the development of Islamic thought, it is clear that, despite the rejection of tribalism inherent in the Quran, tribal traditions were to some extent Islamized and sacralized, obscuring the human origins of certain beliefs and practices.

But then that was even more so in the case of the earlier revelations to the Judaic prophets and Jesus prior to the revelation of the Quran, when Jews and Christians evoked God's "wrath" and went "astray". The rigorously transmitted message of the Quran and the historically documented life of Muhammad have made it much easier to keep to the "straight way". (1:7) The importance of the Quran as the revealed word of God cannot be exaggerated, as it provided a secure basis for maintaining the fundamental truths of Islam over history, and today inspires Muslims in a way unparalleled by other religions.

Not only is there a concern for purifying the practice of tribalism from Islam, there is the dilemma of pushing back and re-evaluating the distortions brought to the umma by imperialism during the past four centuries, with its program for secularizing Muslim societies and integrating them into the capitalist world on the West's terms—using the West's map. This two-pronged re-evaluation requires that the Quran and sunna be interpreted in the historical context, via *tajdid* and *ijtihad*.

The process of *tajdid* and *ijtihad* to derive principles (*maqasid*) for achieving a sustainable society true to the Quran has been the foundation of both the best of Islamic traditionalists and the best of the self-styled Islamic reformers in the past two centuries. In fact, the five pillars of Islam and many of the hadiths are themselves early instances of this careful *tajdid* and *ijtihad*, deriving the fundamental principles of Islam in their day.[54] We invariably are using our reason whenever we think and act, so this process is taking place whether we like it or not. In fact, it is impossible not to do it in any such discourse. For instance, Abduh analyzed the story of David vs the Philistines (2:247-252), deriving 14 propositions about sociopolitical changes, progress and war—"sociological laws of the Quran", with a flavor of social Darwinism, concluding that war was a struggle for existence and hence is part of the natural order. In Chapters 3–4, it was seen how reform programs and actual policies have been hammered out in political, economic and social spheres, using 'reason grounded in revelation', 'revelation grounded in reason'.

Some 'commandments' which fulfill the principles of tawhid, vicegerency and equity of the Quran, and which are also part of the best of western traditionalist/ leftist discourse in some way, would include:

- *Human life is sacrosanct*

"If anyone kills a person unless in retribution for murder or spreading corruption in the land—it is as if he kills all humanity."[55] Capital punishment is a last resort in exceptional cases. "Cut off the hands of thieves ... but if anyone repents after his wrong-doing and makes amends, God will accept his repentance." (5:38–39) The universal principle is justice and fair punishment according to the norms of society. The discourse on murder[56] reveals important principles of Islamic law: equity, compensation and forgiveness. The purpose of punishment is not only retribution, but deterrence and rehabilitation. Concerning *zina* (adultery, rape), the requirements for evidence are rigorous, and confession and repentance are important mitigating factors. (4:15, 24:5)[57]

- *Nature is also sacrosanct*

Man is responsible for God's realm. In the tradition of 'Small is Beautiful',[58] the new science of ecological economics treats the economy as a subcategory of ecology (following the Islamic principle of *tawhid*). We must minimize our use of Nature. "Let there be no change in the work wrought by Allah: that is the true Religion. But most among mankind understand not." (30:30) That *ayat* calls for us to minimize the surplus we extract from Nature, and not to extract for the sole purpose of making profit. Maximize something worthwhile, like efficiency of production, green jobs, renewable energy use, clean air.[59] "If any Muslim plants any plant and a human being or an animal eats of it, he will be rewarded as if he had given that much in charity". Rachel Carson believed that "science and literature had the same aim, which is to 'discover and illuminate truth'." *Silent Spring* (1962) is a model of what Islamic science is about, incorporating the 'Big Three' arts and morality as part of the study of nature. Einstein famously observed that "science without religion is lame, religion without science is blind'."[60]

- *War is strictly circumscribed*

"Fight in the cause of God those who fight you, but do not commit aggression" (2:190). War is for self-defense, the only legitimate enemies are those who wage war against you (22:39). The goal is to persuade the aggressor to cease hostilities. "If they cease, let there be no hostility except to those who practice oppression." (2:193) It is much better to "spend of your substance in the cause of Allah, and make not your own hands contribute to (your) destruction." (2:195) War must fulfill the larger goal of building a just, equitable, open and tolerant society where war no longer necessary (*dar al-islam*). It is not 'war leads to peace' but 'economic development leads to peace.'[61]

- *Usury/ interest must be outlawed*

By removing usury as the basis of our economic relations (2:275–281), we can restore democracy to the economy, and make the state the servant of *people*, not banks and corporations. Usury makes the rich richer and can trap people and states in perpetual debt servitude. Usury undermines the moderation and strong sense of social justice of the (Islamic) 'middle community'. As such,

> usury is a tool of oppression. The Quran is unambiguously on the side of the poor. ... It is not just an issue of social and economic justice but also of morality ... Usury generates a love of wealth per se, makes us selfish, and leads us to think like Gordan Gekko in the film *Wall Street*, that 'Greed is Good'. *R-b-a* contains the idea of 'the exploitation of the economically weak by the strong and resourceful'. These verses were among the last to be revealed, and their vagueness is a blessing in disguise, as exploitation 'morphs into any shape and size, and devours anything in its path. It takes different forms in different societies, depending on the

principle modes of production and technological status.'[62]

In today's context, combating usury demands making banks public utilities. In the Marxian equation

$$M - C - P - C1 - M1,^{63}$$

the M − M1 surplus (realized in capitalism as profit and interest) must be acknowledged as a positive-sum social 'free good' (value added from work, the service of the administrative state, the financier/ capitalist catalyst, etc.), where money is advanced by the state on behalf of the people, and doesn't 'cost' society anything. As Qutb (and Marx) dreamed, the state to a large extent 'withers away', becomes decentralized, a regulatory collection and distribution agency, like the umma, governed by sharia.

- *Distribution must be equitable*

While it's okay to be (slightly) rich, striving for material wealth per se is haram, and wealth should be shared.

> Only two may be rightly envied: a man whom Allah has given wealth and thereupon endowed him with the strength to give it away in the cause of justice, and a man whom Allah has given wisdom and who acts in its spirit and imparts it to others.[64]

There should be a socially agreed system for the just distribution of wealth, beginning with the family and extending to the whole of society and humanity. (2:215, 273–274) Zakat can be reformed to "establish a real system of collective solidarity and social security, woven into the very fabric of society, that aims at freeing the poor from their dependence so that eventually they themselves will pay zakat."[65] This proactive charity is like "grains of corn that produce seven ears, each bearing a hundred grains." (2:264) Charity must be redefined as a right which the poor have on the wealthy, to be regarded as the latter's duty rather than reflecting their generosity. The intent is to try to overcome the divisions in society, not highlight the distinctions between haves and have-nots.

- *There should be a sense of cultural restraint within a moral/ ethical order*

Culture must recognize limits. Art and beauty are integral to science and morality (the Big Three)—David sang praises to God, "You mountains, echo God's praises together with him, and you birds, too." (34:10) But, "There is the sort of person who pays for distracting tales, intending, without any knowledge, to lead others from God's way, and to hold it up to ridicule." (31:6). Art is contemplative, expressing "an encounter with the Divine Presence".[66] Culture must help to improve our ethical behavior, and "turn anger into calm, grief into joy, depression into a state of relaxation, avarice into generosity, cowardice into bravery."[67] Traditional Islamic society operated on the principle of social order, where sanctions on behavior and promotion of art were intended to strengthen society, not artificially create excitement, tension and turmoil, as in the West today.

- *'Means' cannot be separated from 'ends'*

While 'ends' remains theoretical and not part of one's immediate politico-historic reality, 'means' constitutes one's practical activity and lived-experience. It is the means which over time shapes one's ends. That which **leads to** haram **is** haram. The Islamic deen governs one's ego—the inner jihad—as well as society, making sharia, its civilizational legal expression, a societal 'path to salvation' rather than just a 'set of orders'.

> The task of following the right path is extensive and all-inclusive: it touches all aspects of human life ... Balance and equity apply across the whole range of human life. The insights and lessons of spiritual discipline apply to and operate in all the mundane aspects of our human nature and daily life.[68]

Islam overcomes Koestler's commissar-yogi dilemma. Morality doesn't end with the Quran, but rather begins with the Quran ('Don't just adapt to reality, transform it!'). There is much outside the Quran to discover using the moral principles of the Quran and sunna.

- *Muslims have an existential obligation to 'enjoin what is right, and forbid what is wrong' (3:104)*

This fundamentally differentiates the umma from the non-Muslim world, and defines the umma's primary obligation as an embodiment of Divine Will. This includes social and foreign policy as well as personal behavior. At the international level, replacing existing agencies with ones committed to equitable and sustainable distribution of wealth, say, a Global Asset and Investment Agency replacing the WB, a Fair Trade Organization replacing the WTO ("and do not undercut one another in business transactions"[69]), an International Clearing Union replacing the IMF with its own international currency, an Authority for Debt Adjustment and the Elimination of Tax Havens.[70] Where 'wrongs' such as poverty, moral corruption, etc. are a product of the system, Muslim politics must change the system.[71]

These principles and goals can be applied to an analysis of governments struggling to implement an Islamic agenda. It is up to an educated, activist umma to push their governments to follow Islam in their policies, using such principles.

During his presidency, Egyptian President Morsi found himself in an impossible situation, as the system cannot be changed overnight by any party, including the MB. His attempts to implement Islamic civilization met with open sabotage by the still powerful military and secular elites. The constitution which the elected parliament passed and which won 64% in a referendum called for Azhar to be consulted to ensure that laws passed are not in violation with the Quran and sunna.[72] If the new constitution preserves this, there is some hope that the halting steps of Egypt's first Islamic government will not have been in vain.

Though the "nation state" is inherited from imperialism and a given at this stage, will there be a program to unite the broader umma over time? Iran's chairing of the Non-Aligned Movement is an indication of how an "Islamic state" can promote both unification of the umma and religious pluralism.

Morsi continued many of Mubarak's policies, in particular, the IMF loan, the raids on Islamic militants in Sinai, and the continuation of the Peace Accord with Israel. Could these policies have been justified in terms of fiqh principles of necessity (darura) and coercion (mukrih), allowing them as temporary measures or even permanent measures? Because the MB chose "to gain control over a political system which is in itself a proxy regime and of significant geopolitical interest to regional and international hegemonic players",[74] it had to work extra hard to justify itself. It did not get a free ride, as would a secular liberal regime which implicitly accepts assimilation.

Then there is the IMF hovering over the region, trying to make sure there is no radical challenge to its hegemony. Resolving the dilemma of how to extricate the umma from the straightjacket of neocolonialism using Islamic means to achieve Islamic ends requires more than just the electoral assimilationist map. The MB forged a grassroots action program during the twentieth century, based on the revelation-reason dialectic, which will continue to play an important role in mobilizing the umma to support changes. Other forces for change, both secular and religious-based, will also play an important role in moving forward (or undermining any attempt at following an Islamic path, as so far has been the case). Shaping viable and desirable futures for a Muslim civilization must involve the active participation of communities and conscious effort at consultation (*shura*) at all levels of society with the aim of achieving a broad consensus (*ijma*).

***

The three monotheisms have followed very different paths in the past three centuries: Christianity morphed into an embrace of secularism, Judaism morphed into Zionism—a secularized religion of race. Their cooperation extends even to the fundamentalists among them, who—Christian or Jewish—are determined to speed up history and bring the 'end times' closer, defying God with the creation and expansion of the world's last colony, in the heart of the Muslim world.

Islam has not been transformed by capitalism/ imperialism. True, it has spawned many reform movements, determined to use the principles of *ijtihad, ijmaa, shura,* etc. to make sure Islam remains healthy in a very problematic and complex reality. But for those who believe Islam to be the perfection of monotheism, indeed of religion as a whole, containing the seeds for realizing God's order in the world, it is more a matter of rediscovering the essence of Islam, of educating the umma and uniting it again—now via modern telecommunications technology, of adapting the many possibilities inherent in the world order today to the needs of God's order.

All the various currents of Islam in the world today—from premodern accommodationists (Saudi, Qatar, UAE) to quasi-revolutionary traditionalists (the MB and Shia), neo-Wahhabi terrorists and Sufis—are in for the long haul. For them, it is the West that needs another Reformation/ Enlightenment to bring justice and the realm of the spirit back into the daily lives of both humans and the natural world, our inner lives and world culture. To move towards the era of postsecularism.

Who knows, maybe those liberals who opt to work inside the system have time on their side. The premodern Saudis reason that they might as well sit back and enjoy the fruits of capitalism, waiting it out as it declines and Islam endures. Even assimilationists like Mubarak, by allowing enough freedom of organization, and bowing to the continued strength of Islam, wittingly or unwittingly leave room for Islam to return, as was so graphically shown in 2011.

Similarly, those working outside the system, the stubborn Deoband traditionalists, as epitomized by the Muslim Brotherhoods, refuse to lie down and die, rising like the phoenix each time they are banned and/or killed by the fearful capitalists. But both traditionalists and their neo-Wahabbi nemesis should learn from the fate of the Soviet Union, as they ponder their anti-imperialist strategies: mobilizing the people against a formidable empire is a daunting task, and killing innocents in the name of God is not going to lead to a happy ending for anyone.

Then there are the Sufis, who have held aloof during the past centuries of struggle. As the Mongols destroyed the infrastructure of the caliphate and then weakened themselves, the anarchic Sufis were able to pick up the pieces to some extent and propagate a positive vision of the faith in the grim aftermath of the invasions, attracting followers of many ethnic backgrounds. As the various Islamic factions fight it out among themselves and against the imperialists in the political ring, perhaps the Sufis' message of love will be the one that most inspires the post-postmodern world.

Though Sufism has mostly been absent from this consideration of the re-emergent Islamic civilization, it is very much a part of the coming order, as the human world dismantles its obsession with the material and develops a robust "political spirituality". Guenon was convinced that the present order must collapse before a new one based on spirituality arises, in the eastern tradition of cyclical ages which rise and fall. Sufism's behind-the-scenes role throughout this work shows both its enduring value and at the same time its irrelevance for precipitating concrete change in the here and now.

We must marvel at the resilience of Islam, that in the face of the current decline of civilization, it is alive and well, inspiring, providing succor, unlike the tattered threadbare socialist secular ideology or the bankrupt (literally) capitalist one, not to mention the impotent remains of Christianity and the lethal racialist doctrine which Judaism in its Zionist phase has become. After the last bank closes, after the last rainforest is chopped down, after the last Israeli drone drops its bombs and the Jews flee their 'eternal' city for the safety of their true spiritual home—the secular West—people will be spreading their prayer mats in response to the plaintive call of the muezzin and worshipping together, celebrating the oneness of the Almighty.

The very fact that capitalism, having destroyed the socialist alternative, is now so demonizing Islam in western discourse should alert us to its vital role as the last great protagonist to capitalism. The underground political Islam of the past century (the MB, Qutb and the neo-Wahhabis) is the product of imperialism, "the offspring of modernity rather than of tradition".[75]

But that is not to condemn all Islamists who seek to transform the global imperial order. Islam has always been 'political', embraced throughout history by all races and social strata in reaction to oppression, inspired by its positive-sum outcomes, and its ability to address our deepest needs. Rather, it is to recognize the importance of history and the social and economic forces shaping it, for Islam as well as for the rest of us. Today, Islam has 'merely' assumed the anti-imperialist burden which the Soviet Union once carried and collapsed under.

There is a future other than the one of pushing the secular rock up the mountain. It is not one where Muslims come hat in hand to their socialist Sisyphean brothers, but one where people of all faiths come to the support of their Muslim brothers and sisters, as we are in fact witnessing today with the outpouring of sympathy for the Palestinians, unfortunately less so for the Afghans, Iraqis and Iranians resisting the ongoing western colonial steamroller. The struggles of these Muslims today is most definitely a jihad, opposing the forces of dissipation and chaos both within and outside themselves. Defeat does not matter, because it is by fighting this 'war' "that we become what we are".[76]

Eaton's rejection of modernity and embrace of Islam from a conservative inspiration parallels Foucault's rejection and embrace from a leftist one. Many other thinkers, such as Rida and Iqbal made similar journeys over their lifetimes, reaffirming the uniqueness of Islam and its continued relevance today. As Islamic civilization re-emerges, it will inspire others in the two journeys that everyone must make, and where all life and all aspects of our life activity are sacred.

ENDNOTES

1   Comte's positivism and the empirical approach to knowledge grounded upon

observation and verifiable facts.

2   As Marx pointed out, man's nature is shaped by social conditions, so we can never really know what it is. In Islamic thinking, man's nature is similarly shaped by his environment. See, for instance, Yasien Mohamed, "Ibn Taymiyyah's view on Fitrah", islaam.net, 1996.

3   At the 1982 Conservative Party Conference, Prime Minister Thatcher announced, "There is no such thing as society."

4   Though primarily an artistic movement, such writers as Jean Jacques Rousseau, Henry David Thoreau and Thomas Carlyle critiqued modernism from a romantic point of view.

5   Foucault acknowledged this when he added "the axis of ethics" to "the axis of knowledge" and "the axis of power" in his later writing. See Michel Foucault, "What Is Enlightenment? (1984) quoted in Janet Afary and Kevin Anderson, Foucault and the Iranian Revolution: Gender and the Seductions of Islamism, USA: University of Chicago Press, 2005, 137.

6   Sohrab Behdad and Farhad Nomani (eds), Islam and the Everyday World: Public Policy Dilemmas, New York: Routledge, 2006, 114.

7   "Dialogue between Michel Founcault and Baqir Parham", in Afary, Foucault and the Iranian Revolution, 76.

8   "A Powder Keg Called Islam" Corriere della sera, 13 Feburary 1979, in Afany, Foucault and the Iranian Revolution, 108.

9   See Chapter 1 Appendix B: The 'Protestant' ethic, the rise of New Ageism and fundamentalism. Also Hassan Hanafi, "Facts and Values: An Islamic Approach", In Mehran Kamrava (ed.), The New Voices of Islam: Rethinking Politics and Modernity, A Reader, USA: University of California Press, 2006.

10   "Eurocentricity is a singular idea of modernity, which privileged a white band of predatory colonialists in Europe, and disenfranchised the rest of humanity (includlng the disenfranchised classes inside Europe)." Dabashi advocates an alternative socialist, secular "emancipatory and universal modernity". In Hamid Dabashi, Iran: A People Interrupted, New York: New Press, 2007, 98. Bayat talks of "post-Islamism", Dabashi of "post-ideology" and "radical emancipation" and a "new geography of liberation". In Hamid Dabashi interview, jadaliyya. com, 10 June 2012.

11   Originally the intent of 'separation of church and state' was to protect Protestants and Jews from Catholic persecution in Europe, and to ensure no one religious group could monopolize state power in the US (see Chapter 1 Appendix B), not to divorce morality/ ethics from politics.

12   "It is better not to seek paradise but proximity to God. Paradise of the Quran is Paradise of His good pleasure, of the Infinite. Nothing can be added to the Paradise of the Infinite, so only nothing can enter it. Seek to be nothing here and now." In Ziauddin Sardar, Desperately seeking paradise: journeys of a sceptical Muslim, UK: Granta, 2005.

13   Both traditional Muslim teachings and the Sufi mystical trend in Islam fit E. F. Schumacher's (1911–1977) requirement for a balance between the four fields of knowledge arising from combining two pairs: Myself and the World (individual vs social); and Outer Appearance and Inner Experience. Each field of knowledge has its own validity claims and approach to studying the world. See Schumacher's A Guide for the Perplexed (1977).

14   Friedman argues that globalization has made the world a level commercial playing field. See Thomas Friedman, The World is Flat: A Brief History of the Twenty-first Century (2005).

15   Seyyed Hossein Nasr, Islam in the Modern World: Challenged by the West, Threatened by fundamentalism, Keeping faith with Tradition, USA: Harper One, 2010, 142.

16   Ibid., 107.

17   You cannot "choose between liberation and salvation. The end of my libera-

tion should be salvation and the end of salvation is liberation, liberation from my ego, the hold of war, oppression, colonialism, alienation." Tariq Ramadan, lecture at revivingtheislamicspirit.com, 12 December 2012.

18 Nasr, Islam in the Modern World, 277. Nasr argues the traditionalist school opposes the gaining of worldly power and any surrender to worldliness in the name of Islam, never forgetting the Quranic injunction, 'The other world is better for you than this world.' Its sacred name should not be used in the politico-economic arena, where the very nature of the forces involved can only sully it. Ibid., 12, 277.

19 Matthew 4:4. The priority of the spiritual journey is the universal 'truth' of both Christianity and Islam.

20 See Quran 2:62, 5:69.

21 Based on 89:27–28 "(To the righteous soul will be said:) "O (you) soul, in (complete) rest and satisfaction! Come back you to your Lord—well pleased (yourself), and well-pleasing unto Him!" Marcia Hermansen "Eschatology". In Tim Winter (ed.), The Cambridge Companion to Classical Islamic Theology, UK: Cambridge University Press, 2008, 313.

22 Ziauddin Sardar, Reading the Qur'an: The Contemporary Relevance of the Sacred Text of Islam, UK: Oxford University Press, 2011, 276.

23 Sardar, Desperately seeking paradise.

24 Evidence shows the soul level "meditation with form" is characterized subjectively by love, compassion and altruism, and objectively by brain hemispheric synchronization. The spiritual level is characterized subjectively by an expanded sense of self, compassion, love, care, responsibility and objectively the cessation of alpha, beta, theta brainwaves and an increase in delta waves associated with deep, dreamless sleep. The 'highest' level of "formless meditation" is experienced subjectively as infinite freedom, and objectively the cessation of all mental activity. See Ken Wilber, A Brief History of Everything, USA: Shambhala 2000.

25 Robert Wright, Nonzero: the logic of human destiny, USA: Vintage, 2001.

26 War enforces cooperation within the tribe, and stimulates technical invention, but only one side 'benefits', by looting the conquered. Both sides lose men and materiel.

27 Another positive-sum formulation involving no material exchange is the prisoner's dilemma of whether to squeal on your fellow accused, where cooperation also leads to a positive-sum outcome.

28 A leading mainstream neuroscientist posits that the brain could be like a radio receiver, a receptacle for picking up signals from some mysterious 'elsewhere' via neural circuitry, that the scientist's narrow work to study the mechanics of the brain would be like a primitive man analyzing a radio receiver. But, "what about the signals?" David Eagleman, Incognito: The Secret Lives of the Brain, Viking, 2011, 222.

29 Robert Wright, The Evolution of God, USA: Little Brown, 2009, 433.

30 Ibid., 435.

31 <http://www.leftfootforward.org/2012/10/financial-transaction-tax-an-idea-whose-time-has-come/>

32 <http://www.universalnewswires.com/centralasia/tajikistan/viewstory.aspx?id=13799>

33 Dale Eickelman and James Piscatori, Muslim Politics, USA: Princeton University Press, 1996, 27.

34 Sardar, interview by Mustafa Nazir Ahmad, The News on Sunday. In The Reformist, Karachi, 23 November 2008.

35 Eric Walberg, "Turkey and the Middle East: Carpe diem", Al-Ahram Weekly, 23 March 2011.

36 After initially vetoing NATO operations in Libya, Turkey provided five ships, one submarine and a squadron of fighter jets to enforce a narrowly defined

no-fly-zone, the most significant contribution of all NATO members, but on the condition that no Libyans were killed, whoever they supported. Its policy in Syria is much more puzzling.

37 Hamdeen Sabahi interviewed by Ahmed Eleiba, Ahram Online, 6 April 2012. Iran has provided generous subsidies to low income families since the revolution.

38 Israel Shamir, "The Arab Autumn", israelshamir.net, 2012.

39 Eric Walberg, "Turkey redraws Sykes-Picot", Al-Ahram Weekly, 30 September 2011.

40 See Walberg, Postmodern Imperialism.

41 A term coined when Richard Holbrooke became Obama's special envoy to Afghanistan and Pakistan in 2009.

42 Eric Walberg, "When will Pakistan's spring arrive?", Al-Ahram Weekly, 1 December 2011.

43 The Iranian 'nuclear problem' is not enriching uranium for WMDs, but development of the very nuclear power for peaceful purposes which Iran repeatedly cites, supposedly merely to soothe western anxieties.

44 There is a direct linkage between a country being forced to buy oil in dollars and (thus dollar) government reserve requirements that thereby prop up the dollar, no matter how large the US trade imbalance or US government debt. And, 'Beware, potential Husseins/Ahmedinejads, don't even think of boycotting US dollars out of distaste for US wars.'

45 Tariq Ramadan, Radical Reform: Islamic Ethics and Liberation, UK: Oxford University Press, 2009, 266, 287.

46 Ibid., 288.

47 Through the referendum process enshrined in the 2008 constitution (along with rights of Nature), Ecuador's government has the political authority to take on major vested interests and powerful lobbies. A new law in July 2010 increased the government's share in oil revenues from 13% to 87%. The government managed a dramatic increase in direct tax receipts (mainly corporate taxes). Ecuador now has the highest proportion of public investment to GDP (10%) in Latin America, even as social spending has doubled since 2006. Jayati Ghosh, "Could Ecuador be the most radical and exciting place on Earth?" *Guardian*, 19 January 2012. After the election of President Morsi, negotiations with the IMF included a request for over $1 billion reduction in Egypt's debt based on the "odious debt" precedent. *Al-Ahram Online*, 7 January 2013.

48 Postmaterialism assumes an ongoing transformation of individuals and society, which liberates them from the stress of materialistic needs. From 1980–1990 the share of "pure postmaterialists" (Inglehart Index) increased from 13 to 31% in West Germany. After the economic and social stress caused by German reunification in 1990 it dropped to 23% in 1992. (German General Social Survey) The question then arises: Will anti-materialism per se survive austerity without a religious foundation?

49 2009 Rasmussen poll.

50 *www.leftcom.org*, 21 February 2011.

51 Tariq Ramadan, *Western Muslims and the Future of Islam*, UK: Oxford University Press, 2004, 199.

52 Tariq Ramadan, lecture at *www.revivingtheislamicspirit.com*, Toronto, 12 December 2012.

53 Ramadan, *Western Muslims and the Future of Islam*, 220, 224.

54 "For Imam Malik, sunna is simply what came to be accepted by the consent of the Muslim community. 'The actual content of the sunna of the early generations of Muslims was largely the product of ijtihad when this ijtihad, through an incessant interaction of opinion, developed the character of general acceptance or consensus of the community, i.e., ijma." Quote from Fazlur Rahman, Islamic Methodology in History, Karachi: Central Institute of Islamic Research, 1965,

quoted in M. Yahya Birt, "The Message of Fazlur Rahman", freerepublic.com, 27 June 1996. <http://www.freerepublic.com focus/fr/531762/posts />.

55   5:32.

56   2:178.

58   See E.F. Schumacher, Small is Beautiful (1973).

59   Cuba's strict control of the economy to meet society's needs is condemned in the West as inefficient and totalitarian. But efficiency is the main goal only of technopoly, and is a subsidiary goal, a means, for any human- or God-centered society. In a sense, the US-imposed embargo has forced secular Cuba to follow what is also an Islamic economic logic—not developing slick consumer-focused technologies, but becoming a leader in such alternative development areas as organic gardening, environmentally friendly transport, vaccine production and other medical technologies. E.F. Schumacher's 'appropriate technology' is another example, coming from a Christian perspective, which seeks a developmental path which features man/nature as a sacred unity. Carson quoted in Elyssa East, review of William Souder, On a Farther Shore (2012), sfgate.com, 14 September 2012. Einstein quoted in Sardar, The Touch of Midas, 4.

60   Hadith, *Sahih* al-Bukhari, 8:41.

61   The 8th–10th century categories of *dar al-islam* (abode of peace), *dar al-harb* (abode of war), *dar al-ahd* (abode of treaty), and *dar al-kufr* (abode of unbelief, referring to Muhammad's early Meccan period) do not occur in the Quran but only in the much later hadiths, but are now integral to Islamic law, and are being redefined. Formally an abode of war, the West, with its guaranteed civil rights, ironically allows more religious freedom these days than many oppressive, nominally Muslim client states (pre-revolution Egypt being a prime example), where Muslims are in danger and unable to practice their beliefs freely (if only because religion doesn't threaten power in a rigorously secular society like the US). At the same time, mass migration and the globalization of economic, financial and political power means that the concept of physical borders loses its meaning. Sheikh Faysal al-Mawlawi, a founder of the European Council for Fatwa and Research, proposes the concept of *dar al-dawa* (abode of invitation to God) to refer to the early Meccan period and the whole of the Arabian Peninsula at that time, and, by inference, the world today. Ramadan suggests his own characterization of the West as *dar al-shahada* (abode of testimony to the Islamic message). He argues that Muslims are "witnesses before mankind". They must continue to review the fundamental principles of Islam and take responsibility for their faith, building on the *maqasid* (goals) movement within Islamic legal philosophy.

62   Quotes by Muhammad Asad, in Sardar, *Reading the Qur'an,* 195–196.

63   **M**oney (purchases) **C**ommodiy inputs (which undergo) **P**roduction process (which produces) new **C**ommodity (which is sold for) **M**oney

64   *Sahih* al-Buhkari and Muslim, *snad* of Ibn Mas'ud.

65   Tariq Ramadan, *Western Muslims and the Future of Islam.*

66   "Islamic Art", *salaam.co.uk*, 11 February, 2013.

67   Sardar, *Reading the Qur'an,* 367.

68   Ibid., 132–133.

69   Hadith recorded by al-Muslim and al-Bukhari.

70   This is finally getting underway. See Chapter 5 Economics.

71   Ali Harfouch, "Beyond the Mursi Effect: Holding the Egyptian President to account", *New Civilisation*, 1 October 2012.

72   This reasonable proposal was inserted in the new constitution in the teeth of fierce secularist opposition.

73   Imam Abu Hamid al-Ghazali al-Shafi, *Wasit* (7/168).

74   Harfouch, "Beyond the Mursi Effect".

75   Aziz Azmeh, *Islam and Modernities,* UK: Verso, [1996] 2009.

76   Gai Eaton, *King of the Castle: Choice and Responsibility in the Modern World*, UK: Islamic Texts Society, 1977, 198.

BIBLIOGRAPHY

Abdel-Nasser, Gamal, *Filsafa al-thawra (Philosophy of the Revolution),* Cairo: Madbouli, [1955] 2005.

Abdo, Geneive, *No God But God: Egypt and the Triumph of Islam,* UK: Oxford University Press, 2000.

Abrahamian, Ervand, *A History of Modern Iran,* UK: Cambridge University Press, 2008.

Afary, Janet and Anderson, Kevin, *Foucault and the Iranian Revolution: Gender and the Seductions of Islamism,* USA: University of Chicago Press, 2005.

Agha, Hussein, and Malley, Robert, "The Arab Counterrevolution", *New York Review of Books,* 29 September 2011.

Ahmad, Irfan, "How the West de-democratised the Middle East", *informationclearinghouse.info,* <http://www.informationclearinghouse.info/article30946.htm>.

Ahmed, Akbar, *Journey into Islam: The Crisis of Globalization,* Washington DC: Brookings Institution Press, 2007.

al-Amin, Esam, "Showdown in Egypt", *Counterpunch,* 30 November 2012.

Amin, Galal, *Egypt in the Era of Hosni Mubarak 1981-2011,* New York: AUC Press, 2011.

Amin, Samir, "The Electoral Victory of Political Islam in Egypt", *Monthly Review,* 30 June 2012.

Armstrong, Karen, *Islam: A Short History,* USA: Modern Library, 2000.

—*A History of God: The 4000-Year Quest of Judaism, Christianity and Islam,* New York: Alfred Knopf, 1994.

Asad, Muhammad (Leopold Weiss), *The Road to Mecca,* USA: [Simon and Schuster 1954] Fons Vitae 2000.

—*Principles of State and Government in Islam,* USA: University of California, 1961.

Askari, Hussein, et al, *The Stability of Islamic Finance,* India: Wiley, 2010.

Azmeh, Aziz , *Islam and Modernities,* UK: Verso [1996] 2009.

Balci, Kerim, "Philosophical depth: A scholarly talk with the Turkish foreign minister", *turkishreview.org,* 1 November 2010.

al-Banna, Hasan, *Five Tracts of Hasan al-Banna* (1906–1949), tr. Charles Wendell, USA: University of California Press, 1978.

Bayat, Asef, *Making Islam Democratic: Social Movements and the Post-Islamist Turn,* USA: Stanford University Press, 2007.

Beaty, Jonathan and Gwynne, S.C., *The Outlaw Bank: A wild ride into the secret heart of BCCI,* USA: Random House, 1993.

Behdad, Sohrab, *Revolutionary surge and quiet demise of Islamic Economics in Iran,* Denison University, 2005. <http://www.international.ucla.edu/cms/files/behdadtxt.pdf>

—and Nomani, Farhad (eds) *Islam and the Everyday World: Public policy dilemmas,* New York: Routledge, 2006.

Birt, M Yahya, "The Message of Fazlur Rahman", *freerepublic.com,* 27 June 1996.

Blunt, Wilfrid, *The Future of Islam,* London: Kegan Paul, Trench and Co, 1882.

—*Secret History of the English Occupation of Egypt,* USA: A. Knopf, 1922.

Burgat, Francois, *The Islamic Movement in North Africa,* Center for Middle Eastern Studies, USA: University of Texas Press, 1997.

Cinm, Alev, "The Justice and Development Party", *International Journal of Middle East Studies*

(IJMES), 43:3, August 2011.

Clark, Janine, *Islam, Charity and Activism*, USA: Indiana University Press, 2004.

Coll, Steve, *Ghost Wars: The secret history of the CIA, Afghanistan, and Bin Laden, from the Soviet invasion to September 10, 2001*, New York: Penguin, 2004.

Cornell, Svante, "What drives Turkish foreign policy?" *Middle East Quarterly*, Vol. XIX: No. 1, Winter 2012.

Dabashi, Hamid, Iran: *A People Interrupted*, New York: New Press, 2007.

Davutloglu, Ahmet, see Balci, Kerim.

Dreyfuss, Robert, "Cold War Holy Warrior", *Mother Jones*, January 2006.

Eaton, Gai, *King of the Castle: Choice and Responsibility in the Modern World*, UK: Islamic Texts Society, 1977.

—*Islam and the Destiny of Man*, UK: Islamic Texts Society, 1994.

Egger, Vernon, *A History of the Muslim World since 1260: The Making of a Global Community*, New Jersey: Pearson, 2008.

Eickelman, Dale and Piscatori, James, *Muslim Politics*, Princeton University Press, 1996.

Escobar, Pepe, "Why Qatar wants to invade Syria", *Asia Times*, 27 September 2012.

Esposito, John, *Islam and Politics* USA: Syracuse University Press, 1984.

—*Islam: the straight path*, UK: Oxford University Press, [1988] 1998.

—*Islam and Secularism in the Middle East*, USA: NYU Press, 2000.

—and Voll, John, *Makers of Contemporary Islam*, UK: Oxford University Press, 2001.

—and Kalin, Ibrahim, Marques, Ed, Ghazi, Usra (eds), *The 500 Most Influential Muslims in the World*, Georgetown USA: Royal Islamic Strategic Studies Center and Prince Alwaleed Bin Talal Center for Muslim-Christian Understanding, 2009. <http://themuslim500.com/>.

Ghannouchi, Rached, Full Transcript of Rached Ghannouchi's lecture on Secularism, 2 March 2012. <http://blog.sami-aldeeb.com/2012/03/09/full-transcript-of-rached-ghannouchis-lecture-on-secularism-march-2-2012/>.

Guenon, Rene, *Insights into Islamic Esoterism and Taoism*, USA: Sophia Perennis, 2003.

Hallinan, Conn, "Turkey haunted by hubris", *Foreign Policy in Focus*, 3 November 2012.

Hanafi, Hassan, *Islam in the Modern World*, vol. II *Tradition, Revolution and Culture*, Cairo: Anglo-Egyptian Bookshop, 1995, in "Hassan Hanafi", *International Journal of Middle East Studies (IJMES)* 29:3 August 1997.

—"Facts and Values: An Islamic Approach", in Mehran Kamrava (ed.), *The New Voices of Islam: Rethinking Politics and Modernity, A Reader*, USA: University of California Press, 2006.

Hansen, Suzy, "The economic vision of Egypt's Muslim Brotherhood millionaires" *Business Week*, 19 April 2012.

Harfouch, Ali, "Beyond the Mursi Effect: Holding the Egyptian President to account", *New Civilisation*, 1 October 2012.

Herlihy, John (ed.), *The Essential Rene Guenon: Metaphysics, Tradition, and the Crisis of Modernity*, USA: World Wisdom, 2009.

Hodgson, Marshall, edited and introduction by Edmund Burk, *Rethinking World History: Essays on Europe, Islam and World History*, Cambridge University Press, 1993.

Hudson, Michael C. (ed.), *The Middle East Dilemma*, USA: Columbia University Press, 1998.

Iqbal, Muhammad, *Reconstruction of Religious Thought in Islam*, 1930.

Jala, Ayesha, *Partisans of Allah: Jihad in South Asia*, USA: Harvard University Press, 2008.

Kadri, Sadakat, *Heaven on Earth: A Journey Through Sharia Law from the Deserts of Ancient Arabia to the Streets of the Modern Muslim World*, USA: Farrar, Straus and Giroux, 2012.

Kamrava, Mehran (ed.), *The New Voices of Islam: Rethinking Politics and Modernity, A Reader*, USA: University of California Press, 2006.

Khawly, Mohammad, "Egypt: Muslim Brotherhood and al-Azhar follow Salafi lead Bisan Kassab", *al-akhbar.com*, 23 March 2012.

Kirkpatrick, David, "Turkey's Erdogan nurtures new role in the Middle East", *New York Times*, 13 September 2011.

Koestler, Arthur, *The Yogi and the Commissar*, London: Jonathan Cape, 1945.

Kung, Hans, *Islam: Past, Present and Future*, tr. John Bowden, UK: Oneworld, 2004.

Laurence, Jonathan, "How to integrate Europe's Muslims", *New York Times*, 24 January 2012.

Longford, Elizabeth, *A Pilgrimage of Passion: The Life of Wilfrid Scawen Blunt*, New York: Knopf, 1980.

Mansfield, Peter, *A History of the Middle East*, London: Penguin, 1991.

Maududi, Abul Ala, *The Islamic Law and Constitution,* Lahore, 1941.

—*The Meaning of the Qur'an,* <englishtafsir.com>.

el-Messeri, Abdel Wahab, Interview by Mohamed Islam, "Episode 26. Islamic Reformers", <http://www.muslimphilosophy.com/tvtk/ch26.htm>.

Mishra, Pankaj, *From the Ruins of Empire: The Intellectuals Who Remade Asia*, USA: Farrar, Straus and Giroux, 2012.

Moaddel, M., *Islamic Modernism, Nationalism and Fundamentalism: Episode and Discourse*, USA: University of Chicago Press, 2005.

Moussalli, Ahmad S., *Radical Islamic Fundamentalism: the Ideological and Political Discourse of Sayyid Qutb*, American University of Beirut, 1992.

Nasr, Seyyed Hossein, "Islam and Modern Science" Georgetown University lecture, <http://msa.mit.edu/archives/nasrspeech1.html>.

—*Ideals and Realities of Islam*, UK: Allen and Unwin, [1966] 1975.

—*Islam in the Modern World: Challenged by the West, Threatened by fundamentalism, Keeping faith with Tradition*, USA: Harper One, 2010.

Nasr, Vali, *The Shia Revival: How Conflicts within Islam Will Shape the Future*, New York: Norton, 2006.

—*Forces of Fortune: The Rise of the New Muslim Middle Class and What It will Mean for Our World*, USA: Free Press, 2009.

Nieuwkerk (ed.), Karin van, *Women Embracing Islam: Gender and Conversion in the West*, USA: University of Texas, 2006.

Noble, David, *Promised Land: Movement and Myth*, Canada: Between the Lines, 2005.

Noor, Farish, "The responsibilities of the Muslim intellectual in the 21st century: An interview with Abdolkarim Soroush", *muslimwakeup.com*, 2004.

O'Sullivan, Jack, "If you hate the West, emigrate to a Muslim country", *Guardian,* 8 October 2001.

Pargeter, Alison, *Muslim Brotherhood, 2010: The burden of tradition*, London: Saqi, 2010.

Postman, Neil, *Technopoly: The Surrender of Culture to Technology,* USA: Vintage, 1993.

Qutb, Sayyid, *Milestones*, Birmingham UK: Maktaba [1964] 2006.

Rahman, Fazlur, *Islamic Methodology in History*, Karachi: Central Institute of Islamic Research, 1965.

Ramadan, Tariq, *Western Muslims and the Future of Islam*, UK: Oxford University Press, 2004.

—*In the Footsteps of the Prophet: Lessons from the Life of Muhammad*, UK: Oxford University Press, 2007.

—*Radical Reform: Islamic Ethics and Liberation*, UK: Oxford University Press, 2009.

Roy, Olivier, *The Failure of Political Islam*, USA: Harvard University Press, 1994.

Ruthven, Malise, *Fundamentalism: The Search for Meaning*, UK: Oxford University Press, 2003.

Saif, Ibrahim and Rumman, Muhammad Abu, "The Economic Agenda of the Islamist Parties", Carnegie Paper, May 2012.

Sardar, Ziauddin, *"Refloating the Intellectual Enterprises of Islam"*, *Inquiry*, Vol. III, Feb. 1986. <http://www.salaam.co.uk/knowledge/inquiry3.php>.

—*Desperately Seeking Paradise: Journeys of a Sceptical Muslim*, UK: Granta, 2005.

—Interview by Mustafa Nazir Ahmad, *The News on Sunday*, in *The Reformist*, Karachi, 23 November 2008.

—*Reading the Qur'an: The Contemporary Relevance of the Sacred Text of Islam*, UK: Oxford University Press, 2011.

—Introduction to *The Britannica Guide to the Islamic World*, London: Robinson, 2009.

—(ed.), *The Touch of Midas: Science, values and environment in Islam and the West*, UK: Manchester University Press, 1984.

Schumacher, E. F., *A Guide for the Perplexed*, USA: Harper Perennial, 1977.

Shamir, Israel, "The Arab Autumn", *israelshamir.net*, 2012.

Sinclair, Hugh, *Confessions of a Microfinance Heretic*, USA: Berrett-Koehler, 2012.

Slisli, Fouzi, "The Algerian Civil War: Washington's Model for 'The New Middle-East'", Association of Concerned Africa Scholars, August 2007.

Temsamani, Said, "Historical facts about the 'Moroccaness' of the Sahara", *eurasiareview.com*, 6 November, 2012.

Tenet, George, *At the Center of the Storm: My Years at the CIA*, New York: Harper Collins, 2007.

United Nations Development Program, *Arab Human Development Reports, arab-hdr.org*, 2002, 2004, 2009, 2021.

Vadillo, Umar Ibrahim, "Fatwa on Banking and the Use of Interest Received on Bank Deposits", October 2006. <zakat.files.wordpress.com/2006/11/fatwaonbanking.pdf>.

Venner, Dominique, "The Yogi and the Commissar", *countercurrents.com*, 7 September 2011.

Wagemakers, Joas, "The Enduring Legacy of the Second Saudi State", *International Journal of Middle East Studies (IJMES)* 44:1, February 2012.

Wahid, Abdul, "Ghannushi's Political Paradoxes: The Islamic Secular?", *New Civilisation*, 23 March 2012.

Walberg, Eric, "Ever the twain shall meet", *Al-Ahram Weekly*, 13 September 2007.

—"The Quran in translation: Reading Islam's holy book", *Al-Ahram Weekly*, 20 September 2007.

—"Islam and Europe: An equal and opposite reaction", *Al-Ahram Weekly*, 18 August 2011.

—*Postmodern Imperialism: Geopolitics and the Great Games*, USA: Clarity Press, 2011.

Warde, Ibrahim, *Islamic Finance in the Global Economy*, 2nd ed., UK: Edinburgh University Press, 2010.

Wickham, Carrie, *Mobilizing Islam: Religion, Activism and Political Change in Egypt*, USA: Columbia University Press, 2003.

Wilber, Ken, *The Marriage of Sense and Soul: Integrating Science and Religion*, USA: Random House, 1999.

—*A Brief History of Everything*, USA: Shambhala, 2000.

Winter, Tim, *Understanding Islam and the Muslims*, Fons Vitae, 2002.

—Interviewed by John Cleary, Australian Broadcasting Corporation, 18 May 2004.

—(ed.), *The Cambridge Companion to Classical Islamic Theology*, UK: Cambridge University Press, 2008.

Wright, Robert, *Nonzero: The Logic of Human Destiny*, USA: Vintage, 2001.

—*The evolution of God*, USA: Little Brown, 2009.

INDEX